THE DOULA BUSINESS GUIDE

3RD EDITION

How to Succeed as a Birth, Postpartum or End-of-Life Doula

by

PATTY BRENNAN

FOREWORD BY PENNY SIMKIN

2nd Edition 2014
3rd Edition 2019

Published in the United States by DreamStreet Press, Ann Arbor, Michigan
Manufactured in the United States of America
∞ Printed on acid-free paper

The Doula Business Guide, 3rd Edition and companion *Doula Business Guide Workbook, 3rd Edition* are available for purchase from Lifespan Doulas [LifespanDoulas.com]. A 40% wholesale discount is available for orders of six or more copies of a book.

ISBN 978-0-9797247-1-8

To Jerry, who never fails to be on my side,
who believes in me when I doubt myself,
and who sustains me through everything

Acknowledgments

So many people have been part of my journey, not the least of whom are the families I have had the privilege of serving. You have been my greatest teachers and I do not forget you.

Thanks to all the aspiring doulas who have come to me for training. You have humbled me by your dedication and passion. Families and communities benefit when you succeed. You are my inspiration for this book.

Thanks are due to Wende Sharma, for believing in the idea of the Center in the first place and providing the necessary seed money to get me started.

Thanks to Deanna Cochran, Sierra Hillebrand, Kristen Paquin, Toni Auker, Diana Thornton, Stefanie Antunes, Heather Crossan and many others for agreeing to be interviewed for the 3rd edition and sharing unreservedly about their business models. And I am grateful to Debra Catlin for her generous contributions regarding Oregon's process of gaining Medicaid reimbursement for birth doula services.

I am also grateful for the support and collaboration of my business partner Merilynne Rush. Lifespan Doulas would not exist without you.

And finally, thanks to Parvin Keller for her excellent skills, professionalism and responsiveness in designing *The Doula Business Guide, 3rd edition.*

The Doula Business Guide:

How to Succeed as a Birth, Postpartum or End-of-Life Doula

Table of Contents

CHAPTER 6

CHAPTER 7

Foreword

DOULA CARE AND BUSINESS MANAGEMENT—heart and head—do not seem, at first glance, to mix very well to most of us doulas. And yet sustainability depends on our using responsible and rewarding business practices to solidify the foundation from which we spread our birth knowledge and assistance to families.

Until I read Patty Brennan's in-depth coverage of the business side of a private doula practice, I would have told you that the business side is a matter of printing business cards, networking, obtaining a business license, keeping track of expenses and income, paying your taxes, following your Standards of Practice and Code of Ethics, having your ducks lined up (back-up, reliable communication and transportation), plus discussing money without discomfort. By about page 6 of *The Doula Business Guide,* I realized there's much to learn from this book, for me, for you and for all other doulas. And for those of you who plan to form an agency or hospital-based doula program (profit or nonprofit, staffed by volunteers or paid employees), this book is geared for you because Patty has been there, learned what to do and how to do it, and wants to help us avoid reinventing the wheel.

There's more to the business side than what I listed above. It is the make-or-break side of doula care. Without good business practices you won't last very long or, if you last, you'll likely run into some unpleasant situations because you neglected some of the practical down-to-earth nitty gritty things that Patty covers. An appropriate subtitle for this book might be, "Everything You Wanted to Know about Doula Business, but Were Too Naïve to Ask."

Lest I make this book sound daunting to readers, let me assure you that this book is a very good read! Patty's honesty, conversational tone, instructive stories and obvious expertise carry you through each chapter. She shares pearls of wisdom that she has gleaned from years of varied experiences with many types of doula practice. A glance over the Table of Contents shows how complete the book is, covering everything: various models for a private practice or a doula program, how to set it up, market it, remain within the law, finance the practice or program, and manage all possible risks to survival. She also covers, with humor and the voice of experience, such touchy topics as individual lifestyle issues, self-care and personal relationships within the family, community and with clients. She even shows how we can be effective birth activists without jeopardizing our clients' well-being in the birth room. Whew!

We doulas are in a delicate position as we enter hospitals from the outside and introduce a new dynamic in the established hierarchy within the institution. Being an outsider is both a blessing and a curse. We are blessed because we are there because the women want us there. Our role is pure and unconfused—to provide the proven beneficial care that, without us, would either be unavailable or available only when the nurse or midwife has the time, interest and skills to do it. We doulas (at least theoretically) don't answer to other masters who can trump our mandate to address and meet the non-clinical needs of birthing women. Medical and nursing staffs have other important responsibilities besides the laboring woman and her baby—adhering to institutional policies, clinical tasks, caregiver orders, the needs of other laboring women, and their own needs to leave for breaks and shift changes. Clinical care providers must balance the laboring woman's clinical care with all those other demands. The "curse" for doulas is that our position is fragile and depends on the good will of those in the institutional hierarchy who have the authority to remove or ban doulas from the premises without explanation and without recourse for the doula. The best protection against this, of course, is to stick to our standards and scope of practice, which Patty skillfully reviews in a way that is helpful to seasoned doulas and new doulas alike. See Chapter 7.

She shows us, in a number of ways, how to ensure that we can continue to provide doula care and work for change appropriately. If we have a solid infrastructure for our doula businesses and know how to avoid pitfalls (in scope of practice, financial matters, marketing and in relationship building with other doulas, maternity care professionals and clients), we are on surer footing and can perform with confidence. By lining up all our ducks, we can work with confidence and clarity, even in a less-than-receptive environment. It has become clear to me over my many years of doula work, that taking the "high road—sticking to what doulas do best in the birthing room and being respectful, polite and appropriate—we gain in stature in the eyes of others who care for birthing women. Familiarity breeds, not contempt as the adage states, but respect.

As we learn from Patty, good business practices ensure that the wisdom, experience and unique assistance provided by doulas will continue to be available and will grow to benefit more childbearing women and their families. This book is more than an excellent guide to business, but also a guide to the high road for each of us and to positive growth for the entire doula movement.

In the doula spirit,

Penny Simkin, 2010
Author of *The Birth Partner: A Guide to Childbirth for Dads, Doulas, and All Other Labor Companions* and many other books and tools. [PennySimkin.com]

Preface to the 3rd Edition

Right Livelihood

THE CONCEPT OF RIGHT LIVELIHOOD IS KEY TO A FULFILLING LIFE. In Plato's cosmology, each person is born with certain talents and abilities. Some are naturally gifted healers, teachers, farmers, judges, warriors, merchants, priests or artists. Each has unique value as part of a society. It is the individual's task to discover her rightful place in society, that occupation in which the larger portion of daily hours can most effectively and joyfully be invested. In an ideal world, every person would be engaged in work best suited to employing her/his unique gifts. It is not only a good idea to find meaningful work that the worker finds fulfilling, it is THE idea. If you are reading this book, then presumably you are engaged, on some level, in providing doula or related services to families or soon intend to do so. It is my mission to help you be successful in this endeavor. Furthermore, I define "success" to mean work that is both financially and spiritually rewarding, in other words, right livelihood.

Yes, this book is about the nitty-gritty ins and outs of doula businesses. I cover how to go into business for yourself, determine the best business model for your preferences and skills, or launch a doula program and get it funded. I'll teach you the basics of financial record keeping, how to stay out of trouble with the IRS and how to limit any risk associated with doula work. The book is equally about attitudes, beliefs and work habits of successful people. It's about creativity, courage, passion and commanding respect for what we do. It's a how-to manual, and it's my story. It's about hard lessons learned and not reinventing the wheel as we work to create fundamental systemic change. And it's about cultivating a mindset of abundance and worthiness.

The Value of the Mastermind

The mastermind concept comes from Napoleon Hill, author of the 1930s classic *Think and Grow Rich,* and involves formation of a small group of business owners who regularly come together to share ideas, identify opportunities and solve problems related to each member's unique business challenges. The allotted meeting time is divided evenly among the members who come prepared to discuss a specific issue. This can include big picture analysis of their business model, critique of a web page, brainstorming ideas to promote an upcoming event, and so on. The mastermind concept acknowledges that being a business owner is often a lonely pursuit. Most entrepreneurs are struggling with wearing lots of hats and often become overwhelmed with all the tasks and possibilities, leading to a lack of focus. One benefit of a monthly support group is that it builds in some accountability. I mean, you can't come, month after month, with nothing to show the group without feeling incredibly lame. You must prepare so the group can help you set goals for what you will accomplish over the coming month. Accountability helps us get things done. If you are having trouble accomplishing your goals, the group can help.

My first entry into the mastermind was with a group of business owners who were mostly men. Their businesses ranged from carpet cleaning to heating and cooling, tech support, sales training, marketing, and more. It can be mind-blowing to get outside of our little bubbles! Honestly, I had surrounded myself with birth junkies for years. When I first engaged with the mastermind, the guys were trying to figure out what exactly it was that I did. Translating my self-descriptor of "doula trainer and childbirth educator," the group facilitator summarized that I was in the field of "information marketing" and that my niche market was the "childbearing year." That was his take on it. What a spin! Who knew? Entrepreneur, Information Marketing. I found it incredibly helpful, albeit disappointing, to have someone who has no direct connection with my business say, "I don't know what this means" after perusing my freshly completed new web page. Really? It's perfectly clear to me (but then, I wrote it). A mastermind group reminds us that we are not our own customers and we can't see what others see.

In the end, all small business owners have a great deal in common. There is much that we can learn from each other across industries because marketing strategies (e.g., creating effective marketing messages or optimizing a website for the search engines) that work in one business also work in other, completely different types of businesses. There are many shared challenges. My advice? Create a supportive community to make your path—especially at the beginning—a little less lonely. We all benefit from deadlines, accountability, constructive feedback and, especially, getting out of our self-limiting thought bubbles!

What's New in the 3rd Edition?

The doula world is rapidly expanding and evolving! Readers familiar with older editions of *The Doula Business Guide* will find much that is new here.

- While previous editions focused solely on birth and postpartum doulas and maternal–infant health initiatives, many subjects covered were understood to be applicable to any service-oriented small business. In the 3rd edition, we are explicitly including end-of-life doulas (and related practitioners) as well.
- Between the 2nd and 3rd editions of the book, I published *The Doula Business Guide Workbook: Tools to Create a Successful Practice* (2016). Many doula business owners have benefited from the additional business implementation tools available in the *Workbook*. An updated 3rd edition of the *Workbook,* inclusive of end-of-life doulas, is newly available as well (2019). Now, both the *Guide* and the *Workbook* are fully integrated and cross-referenced. Each provides value on its own, but they are conceived as a pair, which is new.
- Essay on "What is the Doula Model of Care?" that seeks to define foundational guiding principles across the doula profession so that, as the profession expands to include a growing variety of types of doulas, we may endeavor to stay true to our essence.
- Expanded and updated material on the pros and cons of various doula business models, especially doula collectives and doula agencies
- How to know the difference between an employee and an independent contractor
- Expanded and updated section on establishing doula programs, including pros and cons of different doula program models
- Thoughts on doula mentoring
- A (controversial) defense of volunteer doulas
- Questions to ask before agreeing to serve on a board of directors
- Updates on the status of third-party reimbursement for doulas
- Updated resources, including technology updates (communication platforms, apps, website plugins, etc.)
- And more! An estimated 30 percent of material is new or significantly updated.

A Word about Pronouns

While more men are being drawn into doula work, especially as end-of-life doulas, the field remains predominantly female. For this reason, I have defaulted (for the most part) to using female pronouns throughout the book. My hope is that male readers will not feel excluded and accept my choice to prioritize readability over cumbersome but inclusive language. It is not a reflection on the value you bring to the doula field or my eagerness to embrace you as a cohort!

Birthing Your Doula Business

Conception, gestation, labor and birth … as doulas, we are intimately familiar with these basic life processes. Birth is the ultimate metaphor for all manner of creative manifestation. As in human gestation and birth, the process of bringing a business to life is one of nurturing an idea, laboring to bring it forth, pushing it out in the world and witnessing it take on a life of its own. It is at this point that both parents and business owners discover that the real work begins! Anyone who has ever given birth, raised a child, written a dissertation or book, taken a daunting project from start to finish, or started a new business knows the meaning of hard work. To enjoy the fruits of our labors, we need to go through the process itself, one step at a time. No way around it. In this book, I doula the doula professional in you, lending the support and (I hope) wisdom of one who has gone before to help you breathe life into your dream of launching a doula business or program. May your work be rewarding and joyful. ◆

Introduction: What is the "Doula Model of Care"?

DOULAS ARE COMING INTO THE CULTURAL MAINSTREAM and they are not just for birthing and postpartum mothers and their families. The emerging role of the end-of-life doula is gaining traction and helping transform how we approach end-of-life care in the United States and beyond. As training and certification programs for doulas of all kinds expand exponentially, there is a danger that each new player in the field will attempt to assert their brand by re-inventing and re-defining the role of the doula, potentially undermining evidence-based core principles of what it means to be a doula. Since current evidence for birth doulas is well established[1] and based on a model of care that is gaining widespread recognition and acceptance by both consumers and medical care providers, it behooves the doula profession to unite in our understanding of the doula model of care, especially as it evolves to serve diverse needs of families throughout the lifespan.

Preliminary definitions are in order as a basis for understanding. A model of care broadly defines the way services are delivered. It outlines best practices for a person, population group or patient cohort as they progress through the stages of a condition or event. It aims to ensure people get the right care, at the right time, by the right team and in the right place. According to the Agency for Clinical Innovation, models of care have the following key elements:

- Quality care—promotes safe, high-quality care
- Patient-centric—focus is on the patient/family
- Integrated care—supports collaboration among all team members
- Cost-effective—promotes efficient use of resources
- Adaptability—localized flexibility; considers equity of access
- Outcome evaluation—has a robust and standardized set of outcome measures and evaluation processes

- Evidence-based—incorporates the best available evidence; links to local and national strategic plans and initiatives
- Innovative—considers new ways of organizing and delivering care
- Visionary—sets a vision for services in the future[2]

The word Doula has Greek origins and means "woman who serves." Service is at the heart of doula work. Throughout time and in cultures all over the world, there have always been those individuals—usually women—who tend to the needs of the mother in labor, nurture the family in the early weeks postpartum, and care for the sick and dying. The concept of the modern-day doula began in 1969, but the word did not come into widespread use until 1992 when Doulas of North America (now known as DONA International) was founded by five visionary maternal and infant health experts. The goal of this new organization was to train and certify doulas to support families in birth and during their early postpartum experiences. Standards of practice and a code of ethics for doulas[3] were thoughtfully articulated to define the doula's scope of practice, thereby professionalizing the time-honored, informal role of the doula. Today, DONA International is the largest doula training organization in the world, serving as the standard-bearer in the doula industry.

The emergence of the end-of-life doula is a 21st century development, and more men are being drawn into the field. With the "silver tsunami" of aging baby boomers upon us—many of whom are proponents of natural lifestyles and holistic approaches to health care—it makes sense that we are seeking new models of care to meet unmet needs at the end of life. Everyone benefits from dedicated support when major life transitions are underway.

Because doulas remain, for the most part, an unregulated profession (only Oregon and Minnesota have passed legislation licensing birth doulas and enabling Medicaid reimbursement for services), there is a great deal of autonomy for doulas to practice freely and evolve businesses that suit each individual doula's interests, strengths and skill set. Today, doulas are working in solo practices, partnerships, collectives and doula agencies. A variety of doula programs have been established, in both the birth and end-of-life fields of care, from community-based nonprofits to hospital-based or hospice-sponsored programs. Some doula programs use volunteer doulas only, while others engage doulas as employees or independent contractors. There is plenty of room for creative visionaries to adapt the doula model of care for a target demographic or specialized care setting. Furthermore, how each doula manifests the doula model of care and delivers services to families will be uniquely her or his own. This freedom, entrepreneurship and diversity benefit the variety of individuals and families with needs that are unmet in existing systems of care delivery. At the same time, we must acknowledge what unites us as doulas and define the core, non-negotiable elements of the doula model of care.

Core Components of the Doula Model of Care

Six Guiding Principles of Doula Support

- **Non-medical support.** Doulas refrain from performing any clinical or medicalized tasks (e.g., monitoring vital signs, dispensing medications, wound care, etc.). This prohibition is fundamental to the role. For example, a retired hospice nurse who has trained as a doula should not call herself a doula if she is also dispensing medications and providing clinical care; rather, she is a nurse with doula support skills.
- **Non-judgmental support.** The doula does not impose her/his values on the client such as acting on biases in favor of one method of giving birth or pre-conceived notions of what constitutes a "good death." The doula does not presume that she/he knows best or somehow confers deeper meaning on the experience, but rather, openly explores the emerging needs of the person/family, what is meaningful/important to them, and how the doula can best support them. *Care is based on the client's values and goals, even if those differ from values cherished by the doula.*
- **Family-centered approach.** The individual and their family form the unit of care. Doulas do not take the place of partners, family members or other care providers. Rather, they seek to support the optimal involvement of loved ones and all available services.
- **Holistic care.** Doulas recognize the biopsychosocial and spiritual aspects of the whole person and provide services in the context of this understanding. Holistic care can also involve information and referrals for complementary healthcare modalities if the client is seeking alternative approaches beyond those embraced by the medical model.
- **Empowerment.** Doulas promote informed decision-making and foster maximum self-determination for the individual and family. They encourage self-efficacy and self-advocacy, based on identified values and preferences, rather than dependency. Doulas are not advocates per se and do not speak for their clients. Their role is better understood as that of a mediator who is facilitating good communication between all parties.

- **Team members.** Doulas are team players with a special role. The doula's areas of expertise may overlap with that of other professionals involved with the client's care, for example, a labor and delivery nurse, lactation consultant or hospice team member. These overlaps are to be expected and need not lead to conflicts provided doulas practice good communication and defer to medical experts for concerns outside their scope. Doulas often have a better grasp of the full continuum of care providers who might be involved in the client's care, as well as where gaps exist that create stress for the client and family. They help provide much needed continuity of care.

Types of Support Provided by Doulas

- **Presence.** Good listener, witness, calming influence, nurturing, support for troubleshooting challenges.
- **Emotional support** (always part of the doula's role).
- **Information sharing.** Education as needed and desired (e.g., how to care for a newborn or what to expect during the dying process). Information provided is non-biased and evidence-based. While encouraging informed decision-making, doulas refrain from giving advice to their clients or promoting a specific choice or course of action.
- **Proactive guidance.** Anticipating needs and making a plan (e.g., birth or vigil planning).
- **Resources and referrals.** Doulas are generalists rather than specialists, though some may have additional training in specialty areas such as massage therapy or spiritual care. When client needs/requests are outside of the doula's scope of practice, personal/professional boundaries, or experience/expertise, the doula is prepared to make referrals to appropriate community resources and care providers, thereby increasing access to all available services.
- **Comfort measures and physical support.** Can include hands-on comfort techniques, help with positioning, visualization, use of the breath and so on. Personal care at the end of life (e.g., helping to keep the person clean, dry and comfortable) may be offered by some end-of-life doulas.
- **Logistical support.** Can include household help, running errands, meal preparation, transportation to medical appointments and so on. Services provided by individual doulas will vary as each establishes her/his own professional boundaries.

Adapting the Doula Model of Care for End of Life

If we reconsider the definition and key elements of a "model of care" discussed above, the doula model of care readily meets the standards of being high quality, patient centric, collaborative, cost-effective, adaptable, innovative and visionary. While the body of literature establishing the benefits of birth doulas is extensive and compelling, standardized outcome measures to evaluate the efficacy of post-partum doulas and, especially, end-of-life doulas are scarce to non-existent. These are urgently-needed areas for research. If the health benefits and cost savings, now in evidence for birth doulas, extends to doulas involved during other phases of the lifespan—as we expect they do—then a strong case can be made for third party reimbursement for doulas and more families will benefit. The more unified the doula profession can be in agreeing on scope of practice, core competencies and guiding principles for doulas, the more successful we will become. In 2018, the National End-of-Life Doula Alliance (NEDA) was formed by a diverse group of trainers and leaders in the field for this very purpose.[4]

In terms of linking to national strategic plans and initiatives, the doula model of care synchronizes well with the public health approach to forming "compassionate communities" for folks at the end of life now being developed and implemented in Australia, the U.K, Canada and the U.S. And it is not a hard case to make that the following recommendations of the Institute of Medicine's landmark report *Dying in America* (2015)[5] are in alignment with the doula model of care:

- Deliver comprehensive end-of-life care by trained caregivers
- Meet Advance Care Planning standards
- Stronger knowledge and skills in palliative care
- Policies and payment systems to support high-quality care
- Public education and engagement

Summary

The emerging field of the end-of-life doula has benefitted greatly from the foundational work completed by leaders in the birth and postpartum doula arena. It would behoove practicing doulas, doula trainers, and hospice and palliative care organizations interested in adopting this new addition to end-of-life care to thoroughly understand and integrate the best of what the established doula model of care has to offer. Within the parameters described, doulas will retain great range for individual expression of their role and the services offered to families.

The core principles can serve as a touchstone for the doula profession, helping us to better serve individuals and families while achieving greater recognition and acceptance worldwide. ◆

References

[1]Dekker, R. (2017). Evidence Based Birth: Evidence on Doulas. Retrieved from evidencebasedbirth.com/the-evidence-for-doulas/.

[2]Agency for Clinical Innovation (2013). Understanding the process to develop a model of care: An ACI framework. Retrieved from www.aci.health.nsw.gov.au/__data/assets/pdf_file/0009/181935/HS13-034_Framework-DevelopMoC_D7.pdf

[3]DONA International (2017). Birth (and Postpartum) Doula Standards of Practice and Code of Ethics. Retrieved from www.dona.org/what-is-a-doula/scope-and-ethics/.

[4]National End-of-Life Doula Alliance (NEDA) (2018). Our Scope of Practice. Retrieved from nedalliance.com/.

[5]Institute of Medicine (2015). *Dying in America. Improving quality and honoring individual preferences near the end of life.* Washington DC, The National Academies Press.

CHAPTER 1

How Doulas Work

THERE ARE SEVERAL PATHS YOU CAN TAKE TO WORK AS A DOULA. In this chapter, we will explore a range of business models and configurations. It is important to understand the different legal structures for operating a business because each has accompanying tax ramifications and government reporting requirements. To further complicate matters, the various business models in use by doulas might fit into more than one legal structure. LLC, S Corporation, 501c3, EINs … it's a virtual alphabet soup! Let's sort it out.

First, consider …

A preliminary discussion of the benefits and disadvantages to being self-employed is in order. The positive aspects are most alluring indeed. You get to pursue your dream job. You no longer *have* a boss; you *are* the boss. Workplace personality issues and power struggles that drain your energy, make you angry and create stress in your life are a thing of the past. If someone is difficult, you can choose not to work with them. You can define your own work schedule and set your own rate of pay. When you want to go on vacation, you are free to do so. You have complete autonomy to please yourself and your clients only. If you have a family to consider, the business can grow at a pace that is consistent with your family's needs or it can slow down as circumstances dictate. Sounds lovely!

What is the down side? No regular, dependable paycheck. No benefits of any kind. No one pays you for anything you don't do. (I have never gotten paid for surfing the net, talking to my girlfriends on the phone or filing my nails while sitting at my desk.) Self-employment FICA taxes of 15.3 percent on your net income (gross income minus allowable business-related expenses) will be assessed. This is a hit! Wage-earners pay only half that amount, with the employer paying the other half. Self-employed individuals are both employer and employee, so they pay the full amount.

But wait, there's more. It can be challenging to carve out time for your business when you work out of your home. Sometimes friends and family members do not acknowledge that you are working. Flexible work hours are not the same as no work hours. If you're a mother and do not have the luxury of a room with a door that can be designated as your office, some clear boundaries will need to be established for when mama is working. If you are home, then you must be available, right? Wrong! There can be a serious lack of distinction between work and home life. On some days, especially when my children were little, I could be fitting in an hour here, two hours there, throughout the day, from eight in the morning to midnight. In a very real sense, I could always be working. At times, I have found myself incapable of simply reading a novel, as the pull of the office two steps away to do "one more thing" has proved overpowering.

Riding the rollercoaster of the work flow can be another challenge of self-employment. While, theoretically at least, we set our own schedule, the reality is that some months are dry and others overly busy. You may need to take on more clients than desirable when the calls are flowing to ride out the quiet months financially. This can be stressful, but if one learns to go with it rather than fight it (remind you of anything?), it can become part of the variety that those of us seeking to avoid the nine-to-five timeclock welcome. The real challenge isn't so much keeping up when it's busy (you just DO) as it is learning to relax and enjoy the down times for the break that they are, rather than stressing out about money. Easier said than done. A lack of clients can provide an opportunity to focus on the development side of the business, such as implementing marketing initiatives. There's always another job around the corner but learning to trust that fact is another matter. On the flip side, when everything is coming down in one week, despite the best laid plans, it is essential to line up sufficient help to get through it. After all, you are just one person and, until cloning becomes perfected, you simply can't be in two places at the same time. There's an art to this and it will likely take some trial and error to get it right.

> Not everyone is cut out to be self-employed and that's okay! Better to go in eyes wide open and make an informed decision.

Finally, since you are the boss, you are setting the agenda. This means that you must set the agenda! No one tells you what to do and when to do it. You must motivate yourself to develop your business forms, create a website, market your business, get out and network, continue to study and learn, return phone calls and emails, and so on. If you have good organizational and time management skills, are self-directed and self-motivated, this will still be challenging at times, but it will suit you well. However, if you struggle with depression, if organization is not your strong suit, or if you function best in community with others, going it alone may not be the best fit for you. Consider ... can you articulate goals, set an agenda and then follow through with implementation? Or do you function best when a daily schedule and structure is imposed on you? Can you impose it on yourself? Where will the motivation come from? Do you need it to come from the promised paycheck every two weeks, or can it come from within, generated by a desire to be successful doing work you love? Do an honest self-assessment and then set yourself up to succeed.

See our Personal Inventory Questionnaire in *The Doula Business Guide Workbook, 3rd Edition.*

Legal Business Structures

As you read through the following options, keep in mind two important points: (1) These categories are not all mutually exclusive; one can, for example, form a limited liability partnership; and (2) you can change your mind about the structure chosen. I have, at different points in my 35-year-long career, operated as a sole proprietor, a limited liability corporation (LLC), an LLC partnership and a nonprofit corporation. Now it appears that an S corporation structure will render significant tax advantages (sufficient to outweigh the drawbacks of this model discussed below) and I am planning to make yet another change. It is to be expected that creative entrepreneurs will evolve their businesses over time. Just do your best to choose a model that strikes the best balance between what makes sense for you today and your vision for where you would like to be in three or five years.

Sole Proprietor

A sole proprietorship is the traditional one-person business model and is the simplest way to set up your business as a self-employed individual. As a sole proprietor, you are responsible for all operational aspects of your business. You provide startup money, assume all debts and obligations, accept all profits and losses, and pay all taxes. The advantages to being a sole proprietor include: low startup costs; ease of startup; freedom from local, state and federal regulations; relatively easy tax reporting; uncomplicated decision making since you alone are in control; and, last but not least, you get to keep all of the profits from the business.

There is one primary disadvantage to sole proprietorship—the business owner has unlimited liability—meaning, in effect, that a client can sue you for everything you own, including both personal and business assets. A corporation, on the other hand, is an entity that is separate and distinct from its shareholders. Therefore, creditors have no rights to the personal assets of shareholders when making a claim against the corporation. (In Chapter 7, I take up the twin issues of liability and risk management in greater detail and suggest strategies for managing risks associated with offering doula services.)

If you do not incorporate your business, you are, by default, a sole proprietor. The simple act of starting a business makes you a sole proprietor. A sole proprietor can use her/his own name and personal bank account for business purposes if desired.

Limited Liability Corporation (LLC)

Simplicity and flexibility are the operational hallmarks of the LLC. In an LLC, the owner or owners are referred to as "members." The LLC entity does not pay federal income taxes. Rather, the members pay income and self-employment taxes on their share of the profits, whether distributed to them or not. There are several potential advantages for doulas adopting this business form:

- Profits and losses pass through the company directly to the owner(s).
- Personal assets are protected from any liability associated with the business (but there are limits on this; see below).
- There is no limitation on the number or nature of owners (such as in an S Corporation); one person can be the sole owner/member of an LLC or you can form a partnership LLC with two or more members.
- An LLC is simpler to operate than other types of corporations.
- LLCs are not subject to corporate formalities.
- Owners may, and typically do, participate in the management of the business.

LLCs are licensed and regulated by the state. If you dissolve the business, you will need to do so formally as well. Many states will charge a renewal fee each year (ranging from $25 in Michigan to $800 in California). It's a fairly straightforward process to establish an LLC however an accountant, lawyer or online service provider (e.g., LegalZoom.com) may be hired to set up the corporate structure for you if you prefer. If you are confident in your ability to research a topic on the web and track the details, you should be able to go it alone. It's not rocket science. You can also call the state for help if you have questions about the process.

Steps to Forming an LLC

To become an LLC, you will have to register with your Secretary of State. Go to your state's government website by entering [StateName].gov in your browser. From there, you can do a search that brings up relevant rules, regulations and forms necessary for the formation of an LLC. Everything can be handled electronically for the application process. (You may be able to opt for snail mail, but it will extend your timeline by many weeks versus a day or two.)

Step One. Search for name availability or "business entity search" to ensure that your chosen name is not already taken (see Chapter 2 for more tips on naming your business).

Step Two. Print out forms for the Articles of Incorporation and follow instructions for completing and filing the Articles (cost of filing differs from state to state, averaging about $100).

Step Three. Apply for an IRS Employer Identification Number (EIN) or Federal Identification Number (FIN). These terms are used interchangeably. You need the EIN even if you don't plan to hire employees. Go to IRS.gov and complete the online application. The EIN can then be used to open a business checking account (see Chapter 2) and is used in place of a social security number for the corporation.

Step Four. Complete an LLC Operating Agreement. The Operating Agreement is used in the formation of an LLC, but it is not filed with any government agencies unless required by state law. If not required by the state, it is simply completed, signed and dated, and filed with your corporate paperwork. While not required in all states, it is nevertheless advisable to have one. The Operating Agreement is extra protection to guard your limited liability status for both single-owner LLCs and partnership LLCs. It helps to ensure that courts will respect your limited personal liability, lending credibility to your LLC's separate existence. In addition, it puts the business owner(s) in control rather than state laws. In the absence of an Operating Agreement, state laws (called "default rules") govern numerous aspects of LLCs. For example, some states' default rules provide that members share equally in the profits, regardless of each member's contribution of capital. Common provisions in an Operating Agreement include:

- a statement of intent
- its business purpose
- the time period during which it will operate
- how it will be taxed
- number of members
- provisions for adding new members
- member capital contributions
- structure of management and sharing of profits

See LegalZoom.com for further detail if desired. If you use a template of some kind, just make sure that your Operating Agreement suits the needs of your business and the laws of your state. For LLC partnerships, the partnership and Operating Agreements can be merged into one document (see our discussion of partnerships below). If there are multiple members, this agreement becomes a binding contract between the members.

Step Five. Complete Membership Certificates for a business LLC. Membership certificates are official documents issued by a company to its members that provide evidence of how much of an ownership stake they have in the corporation. Membership certificates contain the following information:

- Name of the LLC
- State where it was formed
- Number of units issued (100 units for single-owner LLCs and a designated percentage for partnership LLCs)
- Recipient's name

Step Six. Minutes of any Meetings of the Members should also be completed. Minutes provide a clear record of discussions, votes and actions taken by the LLC (especially helpful if a dispute arises among the members). Meetings are only necessary if they are required by the LLC's organizational documents (the Articles of Incorporation and the Operating Agreement). If you are forming a partnership LLC, then stipulating that you will meet annually (or semi-annually) may be a good way to go. For single-owner LLCs, "meetings" seem rather silly, but if required, then go ahead and jump through the hoop and write up a summary of your decisions ("meetings").

Step Seven. A few states may require you to publish a notice of intent to form an LLC, while others may require that you obtain a license or permit.

Once completed, these documents should be stored in a small binder or file folder. No doubt, many owners of LLCs do not bother complying with steps four through six, are completely unaware of these requirements, and likely are not any the worse off for failure to do so, *unless they find themselves in court.* Since doulas are likely motivated to form an LLC for protection of personal assets in the event of a lawsuit, it seems prudent to comply with these steps in the formation process (required in some states) lest legal proceedings in the future question whether the business is indeed operating as an LLC.

It is important to note that while LLC status limits liability, the protection is not absolute. There are some exceptions where an LLC owner can be held personally liable. These include: causing direct personal injury; defaulting on a bank loan or business debt; failure to pay payroll taxes for an employee; fraudulent, illegal or reckless behavior causing harm to another; and treating the LLC as an extension of one's personal affairs or property rather than as a separate legal entity. Under these circumstances, the courts rule that a corporation ceases to exist as the corporate formalities have not been adhered to. Thus, be sure and get the federal employer identification number, open a separate business checking account (see Chapter 2) and keep your personal finances out of your LLC accounting books. And complete an Operating Agreement!

S Corporations

When it comes to taxation, a multi-owner LLC is automatically taxed as a partnership by default, each owner taxed according to their designated share of the profits. LLCs with one owner are taxed like sole proprietorships. However, LLCs can choose to be taxed as an S corporation by filing a document called an "election" with the IRS. In the S corporation model, the owner becomes both an employee who is paid a salary and an owner who receives dividends as a share of the profits. The tax benefit is that FICA taxes (15.3% of net income) are due on the salary amount only.* Dividends are claimed as income but not included in determination of the amount of FICA taxes due. The election may lower the overall tax liability for the individual while it complicates the way the owner pays herself.

Before forming an S-Corp, consider the complication of hiring employees, even if you are the only employee. You will need to comply with a variety of state and federal reporting requirements and pay payroll taxes quarterly. You will be required to purchase Workers' Compensation Insurance and pay into the unemployment fund (though you may be able to defer the latter until a claim is made against you). If you are at the point where you are going to hire help for your business, then you will need to file all these forms anyway so the burden at that point may be a wash. It is worth noting that most accountants will offer a payroll service who handle all the reporting for you for a fee ($50–$75 per month, depending on the number of employees).

* This can come back to bite you later if you are self-employed most of your adult life as I have been. Constant efforts to keep your FICA taxes as low as possible translates into decreased Social Security benefits when you need them. This concern can be addressed if you create a retirement plan as a corporate benefit and regularly invest in it or have some other nest egg or planning in place.

Nonprofit Corporations

A 501c3 nonprofit corporation is a relatively complex entity established for educational, religious, scientific, literary or charitable purposes. Other qualifying purposes include the testing of public safety, fostering amateur sports competitions and the prevention of cruelty to animals or children. Nonprofit status means that the organization enjoys freedom from certain types of taxes and that it is eligible to receive tax-deductible donations and grants from individuals, foundations and government bodies. Startup requirements and costs are considerable. Simply submitting the application to the IRS costs $750 with no guarantee that the application will be approved. The designation "nonprofit" is a bit of a misnomer. Technically, nonprofits must make a profit to remain viable; no business can run at a loss for very long. However, members, officers or directors cannot benefit financially from dissolution of the corporation. If the nonprofit does close its doors at some point in time, all remaining assets must be given, by law, to another nonprofit agency or government body.

While an individual can be the founder and executive director (ED) of a nonprofit corporation, decision-making power and fiduciary responsibility rests with the board of directors. Ongoing rules, regulations and reporting requirements are extensive, requiring the involvement of lawyers, accountants and nonprofit specialists. One risk for the visionary founder/ED is that the board of directors, comprised of good-hearted volunteers who (too often) have no real concept of the day-to-day operations of the business and have minimal overall involvement, nevertheless legally hold full decision-making authority (including the right to hire, fire and replace the ED as well as set her salary). The resulting built-in tension in the relationship between EDs and their boards (especially founder EDs) tends to revolve around accountability issues, which may at times feel like a one-way street from the ED's perspective (e.g., the ED is accountable to the board but can the board be held accountable by the ED and, if so, how?). A founder/ED will understandably have a sense of ownership, while in fact she is an employee, not an owner.

Doula entrepreneurs considering formation of a nonprofit corporation may be motivated to serve low-income families by establishing doula programs, community-based childbirth education centers, breastfeeding clinics, postpartum depression support groups, perinatal hospice doula programs, free-standing hospice homes and the like. These are all worthy enterprises. Given the complexity and challenges in both set up and management of a nonprofit corporation, I have devoted an entire chapter of the book to this subject (see Chapter 4).

Doula Business Models

Next, we consider a variety of ways that doulas take their services out into the world, along with the pros and cons of different business models.

Independent Doulas

The independent doula works in a solo practice and enjoys many benefits. She has complete control over her brand, reputation and all business-related decisions. She sets her own fees and keeps 100 percent of money earned. She can select clients with whom she feels a natural rapport; no one is making matches on her behalf. Because she does not have to coordinate schedules with other doula team members, bosses or managers, her scheduling is highly flexible and she is free to please herself and her clients only. Zero time and energy are spent on the logistics, communication challenges, hassles, emotions and drama often involved in working with others. As she builds trusting one-on-one relationships with her families, she can provide true continuity of care and her clients benefit as a result. For example, they know that the same doula with whom they have been meeting prenatally will be the person at their birth and postpartum visit(s). Families working with end-of-life doulas are not expected to adjust to a variety of different—possibly mis-matched—personalities coming and going at a stressful, yet sacred time. This,

I believe, adds to job satisfaction for the doula. The independent doula's control extends to her choice of a backup doula (or two or three). She can choose someone who has a similar philosophy of care, style, skills, personality. Someone with whom she feels certain her valued clients will feel comfortable. Finally, job security as an independent doula is high. No one can fire you.

The drawbacks of solo practice may also prove considerable, depending on the doula's business skill set, personality, assets, available help and other factors. Independent doulas are 100 percent responsible for everything, including all start-up expenses (e.g., incorporation, liability insurance, website hosting and development, etc.). A big investment of time and creative energy up front is required to launch a business. It takes time to get the business to where you need it to be income-wise and that fact alone may prove the model nonviable for newer doulas who require immediate income. In addition, there is the challenge of finding backup doulas, particularly if there are not many doulas in your area. However, if you make professional networking with other doulas a priority (whether in person or via social media), you should be able to overcome this limitation. It can feel lonely to be doing everything on your own—supplying all the energy, the ideas, the motivation, doing all the business tasks, marketing, finding clients—it's easy to feel overwhelmed (unless you have good help or can afford to hire it). A strong work ethic, focus, motivation, self-discipline and organizational skills are required.

Independent doulas can work as sole proprietors or form an LLC or S Corp. They may also find work as independent contractors (ICs) for agencies or programs.

Doula Partnerships (Think Twice!)

Partnerships are when two (or more) doulas work together and share all the clients, business decisions, income and operating expenses. Perhaps you are considering setting up a doula business with a trusted colleague? At first glance, this may appear to be a good, even fun idea. Certainly, if the idea is to share clients, trade being on call and split up the administrative tasks, the advantages to such an arrangement in preventing doula burnout are clear. In a general partnership, two or more owners share the management of the business, and each is personally liable for all the debts and obligations of the business. Each partner must pay income tax on her share of the profits only.

General partnerships are easy to form. Startup costs may be a bit more if a lawyer is consulted. You can form a general partnership by a simple verbal agreement of involved parties. However, given the not unlikely prospect of future disputes, it's probably a good idea to have an attorney prepare, or at least review, a written understanding or formal Partnership Agreement. A Partnership Agreement spells out the partners' mutual understanding regarding each owner's percentage of ownership, share of profits (or losses), rights and responsibilities, voting powers, management of the business and what will happen to the business and business assets if one of you leaves (buy-sell provisions). The existence of a Partnership Agreement ensures that your business will be governed by your own rules rather than default rules created by the state. Typically, partners make a start-up investment in the business of cash, property and/or services. In return, each partner gets a percentage of ownership in the business assets, usually in proportion to their contributions. The split is often 50/50, however the members are free to divide up ownership in any way they wish. Just remember that in the absence of a signed agreement, the default language in state law will rule in favor of an even division of assets among the partners when/if the time comes to dissolve the corporation.

A Partnership Agreement is designed to head off problems at the pass (just like your doula/client contract). It invites prospective partners to make a cooperative, considered judgment regarding the mutual decision to enter into a partnership and forces them to look at common sticking points for business partners of all kinds. This is a good thing, because there are many pitfalls to partnership. The main disadvantages to partnerships are shared decision making and the near certainty of conflicts arising. It is hard to find the perfect partner. A completely functional, successful, joyful and long-lasting business partnership is a rare bird. Just look around you and ask.

Additional drawbacks include: each partner is exposed to unlimited liability for business expenses; each partner is bound by the actions of the other partner;

Another Take on Partnerships

One doula who has been in a successful partnership practice for five years reported being the primary breadwinner for her family of four. She spoke of "beautiful communication" between the partners. She believes the biggest benefit of the partnership is better support for both clients and doulas. Clients get two experienced doulas supporting them, while the doulas look out for each other and provide relief when needed. Partnership makes it possible for doulas to go off call. Her biggest challenge? Learning to "let go" of her attachment to being at every birth, to be okay with letting her partner step in. "It has evolved so much. I needed to learn to put myself first, to go on vacation."

the loss of one partner may dissolve the business; and the partnership may be difficult to end. When partnerships do end, it is rarely on a good note, thus exposing each partner to the possibility that the other will make disparaging remarks in the community. This type of bad worth of mouth damages your professional image and adversely affects your capacity to continue to earn your living in the field. To protect yourself, you may need to consult a lawyer when dissolving a partnership. A failed partnership is a loss, no way around it. It may be necessary to burn the bridge, but it is always regrettable.

I am not a fan of partnerships. To be fair, I must own that my personality is such that I may be unsuitable for partnership. Perhaps some readers do not share my same failings and tendencies. Three failed attempts would lead any sane person to reflect that perhaps it is not the partner alone who is at fault, but, as in any relationship gone bad, it takes two. Nevertheless, I have noted certain patterns, shared by failed partnerships in general, manifest in my own relationships or those of close contacts. And so, I think it is worth considering in greater detail the various types of challenges common to business partnerships.

Tensions may arise because one partner is more skillful, more knowledgeable, more experienced or better organized than the other. Clients may perceive one partner as being more professional or reliable than the other, or simply prefer to work with one partner over the other. If this happens repeatedly, you have a problem. One partner may have a strong work ethic while the other is more laid back. One partner may be beset with personal problems including marital difficulties, health concerns, a spouse's job loss, or extended family issues, depending heavily on the other to get her through these difficulties while paybacks are slow to manifest. One partner may struggle with depression or addiction (gambling with company funds, for example), while the other is forced to cover for her shortcomings (literally and figuratively). One partner may be coercive or manipulative or have a more dominating personality, bulldozing the other while resentments build. One partner may undermine the other's client relationships or be rude or inconsiderate. There may simply be poor communication between the partners, leading to an array of problems. A common underlying theme is that one partner simply doesn't pull her weight.

Trust me, it gets old fast if you believe you are doing more than half the work while splitting the income 50/50. And, in this case, perception is reality. If that is your perception, then you *will* feel ripped off. In the case of one former partner, I went into the relationship believing that we would both give 100 percent. In the end, I realized that each person's 100 percent was not necessarily equal. That was

Elements of a Partnership Agreement

A partnership agreement addresses the following topics:

- What are the business partners' short- and long-term business goals? Write a short summary statement.
- How much will each partner contribute in cash, property and time, and when will these contributions be made?
- How will each partner share in the profits and losses of the business? Typically, this will be defined as an equal division of profits, however, provisions for an unequal division of profits may be considered in compensation for differences in time or money contributed or differences in ability and experience.
- What are the procedures for withdrawing funds and paying profits? How much and when? This will prevent partners from arbitrarily withdrawing money from the partnership. Who will have the authority to sign checks, for example?
- What about provisions for continuing the business if one partner dies or wants out? Without such a provision, a partner can legally quit or retire any time, sell her share of the partnership to anyone she pleases or demand to be paid fair market value for her share of the partnership. How is value to be determined? The tax consequences of a partnership buyout may be significant. Since the interests of remaining and outgoing partners are often in direct opposition, it is advisable to seek professional advice. Some agreements include a noncompete clause that prevents a departing partner from engaging in a similar business for a specified time and geographic radius.
- Consider the possibility of a partner competing with the partnership and specify whether any of the partners can have a separate outside business.
- If the partnership dissolves, who will own the right to the business name or the URL and website?
- Consider who will own rights to a client database or mailing list in the event of dissolution.
- Consider including a non-disparagement clause stating that the reasons for the breakup of the business partnership cannot be discussed publicly with clients and colleagues.

Note: *A partnership agreement is not binding on third parties such as lenders, creditors or dissatisfied clients who are free to go after all partners in a dispute.*

an eye opener because I had to admit that my partner's perception may very well have been that she was, in fact, giving it her all. But I did not feel that her all was equal to mine. And so, it didn't work for me.

Finally, there is yet another aspect to the dark side of partnerships. Do you think any of us knows, really knows, what we are signing on for when we formalize a partnership, whether it be a marriage or a business partner? I have discovered, as the years unfold, that I have agreed to take on my husband's karma and he mine. It

Partnership Checklist

- ☐ Consider that more than one partner will exponentially increase your risk of problems while also ensuring a more cumbersome (read "slow") decision-making process.
- ☐ Choose a partner who is emotionally and physically healthy and living a relatively stable life.
- ☐ Choose a partner who brings a unique skill or asset to the business venture that you lack. If you are a good fit, you will each contribute different strengths and capitalize on those strengths consciously.
- ☐ Make a list of all the reasons why you desire to form this partnership; ask your intended partner to do the same.
- ☐ Discern whether you are a good match and really be honest about any reservations you may have. If a red flag is waving in your face, don't ignore it and hope it magically resolves; confront the behavior/issue and decide how you are going to address it. In my experience, the handwriting was on the wall, right from the beginning, in each instance, but I chose to ignore it out of a sense of enthusiasm and unexamined optimism. And in every case, the issue that I knew was a problem right from the start was the same issue that came back to bite me, usually sooner rather than later—no big surprises there.
- ☐ Make your mutual expectations explicit and put them in writing. It really isn't fair to be mad at someone for not meeting an expectation that was never communicated.
- ☐ Finally, agree to set up a regular time to meet and hold each other accountable. Acknowledge that there may be challenges that you agree to work through together. Go one step further and ask your partner and yourself to avoid responding defensively if/when issues are aired. Lame excuses, tears or stomping out of the room are manipulative behaviors, pure and simple, and they will not contribute to a healthy partnership. You both need to be able to clear the air and have those hard conversations.

seems to me that we are here on earth to learn certain lessons, to evolve as human beings. Consequently, we draw to ourselves those people who can be teachers and circumstances that aid our growth. If we do not take the time for self-reflection, thus failing to see purpose in our pain, we are doomed to attract the same lesson again and again, until we "get it." It's like the movie *Groundhog Day* with Bill Murray, wherein our protagonist must relive the same day, countless times, until he finally evolves to the point where he gets it right. If our partners—husbands, wives and otherwise—need to learn certain lessons in life, we have signed up for their ride in a sense, and vice versa. In the end, you just really need to be sure that what you are getting out of it is worth it, that it meets your need to be in the relationship in the first place.

Partnerships take some effort. They involve sacrifice. And they require that both individuals make a concerted effort to communicate honestly and respectfully. This all takes time together. When partnerships go bad, the friendships involved go down too, like a bad divorce. Who needs the drama? For my part, I can say unequivocally that one partnership—my 40-year marriage to my wonderful husband—is enough for me. I trust that the lessons we draw are meant for both of us, that we are on our divinely guided path together. I'm not so sure about the hard lessons encountered with my business partners, nor can I be so committed to "for better or worse" in those relationships.

Now, if I haven't scared you off the idea of partnership, and you are intent upon moving forward, at least you will be making an informed choice (be sure and consider the collaborative models discussed below as well). Good luck! You just may be the rare exception and who am I to rain on your parade?

Postscript—Never say "never."

It is four years since I wrote my unequivocal disavowal of business partnerships and two years since I formed a new partnership! What made me do it you ask? I had a compelling reason.

A long-time friend and retired homebirth midwife cohort had been engaging end-of-life work, specializing in advance care planning, facilitating home funerals for families and advocating for green burial while pursuing a master's degree in hospice and palliative care. Meanwhile, I lost two sets of parents in a short time-frame and was intimately involved in their final days. Like so many other families, my siblings and I cared for our dementia-afflicted mother through her years-long decline. My friend and I began to have spirited conversations about the similarities between birth and death, the essence and meaning of support, the role of the doula, and what we were witnessing in our work and extended families.

Our conversations resulted in a collaboration. Together we designed and offered an end-of-life doula training workshop and published a manual of resources. Our first workshop sold out and a substantial number of people were placed on a wait list. A few months later, Lifespan Doulas [LifespanDoulas.com] was born. As you can imagine, I experienced great trepidation about forming another business partnership and potentially placing yet another friendship at risk. I pulled out my own book and we diligently worked our way through the Partnership Checklist and Elements of a Partnership Agreement. Our motives, strengths and weaknesses were openly explored. A few key indicators gave me hope for our mutual success:

- Neither of us felt capable or qualified to launch this initiative on our own, but as a team, our qualifications are impressive and fit the bill. Our choice was either to do it together or not do it.
- Designing the curriculum, publishing the manual and teaching our first workshop was fun! We have shared strengths in these areas and enjoyed the creative synergy of collaborating. Feedback from workshop participants was overwhelmingly enthusiastic.
- While we have both been doulas and caregivers with years of experience supporting families through life's major transitions, we have different skills, strengths and inclinations. Merilynne is extremely social and loves to chat folks up. She enjoys engagement with others and was already actively networking with folks across North America on end-of-life issues (for example, serving on the board of directors of both the National Home Funeral Alliance and the Green Burial Council, among other outreach activities). Consequently, she handles phone support and manages our outreach, public relations and doula mentoring. I, on the other hand, am a writer, a teacher and a details person (dare I say, organizational control freak?). I put our infrastructure into place (incorporation, bookkeeping system, data management, etc.), created and maintain the website, publish a monthly e-newsletter and generally put the polishing touch on all written materials. Thus, we are each speaking to our strengths.

So far, so good. There have been a few rough spots. We work through them respectfully. We set aside time to share our feelings about how the partnership is working, what is going well and what could be improved. Two years later, we remain committed to a shared vision built on trust.

Partnerships can be organized as sole proprietors or incorporate as LLCs or S-Corporations.

Doula Collectives

A collective is a group of independent doulas, from three to six or so, who come together under the banner of one business. Typically, each member of the collective sets her own fees and negotiates her own client contracts, but there may be variations here. There may be a fee to join the collective (a buy-in of sorts) or a monthly or annual fee to cover ongoing expenses of running the collective (e.g., website hosting, marketing, a manager's time). Or it might be arranged more informally with the understanding that everyone is expected to pitch in and help with marketing efforts or other tasks.

Many practitioners have discovered the benefits of pooling resources and working in community with others. The collective business model offers benefits in terms of camaraderie, ease of backup and sharing of marketing and administrative responsibilities, thereby enabling doulas to play to their strengths serving families. In recent years, doula collectives have become an increasingly popular choice. For new doulas, joining an existing collective enables them to bypass the slower start-up and expenses of creating a business from scratch. Doulas working in a collective enjoy the same flexible scheduling as independent doulas, each member maintaining control over the clients she accepts. In this model, job security is high (the same as an independent doula) because each doula is her own boss.

What are the drawbacks of doula collectives? It appears that the primary benefit—working with others—is also at the root of most of the drawbacks. These include: communication challenges, increasing as the collective grows (it can be difficult to find times when everyone can come together); a slower decision-making process based on group consensus; issues with one (or more) member not contributing or reciprocating backup as expected; differences in skills, experience and personality that make some members of the collective more or less suitable as a backup fit for each other; and relationship issues, jealousy and drama among group members that suck time and energy. Furthermore, the group's brand and reputation can be put at risk by one group member behaving in an unprofessional manner. And finally, shared marketing responsibilities is not the same as no marketing; group members must work together to generate clients; one simply cannot abdicate on that front.

Since the doulas working in a collective model are all independent doulas, they have the option of electing to be sole proprietors or forming an LLC or S Corp. They may also find work as Independent Contractors for agencies or programs.

Doula Agencies

A doula agency is run by an owner/manager who hires doulas and matches them with clients. The owner may also take on clients of her own. The owner is responsible for marketing and all business decisions including negotiating doula and client contracts and setting and collecting fees. The doulas may be employees of the agency or, more likely, independent contractors (ICs) who work for more than one agency or have a few clients of their own. It is important to understand the legal distinction between employees and ICs (see below). Whether the doulas are paid as ICs or employees, they receive a percentage of the fee paid by the client, while the owner keeps the rest.

In one agency, birth doulas work in teams of two and rotate being on-call. In another, each doula is matched with a client and can tap available backup if needed. There are many variations on how on-call and backup are handled within each agency so prospective agency doulas should be clear about expectations. One owner instituted a backup relief fund that pays a backup doula to take over if the original doula has been at a birth for 24+ hours. In this model, $25 from every birth goes into the fund and, when needed, the fund pays $25 per hour to a backup doula to step in and provide relief for six hours. After interviewing several agency owners, I find myself marveling at the creativity of the various approaches. Clearly, there is not one right way to do it.

Consumers may be attracted to an agency over a private-practice doula because they value the extra layer of service they are getting. This includes a streamlined interview process with doulas who have already been vetted, a guarantee of backup doulas, and an intermediary if the doula is not meeting client expectations. Vetting of doulas and other caregivers reassures families that they will be matched with trained, experienced and insured doulas. Vetting may include:

- Police background check
- Verification of training and education
- Verification of professional liability insurance
- Driving record check (if applicable)
- Verification of other certificates such as CPR/First Aid (if applicable)

- Reference check
- Personal interview

Let's consider the pros and cons of this model from both perspectives—that of agency doulas and owners.

Agency Doulas

Agency doulas enjoy camaraderie, backup support and flexibility. Some agencies feature a shared on-call system with teams of doulas, thereby ensuring time off call and reduced stress. The doulas are free from many of the concerns of other models as nearly all the administrative tasks and the need to generate clients are the responsibility of the agency owner. This freedom leaves them able to focus solely on clients, engaging aspects of the job that speak to their strengths. If they are short on business skills, it's not a deal breaker. Backup support is readily available and there is no need to communicate with clients about money or have difficult conversations/negotiations. In addition, ICs enjoy flexible scheduling. They can determine their availability, express their scheduling preferences, take on other jobs or enjoy a leave of absence as desired. If a super stressful or challenging client scenario is underway, the agency doula can expect problem-solving support to manage the situation from the owner who, at the end of the day, is responsible for her own brand and reputation. This all helps to avoid burnout and goes a long way toward sustainability for doula work.

The drawbacks of working for a doula agency include the owner keeping a (sometimes significant) percentage of the fee that the client is paying, anywhere from 10–50%. Depending on agency policies which can vary widely, the doula may not have control over clients she is matched with, nor any choice over the backup doula(s) assigned to step in when needed. Overall, the agency doula is likely to have little input on how the

One agency owner I spoke with believes that the birth doula ICs who work for her company are making a more reliable income as new doulas (approximately $22 per hour) than they would be able to do on their own. They can pretty much hit the ground running, with very little start-up cost or investment beyond the cost of training.

In another agency, new doulas earn 70 percent of the client's fee. Certified and experienced doulas earn 80 percent, and when either of the owners attend a birth, they pay themselves 90 percent. If the doula brings a client to the agency, she receives a bonus.

Questions to Ask before Agreeing to be an Independent Contractor for a Doula Agency

- What is the rate of pay? What percentage of the client fee is the agency retaining?
- Am I free to pursue my own clients while working for the agency and after leaving the agency? ***You are looking for an absence of non-compete language!***
- When do I get paid? What if the client doesn't pay the agency on time?
- How does the referral/matching process work?
- What if I am matched with a client and I don't feel it is a good match?
- Can you accommodate my preferred work days and hours?
- What is the work flow like? Can I work as much (or as little) as I want?
- What is your backup system for unavoidable conflicts?
- What expectations do you have of the doula?

agency is managed; it either suits her or it doesn't. If the doula is an IC rather than an employee, she will be responsible for the full 13.5% FICA taxes on her income. *Beware that some agencies require their IC doulas to sign a non-compete agreement.* Technically, this is a non-starter because it is legally incompatible with IC status as defined by the IRS (see below) and therefore unenforceable. Finally, since the doula serves at the pleasure of the agency owner, job security is relatively low.

When working as an IC, the doulas are (by definition) independent. They may elect to be sole proprietors or incorporate as an LLC.

Agency Owners

Doula agencies are often owned by an active doula who divides her time between running the business and taking on her own clients. Some agencies are run by two or more partners. The owner handles all inquiries, but how matches are made varies from agency to agency. Some owners will do the matching, while others have an interview system that includes more choice for both doulas and clients.

What are the benefits of owning a doula agency? Doulas who have invested great effort in building their businesses are prone to feeling dismayed at the idea of turning clients away once they become successful. As an agency owner, they are no longer limited to the hours that one person has available to meet client needs. They can hook the potential client up with another trusted doula, take their cut and still benefit from their efforts to generate that client in the first place. This increases their overall income potential. Agency owners I spoke with identified the following motivations:

- Avoid the isolation of solo practice, preferring to work in community with others
- Create a sustainable pathway for doulas to have long-term careers
- Raise the bar for doulas in their community, setting an example of excellent service for clients and support for doulas
- One owner told me her ultimate goal is to pay herself benefits (e.g., health care, retirement).

There are several potential drawbacks. It is a lot of work! The owner is responsible for all administrative tasks and marketing, and pays all associated expenses. As she expands the number of folks she is dealing with—including both doulas and clients—it is essential to have the proper organizational tracking systems and infrastructure in place. Systems must be vetted, purchased or created from scratch. This requires a considerable investment of both time and money. One agency owner told me that she invested approximately $7000 to get things set up properly, including business training and coaching. Owners may face the dual challenges of generating a steady work flow to keep a sufficient number of doulas working as much as they want to and facing staffing shortages from time to time. Additional drawbacks of running an agency can be summed up with the catchphrase "the buck stops here." The reputation of the agency depends partly on the doula contractors who are working with the families and can be negatively impacted by the actions of one doula. Whenever there is an issue or problem, it is up to the owner to resolve it.

> **"Tenacity is required. We are brilliantly stubborn and will work harder than anyone else."**
>
> —Agency owner Heather Crossan, EliteDoula.com, Alberta, Canada

In response to the question, what lessons have you learned the hard way, owners I spoke with shared the following tips.

"Hire administrative help sooner rather than later."
Love this one!

"Provide crystal clear guidelines to doulas that they are not to make any changes to the client's expectations as specified in the contract."
The owner shared a story. In her agency, the birth doulas work in teams. The client contract promises that the doula will join moms in labor within two hours of notification. Going off call, one doula told the client whose labor was impending not to worry, her doula team member was only "10 minutes away" from the client, thereby setting up a different expectation in terms of response time. Mom waited too long to notify her doula when labor started, the doula missed the birth, and the parents were angry with the agency owner.

"I'm not a free referral agency."
The client contract should include language prohibiting families from attempting to hire the IC doula directly, cutting out the agency owner. In the event the client violates this policy, the client will owe the agency a substantial "finder's fee." To avoid this scenario altogether, owners may require that IC doulas who also have clients of their own refrain from publishing their fees on their website (thereby inviting comparison shopping) or directly advertising against the agency. Note that this is not the same as non-compete.

"Have infrastructure in place."
In one case, two new agency owner partners launched the business from their own successful independent practices. They already had established reputations in the community. They found themselves serving all the clients, doing all the interviews, all the administrative tasks and the record keeping. Meanwhile, they did not have systems, especially bookkeeping, in place to handle their success. She said it was "nuts" as they played catch-up.

"Consider WHY you want to start an agency."
There needs to be passion and a sense of growing your business for the long haul.

"It is a ton of work—way more than I imagined."

The myth that doula agency owners are opportunistically making money off the work of others as they kick back and watch the money roll in needs to be addressed. Owners I interviewed were quick to disavow this notion, one going so far as to call her business a "group" rather than an "agency" because she felt the connotation had become so toxic in doula culture. While there may be some agency

Sample Birth Doula Agency

Ownership. Co-owned by two doulas. One has many years of experience in maternal-infant health, is well-known in the community and has established positive relationships with area health care providers. Her business partner is currently taking a leave of absence from active doula work to focus on the needs of her young son and the growing doula agency. The work is split evenly with the help of an administrative assistant who works 12 hours per week.

The Doulas. Twelve doula ICs are employed by the agency and more are needed. The owners reported that they were willing to hire newly-trained doulas but emphasized that doulas must be mature and have skills. Finding the "right person" is paramount. Requirements for doulas include:

- Completion of doula training
- If not already certified, the doula needs to be pursuing certification. A financial incentive of an additional 10 percent of the client fee is offered for certified doulas.
- Background check
- Each doula must carry her own liability insurance **and** the agency is added on the insurance contract under "additional insured." ***(This is a great tip for agency owners!)***
- Since the agency's service area is defined as a 50-mile radius of their primary location, doulas must be willing and capable of travel within the service area.
- Birth doulas must attend a series of childbirth preparation classes.

How Services are Delivered. Clients seeking services fill out a form on the agency website. In response, one of the owners sets up a phone interview via email and then chooses a doula pair who they believe will be a good match for the client. For the doula team, the owners are looking for doulas who have different strengths and a good chemistry or natural flow between them. Then an interview is set up with the clients and doula team. The client can sign the contract at the end of the interview or do it electronically later.

The Money. The agency charges $1250 for a package of birth doula services that includes:

- One 90-minute prenatal with assigned doula team
- Doulas go on-call as soon as contract is signed.
- A doula will arrive at a birth within two hours of notification.
- If the birth goes longer than 12 hours, the first-call doula can call in her other team member for relief.
- Fourteen hours of face-to-face support in labor are included. Client is charged additional $30-per-hour fee after 14 hours.
- One postpartum visit
- The owners keep 30 percent of the client's fee and the doula team splits the remaining 70 percent.

owners who are taking advantage of their doula ICs, the owners I spoke with sincerely cared about the doulas who contracted with them and wanted to attract quality people who would stay with them and uphold their standards and brand. Owners were willing to engage newly trained, inexperienced doulas provided they were "the right fit." Overall, I was impressed by owners' commitment to properly value the doula's work. Presumably, those few who are pursuing a more opportunistic approach will do themselves in with high turnover among their under-valued doulas, ensuring that they always have the least experienced doula "dabblers" in town rather than committed, professional doulas.

HINT: Look for a 50/50 split on the fees and/or a requirement that ICs provide unpaid help with administrative and marketing tasks as indicators to steer clear. You can do better.

Are Agency Doulas Employees or Independent Contractors (ICs)?

A business may pay an employee and an IC for the same or similar work, but there are important legal differences between the two designations. For the employee, the company withholds income tax, Social Security and Medicare from wages paid. For the IC, the company does not withhold taxes. In addition, employment and labor laws do not apply to ICs. If you are a doula agency owner who hires ICs, you must be vigilant to ensure that government agencies never reclassify your contractors as employees, thereby subjecting you to back taxes and penalties. The following table clarifies the advantages for the doula agency owner of employing ICs rather than hiring doulas as employees. The former saves money for the owner who is not required to pay the employer's share of employees' FICA taxes and is free from the more burdensome complications and reporting regulations associated with hiring employees.

So, how does the IRS decide who is truly an employee versus an independent contractor? One simple way to think of the distinction is that the IC is a separate business entity—he/she is already self-employed and has income from other sources. As a separate business entity, the IC may work under an assumed business name, be incorporated, have employees of her own, work for other companies as an IC, carry insurance, have business cards and invoice forms, and so on. A key indicator of a worker's status is how much control the agency owner has over how, when and where the work is performed.

Variables	Employee	Independent Contractor
Employment Laws	Covered by federal and state employment and labor laws	Not covered by employment and labor laws
Hiring Practice	Prospective employee completes a job application; approved applicant receives a job offer; typically handled by the Human Resources Department in larger companies	Prospective contractor interacts with person or department wanting a specific service or task completed; sometimes a proposal or bid is submitted; contractor enters into a contract with the company
Tax Documents	Provides name, address, Social Security number, tax filing status and number of exemptions on a Form W-4	Provides name, address and Taxpayer Identification Number on a Form W-9
Payer's Tax Reporting Requirements	Reports all money paid to the employee during the tax year on a Form W-2	Reports payments of $600 or more in a calendar year on a Form 1099
Payer's Taxes	Pays payroll taxes quarterly (on the last day of April, July, October and January); responsible for half of FICA taxes on total payroll (7.65%)	Pays quarterly federal and state taxes on net income (gross minus expenses); pays the full 15.3% FICA tax
Reporting to Other Agencies	State and federal Unemployment Insurance and Workmen's Compensation	None
Value of Work or Contract	Earns either an hourly rate or a salary	Contractor submits an invoice based on an hourly, daily or weekly amount, or for a total lump sum when the job is completed
Payment Timeframe	Pay periods may be weekly, bi-weekly or monthly	Contractor paid after submitting an invoice, according to the contract; may require a percentage of the total anticipated amount to be paid up front

10 Distinguishing Features of Independent Consultants

- ICs operate as their own business. An agency's relationship with an IC is a business-to-business relationship.
- ICs are experts in their industry, bringing specialized expertise to a project or task. The client is not responsible for providing an IC with training as they would with an employee.
- ICs openly market their services and work for multiple clients.
- ICs are engaged for a specific project or period. Unlike traditional employees whose jobs may encompass a wide variety of duties and tasks, ICs are only responsible for performing the services outlined in their contract.
- ICs submit invoices for work completed according to a negotiated contract, rather than working for a specific salary.
- ICs determine when they work. Because ICs are their own business entity, a client cannot determine their work hours. They are only responsible for fulfilling the work agreement; when they work and the hours they keep is completely up to them.
- ICs determine how they work, including providing any needed tools or equipment. If a project requires specialized equipment that is only available on site, this should be stipulated in a contract.
- ICs are responsible for their own taxes.
- ICs are not eligible for company benefits.
- ICs can subcontract or delegate work. ICs may have their own employees, subcontractors or partner consultants who help them to complete work tasks. Whether the IC intends to engage other helpers for the job should be clarified up front, during contract negotiations.

Create an Independent Contractor Agreement

A written agreement helps establish a worker's status with the IRS by demonstrating intent to create an agency/IC relationship rather than an employer/employee relationship. Make all arrangements and mutual expectations as transparent as possible. The contract can protect your relationship and limit drama resulting from misunderstandings down the road. It should include the following components:

- a description of the services the IC will perform
- a description of how much the IC will be paid for services rendered
- a description of how and when the IC will be paid
- an explanation of who will be responsible for expenses (true ICs usually pay their own expenses)
- a statement that the agency owner and the doula agree to an IC relationship
- a statement that the IC will pay state and federal income taxes
- an acknowledgment by the IC that she is not entitled to any employee benefits
- a statement by the IC that she carries liability insurance
- a description of the timeframe of the agreement
- a description of the circumstances under which the agency owner or the IC can terminate the agreement
- an explanation of how the agency owner and the IC will resolve any disputes

Additional Resources

- See article "Understanding Employee vs. Contractor Designation" at IRS.gov.
- For tips on structuring your work relationship with an IC in a way that will withstand government scrutiny, see Nolo's article "Working with Independent Contractors: Avoiding Classification Problems" at Nolo.com.
- For general information on ICs and more, see MBOPartners.com.

Agency owners may operate as LLCs or S-Corporations.

Broker (or Referral) Agencies

Like other doula agencies, *My Nanny Rocks* helps prospective clients and service providers find each other. The basic concept is that the agency makes it easier for folks seeking services (doulas, childcare, home health care aides) to go to a trusted and reputable source and find a pre-screened professional who meets their needs. Clients seeking services are interviewed to determine their needs and then given the names of one or two (or more) practitioners who might be a match. In this model, the agent serves as a broker or matchmaker, bringing two parties together and charging a fee for her services. Once a match has successfully been made, the agency is no longer involved in the relationship between the two parties, though their contract may provide provisions for limited follow up in case a match proves unsuitable within a specified time frame.

Doulas may be interested in either starting such an agency of their own or joining an existing agency in their area. By registering yourself with a referral agency, you should not be precluding the possibility of attracting customers on your own. Rather, you are simply expanding your exposure and potential source of customers. Make sure your contract specifies that you are a free agent.

One business in my area, *My Nanny Rocks,* established this model as a partnership LLC. The business is owned and collectively managed by three women who are themselves experienced nannies and postpartum doulas. Following is a description of the business, from their website.

> *We place caregivers for the following types of positions: occasional babysitters, part-time caregivers, temporary caregivers, postpartum doulas, overnight caregivers, full-time nannies (both live-in and live-out) and tutors.*

For the provider:

> *We are a referral agency, meaning that once you complete an application we will interview you and check your background and references. After completing this process, we will match you with a family that fits your desires and job requirements. You and your new employer will negotiate salary and other job benefits; we are here solely to help you find a great position with a lovely family.*

For the customer seeking a service provider:

> *My Nanny Rocks understands the importance of having a trustworthy individual caring for your children. Selecting a caregiver can be daunting but My Nanny*

Rocks makes this task easy for you and your family. We take the legwork out of this process and pre-interview caregivers, check their references, and do a thorough background check so you can be assured that your caregiver is top notch.

Once we have received your family application, My Nanny Rocks' partners will arrange a time to meet with your family to discuss your childcare wishes. After our meeting we will provide you with a choice of caregivers that we believe will be suitable for your family situation. My Nanny Rocks will supply you with the caregiver's contact information so you can schedule a meeting with your prospective caregiver at your convenience. We appreciate your busy lifestyle and our goal is to make this process go as smoothly and quickly as possible.

Business partner, nanny and postpartum doula Lily Sacks reports favorably on the success of this model for her and her two business partners, calling it "financially lucrative." She states that the business can generate a nice income for one person; however, *My Nanny Rocks* partners split profits three ways, thus providing a nice supplemental income for each. Lily shared that the best aspect of the business for her is that she is doing what she likes to do—working with families and getting paid to help families find caregivers. The most challenging aspect of the business is working with families who call and "want perfection in three days." She reports that sometimes it can be difficult to please everyone, especially when customers make their own lack of planning a crisis and draw her and her partners into their drama.

On the partnership aspect of the business, Lily emphasized that it works well because each partner has a different skill set. The "tech savvy" partner is responsible for the website and bookkeeping aspects of the business, while the other two split the interviews, one preferring to work with the caregivers and the other one primarily interfacing with the families. In their model, the caregivers do not pay a fee to be in the approved caregiver group; the families pay the agency's fee after a successful match has been made—essentially, a one-time finder's fee. As the name of the business implies, *My Nanny Rocks* is primarily focused on making matches for long-term child care, however, a percentage of their business involves placing postpartum doulas.

Postscript. This business closed a couple of years ago as the owners went on to prioritize other pursuits, so you will not be able to find them online. The model itself, however, is worthy of your consideration.

Doula Program Employees

Some community-based and hospital-based doula programs hire doulas as employees. Hospices are also coming on board with doula programs though currently, these appear to be limited to volunteer vigil programs like the popular *No One Dies Alone* program. I believe, however, that fee-for-service hospice doula programs will begin to sprout up in the not-too-distant future and will feature a broader, more practical interpretation of the role of the doula beyond planning vigil or guiding legacy projects.

Community-based doula programs typically operate under the umbrella of a nonprofit organization or government agency and are designed to serve a specific target population or demographic (e.g., low-income families, immigrant populations, teen mothers, at-risk groups and so on). Doulas hired to work for these programs are often members of the community served and are culturally aligned with their clients. For example, an initiative designed to reduce premature births and disparities in outcomes for African-American families, might hire African-American doulas who have experienced a premature birth. See Chapter 5 for more information on doula programs of all kinds.

Volunteer Doulas

Many hospitals and a growing number of hospices have volunteer doula programs. There are also community-based programs that make use of volunteer doulas. Program parameters vary. Doulas may sign up for on-call shifts (responding when the call comes in) or they may be pre-assigned one-on-one to a client, building relationships and providing a continuum of care. For birth doulas, this means prenatal visits, birth planning, on-call for the birth, support services through the labor and a postpartum visit or two. Volunteer postpartum doulas might work one-on-one with families or as part of a team if the need is great. For end-of-life doulas, it can mean in-home assessments, advance care planning, guidance/encouragement/support in completing a legacy project, on-call availability for the death vigil and follow-up bereavement support. Requirements for participation in volunteer doula programs typically include completion of doula training and attendance at an orientation program that clarifies any program policies. Of course, there are always the free-lancers too, the folks who simply help, sometimes through their church, family or other community connections. They see a need and they step up.

In Defense of Volunteer Doulas

In recent years, volunteer doula programs have fallen out of favor with an outspoken segment of the birth and postpartum doula community who view them as devaluing the role of the doula. The word "demonization" comes to mind as the tone of the criticisms and pushback on social media has become increasingly polarizing. The arguments against volunteering can be summed up as follows:

1. The notion that every family deserves doula support is ridiculous; doulas provide a luxury service for which clients ought to pay market price.
2. Volunteer doulas are sending a message that doula services have a low value; prospects will be limited for professional (non-volunteer) doulas because people won't want to pay for something they might get for free.
3. Volunteering or low-balling doula fees sets a cultural expectation that doulas aren't worth much and this expectation adversely impacts other doulas' ability to make a living. (One professional doula training and certification agency who espouses this belief goes so far as to ban anyone who condones volunteering as a doula from their business-oriented Facebook group; it is simply not allowed to even discuss the subject.)
4. Doulas should charge top dollar out the gate (immediately after doula training) because they are worth it.
5. Being on-call and the possibility of long, unpredictable work hours make for a stressful lifestyle. Volunteer doulas make it harder for all doulas to earn a decent income for their work resulting in doula careers that are unsustainable and short-lived.

Let me respond to each of these claims.

1. **Doulas are a luxury.** Really? There is an abundance of data in support of the benefits of birth doulas that demonstrate a reduction in cesarean rates and other medical procedures known to increase risks for moms and babies. In addition to a host of established benefits for families directly and society indirectly, doulas save healthcare dollars. The notion that only well-off folks are deserving of the "luxury" of doula support and (excuse my language) screw the rest, seems to me to be essentially incompatible with the concepts of service, empathy and support at the very heart of our work. Can we not say that everyone deserves a doula AND that doulas deserve fair compensation? These beliefs are only fundamentally incompatible if you buy into corollary beliefs #2 and #3 above. Most doulas whom I have trained over the past 20 years view their work as right livelihood but do not equate that with luxury services for only the privileged

among us. Meanwhile, some doulas experience "a calling to serve" while also enjoying the personal freedom of not needing to generate an income from their work. Many of us can't afford to volunteer our doula services, taking time away from family and other commitments while still needing to generate an income, but if someone else can *and wants to,* isn't that a win/win? Isn't there room for all of us?

2. **Volunteering undervalues the doula's role.** This is what we call "scarcity mindset." Doulas who believe in themselves and learn to make the case regarding the value they bring to families, will attract the clients who are a good match for them. Period. Design a luxury service for your market niche and go for it if that is what you want/need to do. Most volunteer programs are targeting low-income or at-risk families. These programs have built-in limitations that private practice doulas are not subject to. My advice? *Stop worrying about what other people are doing and searching for excuses to fail.* Besides, you can refer folks who need help but can't afford your fee to the volunteers, and that's a good thing.
3. **Volunteers set disadvantageous cultural expectations.** Hogwash! Cultivate an abundance mindset, know your own value and learn to communicate it clearly. You will be amazed how people respond positively (you reap what you sow).

   📖 If you need help reframing a scarcity mindset, see the tools available in *The Doula Business Guide Workbook, 3rd edition*—"Examining our Beliefs about Money Exercise," "Scarcity Versus Abundance Worksheet" and "Suggestions for Working with Affirmations."
4. **Completion of a doula training workshop is sufficient preparation for doula work.** Maybe yes, maybe no. If you have some experience and a high level of confidence, absolutely, you should go for it. (I would be the last person to hold someone back from success.) Many times, however, the motivation to volunteer as a doula stems from a lack of experience and the desire to get one's feet wet before rising to the challenge of presenting oneself as a professional and launching a doula business. Volunteering provides the opportunity to gain experience and grow your confidence as a doula. One or two clients later, you will know that you can (and have!) made a positive difference for the families served. Most doulas grow quickly into the role once they engage. But let's not pretend that you won't be a more valuable doula after 10, 50 or 100 families served than you are at the first few you attend.
5. **Sustainability for doulas is compromised when some doulas volunteer their services.** Sorry, but I'm still not getting how one doula's service to lower-income families (through volunteering, reduced fees, community

Thesis, Antithesis, Synthesis

"I am worth something!" is the refrain of someone who, at one point in her life, did not believe she was worth much. As she heals and comes into awareness, there can be a (hopefully short-lived) stage of over-reaction, as she has not yet truly integrated her own value. An unpleasant edge sometimes takes hold as the person rejects the former mindset, guards against limiting holdover ideas and behaviors, and evolves a fragile new self-image. Once the new belief system is fully integrated, defensiveness and aggression (two sides of the same coin) naturally dissipate because they are no longer in service of the growth process. The person has evolved.

programs) translates to a lack of clients for the luxury doula. Let's reframe this assumption as: *Sustainability is the result of doing the hard work of creating a business model that works well for both the doula and her clients.*

Backup-Only Doulas

A small percentage of doulas choose to work only in a backup capacity for other doulas. They get to keep their hand in doula work but are not depending on it for regular income and have none of the responsibility of building a business, marketing or being on-call (except in a very time-limited way, on a case-by-case basis). Thus, they are free to take a leave of absence or commit to other obligations such as school, family, travel, a job and so on.

Backup-only doulas are functioning as ICs, most likely in a sole proprietorship model (for simplicity sake), but they might also incorporate as an LLC.

Other Types of Collaborations

Space-Sharing Collectives

Among other things, my business—*Center for the Childbearing Year*—is a place. It is a collective of businesses centered on the theme of the childbearing year—yet another variation of the collaborative model concept. Each business is separately owned and managed, while sharing physical space and office resources to keep costs down and market visibility high. The name, *Center for the Childbearing Year,* is the actual name of my business as well as the umbrella name for the collective space.

Rather than risking implementation of a grandiose vision, our collective grew organically from modest beginnings, the available space dictating the timing and manner of expansion. An acquaintance familiar with my work approached me one day and asked if I was ever looking for teaching space. My response at the time was, "Am I ever NOT looking for teaching space?" I had been scrambling for years, from one unsuitable windowless basement to another, hauling books, teaching aids, pillows and even TV/LCD equipment, in and out, from week to week, for childbirth classes and doula trainings. My contact reported that she had a friend who was looking to sublet a large room suitable for my classes. I promptly investigated and was delighted at the prospect. My takeover of the space began incrementally, with placement of a bookcase in the corner of the room and then, like a placenta supporting the growth of a baby, all the structures of the business branched out from there and grew.

Over time, as offices adjacent to the teaching space were vacated and the man from whom I was subletting sought to relinquish control, I invited two local, compatible businesses to move into the available spaces, thereby consolidating my presence and control over the space. One was a homebirth midwifery practice. The second tenant was photographer/author Harriette Hartigan, who moved into a sunny studio space in the back. All parties were good friends and got along fabulously well. The walls of the main room/teaching space served as a gallery for Harriette's exquisite photographs. How serendipitous was that?

> **Tip for Managers**
>
> Put everything in writing when a new business joins your collective. If there is room for misunderstanding, there *will be* misunderstanding. Examine your presumptions and spell it out to avoid problems in the future. Friends are friends, and business is business.

My business was originally formed as a 501c3 nonprofit corporation. Our expansion into the physical space mirrored the growth of the nonprofit programs and funding. Our charitable community-based volunteer doula program, known as *Doulas Care,* continued to grow as I hired staff and engaged student interns and work/study help. When the nonprofit ran into a severe funding shortage (see Chapter 4) in its eighth year, the business was split in two, with the educational programs reverting to a for-profit model under my control. Meanwhile, the *Doulas Care* program took on a life of its own as an independent 501c3 nonprofit entity (my baby grew up!) and moved offsite to their new home.

The individual businesses that compose the collective continue to change and evolve. The model is simple. Philosophically compatible businesses, providing complementary but noncompeting services to the same target clientele, share space and resources in a win-win business model. The success of any one of the businesses in attracting customers is beneficial for all via mutual exposure and word of mouth. Setting a high bar for professionalism and excellence, each member of the collective lends credibility to the others. (In other words, be careful who you let in!) And yet, while cooperating and collaborating, we do not cross the line into partnership and the accompanying pitfalls. Rather, each business remains independent. So, for example, when my business underwent a fundamental organizational shift, the other businesses onsite were unaffected.

An added benefit is that the collective provides a sense of community for independent business owners who might otherwise feel isolated in their work. As a benign dictator of sorts, I have final decision-making authority over the composition of the collective. While we are decidedly not a democracy, decision making by consensus is the preferred method of resolving the rare problem. This model has proved sustainable over time and I have had a zero percent vacancy rate in the available space over 20 years.

Community Partnerships

No one experiences success in complete isolation. By forming strategic alliances or joint ventures, you can leverage existing community venues to get your message out and thus create greater public awareness of your services. Likely partners can be found in your local community colleges, universities and hospitals, community nonprofits, and among area care providers who provide services to the same target population.

An example of a successful community partnership is one that I formed with a local community college. I approached the person in charge of the Lifelong Learning Department and inquired whether the college would be interested in offering DONA doula workshops and a small business development class. The administrator jumped at the opportunity. We negotiated my fee at 60 percent of enrollment fees with the department retaining 40 percent. This is a good deal for me! We also agreed that the college would charge the same admission fee as I charge at my local training center. I offered to teach a weeknight class

> **The very best joint ventures** will be ones where it is clear how the relationship benefits both parties, where mutual expectations are well defined, and where there is a means of holding both parties accountable. Beware the one-way street (even if it appears to work to your benefit) because a payback is expected; it just hasn't been defined (yet).

that repeats for five weeks (often requested by Sabbath observers), rather than the weekend intensive workshop format. By hitting a completely different market, I'm not siphoning away my own customers—quite the opposite! I'm getting the word "doula," the concept of doula training, and my name as a trainer in front of an additional 35,000 people, three times per year, who receive a copy of the college's catalog in the mail. Even if I don't achieve my minimum enrollment numbers and the class gets cancelled, the collaboration is a hands-down win for me.

Another community partnership evolved around a friendship with a nurse-midwife who held academic appointments at a local university and nurtured a strong interest in doula programs. Her connections in the academic world, as well as with a clinical nurse-midwifery practice, proved invaluable for securing grant funding for our community-based volunteer doula program, nursing continuing education contact hours for our professional trainings, free labor through student internships, midwife referrals to our programs and more.

Do some research in your community, keep your mind and eyes open, and think outside the box. Are there existing venues or groups with whom you are naturally aligned and with whom you might collaborate?

What's right for you?

Admittedly, an abundance of choices are explored here and, understandably, that can feel overwhelming. There is no straightforward success formula. What does your gut say? As delineated, there are pros and cons to the various business configurations. So much depends on you—your strengths, limitations and skill set—that nothing is set in stone. Any drawbacks identified can be proactively addressed, possibly neutralized. What might be a "con" for one person (e.g., isolation), might rank as a "pro" for someone else. It's all very fluid, adaptable. I interviewed many doulas who shared their stories of creating their businesses. Every single person used the word "evolving" to describe their process over time. It's normal and to be expected. You can't really go wrong because you can always change it up, so relax! Engage and discover where you fit best.

For more help in determining which model best suits your skill set and personality, see our at-a-glance "Comparison of Doula Business Models" table and accompanying "Examining Your Priorities Exercise" in *The Doula Business Guide Workbook, 3rd Edition.*

Your community will play a role in terms of options. Doulas opening practices in large metropolitan areas can expect a good supply of potential backup collaborators as well as existing community forums for doulas (check for local doula groups on Facebook). Rural doulas, especially those from more economically challenged areas, will understandably feel more isolated and need to work harder to identify and connect with their sister/fellow doulas (they are there!). I can't tell you how many times folks in my doula trainings report that there is NO ONE in their area doing doula work when I know that, in fact, their community is not the doula wasteland they fear it to be. Every challenge can be met if you are determined.

For end-of-life doulas, we are pioneering a new trail. I believe there is every reason to be optimistic that end-of-life doulas will hit critical mass and be well integrated into the hospice and palliative care movement in five years or less (by 2024). Together, we will forge this path. Significant headway has already been achieved with the formation of an End-of-Life Doula Advisory Council within the National Hospice and Palliative Care Organization (NHPCO) as well as the National End-of-Life Doula Alliance (NEDA). NEDA [NEDA.org] is a collaboration of several competing end-of-life doula training organizations coming together to define the role of the end-of-life doula, articulate a scope of practice, identify core competencies for end-of-life doulas and create a national credential (a certificate of proficiency) in order to set standards for the new profession. NEDA represents major progress in a short period of time. There is nothing comparable in the birth world where each training organization (at last count, there were 83!) is in its own silo, doing its own thing. What does this all mean for newly trained end-of-life doulas? You may find it challenging to identify potential business partners, backup doulas or members for your collective. Find ways to educate the public and create community among providers (see Chapter 3) and know that this movement is progressing!

The bottom line: There is no one right way to engage doula work. You can always change your mind if a chosen business model isn't serving you well. Businesses can be adapted to meet a variety of challenges and circumstances over time. Regardless of your choice, your approach *will* evolve. You will figure it out. ◆

CHAPTER 2

Building Blocks

Your Creative Vision

Give some thought to the big picture as you set up your business. Think not only of the immediate future but of the long-term possibilities. Where would you like to see your business in two years? Five years? Are there other services that you would like to add? Is there a niche in your community you intend to fill? Dream big or small, whatever best suits your purposes. Don't worry about all the implementation steps and obstacles at this point, just let your imagination flow. The clearer you can be regarding your big-picture intentions, the easier it will be for the details to fall into place.

Create a Mission Statement, Identify Core Values and Articulate Your Vision

Start with a Mission Statement, defined as a succinct summary of your business's overarching purpose for existing. It should be clear, simple and compelling.

What are the Core Values that underlie the mission? In other words, why do you do what you do? Can you articulate your beliefs and philosophy of service? Conscious integration of Core Values into your marketing efforts will enable you to attract your ideal customers. It will make your biases (we all have them!) transparent. If you believe you are best matched with folks planning an unmedicated birth, or mamas who intend to breastfeed, or individuals intent upon a "conscious dying" experience, then go ahead and say so. We are more likely to build good word of mouth about our services if we work with our ideal customers. You can't be all things to all people; you must stand for something. Then trust your potential clients to sort themselves out.

Finally, a Vision Statement affirms your destination. When you put it all together and you are fabulously successful, what have you accomplished? How are your clients different? You? Your community? The world? Time to dream!

📖 See *The Doula Business Guide Workbook, 3rd Edition* for samples and further guidance in the creative process of writing a Mission Statement, identifying your Core Values and defining your Vision.

Naming Your Business

The creative vision you have for your venture should be captured in your business name. It can be a fun and rewarding process, though not a linear one. There are three simultaneous considerations when it comes to choosing a name. In addition to answering the question, "Is it a *good* name?" we need to ask, "Is it available if I want to incorporate?" and "What will the corresponding domain name be and—here's the real kicker—is that URL available?"

📖 See our "Business Name Quiz" in *The Doula Business Guide Workbook, 3rd Edition.*

Is it good?

Perhaps a great idea has already come to you. If not, you might start with a brainstorming session. Simply list, without judgment, words or phrases that best represent you as a doula. Think of it from the clients' perspective. What do you want people to think when they come to your website? What do you want them to feel? What words come to mind? Perhaps an idea will emerge from your list.

Before settling on a name, solicit opinions from a variety of folks who represent your sample target population and be willing to let go of a personal favorite if you need to. Your business name will hopefully be with you for a long time. And while I confess to having changed business names on more than one occasion, *it is not a good marketing strategy to do so.* You want to build up name recognition for your business. This happens due to a consistency of presence and by developing good word of mouth over the years. There are expenses and time involved in changing names and lost name recognition, so it is much better to get it right from the start if possible. Here are a few principles to keep in mind:

- Simplicity is best. The name should be easy to remember and pronounce.
- Think in terms of making it easy for the search engines to find you. "Ann Arbor Doulas," for example, is a name that is really working for this doula

agency vis-à-vis the search engines because it contains keywords (what someone who is looking for your services might type into the search engine) in the name itself.

- Avoid arcane names that may have great personal significance for you but will require explanation to others. If you are constantly explaining why your name is so cool, it may not be as cool as you think.
- If you want people to connect the business with you personally, it's okay to use your own name as the company name.
- Stay away from cute, quirky or intentionally misspelled names and clever word plays.
- Avoid names that are like those of another business.
- Consider choosing a name that does a little advertising for you and tells people what you do. If the word "doula" is not in the name, then perhaps it could be incorporated in a tag line for the business (like a subtitle of a book).
- Avoid names beginning with "the" or "a."
- Names beginning with letters close to the beginning of the alphabet will be given priority in alphabetized lists and directories, which can be an advantage.
- Avoid names that unnecessarily limit you geographically (e.g., Main Street Doula Services).
- Consider whether your chosen business name might not be too limiting down the road. For example, might you potentially want to offer more than postpartum doula services in a couple of years? Choose a name that allows you to grow.

Support for Growing Families is the name chosen by a postpartum doula for her business. After several years, the owner decided to add birth doula services and later, parenting classes and groups. Her business name easily accommodated this expansion of services with no lost name recognition.

Protecting the Name

Once you have settled on a name, there are several levels of protection available to ensure that you retain ownership and the right to use it. For a sole proprietorship, check with your county clerk's office to run a name-availability query. If the name is available, you can file a DBA or "Doing Business As" (at a cost of $10 in my county). You will be issued a certificate good for five years. If anyone else in your county attempts to do business under the same or too similar a name (e.g., Life's Touch Chiropractic vs. Lifetouch Chiropractic), you can order them to "cease and desist" using your protected business name. On the other hand, if you simply print up promotional materials and neglect to protect your business name, you may find yourself on the receiving end of a "cease and desist" letter. In this case, you will need to come up with a new name for your business and will be facing a (potentially substantial) loss in time, money and effort that could easily have been avoided.

Corporations are granted exclusive statewide use of a business name (one more reason to become an LLC). My husband procured a DBA for his business, known as Computer House Call, a sole proprietorship operating primarily in Washtenaw County, Michigan. About a year into the business, he was served with a "cease and desist" letter from a company that had incorporated with the State of Michigan under the same name and was doing business about two hours west of us in a different metropolitan area. The rival company's business plan included eventual expansion throughout the state and it had secured the necessary name protection. Consequently, we were forced to rename my husband's business (Computer Home Service), this time incorporating with the state. If you want statewide protection for your business name, consider the LLC option and check with your state's corporate division regarding availability of your chosen name.

Finally, a more comprehensive level of protection is offered by a federal trademark, though most small businesses operating within a local sphere will not require this. A business with a federally registered trademark has exclusive use of the protected name and/or logo throughout the United States. A trademark is obtained from the U.S. Patent and Trademark Office (USPTO) and it trumps the state name protection or the DBA. You can do a free trademark search at uspto.gov. The cost ranges from $225–$400 for filing, plus additional fees if you use an online legal service such as LegalZoom.com or hire a trademark lawyer for advice. One tip is to be sure to read and follow up on any communication received from the USPTO after filing. Failure to do so in a timely manner can result in abandonment of your application with additional fees assessed for reactivation. Check the status of your application every few weeks to establish "due diligence" until the process is complete or you may find yourself paying additional fees.

Domain Names

While you are choosing names, do not neglect to check and see if the corresponding domain name is available, preferably as a dot.com. If not, you may need to come up with a new business name. If so, reserve the domain name as soon as you have settled on it (approximate cost $13–$16 per year). The availability of the domain name can quickly be determined by going to any URL provider and doing a search (I like SimpleURLSolutions.com but there are many others). The dot.com is most desirable as that is the address people are likely to use if they are unsure and therefore makes it as easy as possible for people to find you. If you are a dot.net or dot.biz, folks may end up on your competitor's site first. Dot.org indicates a nonprofit entity. If you are using your personal name for the business, see if YourName.com is available and reserve it. This is a good idea regardless (who knows how famous you are going to become?). To gain more complete protection over your brand, you may want to own all versions of your URL, or at least the dot.com, dot.net and dot.org variations. The URL does not need to be an exact match with the business name, but it is best if it is close (e.g., Lifespan Doulas / LifespanDoulas.com].

If you should have the good fortune of coming up with a great name and URL that are available, go ahead and reserve them, even if you think you are several months to a year out from being ready to launch your website. Good URLs are being quickly snatched up and there is no guarantee that your favorite will still be available once you are ready. Plus, it's just not that big of an investment, even if you change your mind.

Logos

"Branding" your business entails a consistent repetition and "look" for your business materials. A logo can be part of that. Your business cards, brochures, flyers, ads, website—all reflect the brand. A logo is not necessary and certainly is something you can bring into the picture, so to speak, later. If you are artistic, it may be easy and fun for you to work out a visual representation that is meaningful and eye-catching. If you are artistically impaired (like I am), it is easy to feel stuck at this point. My brain just doesn't work that way. A graphic designer who specializes in logos can guide you through the process, but they will need some idea of what you want as a starting point. Prepare a bit by paying attention to other business's logos and begin to discern elements that you like and don't like. What makes a good logo (unique, simple, clever)? What makes a not-so-good logo (too busy,

My Logos

For years, I used a logo for **Center for the Childbearing Year** that I didn't like. It was created by a friend, on the cheap, when I didn't know what I was doing and was decidedly uninspired. Then, I just felt stuck with it and it fell rather low on the priority "to do" list. About 14 years later, my business went through a major overhaul and re-branding became part of that. I decided to ditch the tired-out logo featuring a spiral (an element integrated on so many birth-related websites that it was pure cliché) along with the silhouette of a pregnant woman's belly and overly-perky breasts. Bleh.

First, I worked out a new tagline for the business: *Guidance, education and support for parents and doulas.* The concept of "guidance" was really speaking to me—pretty much summed up the essence of everything I am about (e.g., *The Doula Business Guide).* Then it was an easy next step to come up with a visual for guidance—a compass. I googled clip-art images of compasses, found one that appealed to me, hired a designer and voila!

The logo creation process with my partner for a new business venture, **Lifespan Doulas,** was more arduous. It was hard to come to agreement. To give you an idea, when our graphic designer provided us with six variations on a logo concept and we were asked to choose our top three ranked in order of preference, there was zero overlap in our selections. And so it went. The process felt a bit like pulling teeth and stretched out over several weeks. Eventually we came to agreement, though neither of us got our way completely.

cliché, unoriginal)? The more direction you can provide your designer, the faster (and cheaper) the process. And be sure to share your mission, values and vision with your designer to increase understanding of the brand you are creating.

An alternative to a logo is to use your picture. After all, if you are offering doula services, YOU are the brand. Put your picture on your business card, brochure, website and social networking profiles. That way, when you attend networking events and give your business card to someone, they have an aid for remembering you, for attaching your name with your face. Avoid pictures that include family members or you on a sailboat or with your dog (unless that is somehow part of your brand). A professional-looking head shot is best. This is business.

In the end, the only thing that matters about a logo or a business name is how it is perceived by others. Get some opinions, from a variety of sources, before you commit to a design.

Pros and Cons of Renting Office Space

Where will you meet with clients? There are basically four choices: (1) rent office space, (2) set up a home office and have clients come to you, (3) conduct all of your visits in clients' homes or (4) meet in a public place, such as a coffee house. Let's consider the pros and cons of each.

Renting office space holds a seductive appeal. Who wouldn't want a lovely space dedicated to the purpose of optimally engaging clients, with tasteful artwork décor, educational materials and a small lending library at your fingertips, and a clean bathroom, all readily available? A place you can escape to and focus, providing a good boundary between work and play, between mama and doula professional? Sounds lovely. Of course, the downside is that the office space costs money, perhaps a prohibitive amount. It may drastically decrease your net income and prove unsustainable in the long run. Do the math! A monthly expense of $325 might strike you as doable. Multiply that by 12 and you are spending almost $4000 annually. What else could you do with $4000 (a gorgeous custom-designed website, more reliable transportation, a fun vacation, an emergency fund)? Perhaps an office space is something you put into your long-term vision—three or five years down the road? Perhaps you could share an office or, better still, sublet from someone who has an office and is looking to cut their overhead. By subletting, you give up some control over décor and hours of use, but you also do not have to furnish an office and are not bound by a lease. Keep thinking outside the box. If funds are tight, there are many creative solutions to finding office space. And remember, any monies paid out for space are a legitimate cost of doing business and can be deducted from your gross income for tax purposes.

Meeting with clients in your home will cut the overhead costs significantly and also offer some tax benefits (see discussion on taxes below). By having your clients come to you, you will spend less time and money commuting to the office or to clients' homes. Minimize the inconvenience of having strangers/clients in your home by considering how to best make a separation of your work and family life. Ideally, clients would enter through a separate entrance leading directly into your office space. Such an ideal space would also have a separate bathroom available and a door that could close off the rest of the family home, at least for the time being.

Anything less than this level of separation will involve clients mixing in with your family life—shared bathroom, access through your living space, exposure of your family with attending loss of privacy, exposure of your private beliefs as displayed on bookshelves, wall hangings and so on. In Chapters 7 and 8, I discuss the importance of setting good boundaries with clients, and I will say emphatically that having clients enter your home through your living room and use your family bathroom is NOT a pathway to good professional boundaries. Home offices may also be perceived by clients as an open invitation to "drop by." I have been put in very uncomfortable positions with beloved clients who dropped by to say "hi" and show me their growing baby just as I was kicking back on a weekend with a glass of wine and about to enjoy an evening with friends.

An additional downside to the home office is the necessity of keeping the home clean and presentable for clients. This is both an advantage and disadvantage. My husband once bemoaned the fact that I no longer taught classes in our living room, observing that tidiness standards had noticeably declined. However, he did *not* miss the nights he was literally kicked out of our home with two kids in tow so that I could teach for two-plus hours, until well after the kids' bedtime. Nor did either of us miss the nerve-wracking hour or so AFTER cleaning and BEFORE class started when I had a tendency to go ballistic over dropped items in the living room and towels left on the newly cleaned bathroom floor. Nor did I miss clients looking suspiciously at my husband's gun book collection or commenting ironically on the Diet Pepsi in the refrigerator (now banished, but an admittedly unfortunate lifestyle inconsistency at that time of my life).

This all brings us to option three, visiting clients in their own homes. This is probably the most cost effective, easy and popular solution embraced by doulas. Certainly, for postpartum and end-of-life doulas, it makes sense to do the initial interview in the client's home as it will give the doula a better feel for the environment in which she will be working. Otherwise, how do you know what you are agreeing to (e.g., what if they are smokers or borderline hoarders and you find yourself unable or unwilling to function in that environment)? While the home visit enables you to gain a more complete appreciation of who your clients are, it also means you retain better control over the start and end time of appointments. It's so much easier to say, "We have just a few minutes left together; do you have anything important you want to cover before I leave?" than "You go now" (or something to that effect) as you attempt to evict clients from your home or office. In addition, your mileage to and from all appointments is tax deductible. Of course, you will have a certain amount of uncompensated commute time with this option. However, this too may be a positive (or a negative), depending upon your perspective. I enjoy my commute time as quiet time to myself, used for reflection or planning. It often creates a space for decompressing. When my kids were little, it was helpful to have that time just to change gears, to get into the right head space before serving clients. The return commute presented yet another opportunity to think, process intense experiences, and enjoy a little peace and quiet before hitting the ground running on the home front. And it was all valid "work time" away from the family that no one (especially me!) was questioning.

Option four is likely not a viable long-term strategy but may be appealing to a specific client. I had one teen mother who did not feel comfortable having me to her parents' home for a visit and wanted to meet at the local Burger King due to transportation issues. I followed her lead and it worked out acceptably. The obvious downside is the lack of privacy that results from meeting in a public venue. I like to be hands-on with my birth doula clients during prenatal visits, to introduce touch into our relationship and begin establishing that critical intimacy before I arrive to support them in labor. I also like to demonstrate the use of the birth ball or teach the partner some massage techniques. Clients love it, but we need a degree of privacy for a more intimate relationship to unfold naturally. Who wants to talk about intact perineums and placentas in the middle of Burger King? On the other hand, some doulas will choose a neutral location, at least for the initial interview, because it feels safer for the doula and less invasive for clients who might be on the fence about using doula services. Navigating neighborhoods in an unfamiliar, dicey section of town may be sufficiently discomforting to throw the doula off her game by the time she settles in for the interview. (See Chapter 7 for safety tips for doulas home visitors.)

My main objective through this discussion is to raise questions for you to consider. Trial and error has been my greatest teacher. My concern here is that some readers may not have the ability to withstand the "error" part of "trial and error" and that a mistake in setting up an office might make the difference between a business that grows and becomes sustainable and one that doesn't make it through its first year, only to become an utterly discouraging life lesson. So, give yourself some time to consider the ins and outs and, at least initially, while you are still acquiring basic skills and building a reputation and client base, keep it simple and keep it cheap. A beautiful office space might just have to be something you earn the right to have, because your business is overwhelming the household or you are spending too many hours commuting. It's a nice problem to have to solve down the road.

Defining Your Service Package

As you begin to shape your business, you will need to design your service package and make a few decisions. This is the true core of your business so take your time to think it through carefully. Your answers to the questions below are multipurpose. They will prepare you to: (1) respond to initial inquiries from prospective clients curious about your services, (2) create a client contract, (3) develop content for the "services offered" page on your website, and (4) begin to set professional boundaries and expectations with your clients. Important work!

Scope of Services

Be specific about your service package(s). What is included? What is optional? What is excluded? What are the timeframes? Are you offering any add-ons or complementary services?

Birth Doulas

Birth doulas typically offer a package of services for a set fee. The package includes the following components, but what each doula or doula business puts together varies. Just start off with what seems reasonable to you and adjust from there till you settle into a comfortable practice.

- **Initial Interview.** How much time will this take? Who should attend? I require that the woman's partner be present and consider it a red flag if the partner doesn't want to come. Will you charge a fee for the interview? Most doulas do not charge as it is an open-ended interview, a chance for both parties to explore whether they are a good fit. In addition, if other doulas are not charging and you are, then the fee could prove to be a barrier as clients might choose to meet with other doulas first. If a fee is charged, it typically gets applied toward your package fee if the client hires you.
- **Prenatal Visits.** How many prenatal visits are included in your service package? How long will each visit be? Think about the purpose of the visits. What do you plan on covering/accomplishing during visits? Your prenatals should be structured and purposeful. How much time do you need?
- **Phone Support.** Most doulas do not set a limit on the number of calls but may specify preferred timing of nonurgent calls/text messages and how long after the birth calls are covered (e.g., through six weeks postpartum). How do you want your clients to communicate with you between visits? Be specific.

- **On-Call.** When does your promise of 24/7 availability begin? Most birth doulas define "on-call" as a two-week period on either side of the expected due date. Outside of those parameters, the doula should still arrange backup for clients when she is going to be unavailable. Two doula agency owners I spoke with promise on-call availability once the contract is signed. In addition to defining the on-call period, you should decide when and where you will join clients in labor. Will you provide in-home support to mothers in early labor? What should clients expect in terms of turn-around time once they have notified you that labor is underway? One hour? Two hours? Realistically, how long will it take you to be on your way, plus the commute?
- **Postpartum Visits.** How many postpartum visits are included in your package? How long will the visit(s) last? They should be short to not exhaust the new mama, perhaps an hour. What expectations do you want to set regarding your role postpartum? How long do you stay involved, available?

Possible Add-On Services/Specialties for Birth Doulas

Beyond the core birth doula service package, doulas may offer a la carte services such as:

- Massage therapy
- Private or group childbirth preparation classes
- Additional prenatal or postpartum visits
- Extended breastfeeding support
- Belly casting, henna art or facilitating Blessingway celebrations
- Placenta encapsulation services
- Photography services
- Sibling support at birth (sometimes needed for families planning homebirths)
- Other?

Sample Birth Doula Partnership Arrangement

Here's how a team of two doula partners has set up their practice.

Sharing the work

- They interview together as a team.
- They do not do all the prenatal visits together but try to do many as they can.
- The on-call schedule identifies first-call/second-call; second-call doula is activated if two women go into labor at once.
- Doulas rotate on-call shifts that run from 7am–7pm.
- They can call in backup support at 24 hours for relief.

Fee Split

- Birth Doula Package fee is $1200.
- Fee includes two prenatal visits, on-call birth support and one postpartum visit.
- These partners split money earned each month according to the following formula:
    - » 5% goes into a business savings account.
    - » Doulas are paid $50 for each prenatal and postpartum visit attended.
    - » The doula who does the birth gets a bonus $250.
    - » 75% of the balance goes to first-call and 25% to second-call (based on number of hours during the month as first or second-call).

Postpartum Doulas

Postpartum doulas work in shifts or blocks of time and charge by the hour. They might create packages with escalating levels of help (see sample). The package structure helps clients consider how much postpartum support they anticipate needing.

- **Initial Interview.** Same as for birth doulas above.
- **Availability.** Set a minimum/maximum number of hours per shift and shifts per week. Many doulas have discovered that a shift needs to be at least 3–4 hours long to make it worthwhile for all parties. On the doula side, there is commute time to and from the client's home, hardly worth it for just two hours of pay. From the client's perspective, it might be

Sample Postpartum Packages

Package 1—Getting Started
6 hours of care
(2 3-hour visits)

Package 2—Building Confidence
12 hours of care
(3 hours minimum per day)

Package 3—A Helping Hand
20 hours of care
(3 hours minimum per day)

Package 4—Extended Care
40 hours of care
(4 hours minimum per day)

Package 5—Ultimate
60 hours of care
(4 hours minimum per day)

Package 6—Overnight Care
10pm–6am
(8 hours)

Are you offering both birth and postpartum doula services?
See this experienced doula's beautiful website for sample service packages that she has designed [SupportForGrowingFamilies.com/doula-packages/].

challenging for the doula to accomplish enough in under three hours to establish her overall value for the family. You really need at least three hours to make a noticeable difference and do it in a graceful, focused, but unrushed way. Availability also includes identifying preferred times and days (mornings, afternoons, evenings, overnights)?

- **Limitations.** Any limitations to tasks performed in relation to household support such as cleaning, child care, animal care, meal preparation, running errands and so on? List any specific exclusions you may have ("I don't clean bathrooms"). Personally, I am willing to scrub out a bathtub so mama can enjoy a hot, healing, herbal bath or feed her some nourishing homemade soup. As a new mama, these would be at the top of my list of needs! That said, I wouldn't appreciate cleaning bathrooms to be a routine expectation. I might just say "light housekeeping" vs. "deep cleaning" to cover what I am willing/not willing to do.
- **Timeframe for Services.** What are your limits here? Do services end at six weeks postpartum? Three months? How will you wean clients from your care? Any exceptions for families with special circumstances who might want extended help (e.g., families with multiples or medically fragile newborns or mamas diagnosed with a postpartum mood disorder)?

What are your motivations?

A postpartum doula friend discovered that some of her clients became "addicted" to her help. One family wanted to keep her employed well beyond expectations for postpartum doula support, essentially expecting her to morph into a nanny. While the positive relationship with the family and the regular, dependable income were great, the doula had to balance that with the limitations of one family claiming all her time. She started to consider her motivations for undertaking doula work in the first place. As a single woman and aspiring homebirth midwife, her motivations were twofold: (1) support herself through her midwifery apprenticeship and (2) continue learning as much as possible about the early postpartum period and challenges faced by families. Clearly, the latter goal was not being met if she chose to stay with one family for six months during which most of her time was spent doing infant care and sibling support. She resolved to set a new boundary on her postpartum services, limiting support to the first six weeks postpartum and referring families who wanted prolonged support to other doulas and/or nannies. Over time, your motivations may change. One of the beautiful things about doula work is that it is very adaptable to your life circumstances.

End-of-Life Doulas

- **Initial Consultation.** Who should be present? What is the anticipated length of the interview? Does the doula charge for this visit? I recommend that the primary family caregiver(s) and decision-maker(s) be present for the interview in addition to the person who is sick/dying, if they are capable of participating. This visit can be structured a bit differently than what we see for birth and postpartum doulas as it may be more of an information session than an interview. The doula can educate the family on the role of the end-of-life doula, explain the differences between palliative care and hospice, provide advance care planning guidance, and/or help the family discern their greatest areas of concern and unmet needs. This can all take a while but should be limited to two hours. Anything longer will likely yield diminishing returns. People can process only so much at one time, especially when they are stressed and not feeling well. The doula should charge for her time for the initial consultation (did you notice I changed from "interview" to "consultation" there?). If the family decides to invest in your services going forward, or later as the death grows near, great, but the initial consultation is a stand-alone fee. Regardless of whether the relationship is ongoing, clients will have benefited from a consultation that clarifies their choices, helps them to identify questions they should be asking and encourages proactive planning for what they are facing.

- **Availability.** Since death vigils can take many days, it is not reasonable to think you will just be there endlessly. How does this work? Everything depends on the type of support you are offering to families. Are you willing to do respite care so that an exhausted primary caregiver can get some much-needed sleep? Do your services include personal care (e.g., keeping the dying person clean and dry)? Are you available to do companion care or "sitting" for someone who is declining but not yet dying? Or are you primarily a "vigiler"? If yes, then how is this handled (e.g., rotating shifts with another doula)? Are you available on an as-need, on-call basis (e.g., patient is having a rough night—can they call you)? If you are going to do shift work, then set a minimum/maximum number of hours per shift and shifts per week that you are available. You will need to set preferred work hours/days (mornings, afternoons, evenings, overnights, weekends, holidays) as well.
- **Limitations.** List any limitations to tasks performed in relation to household support such as cleaning, child care, animal care, meal preparation, running errands and so on. Are you intending to offer personal care services? Does this include managing soiled linen? Think through these details so that no one is caught in the trap of making presumptions leading to disappointment.
- **Timeframe for Services.** How long will you stay involved with families after the death occurs? Do you offer additional services? What expectations do you want to set?
- **Service Packages.** Like postpartum doulas, end-of-life doulas might want to put together care packages—a specified number of hours, including specific services, for a set fee. For extended care packages, the price might drop a bit. Then the family can pick the package and price point that is comfortable for their budget. Be careful with this, however. Too many choices can feel overwhelming and there is a saying, "a confused customer doesn't buy." Keep the choices as simple and straightforward as possible and then test it with a few folks for feedback.

Possible Services/Specialties for End-of-Life Doulas

- Massage therapy, Healing Touch, Reiki, etc.
- Perinatal hospice support (for families who have chosen to let nature take its course after receiving news that their unborn baby has a birth defect incompatible with life)

- Facilitate Advance Care Planning, digital Advance Directives
- Accompany clients to doctor visits as a witness or mediator
- Guidance for legacy projects, video memoirs
- Holding vigil
- Bedside therapeutic harp music
- Animal-assisted therapy
- Personal care services
- Companion care
- Respite for caregiver(s)
- Household support
- Logistical support (e.g., transportation, helping clients get to doctor visits, treatments, etc.)
- Natural after death care, guidance for a home funeral or green burial
- Ongoing bereavement support

Length of Visits

Deciding on a reasonable length of visits with your clients, and sticking to it, is a professional way to proceed. If you are always "winging it," making everything up as you go along, you will invariably get into trouble with folks who will test your boundaries and try to get more for less or who are just unfocused in their conversation with you. Personally, I have felt used and abused after investing three hours of my time in an initial interview, providing lots of free education in the process, only to *not* be hired. Wasn't three hours sufficient to establish rapport? I had to learn to take responsibility for my own lack of boundaries. Once I made a decision that the initial interview for birth and postpartum clients should last between 60 to 75 minutes maximum and communicated that expectation to clients, the abuse magically stopped. The more I thought of myself as a professional whose time was valuable, the more clients responded in kind. *This really is how it works.* Plus, their time is valuable too, and more time in a doula interview is not necessarily viewed as a good thing.

Interview with End-of-Life Doula Deanna Cochran

Deanna is a nurse who has a hospice background and started her own private practice end-of-life doula business in 2005. She is also a doula trainer who has her finger on the pulse of the developing end-of-life doula movement. Deanna believes that it is certainly possible to be an excellent doula with no caregiver experience. The end-of-life doula's scope of practice can encompass or exclude services associated with the caregiver role, but she stressed that it is important for doulas to carve out their niche and make a clear delineation between doulas and caregivers/elder care sitters/companions.

Setting Fees. Like other doula business owners with whom I spoke, Deanna said her business is constantly evolving. I got a glimpse into her fee-setting process as she debated extempore her new pricing system after having recently moved from a metropolitan area to the country. She settled on $500 for a session lasting 3–4 hours, and $100 per hour thereafter if the family felt they needed more. Keep in mind that Deanna is very experienced, not just in palliative care and hospice, but as a business woman. As such, she is positioned to command top dollar for her services. Overall, she reported end-of-life doulas charging prices as low as $20 per hour up to $375 for two hours of care in New York City. Some folks are packaging their services with a single price, such as $1000–1500 per day for vigil support or $1500 for a set of services.

Consultations. Deanna reports that when she is first contacted by a family, they are often in the middle of the dying process and are in full panic mode. Her specialty is palliative consulting. This involves a visit with the family wherein she helps create a vigil plan and then empowers the family to conduct the vigil. "It's their vigil." She ensures that the impending death is not viewed as an emergency, but as the expected conclusion of the process, necessitating a call to hospice rather than 911. Her preference is to help the family be in control and for her to offer paid support sessions.

Death Vigils. Deanna spoke about the importance of boundaries when the doula's presence is desired for the vigil. She requires a space for herself to retreat to, while remaining available to address any urgent needs.

Closure with Clients. Deanna finds that a natural withdrawal of support occurs. She meets at least once after the death when a "re-telling" occurs. This process is directed by the family and she follows their lead. Once this session has ended, "they're done" and everyone moves on.

Deanna Cochran, RN and End-of-Life Doula, Mentor and Trainer, is one of the earliest voices of the end-of-life doula movement. Her heart-centered approach to the human event of dying is practiced worldwide and taught in her School for Accompanying the Dying [QualityOfLifeCare.com]. She is one of the founding members and Chair of the NHPCO End-of-Life Doula Advisory Council and author of the forthcoming book "Accompanying the Dying: Practical, Heart Centered Wisdom for End of Life Doulas and Healthcare Advocates."

Scope of Practice

Are you following formal standards of practice? If so, print them out and provide your clients with a copy. Include any limitations to services in your client contracts as well. See Chapter 7 for a discussion on how a defined scope of practice protects both the doula and her clients. When practitioners identifying themselves as "doulas" offer services outside of recognized doula standards, they are exponentially increasing their own liability risk. Examples include: performing clinical tasks (e.g., checking dilation, doing wound care, dispensing medications); giving medical advice (e.g., "prescribing" herbal treatments, countermanding doctor recommendations); or speaking for the client and interfering with her medical care providers. Here is something to contemplate—what if that Blue Cohosh tincture the birth doula recommended her client take to induce labor causes her blood pressure to drop and this, in turn, has a negative effect on the baby's heart rate? You are not getting paid enough to take on this level of responsibility! Please consider—what is your motive here? To save the woman from the care providers whom *she has chosen* to trust? Why? Because you care more about her birth than she does? Because you know what is best for her and her baby? Because it's all about you? Think about your motives. Doulas are well advised to stick to providing nonjudgmental information and support, trusting their clients to make the decisions that are right for them. Just maybe she knows more about her needs and her path than you do. Empower her to make informed decisions and take responsibility for herself and her baby and don't allow her to cast you in the role of her protector and savior.

Doulas may have their own professional/personal limitations on services offered beyond scope of practice mandates. These are important too and include considerations suggested above under "limitations" when describing services offered.

Number of Clients Served

How many clients can you serve in a month? No one can answer this question but you and, at the beginning, you probably have no idea. The answer will depend on several factors, including your family situation, your need for income, the amount of help you have on the home front, whether you have another job, your health and energy level, your ability to juggle other commitments and so on. Most of us determine what is workable and what is not through a process of trial and error. Often, we discover where the line needs to be drawn after finding ourselves solidly on the wrong side of where it should be drawn, overwhelmed and exhausted. Make your best guess and see what works. Sometimes it looks good on paper, with client due dates nicely spaced, when suddenly one woman births four weeks early, another goes into labor two weeks late and a third (not even on your radar screen yet) is in crisis. On other occasions, I have accepted clients who shared a due date (it didn't look good on paper) and the births sequenced themselves perfectly. It is essentially unpredictable.

Similarly, end-of-life doulas may have several families on their radar, providing some services well ahead of the final days. There is no way to accurately predict when any given family is going to need you unless you are hired to start immediately. Even for postpartum doulas, predicting the work flow is not an exact science unless the family engages your services after the birth. Otherwise, you will be marking out an anticipated window of time when your help will be required.

One way to limit how thinly you are stretched is to define how far you are willing to travel to provide services. If the bulk of your clients live within a half-hour drive of each other and you, then it will certainly be easier to juggle the demands of the practice. On the other hand, if you are driving up to an hour radius of your home, then theoretically you may have clients who live a two-hour drive from each other. You will need to factor distance into the equation of how many clients you can serve each month.

Backup Arrangements

Doulas in solo practice will need to activate backup doula support if:

- You are sick or need emergency dental care
- A close family member is having a medical emergency
- You have a funeral to attend
- Two women in labor at the same time
- Two clients actively dying

These factors are unavoidable and unpredictable, in other words, beyond your control. We might also add to this list "exhaustion to the point of no return" for the doula who has become a liability rather than an asset at a long birth or death vigil. In this situation, the backup doula can be called in and the entire support team will appreciate the breath of fresh air and energy that she brings.

Note what is *not* on this list of reasonable excuses for use of a backup doula: last-minute vacation opportunity, your child's birthday, unreliable transportation, unreliable child care, cell phone malfunction.... In my opinion, these excuses are lame. Either you are a professional or you are not. Your one promise is to *be there.*

If you are not set up to reliably deliver on that promise, then you should find a different career—or be prepared to have angry, disappointed clients demanding their money back. However, if at the time of hiring, you know that you have a pending conflict, you can let folks know from the start that there is a day (or two) during the anticipated on-call period when your backup will take call. If clients proceed to hire you despite the conflict, then they are consenting to the arrangement and there is no problem.

It may not be reasonable to expect your backup doula(s) to meet your clients and vice versa. Do we pay them for their time for this service? If not, then it's a bit of an abuse of the backup. If so, then we are parting with a portion of our fee which unfortunately, for too many doulas, is insufficient to really pay us well for our time in the first place. Perhaps a virtual meeting using Google Hangouts or Zoom will suffice? My recommendation is to introduce the backup doula to your client(s) in direct proportion to the odds of needing to activate her support. If you have a particularly busy month and are concerned about potential overlapping client needs, or if a potential conflict is imminent, then you can certainly afford to pay the backup doula to meet your clients.

Transparency is the bottom line. Have a clear agreement with your backup doula about the logistics of activating her support, fees paid, terms of payment and any other mutual expectations. How quickly will she return calls and text messages? What is the best way to reach her (and does this change if it's the middle of the night)? How long will it take the backup to get to the client when needed? Then put it in writing. When assumptions are made and poor communication rules, you are sure to experience problems.

As to how much to pay your backup doula, err on the side of generosity. For birth doulas, I feel that 50 percent of the fee is reasonable. Postpartum and end-of-life doulas should receive most (if not all) of the hourly wage the client is paying. If the doula goes on-call for you but her services are not needed, she should nevertheless be compensated for keeping herself available and willing. Think of it as a cost of doing business. *We need our backup doulas! You want your backup doula to continue to want to be your backup.* The peace of mind we achieve from having reliable backup support is well worth the price. When you find yourself worrying and stressing about things that are beyond your control, you might ask yourself, "What is the worst thing that can happen here?" The answer is that you will need to ask for help. So be it.

If you work with one reliable backup person who is generally available, you can also try an exchange. I had such an arrangement with a local midwife friend of mine for many years. We agreed to owe each other one birth without pay. If one of us needed to activate the other twice in a row, before the payback had occurred, then we came out of pocket for the fee. We also swapped prenatal meetings for no pay as needed. This worked beautifully.

Doulas should have more than one backup doula if possible. It is not reasonable to expect your backup to always be available for your clients or prioritize her life around your possible need for help. Try to choose folks who have comparable experience and skills, a similar philosophy and personality—in essence, someone with whom your clients will feel comfortable. For example, humor is a very important quality to me in a birth attendant. Personally, I would not respond well to an overly earnest doula, though she may be wonderful for someone else. I also don't need to be mothered. I want a lighthearted doula with a sense of humor and a calm presence (I would value this over experience). Since your clients have chosen *you,* consider the qualities they are likely drawn to and make a comparable choice in your backup doula. As we discuss the need for backup, the advantages of working in a partnership or doula collective with built-in backup become more apparent.

Postpartum and end-of-life doulas may want to team up in any case, as some families will need more help than one doula can provide (e.g., families with twins or multiples, families who need round-the-clock support for a death vigil). It is important to have a good system of communication for shift changes, with one person taking the role of "lead doula" to ensure continuity of care, including follow-up for known issues so nothing important falls through the cracks.

Money Matters!

Yes, indeed, money matters. If you are charging a fee for doula services, then you are, by definition, a professional doula. Just because you love the work does not mean that you should not get paid for it. Just because you *would* do it for free does not mean that you *can or should* do it for free. If you begin to think of yourself as a professional doula, then you will begin to present yourself as one to potential clients. When you present yourself as a professional, you have every expectation of being paid your fee. That is simply how it works. It doesn't work well when we have doubts about ourselves, our worth, our qualifications, our clients' ability to pay or the value of the work itself. If we harbor a belief that true work must be boring and painful, then we will not feel comfortable accepting money for work we simply

Birth Doulas and the 12-Hour Rule

All birth doulas, at some point, become acquainted with the 37-hour labor or three-day induction. Yikes! These situations certainly can be extremely challenging for all involved. In response, some doulas are embracing a 12-hour rule as part of their client contracts—in essence, an overtime clause. The idea is that clients are promised a set number of prenatal and postpartum visits, on-call availability and 12 hours of labor support as part of the service package. If the labor goes longer than 12 hours, then the doula charges an additional hourly fee.

What are we to think of this? The motivation for instituting this policy is clear—it's about offering protection to the doula. One doula whom I interviewed told me she believes in unconditional support for the laboring mother and thinks that penalizing a new mama financially for having a long labor is fundamentally incompatible with her role. We doulas often criticize the medical profession for rushing women in labor and making time an unnecessarily stressful factor in decision making. Now, we're the ones putting the clock front and center. "My doula heart can't do it" she said. I agree. That said, you may want to include provisions for births that go long in terms of calling in backup support so you can grab a few hours of sleep.

For more information, see the summary results of a survey conducted by Penny Simkin and Katie Rohs on doulas' practices in this regard ("The 12-Hour Clause," *International Doula,* Fall 2016).

love to do. And we will find a way to undermine ourselves, to give a mixed message to clients, to present our expectation of being paid as flexible, negotiable and so on. We may even undermine the prospective client's confidence in our capacity and professionalism—because they will read between the lines. They will hear every "but," explicit or implied. ("I charge $25 per hour for postpartum doula services, but . . .") And then, like water running through cracks, the customer finds the opening, and the doula finds herself negotiating her fee down to $22 per hour.

My question is—Does this work for you? Are you okay with negotiating your fee? How low will you go? Do you not believe that you are worthy of the fee that you set in the first place? I cannot overemphasize the importance of examining your own beliefs about your value and worth as you set up your business. Every single time you sell yourself short, you absolutely must observe yourself consciously and admit that you just did it again. Then be curious about your reasons for that behavior and begin to reprogram yourself. Otherwise you will not be in business long because I promise you will keep attracting people who are going to be difficult about money.

For help in changing self-defeating behaviors, see "Examining Our Beliefs about Money Exercise" in *The Doula Business Guide Workbook, 3rd Edition.*

I have always been good at getting paid. It's one of my skills. Many years ago, just after my first son was born, I decided to find a way to work from home so I could take care of him. When he was a few months old, I began taking in typing and editing jobs for the local university and business communities. Once personal computers came on the scene, I switched to editing and word processing and, over a seven-year period, this business grew to provide half of our family's income. You'd better believe that my per-page rate was nonnegotiable. I certainly wasn't doing text entry for the love of the work! I seldom had issues with clients and I always got paid. The best part was that the skills I learned from being self-employed in my crank-it-out job transferred easily to my new vocation once it was revealed to me.

How to Set Your Rates

Fee setting is an important early decision in setting up the business. The answer to the question "How much should I charge?" is based on your composite answer to the following questions.

What are your expenses?

Typically, expenses are minimal for service-oriented businesses. Rarely is it necessary to rent office space, invest in inventory or buy expensive supplies. But that is not to say there are *no* expenses. At a minimum, there is the cost of professional affiliations, continuing education, mileage, marketing, a few supplies and perhaps child care.

Think of the ratio of expenses to income for self-employment in the same way that you might perform a calculation for choosing to work for someone else as their employee. One needs to factor in the cost of a suitable wardrobe, transportation to and from work, parking fees, increased cost of eating more meals out and grabbing food on the go and, last but not least, child care. Tax implications for the additional family income also need to be taken into consideration. When we are self-employed, we also have a cost of doing business and must make similar calculations when setting our fees.

What are similar businesses charging?

The answer to this question will vary widely according to where you live. In Michigan, for example, rates fluctuate based on whether you are operating in larger metropolitan areas such as the greater Detroit–Ann Arbor area where I live or rural communities in more economically depressed areas of the state. In general, rates have been increasing in recent years. Many doulas publish their fees openly on their websites, so do a little digging on the web. You can also call a few doulas, introduce yourself and respectfully ask whether they will engage in a conversation about their rates. Social media is another way to connect—doula groups on Facebook for example.

Since end-of-life doulas are opening a new frontier, there are no established "going rates" but hourly rates for shift work should at least be comparable to what postpartum doulas are charging ($25–$35 per hour, higher for overnight shifts and specialty work). End-of-life doulas may also experiment with creating client packages for a set fee, similar to birth doulas. Build in as much value as you can, but don't short-change yourself. And take care to be explicit about what is included and not included in the package (services, number of hours). An initial consultation or facilitation of an advance care planning session might last 90 minutes to two hours and be valued at $250.

Not all doulas are comparable. Someone with ten years' experience and a strong local reputation is likely to place herself at the higher end of the pay scale, while someone just starting out and still seeking to fulfill certification requirements may offer her services for free or seek only to get her out-of-pocket expenses covered. Determine what the range is and then see where you fit. Keep in mind that your prices are fluid; you very well might decide to increase them as you discover what the market will bear. One way that self-employed people know it is time to raise their fees is when they have more work than they can handle. Starting out on the lower end and increasing as you gain in confidence, experience and skill, makes sense. In the end, it's your call and if the market will bear your price, then more power to you!

> Customers are not as price resistant as we might imagine. They are more afraid of spending their money stupidly, of not receiving good value for their investment.

An associate is a successful postpartum doula. She decided to add birth doula services to her business, primarily because she wanted to offer the service to past postpartum doula clients who were having subsequent babies. After consulting with her peeps (me and a few others), she took the bold move of charging $1000 (high market end at the time) for a package of birth doula services immediately after completing her training. She could pull this off because she was confident in the value she brings to families, based on years of experience, AND she didn't really want to be busy as a birth doula.

What are clients willing and able to pay?

Try to get a sense about the answer to this question in your conversations with other doulas. In the end, there will likely be some guesswork involved. If you set your fee too high, you may find that you are losing potential customers to doulas who are charging significantly less. On the other hand, if you purposely underbid all the other local doulas, consider the message you are sending. Being the cheapest doula (electrician, hair stylist, massage therapist) in town does not necessarily inspire confidence in the consumer. Perhaps there is some ambivalence on your part regarding your value? Are you sending a message that the service itself is not worth more? The psychology of price setting is such that you want to try to hit it just right—professional fees for a professional service. As doulas, we just need to learn how to communicate our true value to the families served and then deliver that value. Clients will be happy to pay your fee!

If you live in an area where there are no other doulas practicing, then it may be advisable to start nearer the lower end of the pay scale as you build up your business and local word of mouth about the value of your services. Focus your efforts on education and marketing to get the word out.

How much money do you need to make per client, as a bottom line?

This final question will lead you to settle on a fee. Ultimately, you must make enough money per client to cover both your expenses and your time. Only you can decide how much this needs to be and you can change your fees at any point. Once you have made a decision, think of it as a jumping off point. You may decide to increase your fees after a couple of families served or you may determine that you are scaring prospective clients off and make adjustments.

The likely prospect of changing your fees dictates that you refrain from publishing them in your print literature (rack card or brochure if you have one). You can, however, publish them on your website where they can be easily updated as needed and you won't have old, discarded fee information floating around. I have seen arguments both pro and con regarding publishing rates online. Those against the practice maintain that it invites price shopping on the consumer end and doesn't give you a chance to establish your value and create rapport with a potential customer. They argue that you want that opportunity rather than attracting folks simply because your prices are on the low end. Those in favor of the practice claim they personally look for prices when shopping for services online and are annoyed if they can't find them. Some will assume that the person's fees are too high and that is why they are absent, generating suspicion rather than rapport. After polling many groups, I am convinced that publishing your prices on your website will serve you better than not. In the end, if the client wants the cheapest doula in town, so be it.

What If They Can't Afford You?

Undoubtedly doulas will cross paths with folks who cannot afford their services. There are several different ways to approach this issue. While your heart may want to say "yes," your pocketbook or your partner may not be down with the sacrifices entailed in doing so. Possible approaches include working out a payment plan, bartering, referral to a doula program providing free services to low-income families (if available in your area), or offering a sliding scale. It has been my experience that people generally do not value services provided at no charge. If they are invested, if they are giving something in return, then they value the service.

Consider also that there is quite a continuum on the theme "I don't have the money." In some cases, such a statement is more perception than reality. One family's "I don't have the money" might best be translated as "I would have to dip into my savings" or "I'm cash poor at the moment because I just bought the new $30,000 vehicle parked in the driveway," while another family's "I don't have money" means they are having trouble buying groceries. You will have to decide if you have the capacity, in terms of available time and need for income, to take on clients who cannot afford your services. This may not necessarily be an all-or-nothing decision or one that can't be revisited as your own circumstances change over time. I decide, on a case-by-case basis, who my gut tells me I should cut a break to. Typically, I ask for something in return. For example, if someone wants to take my childbirth classes and can't afford the fee, I might offer the option of bringing a healthy snack to class to share with the other couples

> **I want to encourage** every professional doula to provide all clients with the opportunity to give back something in return for her services.

or helping me at the office with copying and assembly of course materials. Or they might propose a payment plan that will work for their family. Typically, this includes an initial deposit to hold a spot for them and then authorization to make scheduled charges to their credit card. What I'm not down with is supporting an entitlement mentality. There should be an exchange of energy.

Be sure to explore insurance reimbursement options and strategies with your clients. Some clients may have Health Savings Accounts, Medical Reimbursement Accounts or Flex Accounts available. Encourage them to inquire whether doula services qualify for reimbursement under these pretax medical savings accounts.

I have bartered my services for car repair, massage therapy, graphic design, haircuts and cleaning services. On the other hand, I turned down the offer to exchange palm reading for doula services as palm reading is not something that I value. The barter should be equal in value, dollar for dollar. A major downside to bartering is that it can contribute to sticky or murky relationship boundaries with clients. Once bartering enters the picture, your client is in your life in a new way. The relationship is no longer just about you meeting their needs; they are meeting your needs too. Money is cleaner, less personal and the boundaries are clearer. Be prepared to have a harder time bringing closure to a professional relationship that has crossed this line. If the barter/payment is extending into the future, by definition, you do not have "closure."

Sliding scales can be a bit tricky. I have experienced mixed results with them. For several years I offered a sliding scale for my doula services. When presenting the option of a sliding scale, state the value of the service up front. "I charge $1200 for a package of birth doula services." Then you can say something like … "In consideration of folks for whom this fee presents a hardship, I will *waive a portion of the fee.*" This language is important because it allows you to state your worth and it is a more accurate description of what you are willing to do—waive a portion of your fee rather than devaluing the services. When devising your scale, play with the numbers a bit and come up with something that seems reasonable to you. Be clear about your bottom line (the least amount you will accept) and keep it simple. You don't want to get into the nitty-gritty of their finances and hear all about their college loans,

Sample Sliding Scale

Family income / Birth Doula Service Package Fee
< $30,000 / $400
$30,000–40,000 / $600
$40,000–50,000 / $800
$50,000–60,000 / $1000
> $60,000 / $1200

overall debt load, mortgage payment, tax problems and so on. Nor do you want to deal with complicated algorithms that take into account family size, etc. You are not a government bureaucrat. Obviously, a $60,000 annual income with six dependents is a far cry from that same income supporting two people. Simply present clients with some rough guidelines during the initial interview and then, once hired, ask them to self-identify their fee amount and draw up the contract accordingly.

When a sliding scale was offered, most clients in my area put themselves at the top of my scale. A couple of people took advantage. Since the appreciative folks significantly outnumbered the manipulators, I chose to offer the sliding scale for several years. To play devil's advocate for a moment, however, I will say that I'm guessing your mortgage payment amount doesn't "slide" from month to month, nor does the price your local grocer charges for milk. Doulas are not required to offer a sliding scale.

It's going to break your heart when you are witness to the overwhelming unmet needs of some families. That single immigrant mother of a two-year-old and newborn twins, recently abandoned by her husband, post-cesarean delivery, one baby in neonatal intensive care and the other being released, no family in this country, in poverty. Literally, this happened. How does a caring doula say "no"? It precipitated me to expand an existing nonprofit volunteer doula program I was running to include postpartum doulas! But I realize not everyone has that option. If we get completely swallowed up in the needs of others when our own families are depending on us, it's a sure path to burn-out.

What *can* we do? Consider whether there's a way to serve as a catalyst for organizing help and make a limited contribution such as:

- Meeting with her to come up with a plan
- Helping her create a "circle of support"
- Making a few calls on her behalf to identify potential sources of help
- Identifying community resources
- Posting in a doula Facebook group to solicit volunteer help
- Starting a Go Fund Me campaign to hire a mother's helper
- Identifying a caring neighbor or church group who will organize a Meal Train (notice *you* are not the organizer)

It feels good to do the occasional pro-bono job. I believe this should be a matter of choice on the doula's part, not something she is guilt-tripped or manipulated into doing because someone else feels entitled to her time and expertise. If we can help when someone in great need crosses our path, we do what we can. I think of it as a form of tithing and trust them to pay it forward. And thank God for those volunteer doulas among us. They are needed!

Establishing a Timeframe for Payment

Now that you have set your rates, the next step is to become proficient at collecting your fees. It will help considerably if you have set a fee that you believe is reasonable and feel, in your heart, that you are worth every penny. A written payment policy is an essential component of your client contract. When must payment be made? How much is due each payment? At what point must the client pay in full? Communicate your fees and payment policy without hesitation or apology to the client.

I recommend that birth doulas collect their full fee prior to the start of the "on-call" period as defined by the contract. I ask for 50 percent of the total as a "nonrefundable retainer fee" at the time the client hires me and signs the contract. If you can only accept two clients per month, then you may be turning down other work. You are being asked to make a commitment and you need the client to reciprocate. Commitment is a two-way street. The balance is due at the final prenatal visit, prior to the onset of the "on-call" period, usually around 36–37 weeks. That way, I am not in the position of asking for payment at a postnatal visit—a time when I want to continue my focused, caring support. If I have a tearful postpartum mom who is struggling with breastfeeding and lack of sleep, it can be very difficult to bring myself to ask for payment if she doesn't remember without prompting. And, frankly, it is not likely to be the top thing on new parents' minds. If the situation drags out, it's amazing how quickly the doula will fall down on the list of priorities for who gets paid after the birth has concluded.

Birth doulas should never allow a payment decision to be based on the birth outcome, for example, in the case of a woman whose intention was to have a VBAC (vaginal birth after cesarean) that ended in cesarean. Does she still have to pay her doula? You bet! You are not responsible for her birth outcome. She is. Everything you do in the course of building your relationship with her should communicate this simple fact—she is central to her own experience. You *cannot* protect her from the big, bad medical profession nor save her from a repeat cesarean. You *can* support her in her strengths. Teach her how you will support her and help her set up a plan to succeed. Do your best but, in the end, it's all on her and you get paid regardless. Collecting your full fee in advance of the birth is another way of delivering this message and heading off any unpleasantness about money.

My way is not necessarily the only way or the best way. I am simply sharing the model that I settled into after years of experimenting. At a minimum, doulas should be paid something to reserve time in their schedule and at least 50 percent (if not 100 percent) of the full fee paid prior to the birth. Exceptions can be made on occasion; however, if you are using a credit card to buy groceries so that your client doesn't have to use her credit card to pay you, then there is something very wrong with this picture.

Postpartum doulas will also want to get a nonrefundable retainer fee to hold time in their schedules for clients who hire them prior to the anticipated event. It might be payment in full for the first week of anticipated services upon signing the contract. Or, the retainer fee may be based on a percentage of the anticipated overall contract price. This protects the doula, especially in situations where the family anticipates needing regular help. I recommend that doulas apply the retainer fee toward the final portion of the contracted hours rather than the front end, and then invoice the client, as agreed, at the hourly/weekly rate as you go.

The importance of the retainer representing the true value of the overall contract was recently brought home to a pair of postpartum doula partners. A family expecting multiples hired them for anticipated months of support. The doulas cleared their schedules, turning away other queries. The total contract represented several thousand dollars. As the birth grew near, the mother added special requests with which the doulas felt uncomfortable and subsequently were fired. It was quite a hit to absorb, a lesson learned the hard way.

For end-of-life doulas, retainer fees are a bit tricky due to the extreme unpredictability of the dying process. I have seen people who appeared to be actively dying, unexpectedly recover sufficiently to be discharged from hospice. And another case where a man decided to stop dialysis treatments which had kept him alive for five years. After entering hospice care, he surprised us all by living for two months instead of the expected week or less. It may work best to simply charge fees for services rendered as you go. However, if you are engaging with families well upstream of the anticipated death AND they are seeking to secure your services for significant shift work (that entails you potentially turning away other jobs), then you should work out an upfront retainer fee for the job. We must constantly balance the shifting needs of families with our own need for a secure, steady income. And keep in mind that on-call availability is a huge commitment on the part of the doula and it requires compensation as a service for its own sake.

Refund Policy—Be Careful Here

You will also need to articulate a refund policy. Under what circumstances might you refund a retainer fee? Under what circumstances might you refund a client's full pre-paid fee? Under what circumstances would you not refund any portion of the fee? What is the timeframe for refunds? Since the issue of refunds likely is arising from misfortune or is fraught with the potential of a disintegrating doula–client relationship, it is covered in detail in our risk management section (see Chapter 7).

Collecting Your Paycheck

Consistency is important. Hold clients responsible to the agreement and call them on it if they are engaged in shenanigans. The old "I forgot my checkbook" or "the check's in the mail" (when it's not!) doesn't work well if you are counting on getting paid today and it's not forthcoming. I have sometimes sat in uncomfortable silence as a response to the "I forgot my checkbook" claim, waiting for the client to work through how she's going to solve the problem. If she's not forthcoming, I might say "That's a problem for me today. How soon can you take care of this?" Being "sweet" when someone is neglecting their responsibility to you is an invitation for that person to continue bad behavior. You are not the one who caused this problem and it is not up to you to fix it. Sweet isn't truly sweet when resentment is behind it.

> **TIP:** *Always* accept money when someone is ready to pay. If the client asks, "Can I write you a check now?" the answer is "yes, thanks." "That would be lovely."

What about the client who forgets to pay you? You have a lovely prenatal visit together. You like her and her partner a lot. You are all excited about their upcoming birth. It's time for you to hit the road. According to your contract together, their final payment is due tonight and you really wish they would just pull out the checkbook and pay you. Here are some options for bringing up the subject:

"Do you have that final payment for me tonight?"
"Can we take care of payment before I leave?"

Whatever you do, don't walk out of that house knowing that they should have paid you but you neglected to remind them to do so. Remember, you are a professional with every expectation of getting paid. As you step into that role, as you own it and take pride in your work, all uneasy feelings about being paid and paid well for your

A Lesson Learned

One homebirth midwifery client of mine was a lovely, fun woman with a great sense of humor. I enjoyed her company at prenatal visits and the feeling was mutual. However, she repeatedly "forgot" to bring her checkbook to prenatals, the bulk of my fee was still unpaid and her due date was looming in the near future. In addition, she was often late to prenatal visits, sometimes calling when she was already fifteen minutes late to say that she was on her way and, on one occasion, not showing at all. Underneath the pleasantness at prenatal visits there was a layer of anger and irritation for me, but I chose not to address it with her. Instead, I complained to my husband about her on a fairly regular basis. At one point he finally said, "Patty, you're telling the wrong person."

This obvious observation forced me to confront the issue. How many of us will go to great lengths to avoid confrontation? We want to be "nice" even when others are taking advantage of us, when they aren't being nice. I gathered my resolve and called her, fighting a sick feeling in my stomach. I told her that I did not feel that I could continue as her midwife because I was feeling angry with her for not valuing my time. She was shocked. I explained that she demonstrated over and over again that she did not value my time when she was repeatedly late to prenatals or skipped them without notice and when she failed to make payments according to her contract. I asked her if she really wanted to be attended in labor by an angry midwife.

She promised to remedy the situation immediately and somehow came up with the balance of the fee. The air was cleared and she started showing up on time for the remaining prenatal visits. When she became pregnant with her next baby, she and her husband hired me to be their midwife again. On the first prenatal visit, she handed me a check and a written payment plan for the balance of my fee. I don't know who else among their creditors were not getting paid, but clearly I had moved up on her list of priorities. Buy groceries, make rent, pay utility bills, pay Patty ... that's where I want to be on the list.

My failure to confront this issue earlier was pure cowardice disguised as wishful thinking. I liked her. I wanted to keep liking her. We had a good rapport. I wanted to pretend it was all fine, but it wasn't fine. The ability to be honest in the moment with others, to confront bad behavior, to lay down a boundary and state that you don't give your consent to be in relationship with them if the behavior continues, is a skill. Like all skills, it gets easier with practice.

time will drop away. The key to having clients who pay you faithfully is to have a matter-of-fact attitude about the business part of your business. Some people will try to make their money problems be *your* money problems, showing obvious pain as they make a payment or telling you about what they just had to spend to get their car fixed and so on. You don't need to engage and you certainly don't need to feel guilty (presumably they want *your* car in working order so you can make it to their birth!). Simply smile and say "thank you" when they hand you your check. It's just business.

Checking Accounts

If you are a sole proprietor with a DBA, simply take the certificate to your bank. You have two choices here: set up a separate business account or add your DBA to your personal/family account. By adding the DBA to your existing account, you can most efficiently access your money. All deposits go immediately into your personal checking account. A separate business account will require you to transfer funds, after deposit, to the personal account when you want to pay yourself.

If you have formed a corporation of one kind or another, a separate business checking account will be required. First, you will need to obtain a federal Employer Identification Number (EIN). This can be done easily online at IRS.gov. Take the certified Articles of Incorporation from the state and the letter from the IRS assigning your EIN with you to the bank.

The primary advantage of a separate business checking account is that the bookkeeping is cleaner. Psychologically, it may be less painful to pay business-related expenses from a business account than it is from a personal checking account. It is much easier to track what is actually going on with the business if it is separate from your personal finances. You will have income, minus expenses, including taxes that need to be set aside. What's left over is what you can afford to pay yourself as an "owner's draw." I think that the separate account helps independent business owners develop a business mindset and good habits around money. At the end of the year, your tax picture will be much cleaner as well. However, if you are just doing a little bit of doula work, supplementing family income here and there, you might want to forego the complication of a separate bank account. There will also be a monthly fee assessed for a business account.

Cash Payments

Some self-employed business owners prefer cash payments only, "under the table," to avoid tax liability. Or they may attempt to cash checks directly at the banks where they were issued rather than depositing to their own account, again in an effort to avoid the paper trail and tax liabilities. Today, banks have made it increasingly difficult for people to engage in the practice of cashing checks unless you are an account holder at their bank. A check cashing fee will likely be charged and many banks will thumbprint you for this service. In addition, whenever your social security number is requested, you can assume that the related income is being reported to the IRS. Finally, if you should ever be audited by the IRS, one of the pieces of financial documentation they review is your bank statements. So, if you are using cash to pay your bills, then the gaps in the paper trail may be discernable. Ethical considerations aside, this is not a viable way of doing business and will not build trust with your clients.

Accepting Electronic Payments

Accepting credit/debit cards will give your clients options for paying for services that they may need or appreciate. The upside is that having the credit option available may increase your income because you are making it easier for people to pay you. The obvious downside to accepting credit cards is that the credit card company will charge you a percentage of the sale for the privilege. If you decide to move forward on this option, shop around for vendors and get some competitive bids before you choose a company. Many doulas use PayPal for the ease of set up. PayPal takes three percent of all money transfers which is on the high side. It's also possible to get a small card reader that attaches to your phone, such as Square, so that getting paid on the spot is as simple as a quick electronic transfer (thereby making the old "forgot my checkbook" excuse moot).

Third Party Reimbursement for Doula Services

Currently, third party reimbursement for birth and postpartum doula services is unreliable but may be possible. For end-of-life doulas, we are on the frontier, though development of the profession is happening rapidly. Leadership and political advocacy are needed to advance this agenda on all fronts. Think "pioneer."

It was due to the efforts of one doula from South Carolina, Pat Burrell, that an important first step towards reimbursement—that of recognizing doulas as

Leadership and political advocacy are needed to make consistent third-party reimbursement for doula services a reality.

providers and assigning them a unique provider number—was accomplished several years ago. She has proven that one person can make a difference as she relentlessly pushed the National Uniform Claim Committee [NUCC.org] to add a provider number for doulas. Prior to this feat, the lack of a taxonomy code and provider number were impediments to reimbursement. Pat made repeated phone calls and engaged in dogged follow-up over months to accomplish this goal.

Procuring a National Provider Identifier (NPI)

The NPI is used, in conjunction with applicable CPT codes (see more below), when submitting claims for reimbursement through third party providers. Doulas will need to file for an NPI number through the National Plan and Provider Enumerator Systems (NPPES) [NPPES.cms.hhs.gov]. Doulas can be found under Nursing Service Related Provider (Provider Type Code 37). You will need the taxonomy code for doulas (#374J00000X) to complete the application. A definition of "doula" has now been formalized by the NUCC as follows:

> ***Doulas*** *work in a variety of settings and have been trained to provide physical, emotional and informational support to a mother before, during and just after birth and/or provide emotional and practical support to a mother during the postpartum period.*

Note that end-of-life doulas are not yet included in this definition. There are other provider types listed that might apply to select end-of-life doula services, however, including home health aide, religious nonmedical practitioner, and possibly others that fit, depending on training, credentials and services provided. Ultimately, we will need to lobby the NUCC to add end-of-life doulas to the provider type definition.

The taxonomy code for Health Educators is #174H00000X. The code is listed under "Other Service Providers Type." This may be an additional option for third party reimbursement to cover childbirth educators, breastfeeding educators, infant massage educators and so on. "Health educator" is defined as follows:

> ***Health Educators*** *work in a variety of settings providing education to individuals or groups of individuals on healthy behaviors, wellness and health-related topics*

with the goal of preventing disease and health problems. Health educators generally require a bachelor's degree and may receive additional training, such as through mentoring, internships or volunteer work.

Current Procedural Terminology (CPT) Codes

The CPT medical code set is maintained by the American Medical Association. It describes medical, surgical and diagnostic services and is designed to communicate uniform information about medical services and procedures among physicians, coders, patients, accreditation organizations and payers. New editions of the code set are released each October.

While recognition of doulas as providers is an important step towards third party reimbursement, it is far from a guarantee. Individual health plans may accept or deny doula services as a covered expense and the American Medical Association (AMA) has yet to assign billing codes that are doula specific. Sadly, codes that had been used, with limited success, for reimbursement of birth doula services prior to 2014, have since been rewritten using more restrictive language—specifically, "labor support by a midwife." Doulas risk insurance fraud for continued use of the code, though other codes may work for specific services such as lactation support, childbirth education, postpartum visits and so on. It may be possible to write a description of services in place of non-existent CPT codes. Until proper codes are made available, doulas should take care to be explicit that submitted claims are for *doula* services. Clearly, the success formula for reimbursement that one might hope for does not exist at this time.

Submitting a Private-Paid Insurance Claim

Nevertheless, I am including here information on how the claim submissions process was working prior to 2014 because it may prove helpful to a few people and my hope is that the much-needed doula-specific CPT codes will be forthcoming from the AMA. If an intrepid doula client wants to tangle with her private-paid health insurance company to advocate for claim reimbursement, here's a few recommendations. Keep in mind that the insurance company works for the policy holder (your client) and not for the provider (in this case, you). This means that your motivated client needs to do the legwork and be willing to see the claim process through. She has the power.

Determine whether services are covered.

The client starts by contacting her insurance provider and inquiring whether doula services are a covered benefit. Some health plans may state explicitly that doula services are covered or excluded. If the answer is "yes," then all parties can proceed with confidence that the claim should be covered. On the other hand, if your client's plan explicitly excludes doulas services, then it is unlikely her claim for reimbursement will be successful. Be aware that many benefits agents may not be familiar with doulas and may simply state that their services are not covered. *This does not mean that there is no chance of getting doula services covered* (see "making the call" below).

Reimbursement often requires advocacy and a policy review. It can be a lengthy, but not difficult, process which cannot begin until after services have been completed and billed to the provider. Your client can expect to submit a claim, wait for the claim to be denied, challenge the denial, and await a review process which may include requests for additional information and supporting documents. There is no guarantee that the claim will be approved, but if it is, reimbursement is likely to take several months. Due to the uncertainty, it is recommended that the doula collect her full fee up front and then provide the client with the needed documentation for her insurance provider. If reimbursement (partial or full) does occur, the check will go directly to the client.

Making the call

Have your client call the customer service number for her health plan and ask a benefits specialist the following questions:

- **Are doula services a covered benefit under my health plan? Are doulas an accepted provider type?** If the answer is "yes," write down the name of the agent, date and time and any details they explain. Your client should write down the phone number she dialed to reach the person she is speaking with or ask them for the best number to contact if she has additional questions. *She must document as she goes and keep records.* If the answer is "no," move onto the next question.
- **Are doulas or doula services specifically excluded?** If the answer is "yes," she should ask them to send her a copy of the exclusion in writing. If she receives this proof, then it is not worth anyone's time to bill for doula services. However, if the answer is "no," you may consider submitting a claim and your chances for reimbursement are fair.

Submit the claim.

If the insurance company provides their own claim forms, your client should use the company's form, sometimes referred to as a Request for Self-Paid Services Form. Otherwise, complete a Universal Claim Form known as the **1500 Health Insurance Claim Form,** available online [mdcodewizard.com/CMS1500/]. You will need the following information:

- Doula's tax ID number (either the EIN or social security number)
- Doula's address
- Dates of services for all visits
- Client's date of last menstrual period (for birth and postpartum services)
- Fee for services (if you charge one fee for a package of services, you will need to break it down)
- Diagnosis code(s)
- CPT code(s)
- Location code
- Policy/plan/group number
- Claim submission address

Follow-up

The client will receive an explanation of benefits from her insurance company, typically within 2–6 weeks after submitting the claim. If the claim is denied, there will be an explanation. If the denial is due to a mistake or missing information on the form, the form can be corrected and resubmitted. *If the denial is because of questions about the provider or type of services rendered, the claim should be resubmitted.* The company may request certain documentation, or the client might need to initiate an appeals process. The following documents may be helpful to include after an initial rejection:

- Letter from client explaining why she feels the insurance company should reimburse for doula services
- Copies of her medical records
- Verification from her doctor or midwife that a doula was present at her birth and that the doula provided a valuable service, helped to improve outcomes or lowered costs; completion of this task will likely be expedited if

the client writes the letter and asks her doctor or midwife to put it on their letterhead and sign it

- Doula scope of practice (on letterhead of doula's professional organization)
- Summary of research regarding the role and effectiveness of doulas
- Summary of research regarding the cost benefits, for insurance providers, of doula services (see Issue Brief cited below)

Ask clients to keep you posted on their progress and follow up with them. Get electronic copies of letters that resulted in reimbursement, remove all the identifiers and share these widely. Consider posting information on your website, blog or via social media. Ultimately, we should be enabling our future customers to select insurance options that cover desired forms of health care known to improve outcomes, namely, doula services. Most folks simply don't know the questions they should be asking when it comes time to select a plan or change an existing one.

What if my client is on Medicaid?

Oregon and Minnesota are the only states that have passed legislation enabling Medicaid reimbursement for birth doula services. In 2016, Choices in Childbirth [ChoicesInChildbirth.org] and the National Partnership for Women & Families [NationalPartnership.org] published a joint Issue Brief entitled *Overdue: Medicaid and Private Insurance Coverage of Doula Care to Strengthen Maternal and Infant Health.* In addition to summarizing arguments in favor of doulas as a means of improving outcomes and lowering costs, the report analyzes the current state of third party reimbursement for doula services in the U.S. and makes recommendations to expand reimbursement. It is worth your time to read this report. Specifically, it addresses:

- What is doula care?
- Why do women need doula care?
- Improving the health of women and babies
- Eliminating disparities
- Enhancing women's experience of care
- Reducing the cost of care
- Innovative program models
- The path forward (the role of Medicaid and private insurance; and federal, state and community level recommendations)

In an interview with Debra Catlin of the Oregon Doula Association [OregonDoulas.org], she confirmed that, after legislation enabling birth doulas to receive reimbursement through Medicaid became law in 2013, an Oregon state doula registry was established, and doulas began to enroll. Because these doula visionaries were pioneering new territory, it took time to work out all the details and nuances of working with the healthcare industry. These challenges were summarized in the Issue Brief:

> *Both Oregon and Minnesota have been taking steps to identify or create certifying bodies, registration procedures, core competencies, scope of services, supervision arrangements and reimbursement procedures. Because of the extensive work involved in developing the needed infrastructure, it has taken significant time for these states to begin reimbursement.*

The original Oregon legislation required healthcare providers to bill for doula services and many were unwilling to do so. After a new rule enabling doulas to do direct billing went into effect on July 1, 2018, doulas in Oregon can finally accept clients on Medicaid, submit claims and receive reimbursement for a package of birth doula services that includes two prenatal visits, labor support and two postpartum visits. The state base rate for this care package was set at $350 in 2015, which is the minimum that must be paid for uncontracted services. However, some health care payers have begun contracting with state certified doulas as preferred providers at $600–700 per care package.

> **The wheels grind slowly.** But keep in mind that five years (or ten) have a way of passing, one way or the other. The question is, where do you want to be in five years?

The Blessings and Pitfalls of Legislation

Arguments in favor of enabling government reimbursement for doula services revolve around access to care and reduction of disparities, certainly worthy causes. In the absence of Medicaid reimbursement, doulas are essentially a luxury service, leaving out marginalized populations who lack other resources and face an increased risk of poor outcomes. Everyone can benefit from doula support! Doulas who come from lower-income or at-risk communities and wish to serve families in their community face severe sustainability challenges. How can they attend births if they must maintain another job to pay their bills and keep their gas tank full?

> **Side Rant**
>
> **Have you ever noticed** how what passes for preventive health care is often actually screening and early detection? For example, taking a blood pressure or screening for a postpartum mood disorder are both activities that are often presented as "prevention." Of course, catching high blood pressure or a postpartum mama who is suffering emotionally, and intervening sooner rather than later is a good thing. But what if we could prevent the high blood pressure, depression or PTSD from developing in the first place? Doulas can proactively help to address the underlying causes for poor outcomes by providing emotional support, reducing isolation, increasing access to services, promoting evidence-based strategies, providing education on healthy choices, reducing stress and more. **This is the true prevention argument!**

Or if they face losing a day's wages in order to attend a birth? Our world will be a better place and health care dollars saved if dedicated community doulas are paid a living wage for their efforts. Third-party reimbursement is the only way to achieve this goal.

Whenever there is a push for legislation of this kind (e.g., recently-enacted legislation in Michigan legalizing and regulating homebirth midwives), there will always be pushback, from within the profession itself, by folks with *legitimate concerns*. Primary among these are the fear that doulas will become co-opted by the medical system thereby compromising the client advocacy role, and that we will be inviting all-powerful vested interests to exert control over the profession. Ethical mandates regarding the doula's responsibility to the primacy of her client's interests could be compromised as regulation opens a pathway for the promotion of other agendas. For example, doulas might be mandated to push vaccination or safe sleep agendas rather than presenting information to promote informed decision making and client autonomy (our true bailiwick).

> Ethical mandates regarding the doula's responsibility to the **primacy of clients' interests** could be compromised ...

For 35 years, I offered community-based childbirth education programs, purposefully steering clear of hospital-based settings that might have proved more lucrative. The reason? If the hospital has authority over me and my job is on the line, then I can be held accountable to their agenda (selling epidurals or routine induction of labor, for example). Even as a community-based educator, I have faced repeated confrontations by medical care providers regarding my encouragement for *informed choice* on routine active management of third stage of labor, as just one example. Had I worked for the hospital and continued to present both pros and cons to this practice, I surely would have been fired. As it is, I suffered a reduction in referrals to my classes from some providers—a price I am willing to pay to keep my purpose and integrity intact.

To balance the blessings and pitfalls, efforts to advance the cause of third-party reimbursement for doula services must seek to rigorously protect the core principles of the **Doula Model of Care** (see Introduction) and represent the doulas' interests. This might be accomplished through a national organization that promotes mainstreaming doulas while defining scope of practice, establishing core competencies and setting high training standards for doulas. For end-of-life doulas, such an organization now exists with the 2018 launch of the National End-of-Life Doula Alliance (NEDA) [Nedalliance.com]. Current leaders in the birth and postpartum doula movement, however, are in their own competitive silos, each doing their own thing, and this will not work in our favor as a path forward. Is it possible to work together and agree to protect essential components of the Doula Model of Care? What are the common denominators among the 83+ birth and postpartum doula training organizations? Do we want to be in the mainstream and become the standard of care or do we want to remain a luxury service on the fringe?

The Path Forward

You can help! Following are some possible ways to proceed if you believe that third-party reimbursement for doula services is desirable.

- **Partner with professional organizations and advocacy groups.** Stay abreast of progress being made. Generously share information about companies that are paying and reimbursement strategies that are working. Ideally, we would see cooperation between training organizations or a central organization that represents us all. For end-of-life doulas, NEDA can serve this function.
- **Pressure the AMA for the needed CPT codes.** Advocacy efforts can be informed by a trained, educated biller, someone on the inside of the process of establishing the CPT codes who can work with representatives from the professional doula associations to better understand the role of the doula and services provided.
- **Lobby the unions.** Since unions are negotiating the terms of health insurance policies for their members, helping union leaders to understand the

cost-saving benefits of doulas and exerting pressure to cover doula services might prove an effective strategy. To my knowledge, this has not been tried but has been recommended by insiders in the insurance world as a possible approach.

- **Support research on doulas.** We need evidence that demonstrates the benefits of doulas, especially if those benefits can translate into healthcare dollars saved. There is a strong evidence base in support of birth doulas—especially a reduction in cesarean delivery rates—which is leading more hospitals to initiate hospital-based doula programs. But hard data in support of the projected benefits of postpartum doulas (e.g., reduction in number of ER visits post-discharge; increased breastfeeding success; prevention, screening and early intervention for women suffering from postpartum mood disorders; etc.) is scant. And research on end-of-life doulas is just getting underway with qualitative studies. Ultimately, quantitative research on outcomes related to use of end-of-life doulas (e.g., increased use of palliative care; earlier engagement with hospice; fewer 911 calls or ER visits in the last days and weeks; diminishing caregiver stress) is needed. What does "support research" mean? Say "yes" to participating in research studies and help recruit clients to participate. Or, if you have the interest, credentials and skills, undertake the research! This is the long game.

While the legwork necessary to get the third-party reimbursement ball rolling is heavy up front, once we are mainstreamed into the system, more families can benefit from doula support regardless of ability to pay.

Resources

The Oregon Doula Association (ODA) has created a *Roadmap to Doula Care for Medicaid Clients* that outlines steps to creating similar programs in other states based on lessons learned the hard way (thank you ODA!). As more states take on this fight and share their own lessons learned, we can expect the path to get easier. While the process will vary from state to state, *Roadmap* recommendations can be broadly summarized as follows:

- Gather the stakeholders
- Gather the information
- Determine the care model
- Learn state's Medicaid system

- Assess current workforce
- Petition legislators to sponsor the bill
- Create rules advisory committee
- State system responsibilities
- Educate doulas on state program
- Educate health care systems
- Educate the public

Contact DebCatlin@aol.com for a full text of the *Roadmap* and more information.

DONA International is committed to sustainability for doulas, including advancing the cause of third party reimbursement. Their advocacy efforts are summarized here: DONA.org/the-dona-advantage/get-involved/advocacy/.

Tax Primer for Small Business Owners

No doubt we are all motivated to avoid time-wasting scrutiny, stress and trouble with the IRS. To do so, we must develop a basic awareness of what is required and then set up a system to enable requirements to be met. An accountant can be hired to give advice and file necessary forms if you are not a do-it-yourselfer. However, the accountant can only work with the data that you provide. He/she cannot manufacture the numbers needed to complete the forms nor provide you with evidence to back up your deductions, so you must do your part. Ignorance is not a defense.

Financial Record-Keeping Basics (4 Steps)

1. Set up a system to keep track of your income and expenses as you go.
2. Keep receipts for your expenses.
3. Keep a written record that tracks your business-related mileage.
4. Keep all records in storage for a minimum of seven years (for more information on storage requirements, see IRS.gov).

Overview

You must have business-related income during the year for which you are claiming expenses. In other words, if you don't have income against which to write off the expenses, then you don't actually have a business. IRS Schedule C, along with instructions for completing it, can be downloaded at IRS.gov. Take a look at the form now, when you are in the setup phase for your business. Gross business-related income for the year is reported on the top part of the form. The bottom half and the back of the form are used to report allowable deductions. If the expense categories on the form don't match yours, you can report expenses under "other" on the back of the form. Expenses are then deducted from income to yield your net (taxable) income. That is the number to report as income (profit or loss) on your Form 1040.

Now, on occasion, especially in the first year of a new business venture, the net number can be a negative amount. In other words, you spent more money than you made. This loss can be deducted on your Form 1040 in the income reporting section resulting in lowering your overall taxable income. Prevailing wisdom on small business start-up is that it can take up to three years before the business becomes profitable. The IRS understands this. That doesn't mean you aren't earning income during that timeframe; it simply means that it takes persistence to grow a business to the point where you are solidly over the hump and your investment in time, money and effort is really paying off. If you can be ahead of this curve, so much the better. However, if you are claiming a loss (or negative net income from the "business") for three consecutive years, the IRS is likely to determine that you don't actually have a business, but rather an expensive hobby. Accordingly, they will disallow the write-off, not only for the current tax year, but making the determination retroactive as well. So, don't attempt to claim a loss three years in a row on the same business.

If your net income on Schedule C is $400 or more, then you must pay FICA taxes of 15.3%. Use Schedule SE for the purpose of calculating and reporting FICA taxes. If, at the end of the year, your overall tax liability is $1,000 or more owed to the IRS, then you will need to start filing Quarterly Estimated Tax Payments in the subsequent tax year. If the amount owed to the IRS is under the $1,000 threshold, then you do not need to worry about estimated payments. One strategy that I employed for years, in order to avoid doing estimated tax payments, was to claim zero deductions on my husband's W-2 income from his job. Thus, money was coming out of his paycheck at a high enough rate to cover (or almost cover) our overall tax liability once my Schedule C income was plugged into the equation. One year we nevertheless ended up with a significant amount owed and so we elected going forward to have an additional $75 taken out of his biweekly paychecks, some going to the IRS and some to the state. These changes can all be made on the W-4 form provided by the employer and is only applicable to readers with W-2 family income.

Deductible Business Expenses

When thinking of deductible expenses, think in terms of capturing and recording every penny you spend on your business. Anything reasonably related can be deducted, but you must be able to substantiate each deduction if you are selected for an IRS audit. Careful record keeping is required and it cannot be done adequately next April (for the prior year) by searching through a messy heap on your desk or pile of papers in the corner of your "office." Please consider:

- Are you organizationally impaired?
- Do you have a problem following through on details?
- Does depression get the best of you at times?

If so, then, at a *minimum,* get yourself one big envelope that you put your receipts in and *DO IT AS YOU GO.* Keep your appointment book and client records and you should be able to reconstruct mileage using MapQuest online (though it is likely you will underreport your overall business mileage using this method). With the envelope and client records method, at least you will have something to work with come tax time. But it is sure to be a daunting process, making procrastination appear infinitely preferable to tackling the job.

The alternative is to put a system in place and exercise self-discipline in order to develop good habits in using the system. Your system can be accounting software such as QuickBooks, though for many small, service-oriented businesses, a two-ledger account book purchased at your local office supply store will suffice. For many years, I used the ledger book method. On the left-hand side of the page, I labeled at the top "October Income" and on the right-hand side "October Expenses." For each income entry, I put a date, name and amount. On the expense side, I put date, expense category and amount. All receipts then go in an envelope titled "October Expenses." At the end of the month, that envelope is sealed and filed away and a new one is started. (I should never have to open up the receipts envelope again, unless I am audited, knock on wood.)

If you decide to use a software program, you may want to check with your accountant, if you have one. See what he/she recommends and what will be compatible with their system. Accounting software will incorporate functions well beyond the needs of doulas who are offering a fairly straightforward set of services.

However, if retail sales, employees or multiple types of services are integrated into the business model, the software makes it much easier to track income from various revenue streams, track expenses and generate reports or snapshots of your business at any point in time. All of this can be immensely helpful for planning purposes and generating reports as proof of income for loan applications or other purposes.

Following are some expense categories. The list is meant to get you thinking in terms of possible deductions, but it is not necessarily exhaustive.

Child Care

Child-care expenses are not claimed on Schedule C. There is a place on Form 1040, page two, for this exemption. Follow the instructions accompanying the form to see if you qualify and how to make the claim.

Education

- Books
- Continuing-education classes, conferences, seminars, webinars and so on
- Subscriptions to professional journals, magazines

The cost of continuing education is 100% deductible. The education must meet the test of maintaining or improving a skill required in your business. It is not deductible if it is required to meet the minimum educational requirements of your present business or if the education will qualify you for a new trade or business, such as your basic doula training. However, a massage therapist, nanny or yoga instructor who has an existing business requiring Schedule C reporting to the IRS, and who has decided to enhance her business with the addition of doula services, can deduct the cost of basic training. Likewise, a birth doula who takes post-partum or bereavement doula training to enhance her existing skill set or expand services may deduct the cost of training. If the education qualifies as continuing education, such as taking a business development class or attending a professional conference, then all related expenses are deductible, including:

- Food when traveling for business purposes (50%)
- Lodging (100%)
- Travel expenses (airfare, train fare, bus fare, shuttles, taxis, mileage) (100%)
- Tuition and fees (100%)

Equipment and Furnishings (Form 4562, Depreciation and Amortization)

- Computer, printer, software
- Office furnishings (desk, file cabinet, bookcase, etc.)
- Phone (dedicated business line)

Home Office (Form 8829, Business Use of Home)

You can deduct a percentage of your utilities and rent or interest on your mortgage for a home office. The IRS has strict rules governing deductions for home offices but if you follow the rules, it is legal to do so. Be careful here and consider getting professional advice from an accountant as high deductions for a home office constitute a red flag to the IRS.

Here's how it works: (1) calculate the total square footage of your home or apartment; (2) calculate the total square footage of the space singularly dedicated to business use; (3) calculate the percentage that the business use represents of the total number; (4) plug this number into IRS Form 8829 and follow the directions to figure your deduction; (5) keep all utility and insurance bills for the year, add these up and multiply by the same percentage.

Some capital improvements and repairs to your home may also be deductible, using the same percentage. Be careful, however. A plumbing repair to keep your bathroom operational may qualify, while a washing machine repair probably does not (unless you are also a massage therapist and laundering linen is required to do business).

A key qualification to keep in mind is whether or not the space being designated as "home office" is a dedicated workspace. If you are using the kitchen table to conduct business, this will be a hard case to make. If you are using a room for two purposes, say as an office and a guest bedroom, you cannot deduct that entire space, but only the space used for business purposes. If you have the luxury of having a dedicated office space, then the entire space is deductible.

Insurance (See discussion on insurance in Chapter 7)

- Automobile rider on your car insurance (for transport of clients in your vehicle)
- Commercial insurance (protects place of business from loss in case of fire, theft, slip and fall)
- Professional liability insurance ("Errors and Omissions")

Inventory

Taxes are more complicated if you plan to sell products. I recommend that you talk to an accountant. You will need to apply for a sales tax license, if required by your state, and do an inventory at the end of each tax year.

Marketing

- Advertising
- Booth fees for community events
- Business cards, brochures or rack cards
- Graphic design services
- Postage, printing for direct mailing costs
- Signage
- Social media consultant
- Web design/hosting and domain fees

Mileage

Question: What is the best system for tracking mileage?
Answer: *The one that you use.*

A simple mileage log can be purchased at any office supply store. Keep it in your vehicle and track all business-related miles. There are also phone apps that will track mileage if you prefer. Just google "best phone apps to track mileage" and you will find more than enough information to help you select one. While doulas cannot claim mileage to commute to an office outside the home (if you have one), they can claim miles driven to meet with or serve clients, attend work-related events and run business-related errands. The IRS determines the reimbursement rate annually, or semiannually if there are significant increases or decreases in the price of gas. Currently, the reimbursement rate is $.545 per mile. This can really add up to a significant deduction!

See our mileage tracking guides in *The Doula Business Guide Workbook, 3rd Edition.*

Miscellaneous

- Business lunches
- Copying costs

- Gifts
- Parking fees, tolls (you may want to set up a petty cash account for these)

Professional Fees

- Accountant fees
- Backup doula fees
- Business-name registration fee
- Certification fees
- Incorporation fees
- Lawyer fees
- Membership dues

Record Keeping and Accounting

- Accounting software
- Bank fees
- Ledger, day planner

Rent and Utilities

If you rent office space separate from your home, rent and utilities are 100% deductible.

Supplies

Office Supplies

- Binders, file folders, etc.
- Paper, envelopes
- Pens, stapler, etc.
- Printer cartridges
- Stamps

Doula Supplies

- Birth ball, rebozo
- Carrying bag
- Educational materials, reference books

- Massage lotion
- Other?

Telecommunications

- Phone (claim only the percentage used for business; be careful about writing off 100% of a cell phone bill unless you have two separate lines, one for personal use and one for business)
- Internet access (deduct only the estimated percentage of the monthly bill that represents use for business purposes)

IRS Forms Summary

Schedules C & SE

Use Schedule C to report self-employment income and Schedule SE to compute and report FICA taxes of 15.3% on net earnings. You may also need separate forms for business use of your home or depreciation on equipment purchased for your business (e.g., a laptop) to complete the Schedule C. *If you are an LLC partnership, an S corporation or a nonprofit corporation, you do not use Schedule C and I recommend consulting an accountant.*

Payroll Taxes

If you have employees and payroll is involved, then it is more complicated. You will have both federal and state requirements to meet. Consider hiring an accountant to set it up for you, hire a payroll service or purchase tracking software such as QuickBooks payroll. The latter is a relatively expensive option when you consider the subscription service you will need for tax updates, so this is not just a one-time purchase. I recommend that you price out these different options and take the hassle factor of doing it all yourself (which is huge!) into consideration before you make a final decision.

Forms 1099 and 1096

If you pay out $600 or more in a given tax year to an individual or business for services rendered, then you must issue a Form 1099 to individual payees and report these payments to the IRS on Form 1096. The deadlines for sending out these forms is the end of January for the previous year. Check the IRS.gov website for the most up-to-date requirements.

As an example, I contract with teachers (who are not my employees) to teach childbirth preparation and other classes at my Center and each receives a 1099. My website developer, tech support person, graphic designer and landlord for the business property also qualify for a 1099. To be compliant with IRS regulations, require all contract service providers to include their social security numbers and addresses on invoices for services rendered. It's always easier to get the social security number up front than to try and track someone down after the fact.

The corollary to the above is if you provide services as an individual contractor and are paid $600 or more in a given tax year by one business owner, then you will be on the receiving end of a Form 1099 and will be held accountable for taxes on the reported income.

For further guidance, see "Setting Up Your Chart of Accounts in QuickBooks," "Staying Out of Trouble with the IRS—Startup Exercises" and our "Bookkeeping System Checklist" in *The Doula Business Guide Workbook, 3rd Edition.*

Getting the Paperwork Together

At a minimum, doulas will need to create:

- A contract for services (see Chapter 7 for more on contracts).
- An invoice for services rendered. Invoices should include the client's name and address, dates and location of services, description of services provided, hours worked, rate of pay and total amount due. Put this on your letterhead and make it look professional.
- A receipt for payment. Receipts will contain the same information but will show total amount paid. If clients are attempting to seek reimbursement for services through insurance companies, Medical Savings Accounts, Health Reimbursement Accounts or Flex Accounts, then the issuer's social security number or federal identification number (FIN, same as EIN) and the client's social security number will also be required. Ditto on letterhead.
- On-call doulas will need to write up simple instructions regarding how and when they want to be contacted when support services are needed—ideally a one-page summary that can be posted on the client's refrigerator or other prominent location in the home.

Beyond these essentials, doulas may want to use a variety of forms or questionnaires that have been developed by others or that they create for specific purposes, such as client intake. Samples of such forms are often included in doula training manuals, can be found through an online search and are available for purchase from doula business support vendors. I am not going to reinvent that wheel here. I do, however, want to invite you to think critically about the use of forms and paperwork in your doula practice. Here are some considerations:

- Does the form help you provide better care to your client (special needs, requests)?
- Does the form contain important information that you will need to access (directions to their home, names of key family members)?
- Does the form enhance your understanding of your client's motivations and needs without being unnecessarily intrusive?
- Is it a good tool for self-discovery for the client?
- Is it a good tool to facilitate communication between all parties (among family members, between the doula and her clients, among the entire support team)?
- Does the form ask for a health history and other specific medical information? If so, why are you, the doula, asking this information? How is it going to change the care you provide? An alternative approach is simply to ask a more general question such as, "Have you been experiencing any health-related concerns that you would like me to be aware of?" or "Is your pain being adequately managed?"
- Is the form primarily for your benefit, for example forms needed for certification purposes?
- Is the form required by the hospital, doula program or hospice with which you are affiliated?

In my experience, less may be more (as in better) when it comes to forms. Some clients, recent immigrants in particular, may be intimidated by or suspicious of forms, or have privacy concerns (see the section on HIPAA and the doula in Chapter 7). The formality of creating documentation, however benign, can introduce both medical and governmental overtones into your relationship. My advice is to be ruthless in eliminating unnecessary paperwork! And keep in mind, the forms serve you, not the other way around (with the notable exception of forms required for certification or by program managers to whom you are accountable).

Doulas provide a simple service with a loving heart. Let that be reflected in the tone and quantity of your paperwork lest you give the impression that you are a medical care provider.

Publishing a list of select educational or community resources, on the other hand, is a good idea. Many doulas have found that putting together a folder of materials or a Client Welcome Packet is much appreciated. I like to include professional scope of practice documents in my client packets. For birth doula clients, I also provide one-page summary sheets on what to do in early labor, possible supplies to bring to the hospital, how partners and doulas work together, postpartum self-care, how to know whether breastfeeding is going well, and a birth planning template. Community resources include available childbirth classes, pediatricians, postpartum doulas, chiropractors and so on. For postpartum clients, I provide a list of mother-baby support groups, breastfeeding resources (where to go for pumps, parts, nursing bras, professional help) postpartum fitness resources, and counselors/clinics offering help for postpartum mood disorders. End-of-life doulas can share resources on advance care planning, after death care options, Threshold Choir and so on—whatever you think your clients might need. Keep the materials you provide to clients simple and brief, emphasizing key information. It's easy for folks to become overwhelmed with too much information when hormones are raging or they are in an emotional crisis. Resources can include online favorites such as helpful websites, Facebook groups and YouTube videos. Don't forget to include community resources for low-income families as well. You might publish your resources on your website as a way of driving traffic to the site and a reason for folks to come back while you're at it.

> **A list of local resources** serves a dual purpose: (1) It empowers clients to get their needs met from a variety of sources, thereby freeing up any tendency to become overly dependent upon the doula and (2) it is comprised of folks with whom you should be networking and co-marketing since you are serving the same target audience.

See "Assembling a Welcome Packet" and our "Forms Checklist" in *The Doula Business Guide Workbook, 3rd Edition.*

A Word about "The Stuff"

I heard Penny Simkin speak at a conference where she was deploring the notion that doulas should bring a rolling suitcase full of supplies to a birth. I couldn't agree more! I think it is a true sign of being a rookie and feeling insecure to focus extensively on accumulating "stuff." I will go so far as to say, categorically, that "stuff" will not make you a better doula. I have two stories to share.

My First Catch

Many years ago, I was an inexperienced apprentice homebirth midwife. As I arrived at the client's home in labor, I was greeted by a visibly relieved grandmother-to-be and grunting sounds coming from the bedroom. A mere half hour earlier, I had spoken by phone with the laboring mother, who reported feeling discouraged that, while she wasn't able to sleep much through the night, she did not think she was making any progress. Upon hearing the unmistakable sounds of an imminent birth on my arrival, I asked whether or not the midwife had also been called. The grandmother's facial expression sank as she asked, "You mean you're not the midwife?" I quickly recovered with, "Yes, I mean did you call the *other* midwife?" privately thinking "be careful what you ask for" regarding my dream of becoming a baby catcher.

I had been to a total of twelve births at the time and carried a very small bag of birth supplies. My brain went into overdrive as I walked into the bedroom to attend the mother. One of my roles at births up to this point had been to lay out all the stuff neatly and ensure that everything the midwife might need was on hand. Clearly there would not be time to fuss over this, but I was nevertheless thinking about the stuff. What was absolutely needed? Did I have what I needed in my bag? And so on. The mother was in a panic, primarily because her husband and mother had been exhorting her to stop pushing while her body was refusing to heed their commands. She urgently directed me with these words: "Patty, you have to help me keep it together!" I remember gratefully dropping thoughts of anything else. I moved in close as I thought, "I can do that." As the baby's head began to birth, she called out "support my perineum," and my hands slid into place as her baby birthed over an intact perineum. What a great teacher she was! The lesson she taught me—focus on the mother—has stayed with me throughout my career.

"I Sing"

Years ago, I remember attending a Midwives Alliance of North America (MANA) Regional Conference in Chicago where Nan Koehler (author of *Artemis Speaks*) was teaching. An expert on herbs, Nan was seen roaming the college campus prior to her presentation, picking various wildflowers and plants. I found her anecdotal presentation style delightful as she spoke about her "friends," the plants. There were a few attendees who were getting a bit restless as the class was coming to a close. They had clearly come to her presentation with an expectation of a more linear discussion of herbs, such as recipes and precise dosages—"use this for that." And their frustration was building. One woman, pen poised to paper, suddenly burst out, "What herbs do you take with you to births?" Surprised, Nan replied, "Well, I don't really take much to births anymore. You know, really, I find myself doing a lot of singing at births these days."

Interesting how the wise women come full circle, back to basics. Heart and hands. Focus on the mother. If you don't have a lot of money to invest in doula supplies, so much the better! It's just not a problem. You have what you need and you can improvise the rest.

Supplies for Your Business

So, what supplies are necessary for your business? Here's a suggestion. Make a list following these principles:

- things you need
- things you require
- things you desire

"Need" implies that you cannot do the work without the items on this list. At a minimum, you need a phone and a reliable form of transportation. Computer access, a printer and paper are necessary for business forms, receipts and so on. These are "need" items.

"Desire" items are things you simply want—those things that perhaps you cannot afford but nevertheless compose your ideal vision. In the realm of desire, we are thinking big, dreaming. I recently purchased one of my desire items for the Center—a 75" flat-screen television, wall-mounted with plug-ins for a laptop. Prior to this purchase we were using a combination of pull-down screen and LCD projector for use with PowerPoint presentations and a separate TV/DVD player for additional audio-visual capacity. Technically, we did not "need" the upgrade to the teaching space, but I did desire it and the investment made sense for my business.

"Require" falls somewhere in between "need" and "desire." You could do business without these things, but you really don't want to, or you will be limited. You simply require them. Development of a website will likely fall on your list of requirements. Perhaps you want to become certified or purchase a key reference book or two. Once you have your list, you can price everything out and set priorities based on your budget. The beauty of a service-oriented business is that startup costs are low. You do not need office space and a large inventory of products, nor do you need to invest heavily in expensive advertising (see Chapter 3) or

Possible Supplies for a Doula Bag

Doula self-care items (Most experienced doulas primarily carry self-care items, with perhaps a few other favorites from the list below.)

- change of clothes
- slippers or socks with non-slip soles (helpful when working in homes with wood floors)
- sweater, sweatshirt with hood (hospitals can be cold, especially if you lie down for a nap; hood can also help to block light)
- extra pads, tampons
- toothpaste, toothbrush
- brush, hair ties
- Emergen-C packets (add to water for electrolyte boost)
- protein bars, trail mix, snacks, breath mints
- phone charger

For use with clients

- client records
- key reference book(s)
- pure essential oils and diffuser, cotton balls
- battery candle lights
- massage tools
- rice sock or hot water bottle
- unscented massage oil or lotion
- mini portable battery powered fans (birth doulas)
- gardening knee pad (birth doulas)
- rebozos (birth doulas)
- peanut ball (birth doulas)
- favorite babywearing carrier or wrap (postpartum doulas)

equipment. If you proceed in a thoughtful, disciplined manner, you can work your way through your needs, up to the requirements and then, once your income can cover it, your desires.

Invite input on your priorities, possibly from a spouse if you have one. Partners will be more supportive if they understand that your work is a business (not just an expensive hobby) and that you have to spend money in order to make it. By engaging them in your process, they will also learn what is on your wish list and may be able to help materialize your wishes in the form of gifts. The simple act of committing to paper what you want is the first step toward manifesting it in your life.

See "Create a Budget for Your Business" and our "Budget Worksheet" in *The Doula Business Guide Workbook, 3rd Edition.*

Commanding Respect

Respect is not something that one person gives to another. Respect from others is the direct result of self-respect and self-esteem. It is commanded. In order to be credible as a professional, you must command respect and accept nothing less. Frankly, you don't deserve to call yourself a doula if you think that respect is something that medical or hospice staff (or others) retain the power to bestow on you. You must do better for your clients than that! They have, after all, placed their trust in you and are paying you for a professional service. You have the right to be present because they want you there. If you do not command respect in your role, then, by association, your clients are being disrespected and you are a poor role model for them.

So, just as we empower our mamas and families to access their inner strength, we must also access our own. What is our value as a doula? What is our purpose? In challenging circumstances, we must tap into that inner core of our being that drew us to the work in the first place. Banish lame excuses. In fact, banish all excuses and the word "but" from your vocabulary. If you are in the process of landing your first client, don't apologize for that; turn it into an asset. How lucky is the family who gets you as you take this amazing first step on your path engaged in work you love and feel privileged to do! I'd rather have a new doula, passionate about her work, any day than a highly experienced but jaded and burned-out doula on the verge of retiring. No apologies for inexperience are necessary. Just like the person/family you are supporting, you are on a path and it is what it is.

Accentuate the positive!

It is okay to be privately mindful about your areas of weakness as you work toward addressing those weaknesses, but when you are with your clients, focus instead on what you *can* do for them rather than on what you *can't* do. That said, it is always preferable to be honest when asked directly. If a prospective postpartum client wants to know about your experience level in helping her to avoid or address breastfeeding issues experienced with her last baby, you should be truthful if you lack the necessary expertise. Don't hesitate to refer her elsewhere while you continue to work on developing your skills. That is the sign of a true professional and it will serve you well in the long run. It's also okay to say "I don't know" to client questions. It's not okay, however, to let that be your final answer. Resourcefulness is the key to excellence. If you search for and find the answer to her question, you will always remember it and will have attained in the process a higher level of professionalism.

Appearance Do's and Don'ts

Dress as a professional and pay attention to personal hygiene. You might dress a bit more formally for an interview/consultation (business casual) than when you are engaged in the trenches. Do not wear blue jeans or ragged, dirty, sloppy or overly revealing (no cleavage!) clothes. This seems obvious, but I have witnessed more than one doula violation in this area. Do not wear perfume or strong-smelling scents, including clothes dried with those noncling dryer sheets. Do not wear t-shirts displaying political/controversial messages. Unless you are a member of a hospital doula group that requires scrubs to be worn, doulas should not wear scrubs. Scrubs imply that you have a clinical role, thereby sending the wrong message to both clients and health care providers.

Do wear comfortable, modest and nonbinding clothes. Bring an extra layer for warmth (especially in the summer) and a change of clothes. Wear sensible shoes with good support that will enable you to be on your feet for long hours if necessary. Do comb your hair, secure long hair, use deodorant and brush your teeth. In short, do your best to ensure that your appearance is an asset in helping you build rapport with both clients and other professionals. If first impressions are that you look like something the cat dragged in during the night, then commanding respect as a professional will absolutely be an uphill battle. Given that you might take a nap in the middle of a long vigil or birth, it is helpful to keep a dedicated self-care bag with personal care items and a change of clothes in your car at all times.

Use of a nametag may be helpful in building bridges when you work in institutional settings. Identify yourself as a doula when new staff members come on the scene. Smile. Note the labor and delivery nurse's name and use it. Same goes for the hospice nurse, home health aide and chaplain. Make every effort to build rapport. Act like a team member and you will be treated like one. Remember always: your clients wants you there and they are in charge.

Understand that if you are making a strong statement about your lifestyle and your beliefs through your appearance and choice of clothing and jewelry, the statement will serve as a type of filter for or against you. It may attract those who are

Tips for Presenting a Professional Image

- Make it easy for potential clients to get in touch with you.
- Your phone message should identify you as a doula.
- Respond promptly! (Who wants an unresponsive doula?)
- Follow up on client concerns and requests for information. (This establishes trust.)
- Be ready with answers about your doula services when potential clients call you.
- Allow a chunk of time to talk on the phone without interruption (teach your family/housemates to respect this or set up a time to speak with clients when you won't be interrupted).
- Have your paperwork together and handy.
- Make sure all written materials are grammatically correct and absent of spelling errors; if this is not your strong suit, get help.
- Pursue formal training and certification.
- Pursue continuing education, such as attending classes and conferences as well as reading.
- Become a member of professional organizations.
- Subscribe to professional journals and stay abreast of the most recent research in your field.
- Never stop learning!
- Always wash your hands after arriving at a birth, upon entering a client's home, after changing a diaper, before preparing a meal and so on.
- Master the voice in your head that tells you negative messages about yourself (you know, the voice that tells you you're not thin enough, smart enough, experienced enough, etc.); create a new script that sends positive messages.
- Always be on time, including keeping to your timeframe for length of visits.
- Do not concern clients with problems in your life.
- At interviews, listen more than you talk.
- Look for ways to be helpful; try to anticipate the needs of the client.
- When working in clients' homes, be polite and friendly to every member of the family (including pets); write down their names so you'll remember them.
- Support, rather than judge, your client's choices.
- Make each client feel important.
- Do what you say you are going to do.

(This list has been around for a while. I'm not sure who to credit for the original version, but I have put my own spin on it.)

in sync with you and repel those who are not. Perhaps that is your intention. I am just suggesting that you accept the truth of it and make it a conscious intention, as it will undoubtedly limit your potential client base.

If Respect Is Not Given ...

Some years ago, I was the doula for a mother whose planned homebirth resulted in a hospital transport during labor for decelerations in the baby's heart rate. Upon arrival at the hospital, the laboring mother was attended by a nurse who was also her friend. Knowing the mother's wishes for a natural and nonmedicalized birth, the nurse began to facilitate numerous waivers, especially in regard to anticipated care of the newborn baby. These included declining routine Vitamin K injection, eye prophylaxis and the Hepatitis B vaccine. Throughout labor, the baby continued to have occasional decelerations, but the birth nevertheless proceeded to a vaginal delivery of a healthy baby girl.

After the birth, heavy pressure was brought to bear on the parents to forego their preferences regarding medical care of the newborn. I suggested to the parents that the process of getting an early discharge might be facilitated by their private pediatrician, but they had not yet hired one. They then began the process of engaging their preferred provider, Dr. D., who agreed to come over to the hospital.

Meanwhile, two doctors approached me and asked me to step out in the hallway. Clearly they were preparing to mount an attack. Being mindful to protect our very helpful nurse, I silently began to implement a technique that I had learned in yoga class—I began to practice tadasana, which translates as "mountain pose." Tadasana involves simply standing up straight and tall. It's the perfect antidote when someone is "dumping" on you, as your body language is such that you do not make an easy target for the dumping.

The entire confrontation took place a few feet away from the nurses' station, in the middle of the hallway. One of the doctors did all the talking. I was asked who I thought I was to make promises to clients that they would not have to submit their baby to standard pediatric procedures. And didn't I know that these procedures were necessary for the well-being of the baby? She threatened to hold me responsible for making such promises and told me I would not be allowed back in this hospital. I was accused of lying to the staff that Dr. D. was the woman's pediatrician when Dr. D. had never even heard of this couple and so on.

From my mountain height, I calmly allowed her to finish venting her full range of accusations. I answered her objections dispassionately, one at a time. I informed her that I made none of the promises to my clients that she alleged. I told her that these parents are informed consumers who were making their own preferences known and that it was my job to support them in their choices WHICH, by the way, I believed they had every right to make. I told her that I would never lie to the staff and that I objected to her accusing me of lying about Dr. D. The couple had planned to hire him but had not yet done so and none of us had claimed otherwise. Big Breath.

When she saw that she couldn't intimidate me, she became even more frustrated and angry. She began to repeat herself, but in a louder voice, and we came full circle through the same set of accusations but with more passion and the Big Finish. She threatened to go get Dr. Bigwig-in-Charge-of-the-Whole-Hospital to enforce her assertion that my presence will not be tolerated.

I responded that I thought it might be a good idea to get Dr. Bigwig down here right now. I added that she had begun to repeat herself, that I didn't appreciate her maligning my good name by calling me a liar, that I had been attending births at this hospital for over fifteen years and planned to continue to do so and that I never wanted to have to face this kind of harassment for doing my job again!

End of story. Three nurses came up afterward, squeezed my arm, and congratulated me on how I handled myself. "Good for you." And, instead of tossing and turning all night in burning humiliation and indignation (been there), thinking about what I should have said but didn't, I slept really well that night.

If respect is not simply implied or given, we must command it.

Become a Mountain

Poses are built from the bottom up, from the reference point where one's body is in contact with the earth. In the case of tadasana, it starts with the feet together and firmly planted, toes spread. Next, the practitioner moves her attention up her legs, lifting the kneecaps by activating the thigh muscles, feeling the lift move on up through the center core of the body, engaging the pelvic floor in the process. The tailbone is slightly tucked. The chest opens as the sternum lifts (this is really powerful). The shoulders relax as the arms fall gently to the side of the body, palms facing inward. Viewed from the side of the body, an imaginary straight line intersects the ankle bone, knee, hip, shoulder, and crown of the head. The crown of the head is balanced as though supporting a book. The entire spine moves vertically in space, stretching upwards. The breath is deep and slow. Practice of the pose builds character and strength. ◆

tadasana
(mountain pose)

CHAPTER 3

How to Market Your Practice

FOR MANY YEARS, I THOUGHT OF MARKETING AS A "BUSINESS" ASPECT OF MY WORK, something that was necessary, but distasteful, and essentially different from the work itself. I have learned to reframe that perception. A good doula has *the heart of a teacher.* Education is integral to the role. I began to realize that marketing is really just another form of education, that it is incumbent on doulas to get the message out about why our services matter in the world. Why should an expectant couple want to consider hiring a doula? How do postpartum doulas meet the needs of new moms and their families? Why does that matter? How do end-of-life doulas complement hospice services? How can they help the dying person and their loved ones? Why am I the best available choice (among all available options) to meet client needs? What makes me unique? Marketing answers the question "Why?" When I began to think of marketing as education, I started to make peace with it and even embrace the process. It is critical that we continue to articulate the reasons why doulas make a difference for families at life's critical periods of transition. We must become good sales people, whether our efforts are aimed at building a private practice or getting our doula program funded.

Marketing is not a single act. It is an ongoing process.

Marketing is not something you do once and then you are done, like a hit and run. Even successful business owners who claim to have more work than they can handle, nevertheless need to continually market their businesses. I have watched highly experienced and skilled doulas fall by the wayside and struggle financially because they made the mistake of thinking they were the queen bee, top of the heap so to speak, and did not need to do anything quite so crass as marketing, let alone become knowledgeable about developing an online presence. While they were busy being impressed with themselves, a younger generation of savvy young

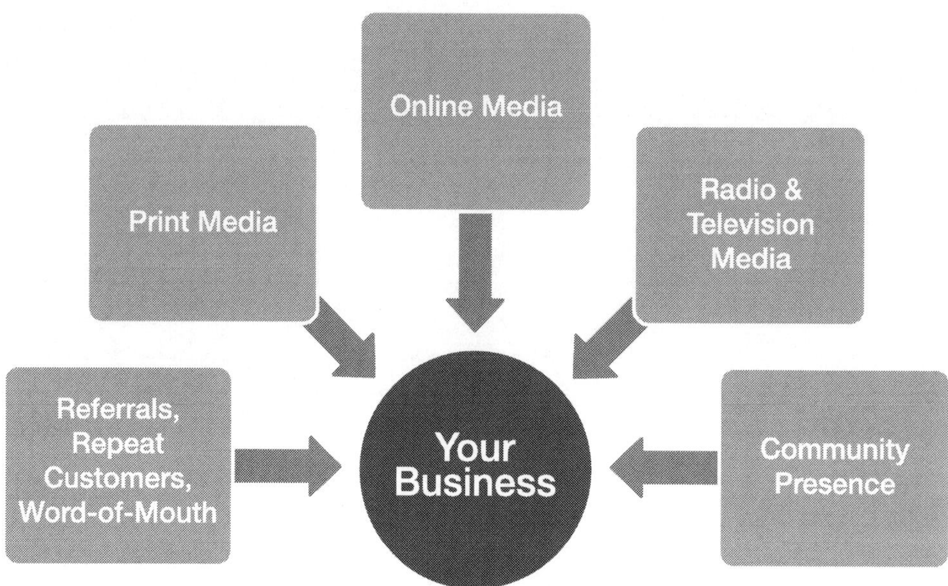

businesswomen moved to town and set up shop, establishing a quick competitive edge with unrelenting, smart outreach efforts.

How will prospective clients hear about you? The marketing principle of "name times three" states that, once a prospective customer has seen or heard about you or your business name three times, she/he will be more likely to think of you when your services are needed. This means that almost every effort you make to get your name "out there" will ultimately result in a return on your efforts, and this has been my experience. See the diagram above for a visual on how we might put the principle of "name times three" into action. To attract customers, you will need to get all vectors pointing to you.

Your future clients are out there. It is part of your job to make it easy for them to find you. In this chapter, I will give you pieces of the marketing jigsaw puzzle. If one section of the puzzle feels overwhelming to you, work on a different aspect. As the pieces come together, sections that previously felt daunting may fall into place. Or you will attract the right help at the right time. If you are just starting out, then simply follow the path of least resistance (go with your strengths and ideas that strike you as fun) and keep chipping away at it. You WILL get a return on every effort, every hour invested, though it may not be immediate. Remember, all entrepreneurs wear more than one hat. There is the work itself. And then there is the selling of the work. And both are important. Otherwise, we are the proud owners of the best-kept secret in town! And of what possible use is that? So, come up with some goals and a plan and set aside some time (and a little money) each week to market your business. And we'll walk you through it.

The Doula Business Guide Workbook, 3rd Edition contains a "Marketing Plan Checklist" to help you track your planning and celebrate your progress through the various components.

The Big Picture—Marketing Overview

Consider first who your market is, your target customers. See these people in your mind clearly. Where do they live? What is their income? How old are they? What do they like to do in their spare time? Where do they get their information? What needs do they have that you are ready to meet? What might motivate them to purchase your services? These might seem, on the surface, to be simple and straightforward questions. In fact, understanding the motivations of your target customers may be one of the most (unfortunately) overlooked aspects of many business owners' marketing efforts. If we really engage in exploring the needs of our potential customers, it is possible we might discover that an entire new niche market exists for our services or products.

See "Your Ideal Customer Questionnaire" and "Competition Makes Us Stronger" in *The Doula Business Guide Workbook, 3rd Edition* for guidance in defining your best prospective customers and potential niche market.

Second, we must craft a message for our target customers. The message needs to be compelling. A business card is not a message, yet many business owners spend good money on ads that are essentially nothing more than what they have on their business card—the business name, a brief list of one or two services offered and contact information. How boring! Think in terms of attention-getting headlines and customer benefits. Your pitch answers the question, "What is the benefit to the customer?" For example, once I started to grasp this concept, the headline in my monthly e-newsletter designed to promote doula training went from "Doula Training Spring Schedule" to "Launch your New MotherBaby Business Today!" I moved from "what" to "why." In other words, the message is not about me and what I do; it is about the customer and how my product meets their needs. We are not simply selling a service, we are selling a solution—that's the message. Think about it from the client's perspective.

The final component of marketing is the media or the means of delivering your compelling message to the right market. Considerations regarding the various media or methods for getting the word out are detailed below. Diversify your use of media as much as possible—the more the merrier.

Put all three components together—market, message and media—and do it well, and you have a viable business, *provided you can deliver on your promises.* Eventually, a poor product or unscrupulous business practices will be the undoing of even the most successful salesperson. If the emperor has no clothes, sooner or later someone will make this observation publicly.

Networking and Cultivating Referrals

The single most effective thing you can do to build your business is to create excellent word of mouth about your services. Happy, satisfied clients will turn into repeat customers and help spread the word about how wonderful you are. Imagine an upside-down triangle. The tip at the bottom is the starting point. It's a bit lonely at the beginning. But, as you provide excellent care to each person who comes your way, that person touches many others and they, in turn, have their own realms of influence and contacts. As a few more people come your way, each person presents an opportunity to enlarge your sphere of influence. Over time, the number of people who are potentially exposed to you and your services is expanding, like the base of the flipped triangle, and your business grows exponentially.

Marketing is about building relationships.

The reverse is also true. One really unhappy or angry customer is likely to tell many more folks about their disappointment than a happy one. Your reputation is a precious asset and negative word of mouth, justified or not, can do a lot of damage. Chapter 7 takes up the topic of risk management, including identification of high-risk scenarios, how to manage difficult people and damage control after an incident—all with an emphasis on preventing harm to your reputation and pocketbook.

Networking is another word for building professional relationships, for connecting with people who are in the business of providing goods and services to the same target population. No one builds a referral base by sitting in a chair and bemoaning a lack of business. It's akin to a lonely person staying at home and watching TV while complaining about being lonely. You must get involved, give

All of your clients' family members, friends, and contacts

Your immediate contacts

Doula

people the opportunity to get to know you and vice versa. Networking is the conscious act of making these connections. Potential networking venues include doula support groups, membership organizations that meet regularly, coalitions and task forces, celebrations or fundraisers sponsored by local groups in your field, health fairs, trade shows, continuing education events, conferences and so on.

How is networking done? When attending a networking event, your goal is not to put your business card in as many people's hands as possible. That will likely result in your cards ending up in the wastebasket later. Rather, make it your goal to have a meaningful conversation with five people, to make a connection. A conversation involves a nice (hopefully interesting and/or funny) exchange of energy. It goes two ways, so be sure that you spend some time listening and asking thoughtful questions and conveying a genuine interest in the other person. As you wind up the exchange, ask for their business card (and give them yours). One way to keep it moving, so that you don't end up in a corner with just one individual for the entire event, is to introduce that person to someone else, helping him or her move on to another connection as well. Or perhaps, during the conversation, if someone suggests a person you should know, ask to be introduced. Quality over quantity. If your business card contains your picture, it will serve to help people remember you.

Begin by brainstorming a list of everyone in your extended community who is offering services or products to the same target customers. See pp.108-109 for a generic list and then fill in the specifics for your area. The beauty of your list is that it will serve the dual purpose of identifying community resources for clients as well as potential networking connections. Anyone to whom you are making referrals is also a candidate for reciprocating with referrals to you. Referrals from

Networking Contacts for All Doulas

- Acupuncturists, Traditional Chinese Medicine practitioners
- Aromatherapists
- Chiropractors
- Energy workers, Reiki practitioners, Healing Touch practitioners
- Flower Essence practitioners
- Health food stores
- Homeopaths, homeopathic pharmacies
- Massage and cranial-sacral therapists, therapeutic body workers
- Naturopaths
- Osteopaths
- Perinatal loss support groups

Networking Contacts for Birth & Postpartum Doulas

- Birth centers (free-standing and hospital based)
- Birth doulas
- Breastfeeding equipment suppliers
- Breastfeeding support groups, clinics, classes
- Cesarean recovery/prevention/VBAC promotion support groups
- Childbirth educators (community-based and hospital programs)
- Childcare providers (daycare centers, in-home providers)
- Clinics (prenatal, well-baby)
- Community services and programs for pregnant women and families
- Counselors, psychotherapists (especially those specializing in perinatal issues)
- Diaper services, cloth diaper outlets
- Doctors' offices (obstetricians, family practice doctors, pediatricians)
- Early intervention programs for babies with special needs
- Exercise/yoga classes (prenatal, postpartum, mother-baby)
- Fathers' resources (classes, support groups, counselors)
- Infant massage classes and services
- Lactation consultants
- La Leche League leaders
- Nursing bra suppliers/fitters
- Maternity/nursing clothes retailers (new and used)
- Maternity stores, baby equipment
- Midwives (homebirth, birth centers, hospital based)
- Mother-baby support groups
- Mothers of Multiples groups
- Nanny agencies
- Natural baby product sources, boutique stores
- Nutrition counseling, education, WIC
- Parenting classes, support groups, play groups
- Postpartum depression support groups
- Postpartum doulas
- Public Health Department (Maternal and Infant Services)

Networking Contacts for End-of-Life Doulas

- Advance Care Planning Facilitators
- Agencies that provide companion care or "sitting"
- Celebrants, chaplains, pastoral counselors, shamans
- Community services and programs for the elderly and infirm
- Counselors, psychotherapists (especially those specializing in aging issues, bereavement, caregiver burnout)
- End-of-life doulas, death doulas, death midwives
- Estate sale planners, auction houses
- Funeral homes
- Gerontology clinics
- Grief support groups
- Home funeral guides
- Home health care agencies, suppliers
- Hospices
- Lawyers (specializing in wills, estate planning)
- Legacy planners
- Music thanatologists, Threshold Choir
- Natural health stores
- Palliative care specialists, clinics
- Private-duty nurses

doula colleagues can serve as a significant source of business. This takes some time because it is a matter of getting to know people and establishing trust.

See our "Professional Networking Worksheet" in *The Doula Business Guide Workbook, 3rd Edition* to identify your top networking contacts and track your progress.

Referrals and repeat customers can be purposefully cultivated. There is room to get creative here. It is all based on the simple idea that people who have bought something from you once are likely to buy from you again. Start noticing the marketing strategies employed by other businesses as you go through your day. What's effective? What's obnoxious? Rewards programs at my local grocery market and office supply stores are very effective with me. Coupons for twenty percent off work too. How might doulas encourage referrals and repeat business? Here are just a couple of ideas:

- If offering classes, give clients a discount for taking multiple classes (the "upsell" in marketing language).
- Design a gift certificate for a specified amount off products or services (put in a deadline in the not-too-distant future); tie this to an event such as Mother's Day and promote on social media.

- At my center, we send a postcard a few weeks after the baby's expected due date inviting all former class participants to join a MotherBaby support group, reminding them of available parenting resources and suggesting options for moms who may be struggling with depression (nurturing connection and keeping my business "front of mind").
- Host a client/family appreciation day and encourage families to bring interested friends (include an inducement).
- Sponsor a "milk and cookies with the doulas" lunch/snack break with a local OB practice, family practice doctor group or midwifery service on one of their prenatal office days. If you can manage to coordinate with a staff meeting, you may be able to make a brief (ten-minute) presentation on the benefits of doulas and your services. Bring your Scope of Practice document(s) and ask how you might best partner with them to help families achieve their goals. Leave your literature with the office manager. This strategy will be especially effective if you are doing outreach for a doula program or have supports in place for low-income families.
- Many massage therapists/body workers have offered me complimentary sessions over the years, understanding that if I liked their work, I would be likely to refer customers their way. They were right.
- Whatever you can dream up!

For many years, I hosted a drop-in "Seasonal Tea" four times per year at my home for past clients and their families. My husband called it my "breastfeeding party." I provided the tea and clients brought snacks. In nice weather, we were able to flow outside, as my home bordered a park. A few weeks prior to the event, I mailed out a postcard invitation to my clients (now you could use email or Facebook to save time and money). These teas served multiple purposes—not all premeditated when I first came up with the idea. First, they provided an opportunity for me to see the babies growing over time and to reconnect with all the lovely families from my practice. Secondly, as I realized the delight in this ongoing connection, I began to use it as a way to ease the transition into closure of the immediate client relationships. Instead of saying "goodbye," I could say "goodbye" and "I hope to see you at the Spring Tea." Families felt less of a sense of abandonment when they got a glimpse of an open door in the near future. Third, it ensured that my contact list got updated from time to time. As my clients moved and postcards were returned, I was able to capture their new addresses and contact information. A few began to ensure that I had this information. A surprise bonus was when some clients invited pregnant friends along to the teas so that they could introduce us to each other. All in all, the teas proved to be a successful way for me to build and nurture a community of supporters.

Be sure to express appreciation to folks who refer business to you. Reciprocation in the form of referrals, support of *their* community events or other expressions of gratitude will go a long way toward building a mutually satisfying professional relationship. It can't all be about you. A prompt, handwritten thank-you note never misses. Whenever possible, make a personal connection. If there are one or two people who send a lot of business your way, send them a gift with a note (can even be gift card to Amazon or Starbucks or, better still, a local business you want to support) as a thank you. The psychology of referrals is that, many times, people simply forget to make one. By expressing appreciation in a way that gets noticed, you remind them to continue making referrals to you. They feel appreciated and you stay on their radar screen.

Bottom line: Never take referrals for granted.

Yikes!

At one time, my childbirth preparation classes were heavily populated by referrals from the nurse-midwifery service at the local hospital. Perhaps as many as eight out of ten couples were referred to us by the midwife practice. One afternoon, on my commute home, I was listening to a marketing education program that discussed the importance of saying "thank you" for referrals. I realized, with shock and a sense of urgency, that I had never thanked the midwives for all the business they were sending my way. Unconsciously, I had taken it as my due because I was offering a premium product and people loved the classes. I went home and contacted the midwife in charge of the practice. I told her that I wanted to sponsor a breakfast, lunch or snack for the group's next meeting as a thank you for their many referrals. She graciously accepted my offer and I continued to do this annually, making sure not to use it as a promotion, but as a straight-up thank you. One time, she invited me to join the meeting and make a brief presentation on classes and services offered through our Center, with time for the midwives to ask any questions they might have.

Print Media

The many forms of print media include your own promotional literature, purchased advertising in local publications, calendar listings for classes and events (often free), provider directory listings, direct mailings, articles written about you and articles written by you. At a minimum, you will need a business card. All print media should be spell-checked and edited for proper grammar and syntax. Make it look appealing as well and use photos to draw interest. You may be an excellent doula but if writing well and spelling are not your strong suits, then get some help to make you look good on paper. Poor grammar and misspelled words will undermine your professional image.

Business Cards

The small size makes business cards easy to carry around and stock in public venues that are likely to reach your target market. Keep some cards in your wallet and car. Your card should contain your business name (if any), your name, logo (if you have one), area served, phone number, email address and website URL. Business cards and other literature can be made up on your home computer, using design templates, and then printed on special business card stock from the office supply store. Or you can go online to a self-serve design and printing company such as VistaPrint.com and create a design using one of their templates that they will print and mail to you. A third possibility, if your budget allows, is to have a professional graphic artist format your literature for you and upload your customized design to VistaPrint.com for printing.

Brochures or Rack Cards

A tri-fold brochure or rack card (the equivalent of one panel of a tri-fold printed on cardstock) can also be useful. The brochure format allows you to describe your business in detail and serves as an educational tool. Brochures should be distributed to anyone who is in a position to make referrals to you. Ideally, take them around in person, introduce yourself, show interest in the other provider's business, offer to take some of their literature for distribution and ask if they will share yours. Most businesses don't have space to display fifty brochures. Leave ten to fifteen and then check back in a couple of months to see if they need replenishment. While full-color brochures look great, they are relatively expensive to print. I find the rack card format to be a great alternative at a third the price. Refining what you want to say so that it fits into two panels (front and back) is a good mental exercise. It forces you to be succinct and, honestly, most folks aren't going to read an overly-wordy jam-packed brochure all about you and your services anyway.

Keep waste to a minimum by printing up smaller quantities of promotional materials at a time (e.g., 250 rather than 1,000). You may want to make changes in a few months as you refine your business or add services. Distribution is key, so get those materials off the shelf and out in the world!

As a business that provides a space for folks to display their promotional literature, I find it hard to accommodate odd-shaped pieces such as postcards, both big and small. The office supply stores sell standard-size literature display units designed to hold business cards, brochures or flyers. Variable sizes make your stuff more difficult to display.

Flyers

Flyers are best used to promote a specific event or class. Flyers should be visually appealing and attention getting. An effective flyer contains only enough information to pique interest and should not be word heavy. Tricks include using photos, clip art, text boxes, a variety of fonts and font sizes, and colored paper for printing/copying. Microsoft Publisher is a good design tool with a bit of a learning curve. Not all clip art is free, but some is available in the public domain. Just google "clip art" and then visit some of the sites to see what is out there. While you're surfing, bookmark your favorite free site(s), for future searches.

Patty Brennan's Rules of Bulletin Board Etiquette

As you pass through your community, begin taking note of where the bulletin boards are located. Note whether or not they are maintained boards or ones that become quickly trashed with postings on top of postings. Some boards aren't worth bothering with and it is a waste of resources to post on them. I have found that the upper left-hand corner is the premier spot for posting. If I claim that spot and maintain it regularly (every two to three weeks), it is rare that someone moves me out of it.

When posting on a board, it is not okay to post on top of someone else's literature. It is okay to make some adjustments in order to create space for your stuff.

Show some consideration as you do this, and take care that other folks' stuff is still visible. If an outdated flyer for a particular event is using up limited space, it is okay to pitch it. It is also okay to pitch stuff that has been posted on top of yours. Bottom line is that those folks who maintain their postings with the greatest vigilance will remain the most visible. What gives me the right to make these rules? Who can say?

If a bulletin board is owned by a particular business and appears to be meticulously maintained, then it is a good idea to ask permission before posting on it. Some boards will have a visible policy to this effect, while others will regularly sweep away anything that is not dated. In some public display venues, such as libraries, literature postings may be limited to nonprofit businesses only.

An excellent tool to use for display purposes is a "vinyl envelope" sized to hold business cards or brochures. Check online at Uline.com. This is extremely inexpensive advertising and it works. The envelopes are neater looking than tacking up several brochures or cards with a thumbtack and they make it easier for folks to help themselves to one without having to take the whole stack down and then repost it (thereby making a mess of your display). Oh, and if someone removes your stuff from the vinyl envelope and puts their stuff in it (or puts their stuff in your envelope on top of yours), then the rules further state that you can dispose of their literature with great prejudice.

I like to keep a stash of brochures and business cards inside of vinyl envelopes in my car, tucked in the pocket behind the driver's seat. Sometimes I have flyers for an event or class that I want to promote. When I find myself doing errands in a venue where a bulletin board is located, I check on my materials and restock as needed. It's cheap, easy and systematic!

Create a Portfolio

A portfolio allows you to display your training and credentials and/or boost your professional appearance. This can be a simple binder with clear plastic inserts in which you place certificates (or other proof) of training, continuing education or certification. You can include articles written about you and your business, photographs of clients you have helped (with their permission), your curriculum vitae or résumé, client testimonials or letters of recommendation. Your portfolio will be a work in progress. You can bring it along to that initial client interview or have it on display at promotional events in the community.

When we are self-employed, it is a good idea to document our accomplishments. A portfolio can serve this purpose. In the future (and who among us ever knows what's really around the next bend in our road?), an up-to-date portfolio may come in very handy if you find yourself in the job market or applying to a post-graduate school program. Certainly a portfolio is not something you need right from the start, but if you begin the process, then it will be easy to build it as you go.

Press Releases

Press releases are submitted to members of the media, via email, in order to draw their interest to your business and thereby gain free publicity. Writers are always looking for stories. Often a story will be taken word-for-word from your press release, with perhaps a quote or two thrown in. Your chances of getting your release published or read on air will be greatly increased if you do a little homework and send the press release to a journalist who is interested in your area of expertise. This requires familiarity with the publication, so you need to start paying attention to where you fit in.

To boost your credibility and chances of being published, use a standard format for creating press releases. Your release should be newsworthy and factual; don't make it a sales pitch or it is likely to end up in the trash. Report in the third person and avoid the use of exclamation points and ALL CAPS. Your purpose is to get media attention, so think in terms of an angle that will appeal to journalists, such as connecting your release to current events or issues. For example, if you just read a New York Times article about the "silver tsunami" of aging baby boomers, use their data and phrase to demonstrate your relevance. Effective releases use a strategy known as the inverted pyramid, which is written with the most important information and quotes first. All of the essential information—who, what, when, where, why—is contained in the first paragraph. If a busy editor grabs your release for publication and needs to chop off the bottom third or more due to space issues, you want to ensure that your message makes sense as a stand-alone, single paragraph. Each paragraph expands, in a bit more detail, on the key information. Keep it on the short side. Press releases are most effective when they are under 500 words (generally two to three paragraphs) and have an attention-grabbing headline. Finally, use the grammar and spell-check functions before sending.

If an editor must sift through several paragraphs to draw out the key information and rewrite what you sent, or you send it to the wrong person, or you send it

Standard Press Release Template

FOR IMMEDIATE RELEASE

These words should appear at the top, in upper case, informing the editor that you are submitting a press release and the information is to be made available immediately. Approximately two weeks' notice is best.

Contact

Make it easy for the reader to contact you for more information or follow up. Put this information right below the release date.

Contact Person

Company Name

Best Phone Number

Email Address

Website Address

Headline

The headline is one of the most critical components of a press release. It must be written in a creative and captivating way to capture the attention of the reader and entice her to read the remainder of the release. Ask yourself, "Why should anyone care?" and then write your headline to make them care. ***(The headline's only function is to grab the attention of the editor to read on.)*** Put the headline in bold type and a font that is a little larger than the body text. Preferred type fonts are Arial, Times New Roman or Verdana. Keep the headline between 80 and 125 characters. Use Initial Caps, but not ALL CAPS.

First Paragraph

Include city, state and date. The opening sentence contains the most important information; keep it to 25 words or less. Never take for granted that the reader has read your headline. Answer the questions who, what, when, where, why and how. Your text should include pertinent information about your product, service or event. This paragraph should summarize the news release such that if it were the only part seen by a reader, it would tell your entire message. It should include a hook to get your audience interested in reading more.

Subsequent Paragraphs

These paragraphs should contain more detailed information and make up the body of the release. Expand on information provided in your first paragraph, including a quote from someone who is a credible source of information; include that person's title or position and information on any awards they have won, articles they've published or interviews they have given.

Last Paragraph

The last paragraph before the company information should read: For additional information on (put in the subject of this release), contact (name) or visit yourwebsite.com. If you offer a free sample or demo, include that information here as well.

About Your Company

Conclude with a brief paragraph describing your company, products and services along with a short company history.

###

Put these characters, centered, at the very end of the release.

via snail mail, your efforts are likely to be filed it in the circular file. On the other hand, if an editor has room AND you sent the release via email to the right person AND you sent it in the proper time frame (two weeks prior if publicizing an upcoming event) AND it is well written, then you have a good chance of it not only being included in the paper, online media, or on-air announcements, you may very well stimulate an inquiry for an interview or story about your business.

Articles

An alternative to the press release is to write your own article to get some print exposure. The article does not need to be explicitly about your business. Rather, it can address an issue or topic relevant to your target customer, such as choosing a care provider, the importance of advance care planning or the benefits of baby wearing. By offering *content value,* you create interest in your business. If you have a local publication directed at families or the elderly in your community, an informative article about doulas, for example, would make a perfect submission. Authoring an article establishes you as an expert and this is key. Be sure to include your contact information (website and phone number) at the end of the article. This may need to be negotiated up front with the editor. Even if the article is not accepted for publication, your effort is not wasted. You can pass it out to potential clients, include it in your information packets, make it into a blog post and publish it on your website. I proposed a column on the childbearing year for my local food coop's newsletter a number of years ago. This regular series of articles was a great way to establish myself as a local authority in the field of childbirth and get my name out there. As a bonus, I earned a discount on my groceries for my efforts. Perhaps you are not a writer, but one of your clients is? How about asking her (or her partner) to write an article about postpartum doulas and include an interview with you? There is more than one way to beat this bush.

Establish yourself as an expert.

Print Ads

Print advertising is relatively expensive, for the most part. For a few years now, it has become increasingly apparent that print ads are not yielding good results for my business. All customers are surveyed via an evaluation form at the close of each training or class series to learn how they found out about the Center and our programs. The responses confirm that the bulk of my business appears to be evenly split between referrals and internet searches. It is extremely rare that a print ad is mentioned. Accordingly, I have been directing an increasing percentage of resources toward optimizing my online visibility. I'm not saying that all forms of print advertising are worthless, but I do want to encourage business owners to think strategically about their choices, especially when funds are limited.

An important part of the cost-benefit equation for print ads is the frequency of publication. Advertising in daily or weekly publications is likely to be prohibitively expensive for most small business owners. Look at monthly, bimonthly or annual publications—something that stays around for a while, that people are likely to refer back to for calendar listings, for example. Purchase of an annual listing in targeted online directories is a much better use of resources. Do a little research online to see what's available in this regard. If a print ad venue includes an online ad or listing as part of a package, then it may start to pay for itself.

Consistency of presence is also a factor. It does not make sense to purchase an ad as a one-time experiment "to see if it works." Not everyone needs doula services at the moment the ad catches the eye. However, if the potential customer knows that she can reliably find "that doula who advertises in such-and-such magazine," she will seek you there when the time comes. The advertiser needs to make a commitment of at least six months, even a year, to really judge the effectiveness of an advertising venue. If you can't afford to take this risk, then don't.

Depending on the venue, classified ads will be the most affordable, costing anywhere from $.15 to $3 per word. An ad can't say much in ten words and the price may already be up to $30 so "affordable" is definitely in the eye of the beholder. My local food coop, however, charges $.15 per word for advertising in their newsletter, which it publishes quarterly. This is so inexpensive that I have chosen to keep a consistent presence in this publication over the years. I'm also likely to find my target audience here—families who are health conscious and actively seeking out alternatives in the community.

Miscellaneous Stuff

Bumper stickers, magnetic car signs and customized t-shirts with your business name and/or logo are other inexpensive ways to get the word out about your business. Be sure to have business cards with you when you are out and about so that you can maximize the return on this particular form of advertising. My husband ordered a shop coat, with his business name above a front pocket at eye level. He wears it all day as he goes about his business and has had many business owners and fellow shoppers ask for a business card while he is out doing errands or grabbing lunch on the go ("Hey, this guy doesn't look too scary ... maybe he can help me"). Check out CaféPress.com or VistaPrint.com for more ideas and resources. Personally, this is one of my least favorite ways to advertise because I don't really enjoy having random conversations with complete strangers or chatting-it-up with folks. I'd be the last person to wear an "Ask me what an end-of-life doula is" t-shirt, but that's just me.

The Value of Testimonials

Testimonials create social proof and help establish your credibility. They can be written, audio or visual. Every business owner should be using client testimonials in all marketing efforts because what others say about us is ten times more powerful (and believable!) than any claims we make about ourselves. If a client writes you a glowing evaluation or a raving thank-you note after services are completed, ask for permission to use her words as a testimonial on your website and promotional literature. Attach her name and city to the quote to give more credence to it. Publish a photo of the happy family to accompany the words—with their permission, of course. If the client's rave is expressed verbally, ask if she would be willing to put it in writing for you. If she agrees, don't wait for her to remember to do it; capture it in writing yourself and email it to her for approval. With this prompt, you are much more likely to get the testimonial and it is quite likely to be further embellished.

The best time to ask a client for a testimonial is right after the completion of services. Results-based testimonials will be most effective. Here are some sample questions to ask customers for soliciting testimonials regarding the major benefits of your products or services:

- What problem were you facing that I was able to help you with?
- What did you like about the experience of working with me?
- Were you pleasantly surprised by any part of the experience?
- If you were to tell someone about [my business], what would you say?

It is okay to correct spelling or rewrite a testimonial for clarity or to condense the message. However, be careful not to polish it too much. You don't want to make it too slick. Testimonials are conversational, and they will be more authentic in the person's own words even if their grammar isn't perfect. And don't forget to include family members when soliciting testimonials. They are often your biggest fans. You must be willing to become your own best promoter because no one is going to do this for you. You can let others sing your praises for you, but you must provide them with the vehicle to do so (they won't mind). Then display those testimonials—on your website, in your brochures, flyers, annual reports and promotional literature of all kinds. There's a science to marketing and testimonials are a proven strategy.

Online Media

Online media is an essential tool for making your business visible and reaching your target market. An online presence can be established by:

- developing a website, optimized for the search engines
- developing a list of professional contacts and customers that includes, at a minimum, their names and email addresses
- publishing an electronic newsletter, emailed to your subscriber list at regular intervals
- publishing a blog
- engaging in social media

I can sense a few of you beginning to hyperventilate, but keep in mind that there are numerous ways to build an online presence and none of this is accomplished overnight. Take bite-sized pieces, one at a time, and follow the path of least resistance. Certainly not every doula needs to publish an electronic newsletter or start a blog but when you're ready for it, these are powerful tools. An email account *(checked regularly)* and a simple website, however, are mandatory. Keep your radar up for someone who can assist in the development of your site and get you set up. It might be a friend or friend of a friend. Perhaps you can barter for services, or budget to hire a professional.

Website Development

We discussed securing a domain name or URL in Chapter 2. You will also need to secure a hosting service for your website. If you are working with a professional designer, they may have a hosting service that they recommend. Some host services are free but may have built-in limitations, for example, appending their name to your business URL (weebly.YourBusiness.com). Not a good trade off. Others may or may not have storage space for video and PDF uploads. Ultimately, the best option depends on your needs. Personally, I sell access to content on my website in the form of recorded webinars and online classes, so I need the storage space. I've been happy with the customer tech support available at BlueHost.com for the two websites that I maintain through them and pay less than $200 per year to host each site.

Next, you need to choose a "platform" for designing the site. Again, your consultant can help you with this. Most experts recommend WordPress which is user friendly with a short learning curve. I paid a website professional to design my WordPress sites, create the framework, set up a shopping cart (you may not require this) and make it all functional. In addition, early on, I paid her to teach me how to enter content and do updates. Over the years, I have experimented and taught myself quite a bit as well. If you use the internet a little and are familiar with any basic word processing software, then navigating your way around WordPress is an easy transference of skills. WordPress also provides the best and most user-friendly platform for blogging available, so it's helpful to have that capacity too, even if you're not using it at the start. A final point in its favor is that the WordPress platform has unmatched SEO (search engine optimization) potential—not a minor consideration!

An important consideration is that all websites should be mobile friendly. Today, approximately 53 percent of web traffic originates on a mobile device and this percentage is expected to increase. Thus, it is critical that a mobile-friendly template be used for your website design. This technology advance has been a big adjustment for me, as web-based mobile devices were non-existent when my website was first created in 2006. I really like to make everything look pretty. So, when I am sitting at my computer and viewing my website, I have historically thought of creating a page and making it look attractive as a page. If there is a sidebar, for example, I worked with the gestalt view in mind rather than considering that the sidebar might get stacked with the other content on a mobile device. Perhaps it will even show up first (not a good idea as it is SIDEBAR material). I am making the switch to thinking differently about web page design but nevertheless can't help admiring how the page looks on a computer screen. That's okay, provided the most important content is showing up first and is optimized for mobile devices too. Old habits die hard.

A preliminary step to working with a web designer is to clarify your goals for the site. Designers think in terms of a "site map." I have a relatively complex, mature website for my current business at LifespanDoulas.com. There are several categories across the task bar and then each of these has a drop-down menu of further choices. Doulas and other small business owners just starting out, however, may

Website Tips

- Make your contact information (phone and email) and service area easy to find on the homepage.
- Make your contact information (phone and email) and service area easy to find on the homepage. (Did I just say that? It's worth repeating! So many infractions ...)
- Create an "opt-in" for building your email list, connect it to a list service such as MailChimp or Constant Contact and have it visible in the upper right-hand corner of your homepage.

want to keep it simple. As you add services and resources/content, your website can expand to have more layers and depth to accommodate whatever you want. A simple site map for start-up doula businesses might have the following categories across the main navigation bar on your homepage, each consisting of one page: Home / My Services / Benefits of Doulas / Favorite Resources / About Me / Contact.

WordPress has a variety of templates for creating the look of your homepage or a designer can custom design a look for you. It is worth your time to browse other doula websites and make a note of design elements you like and don't like. You can also go to the WordPress.com site and look at the pre-designed templates they have available. Any template can be adapted or customized. Play with color pallets that appeal to you and let your own vision come forth. The more you have an appreciation for all the nitty-gritty details that go into creating a website, the more you will appreciate the process from the designer's perspective. There are lots of small decisions that go into creating a site. Knowing what you like and don't like, and communicating that at the beginning of the process, will save time and money.

Thinking through how you would like the site to function—how the user will navigate your site—is a logical, left-brain process. The look and feel of the site is a more creative, right-brain process. You need both! A visually appealing site, with photos and educational content, will induce visitors to stay on your site longer as well as make return visits. Incorporation of audio and video clips also enhances the attractiveness of your site while encouraging visitors to engage. Content that changes (at least on the homepage) and is dynamic in nature (e.g., a blog, events calendar) also enhances the value and relevancy of your website and provides a reason for people to come back. This will increase your rating with the search engines over time.

While your designer creates the look and framework for the site, you can begin to work on content. This can all be done in a Word file and then simply copy and paste the content to your new web pages. Your designer can show you how to format the content, but it's pretty much the same as a Word menu, so not difficult to learn. Keep creating fresh, high-quality content for the site! It's not a one-off task.

See our "Website Planning Guide Checklist" in *The Doula Business Guide Workbook, 3rd Edition.*

Comments on Hiring a Web Designer

I'm afraid I have fired more designers than seems reasonable. And I've been frustrated a lot, as have many of my colleagues. I have found that many self-employed small business people appear to think that a particular skill or talent is all they need to be in business. In fact, knowledge and skill are only about half of the equation. Whether you are a contractor doing odd jobs in people's homes, a web designer, a hair stylist or a doula, it is not enough to just know your trade. You have to be able to communicate with folks about their needs, assess whether or not you are a good match for their needs, manage your time effectively so as to serve more than one client at a time, meet deadlines and be accountable for delivering on what you say you will do. Oh yes, and you also need to have a Work Ethic. Many, if not most people do not seem to be able to put the whole package together. Red flags will really start waving when they don't deliver the product or service on time and refuse to be held accountable, neglecting to even return a phone call or answer an email. This can be absolutely maddening. If they don't respond to an initial inquiry by phone or email in a timely manner, is it reasonable to think that once you have engaged their services they will suddenly become more responsive?

Time and work flow management are often at the root of the problem. I'm learning to communicate my needs more effectively with prospective independent contractors. I now think in terms of "what is the deliverable?" What, precisely, do I want done and by when? If a job has discreet tasks associated with it, then it may be best to take it one task at a time and see how they do. If the first task is done to your satisfaction and the quality/cost ratio is in balance, then you can move on to your next priority task. Don't muddy the picture talking about potential future

Questions to Ask a Prospective Web Designer

- What hosting services have you used? Do you have a preference?
- Have you built websites using WordPress?
- Do you incorporate any strategies to enhance SEO when building the site? If so, which ones?
- Can you install Google Analytics code on every page of my website?
- Can you put a shopping cart on my site? Is there one that you recommend?
- Do you charge by the job or by the hour? If by the job, how do you handle changes/feedback in the design process?
- Do I pay you when the job is done or do you require a deposit up front?
- Can you meet a deadline?
- What do you need from me and when?

needs. The contractor needs to earn your business by doing their job, doing it well and completing it on time.

Keep in mind, you get what you pay for. A true professional will charge more for their time because they're worth it. $25 per hour for website design may sound like a great deal on the face of it, but what can that person accomplish in an hour? And how much time will be wasted by mistakes that a more seasoned professional would steer well clear of? In the end, the person charging $80 per hour might be a better deal on all fronts, including cost. It's like buying a used car—it's inherently risky and unknown. Hindsight will absolutely tell the story but the right choice in the moment is unclear.

Driving Traffic to Your Website (a.k.a. Search Engine Optimization or SEO)

Once you build it, they will come. Well, no, not really. You must actively employ strategies to get noticed online by the search engines. Keep in mind that the more people who visit a site, the higher the ranking in the search engines. Your goal is to show up on the first page of organic search results and, if not the top ranking, then as close to the top as possible. Most people do not look past the first page of results after performing a Google search. Non-organic results are paid ads, notated as such, and accordingly not as valuable from the consumer's perspective, despite

> **SEO keywords** are the key words and phrases in your web content that make it possible for people to find your site via the search engines. Every online search is an expression of people's needs, wants, interests and desires. Keywords are the words they use to start the search.

appearing at the top. There are many SEO tricks, so optimization is an activity that can take a fair amount of time and expertise (read money). That said, here are a few strategies:

- Include the business name or primary key words in the website's domain name, if possible.
- The business name should also be mentioned on the site's homepage (and not just in a logo jpg file), as well as in the title tag and meta description. (For the uninitiated, these terms refer to the back end of your website where you are creating and posting content. Your designer/consultant can show you or do it for you.)
- Think in terms of "keywords." Start by brainstorming a list of possible words or phrases that folks might use when searching for your services. *Keyword Tool* is a free online research instrument that identifies what your potential customers or readers are searching for on Google.
- The keywords then need to be strategically integrated on your website. In particular, make the keywords prominent on your homepage, in your page headers (especially level-one headings) and in the permalinks for each page or post.
- Ensure that each page of your site has clean, user-friendly URLs (aka "permalinks"); remove extensions and query strings to make them more SEO friendly.
- Each page should have a unique descriptive title (between 10 and 70 characters).
- When it comes to formatting, use html headings <h1> <h2> rather than mere boldfacing to highlight content and use only one <h1> heading per page. This practice helps the search engines know what is on the page and which content is most important.
- Enter meta descriptions to highlight content on each web page. Meta descriptions should be between 70 and 160 characters. This influcnces how your web page is displayed in search results. Google will pull a meta description for you and display it with search results, but by doing it yourself,

you can be more strategic and increase your click through rates, turning it into an organic ad that contains your most important keywords.

- Pictures and media are great additions to your site. People like them and so do the search engines. Be sure and identify the content by using the keywords in the "alt tags."
- List your services in online provider directories and take advantage of the free Google, Yahoo and Bing listings (there are others, but these are the top three). The Google Pages and Google Plus local listings for the business should be found and updated to match the business website. There are other local directories too such as Yellow Pages, Super Pages and more. Max out what these listings offer; for example, if "up to five keywords" are allowed in your description, use five keywords; if ten photos are allowed, then upload ten photos.
- Exchange links with others. Back links to your site are especially desirable and they need not be from folks offering related services. Exchange links with local businesses and your vendors. More links = more page rank. Incoming links are especially valuable, but outgoing links are good too and certainly will not hurt you.
- Google ranks each page on a site for its importance. You can raise the importance of a page by linking to it, either internally on the site itself, via an electronic newsletter or blog, or via back links from other sites.
- Use your best keywords for "anchor text." For example, when linking, do not hotlink the words "click here" for more information on end-of-life doulas. Rather, hotlink it this way: "for more information on end-of-life doulas."
- A "sitemap" plugin, such as Google's XML, should be included on the website to allow search engines to pick up every page.
- Have your designer install Google Analytics code on every page of your website. The code provides valuable information about the popularity and functionality of your site. If you decide to do pay-per-click advertising (see below), you will need this code to learn what is working and what is not in your ad campaigns.

WordPress has a free plug-in known as **Yoast SEO.** This tool is an extremely helpful and user-friendly way to optimize your pages for search engine visibility. I give it 10 thumbs up! Here's how it works. First I create a page, highlighting the most important information first and laying it all out in a way that makes sense to me. And, of course, making it look pretty (because I just can't help myself). Then

I use the Yoast SEO tool which conveniently displays right under the new page on the back end of the site. After identifying the unique keywords that I want the page to rank for, Yoast gives me a score—red light (stop and fix this; lots of ways to make it more SEO friendly), orange light (pretty good; fix a few things) or green light (great job; good to go). Then there follows a bulleted list of specific fixes or ways that the page could be better optimized. As you fix these, the score improves. Keep going till you get to green.

I must confess that I call this part of web page creation "dumbing it down for the search engines." I don't necessarily want to communicate via repetitive keywords, though repeating the keywords that you want the page to rank for in the page title, major headings and subheadings, in the text itself, and in the alt tags for any photos will undoubtedly result in better search engine results. So, it's a bit of a balancing act between getting the page to rank and making it enjoyable to read. On occasion, I refuse the tyranny of the plug-in because I just don't want to do what they are suggesting.

📖 See "Understanding Keywords" in *The Doula Business Guide Workbook: Tools to Create a Thriving Practice, 3rd Edition.*

Pay-Per-Click (PPC) Advertising

Another idea, not so simple, is to create an Adwords campaign with Google. Adwords is pay-per-click online advertising. You (or your Adwords campaign manager) create ads that pop up when folks are doing online searches tied to your keywords. If the searcher clicks on your ad and goes to your website, you pay Google. A budget is set for the month as the maximum amount you are willing to spend. Google will assign a dollar value to different keywords. Working with an Adwords consultant, I have learned that identifying the correct keywords and building the ad campaigns is a fairly complex process. Perhaps it's not beyond my capacity, but I just don't want to invest time in becoming fabulously knowledgeable about Adwords (call me crazy). So, I am taking some of the money I formerly invested in print advertising and paying a consultant to help me with this. As part of the service, she monitors the campaigns monthly and tweaks them based on the results. I have learned that if you're not monitoring your campaigns—determining which keywords are converting to clicks—then you don't really know what you are doing with Adwords and are probably wasting your money. Facebook is also now providing PPC advertising as well. Targeted keywords are matched to keywords present in individual profiles. Overall, PPC is sophisticated, highly targeted advertising—so definitely something to keep in mind though it might understandably get put on the back burner for start-up businesses.

Your All-Important "List"

Targeted email addresses are an asset. An excellent way to stay in touch with past customers is to collect and store their contact information, especially emails, for your all-important "list." Think about ways to maintain a connection with anyone who has established that they like you and are willing to do business with you. Once you have generated an interested prospect or made contact, it behooves you to find a way to stay in touch with these folks. You can send them coupons, helpful and timely information, sales promotions, invitations to customer appreciation events and so on. At the beginning, don't worry over the details of how you will use your list (we'll get to that), but do not fail to develop one. Every single person who expresses interest in your services, even other providers, should be captured for your list. Start today!

Who is the easiest person to sell to?

#1 Someone who has bought from you in the past

#2 Someone who has been referred to you

#3 Someone who is actively searching for what you have to offer (think search engine)

Who is the hardest person to sell to?

#1 Anyone who is not actively searching for what you have to offer (think "cold call")

A technique for capturing the email addresses of people who visit your website is to have what's known as an "opt-in" on your homepage. For the best response, the opt-in should be placed in the upper right-hand corner. It typically appears in the form of a box where the visitor enters her/his email address, often in exchange for a benefit (e.g., free newsletter, free report, coupons, etc.). The email address of an individual who has already found their way to your website is a valuable commodity. Your web designer can set it up so that all email addresses entered will feed directly into the list management system of your choice (see more on this under Electronic Newsletters below).

In addition to the opt-in, I'm always building my list by capturing every single email address of someone who contacts me regarding my business and adding them to the subscription list. With this method, it has been extremely rare (three in about 10,000 over a ten-year period) to have someone designate my e-newsletter as spam, though approximately 30 or so people unsubscribe each month when the

Email Etiquette Hint

If you are emailing a membership group, protect the identity of members by placing their addresses in the blind copy box (Bcc:). Or you can create a "list serve" or segmented list with your email program. This will prevent others from importing whole lists into their own lists, which is basically a spamming technique.

newsletter goes out. Do not capture and add to your list the email address lists of entire groups of people with whom you have no personal connection. This will definitely get you into trouble with the spam detectors.

Electronic Newsletters

Electronic newsletters are an inexpensive way to keep in touch with your list. The first order of business is to choose a service provider. What will a service do for you?

- Safeguard your list as you build it
- Protect promotional emails from being identified as spam
- Allow customers to unsubscribe, ensuring you don't make a pest of yourself with folks who don't want to hear from you
- Allow you to sort your list into segments for more sophisticated, targeted marketing
- Allow you to monitor your results (e.g., open rates, click-through rates and more)
- Enable you to have regular contact with your customers
- Allow you to create a customized template for emails that duplicates the look of your website and works with different browsers and smart phones

Your web designer may be able to help you with weighing the pros and cons of various providers. Ask your colleagues what service they use and if they are happy with it and why. You will need to do some exploring here. I have switched from Campaign Monitor to Constant Contact to MailChimp and found some fairly significant differences between these services. Pricing was my main motivator in choosing MailChimp because it allows me to send as many emails per month as I want for one monthly fee and I like how they allow me to segment my list. Campaign Monitor served me well previously because they only charge when you actually send an email. A service might not be necessary if you are just starting out, your list is small and your needs straightforward. If you are not sending out monthly emails at the very least, then why would you want to pay a monthly fee? I'm not sure at what point the spam detectors go off, but your email service provider might start balking if you are attempting to cut and paste a hundred or more email addresses into an outgoing email.

Frequency. People are bombarded by spam. If you are constantly in their face, trying to sell them something or begging for money, they will tag you for the trash bin. Decide on a reasonable frequency for your newsletter, perhaps monthly. If you don't think you want to put yourself on a schedule to create fresh content so regularly, then perhaps a quarterly newsletter makes more sense.

Timing. Marketing research reveals that the best days to send out an email campaign are Tuesday, Wednesday and Thursday, in that order. Why? Because on Mondays, people are too busy getting up to speed after the weekend and are more likely to delete e-newsletters that compete for their time. By Friday, they are thinking about the weekend. So, our best opportunity is to reach folks mid-week. Following similar reasoning for each day's work flow, the best times to send out an e-newsletter are 10:30 am and 1:30 pm, or mid-morning and right after the lunch hour.

Opt-out capability. The service you choose to manage your subscriber list should offer folks the option of unsubscribing from your list. Every newsletter that goes out will include a link to unsubscribe from the list easily and quickly. Once someone has unsubscribed, the system will not allow the list owner to re-subscribe that person accidentally, so you can be ensured that you won't make a pest of yourself.

Content. Your content should be 80 percent informational/entertaining and 20 percent promotion. Or, another way of saying this is 80 percent should be about your readers and 20 percent about you and what you are doing.

Use links. Think strategically about the purpose of your newsletter. Each entry/item should be a Call to Action. What do you want the reader to do? The purpose of the newsletter is to keep you front of mind and to drive traffic to your website where, hopefully, potential customers will learn more about you and eventually buy something (products, services, classes, etc.). Use a hotlink to take them to the appropriate page on your website. Occasionally I link to another website, such as a conference registration page or a blog that I like. By doing so, I am establishing the newsletter as an object of interest, something that provides valuable, up-to-date information and resources for my readers. They will open it again next time because it contained information that was useful. And, who knows, perhaps they will click on a link next time that takes them to my site. Linking to other sites also

More E-Newsletter Tips

- Whether people open an email or not: 60 percent determined by who it's from and 30 percent by subject line
- Keep the subject line of your newsletter pithy, less than 50 characters.
- Subject line should incorporate a specific benefit.
- Aria, Verdana and Tahoma fonts are better for conversion rates in headlines.
- Deep red headline = better open rates
- Make headlines relevant to search terms on Google.
- Use action verbs.
- Benefit stacking increases value.
- Multiple choices, options, sales, premiums will outsell one offer.
- Images and headers may show as empty boxes, unless folks specifically choose to enable the images to be displayed. Add text for each image to avoid displaying the empty box.
- Limit the header in your newsletter design template to a maximum of 150–175 pixels.
- Change links to blue so they are easily recognized as links by the reader.

establishes a willingness to help others and recognize their good work. What goes around, comes around.

Keep it brief. An e-newsletter is just a tool; it is not an end in itself. Folks are not likely to want to spend more than three minutes reading your newsletter. If it's too beefy and content-heavy, then you are in danger of putting folks on information overload. Go for variety and interest. If they want more information, take them to your online home and voila! I might have six to eight entries in my monthly e-newsletter in any given month. Each entry is one to three sentences long and absolutely every entry has at least one link.

Design considerations. For the initial set up, I paid my web designer to create "the look" of the newsletter so that it was consistent with my website. Different browsers used by your customers can skew "the look" of your newsletter, which can be frustrating. In other words, how the newsletter looks on your screen is no guarantee that all your recipients will receive an identical version. You want your

Five Essential Elements of a Good Marketing Piece

- Make an **Irresistible Offer** (usually something of value is given away at no cost).
- Provide a **Guarantee** thereby removing the risk for the customer; make it specific, succinct and meaningful.
- A **Deadline** or **Call to Action** conveys a sense of urgency by stating a deadline in the near future rather than an open-ended offer; you are enticing people to act now.
- Publish **Testimonials** to overcome objections (see page 120 for more on testimonials).
- Include a **Response Mechanism.** What precisely do you want the person to do in response? Go to your website? Use an order form? Cash in a gift certificate or coupon? Don't make them guess what the next step is.

newsletter to be readable on a smart phone too. A service that takes this fact into consideration, in an effort to standardize the end product generated by all the email service providers, is important, though by no means infallible.

Monitor your results. Email list services have some fascinating features that I have used extensively, at the same time becoming acutely aware of one's absolute lack of privacy on the web. After sending out a campaign, I am able to monitor at a glance: what percentage of people opened the newsletter (who did and who did not); whether or not they clicked on a link and, if so, what links and how many times; how many people unsubscribed, who they are and why they unsubscribed; which email addresses bounced; and more. In evaluating my results, I have been able to increase my open and click rates over time, thereby accomplishing the goal of driving traffic to my website.

Send it out twice. I am super regular with my monthly e-newsletter, typically sending it out at the beginning of each month. To increase my open and click-through rates, I resend the newsletter to anyone who didn't open it the first time about five days later. I typically get another 10 percent to open on the second mailing.

Social Media Platforms

There are many social networking sites and more emerging periodically. Facebook, Instagram, Twitter, Linked-In and Pinterest might all be useful. Social media allows us to do viral marketing, meaning that the marketer crafts a message that is shareable—one that people are likely to forward or pass on to others. We discussed earlier the importance of testimonials. Marketing experts have found that up to 78 percent of people take a third-party referral seriously, while 14 percent think ads are a lie. Social media allows you to concentrate marketing efforts on people who are already your advocates and lets them help you get your message out. Social media is not a place to sell directly and your message should not be "come buy my stuff." Rather, interaction is the goal. Via social media, the business promoter engages in a two-way conversation with existing and potential customers. It is a place to inform and create awareness about you and what you do. Overall, your strategy online is to develop relationships and get people to visit your website. Remember the upside-down triangle at the beginning of this chapter? Well, your sphere of influence online is another whole realm of possible contacts and sources of referrals for your business and it works the same way. It's simply word of mouth but it's happening virtually on the internet. The best part about it is that it's free. It's also extremely targeted marketing. How cool is that? The down side is that it can be a time suck like no other.

Facebook

As of this writing, there are over 1.47 billion daily active users on Facebook. You start by creating a personal profile and timeline. Next, you can create business pages and groups. Facebook keeps changing where things show up and how the site functions, adding new features and changing ones with which you may have been comfortable. Personally, I do not find it to be an especially intuitive or user-friendly website. If you need help, sit down with a friend who can show you around a bit. Here's how to get started:

1. Go ahead and set up your account and create your personal timeline. Be sure to use the box under your profile picture to highlight the most important information (think keywords) you want to be known for. Make it interesting and engaging.
2. Grab your Facebook business page name right away. You don't have to create the page if you're not ready, but you do want to reserve the name. Most likely this will be your business name.
3. Start to build your "friends" network. Facebook will give you options and prompts for doing this. Ideally, you want to "friend" folks who are in sympathy with what you are all about.

4. Just take a playful approach but you might want to set a limit on how much time you invest there for business purposes (setting a timer works). You can visit (and Like) other related business pages, post something on your wall or on a friend's wall, join groups and make connections. Find a way to be helpful rather than engaging in straight-up promotion (though a little bit of this is okay).
5. When you are ready, go ahead and create your own business page and make it positive, compelling and interesting. Then you can invite your supporters to "like" your page.

Here are some suggestions for encouraging interaction on your business page:

- Don't just make statements and announcements; ask questions.
- Link to YouTube videos with a question.
- Link to others' blogs with a question.
- Post a quote or statement and ask followers if they agree or disagree.
- Post questions on topics your followers care about.
- Initially, refrain from engaging in overt promotion.

As with all forms of electronic communication, remember that, literally, the whole world can see what you post and it never goes away. Be careful! Respect your clients' privacy. Only upload photos with permission. Keep it positive, never vitriolic. If you need to vent, social media is *not* the place to do it. The owner of the business page or moderator of a group retains the right and ability to remove any posts or comments that she/he doesn't want on the page. If someone is behaving inappropriately you can delete and/or block their posts. Finally, if you are using Facebook for business purposes, then stay away from politics. You're pretty much guaranteed to offend the approximate 50 percent of folks who see things from a very different perspective. Some of these folks will respond in kind and attack. Now you are in the position of defending your position or they get the last word (and some will keep it going because they have a pathological need to have the last word). At the end of the day, you have gained new enemies to say bad things about you publicly. Obviously a counter-productive way to proceed, right?

Twitter

Twitter is a micro blog, limited to 280 characters or approximately 3 sentences. "Tweets" (messages sent out on Twitter) are outgoing messages and may contain a quick link back to your website. On Twitter, the user has followers rather than friends. You can also find people whom you find interesting and follow them. This is the best way to get a sense of how it all works. Initially, your interaction on Twitter should be a two-way street. Once you reach a thousand followers, however, it is not so much about building relationships as it is simply getting your message out. As in all of social media marketing, your ultimate aim is to get them to go to your website for more.

A business can grow by retweeting content on Twitter and thereby increasing awareness of your brand. Instead of simply retweeting, the original tweet should be edited or quoted in a way that reflects your mission and adds something unique. Before beginning, determine how many tweets will be about business and how many will be items of interest which may draw a reaction. While some Twitter experts suggest only 20 percent of retweets should be about business, others suggest a 50/50 split. Leaders in any field are significant sources of retweetable material. Industry trade magazines, blogs and newsletters can also be great sources for knowing what is trending and drawing interest.

Linked-In

This is the most professional of the social networking sites. The biggest benefit of this site is the recommendations section. Solicit recommendations and recommend others. This is the same thing as testimonials.

Instagram

This photo and video-sharing social networking service is owned by Facebook and is accessed via a phone app. The app allows users to upload photos and videos to the service that can be edited with various filters and organized with tags and location information. Users can browse other users' content and view trending content. The bulk of users on Instagram are between the ages of 18 and 35, with 77 percent being women. If this is your demographic, then this is a place to be.

Pinterest

Pinterest is an online pinboard for collecting visual pieces of multimedia (mostly images). You can create as many boards for your pins as you want, which is great for organization. For example, an end-of-life doula could create one board labeled "Home Funeral" and another one labeled "Green Burial" and so on. Pinterest users interact with each other through liking, commenting and repinning each other's stuff.

Blogs

Blogging is the foundation of a social media strategy. A blog (a contraction of the term "web log") is a type of website containing regular entries of commentary, descriptions of events, or other material such as graphics, sound or video. Many blogs are thematic, sticking to a particular subject area while others function as more personal online diaries. Entries are displayed in reverse-chronological order, so the latest entry displays first. "Blog" can also be used as a verb, meaning to maintain or add content to a blog. Your blog should not overtly sell anything. If you are always selling, people will turn you off quickly. People read blogs to be informed, entertained, motivated and inspired. The bottom line is, all roads lead back to your website. Your website/blog is the hub of the wheel and all your social media and internet marketing efforts are the spokes of the wheel.

Frequency. When launching a blog, you are making a commitment to blog on a regular basis. It will take a while to build a following for your blog, so consistency is the key. Google loves fresh content so if you want to get indexed on the first page of results, consider blogging regularly, perhaps weekly. WordPress allows the blogger to set the exact time and date when a blog post will be published so you can work on your blog anytime you want and then just schedule the publication dates to roll forward. This means you can plan out a month's worth of blog posts at one sitting if it's easier for you to do it that way.

Length. Blog posts tend to be anywhere from 100–400 words in length.

Use Keywords. Use the major keywords in your title and at least twice within the text. If you have a subheading, use keywords there as well. If a photo is included, insert the keywords in the ALT tag.

Encourage interaction. The ability of readers to leave comments in an interactive format is an integral part of a blog. The most important parts of a blog post are the headline and the first and last sentences. To encourage interaction, you can start and end your blog posts with a question. In the comments section of a blog, the blogger maintains control over what gets posted or not. Any content that you don't want on your site, you can remove.

RSS Feed. RSS stands for Really Simple Syndication and it is just that—a method for automating a blog to feed out to social networking sites and notify followers that the blog has been updated. Do it! The RSS feed also allows followers to subscribe to the blog feed if they choose.

Radio and Television

I will admit to feeling a bit intimidated at the thought of the camera, but the voice in my head clearly says, "Get over it!" A radio or TV interview can reach a huge audience and build tremendous interest in your work, whether you are just trying to get the word out about doulas or fundraising for a charitable doula program. In order to be successful in this media, you will need to be very comfortable and confident in your subject matter. You want to be sure that you are a good speaker, that the word "um" is not in your vocabulary and that you do not waste words with phrases like "you know," "if you will" or similar meaningless or pretentious violations.

You will need to identify your local media contacts and note which programs and hosts would be a good match for a story on your business. Search online for Fox, ABC, NBC and CBS affiliate stations in the closest major city. Contact an assignments editor, health reporter and/or morning producer. It's okay to send to more than one person at the same outlet—you might just happen to hit on someone who used a doula. Send them a press release, via email (not as an attachment), with your pitch for a story. The more time sensitive it is, the more likely it is to be covered, so tying it in with an event or responding to a national headline are good ideas. If you don't hear back right away, follow up with a call to see if they received your press release and whether there is any interest.

Prior to an interview, prepare the key points you feel are essential to convey. Write them down and look for opportunities to get your points across. The interviewer, after all, is not an expert in your field. He/she will not necessarily know the right questions to ask or may ask downright stupid questions. In these situations, the interviewee must take charge of the interview and redirect, or otherwise risk wasting time talking about irrelevant subjects. This may be one reason why so many politicians refuse to answer direct questions. They go into an interview with a message they are determined to convey and use the available (limited) air time to accomplish their purpose. Take a similarly proactive approach. Don't script your responses; just sketch out your main points. You will be ahead of the game if you think, "this interview will be a success IF . . ." Then you are seizing power, rather than allowing yourself to be merely responsive.

Becoming a spokesperson and looking good on camera are skills for which training is helpful. Talk to an expert. Check what's available regarding training at your local public TV station. There are all kinds of tricks, including choice of clothing, colors, eye contact, hand gestures and so on. We all have little unconscious, nervous habits that may be very distracting on camera. The good news is that training can help us overcome these. There may even be an opportunity for you to use public access to host your own series of presentations on childbirth or end-of-life topics.

Establishing a Community Presence

Become an Exhibitor

There are numerous events at which doulas or doula programs may want to have a presence. Typically, the price of an exhibitor's table for most community-based events is $100 or less and, in some cases, it will be free. For larger conferences, or groups that are nationally based, the price will be higher, perhaps hundreds of dollars. Nonprofits can often get tables at a substantially reduced price.

Set up a visually appealing display. Ask whether or not the sponsoring group provides the table, chair(s) and a tablecloth (some do and some don't). Even if they do provide a table covering, you might want to bring your own cloth, for visual appeal. I designed a sign for my business at the local Kinko's store. For less than $200, they created a full-color banner—approximately 5' x 3'— that comes with an adjustable, collapsible stand. It's a great solution because of its easy portability (the banner rolls up and fits in a tube), as well as the fact that it can be set up behind my table rather than on the table. For years I struggled with an accordion-fold display board, a commonly used tool. They're expensive ($300 or more), awkward for transport, nondurable, and take up most of the available display space. The person attending the table is forced to sit to the side of the table (if there is room) or stand in front of it. The standing sign is a great solution and allows for the greatest flexibility in any venue, including out of doors. Don't assume there will be a wall available behind your table that you can hang a banner on; you'll have to ask.

Mixed media can be a draw, as well as giveaways (anything from candy to a raffle ticket for a free gift at the end of the day). Other strategies include doing something interactive at your booth such as demonstrating the use of a birth ball, belly mapping, henna tattoos, inviting visitors to make their own lavender rice sock, providing short neck and shoulder massages or whatever else you can think of.

Make sure to have plenty of literature on hand as well, including complimentary educational handouts. Check out the other vendors at these events and critically assess their displays, noting what works and what doesn't work. Whose table is drawing the most attention? This principle—noticing the marketing techniques that work on you and others—pretty much applies across the board. If the technique induces you to stop at someone else's table or buy their product, then it's a technique worth replicating. Finally, the other vendors at an event are also part of your network. Make it a priority to get around, meet people and make some new connections.

See our "Outreach Events/Venues Worksheet" and "Event Planning Guide" in *The Doula Business Guide Workbook, 3rd Edition.*

Volunteer Work

Community volunteer work is another great way to make connections and expand your field of contacts. You can become a member of a group or even serve on the board of directors for a local nonprofit or doula organization (see Chapter 4, "Questions to Ask Before Agreeing to Serve on a Nonprofit Board of Directors"). Try to have a targeted and focused idea of what you can do for/with any given group or you can be sucked into a black hole of need that leaves little time for you to focus on your business. Think, "How will the group be different due to my contribution?" Answering this question will bring focus to your involvement, while follow-through will establish your reputation as a competent "do-er." Since the need for good volunteers is unlimited, it will be easy to be induced into overcommitting—hence the admonition for placing limits on what you can and cannot do.

Community Appearances

Teaching/public speaking are excellent ways to be out in the community, putting your best professional foot forward. I have done gigs at my local library's Lunch & Learn program, the local Whole Foods store, food coop and bookstores. I have been a guest speaker at the local high school, community college and university classrooms, presenting on doulas in women's studies classes, nursing courses, child development classes and even a club of medical students. Any venue that sponsors educational events or a series of talks is a candidate for doula participation. Even if only a handful of people show up for the actual event (and in some cases I have done much better than that), it is worth the time and effort because the sponsor will do the promotion for you, thereby helping to establish your status as an expert in the field. This all amounts to free publicity for a small investment of time on your part.

Evaluation of Marketing Efforts

How do you know what's working and what's not working? Which efforts are worth pursuing and which are not? This is really important because it speaks to how you need to think about your advertising and marketing dollars. Here's the key question: What is a customer worth to you? Next: How much are you willing to pay to secure that customer? Or, another way to say this is: What is the return on your investment (ROI)? Now, if you pay $50 annually to be listed in my online directory of professionals and this listing generates 10 inquiries per year regarding your services, is that worth it? Let's say out of the 10 inquiries, two families hire you. Is that still worth it? (Absolutely!) The ROI is the real deal. No specific ad purchased is "too much" if it more than pays for itself (despite the initial pain of parting with the money). So, be sure and ask each and every client how he or she heard about you. And, as discussed earlier, enable Google Analytics on your website so you can track results of your online marketing efforts. ◆

> **P. T. Barnum once lamented,** "Half of my marketing is paying off; if only I knew which half!" Can you afford to waste time and money? Track your responses to eliminate waste and take the guesswork out of marketing.

CHAPTER 4

Nonprofit Primer—To Be or Not to Be?

Had I known then what I know now . . .

ON THE FACE OF IT, STARTING UP YOUR OWN NONPROFIT BUSINESS that helps vulnerable families through critical life transitions appears to be a noble undertaking indeed. But is the formation of a nonprofit the best vehicle for realization of your goals? The purpose of this chapter is to help the uninitiated understand the full scope of such a task, from dream to reality. Consider the following questions:

- What problem are you intending to solve?
- Who will benefit from your efforts?
- Who are your collaborators?
- What are your strengths and skills?
- What skills will be required for success?
- Why are you the right person for the job?
- Where will the money come from?
- What is your plan for sustainability?

It is okay if you don't have all the answers right now, but these ARE the questions.

What Is a Nonprofit Corporation?

To qualify as a 501c3 nonprofit corporation in the U.S., the following five criteria must be met:

1. It has a public service mission.
2. It is organized as a not-for-profit or charitable corporation.

3. Its governance structures preclude self-interest and private financial gain.
4. It is exempt from paying federal tax.
5. It possesses the special legal status that stipulates gifts made to it are tax deductible.

A 501c3 entity must be organized for religious, charitable, educational, scientific or literary purposes and is prohibited from engaging in political lobbying.

The term "nonprofit" is a bit of a misnomer since technically any business must make a profit in order to be viable. Whereas the ultimate mission of the profit-making enterprise is to make money for its owners, the concept of ownership is completely absent from a nonprofit. The public service mission of the nonprofit organization is articulated in its *mission statement.* All programs and services offered are designed to serve the mission. Thus, the mission statement provides identity, limitations and focus for future growth of the organization.

The organizational structure of a nonprofit involves a volunteer board of directors (trustees), who hold legal and fiduciary responsibility for the organization. What does this mean? Given the substantial tax benefits bestowed on nonprofits, the government has a duty to ensure that the nonprofit is, indeed, serving the public interest. The trustees, therefore, serve as guardians of the public trust. As such, no member of the board of directors can derive financial benefit from his/her board service. Trustees are expected to serve without compensation, except for reimbursement for reasonable out-of-pocket expenses made on behalf of the organization. According to nonprofit expert Thomas Wolf (see Resources), their job is to:

> **Fiduciary** = a person to whom property or power is entrusted for the benefit of another

> *Make sure the organizations they are serving are carrying out their missions as articulated in the articles of incorporation and that their financial activities are both legal and proper, given federal and state requirements.*

Beyond basic oversight, the board is responsible for ensuring that the organization has the capacity (e.g., finances, staff, space) to complete its mission and provides direction and support, leveraging personal connections in the community toward that end. The board is concerned with the big picture and does not involve itself in programmatic details or day-to-day decision making. Such micro-management by the board is anathema among the nonprofit community.

The executive director (ED), on the other hand, is responsible for the day-to-day management of the nonprofit. She hires necessary staff, oversees the development and delivery of programs, provides leadership for fundraising, administers the budget and typically wears a number of hats (too many!), especially in small startup organizations. While there is a great deal of autonomy in her decision-making capacity, the ED is nevertheless accountable to the board. Ideally, the relationship between the ED and the board of directors is one of dynamic and productive partnership—easier said than done.

When the ED is also the founder of the organization, a unique set of challenges emerges, often emanating from the simple fact that the founder ED retains a sense of ownership over the organization. Nevermind that technically there can be no owners in a nonprofit. The person whose vision, passion, energy and hard work brought about the very existence of the organization, and whose ongoing daily commitment sustains it, cannot help but feel entitled to a special claim. And yet, legally, this person can be fired by the board. Therein lays the inherent tension in the relationship between founder EDs and their boards. The ED is the only staff member that the board has the power to hire and fire.

Tip for the Founder ED

Have your board set a salary level for you and note it in the minutes of the meeting of the board of directors. (These are required legal records for the nonprofit and will substantiate any claims you might make in the future.) If it takes a few years to get sufficient revenue rolling in to pay you the promised salary, then you have a legal basis for being awarded assets of the organization (in lieu of unpaid salary owed) should the organization fold.

While the nonprofit ED cannot claim ownership of profits or property generated by or belonging to the organization, she can be paid a competitive salary for her work and the board of directors can award her raises and bonuses for work well done *if funds are available to do so.* Federal law states that if a nonprofit organization goes out of business, all funds remaining after creditors are paid must be passed on to another nonprofit organization or government body. Keep in mind that it may take two to three years for any new business venture to become profitable. In the beginning stages, it is not uncommon for a founder ED to be working for minimal compensation.

Pros and Cons of Nonprofits

The benefits of organizing your business as a nonprofit are primarily the following:

- Enables the social entrepreneur to become part of the solution through charitable work
- Qualifies the organization to receive grants from government bodies, foundations and individuals
- Allows individuals to support the mission through tax-deductible donations
- Frees the organization from paying state sales taxes and local property taxes
- Provides satisfaction derived from public service

On the "con" side of the decision, the founder faces a rather daunting task. It is important to understand that there is nothing miraculous about gaining the 501c3 designation. Money does not necessarily start flowing in the door via magical thinking. By successfully completing the application and approval process, you have now earned the right to fundraise and apply for grants. That's it. Without part two of the equation (fundraising and grant writing), part one is a waste of time, energy and money (it costs $400–750 to file your nonprofit application with the IRS, with no guarantee of approval). The drawbacks include the following:

- The nonprofit business model is decidedly more complex than the sole proprietorship or LLC for-profit models. For example, this model introduces multiple layers of partnership/accountability with the board of directors, community collaborators, funders, constituents, volunteers, interns, staff, etc.
- Increased federal and state reporting and licensing requirements
- Increased number of people involved in decision making; the more people, the *slower* the process, which can lead to frustration for folks intent upon achieving goals with a sense of urgency
- Conservative (possibly paralyzing) approach to risk taking
- Ongoing challenge of identifying and recruiting *good* (to be defined below) board members
- Challenge of demanding accountability from volunteers of all types
- Probable need for legal and accounting advice (though it may be possible to find someone who will donate these skills for the cause)

- Challenge of covering indirect program costs (ED salary, rent, operations) as many grant funders prohibit use of funds for these purposes, preferring rather to focus on funding for specific programs or initiatives
- Fundraising never ends
- Endless grant writing; one cycle finishes and another begins
- A wide range of skills are needed
- The founder must be more than a visionary; she must actually be capable of grinding out the details
- High burnout potential for the ED who is involved in direct delivery of programs AND overseeing all other aspects of the organization

In addition, there is the theory that the federally-mandated structure of a nonprofit is an essentially flawed concept. But I get ahead of my story here ... we'll get to that later.

For-profit companies, by comparison, offer the following benefits:

- Independent, quick decision making
- Ability to assume risk without spending excessive energy (time and money) on a "strategic planning process" involving groups of people, consultants, etc.
- Zero energy expended to appease ineffective volunteers
- Simplified business structure; accountability to self, family and constituents only
- Streamlined focus of goals and talents

Step-by-Step Setup

If you are convinced that nonprofit is the way you want to go, I highly recommend the latest edition of the book *How to Form a Nonprofit Corporation* by Anthony Mancuso which contains all forms on CD-ROM or available as a download (see Resources). Apparently, California law is so unique as to merit its own version of this book, *How to Form a Nonprofit Corporation in California*.

Step One. Choose an available business name that meets the requirements of state law. Start with your state's government website (e.g., Kansas.gov) and do a search for requirements and forms for incorporating as a nonprofit. The site should be able to walk you through the steps for choosing and reserving a business name. See our earlier discussion in Chapter 2 on "What's in a Name?" to grasp the multiple layers of consideration regarding naming your business. Some states may require that a corporate designator (e.g., Inc., Ltd.) be part of the name and certain words may be prohibited (e.g., bank, federal, etc.).

Step Two. File the required paperwork, typically referred to as Articles of Incorporation. Your state's corporate division may have a packet of nonprofit materials available. Typically, sample language is given for the Articles of Incorporation, and it is okay to fill in the blanks and accept the default language. Be sure you are using required language for nonprofits in order to ensure you will qualify for tax-exempt status. If you have a lawyer available to advise you, you can consult one before filing, but do not let lack of funds for legal advice be an obstacle here. Articles can be amended later, as needed, and the default language will serve to move you through the process efficiently.

> **TIP:** Read through the IRS tax exemption application *before* filing your Articles of Incorporation. Spending time upfront to become familiar with what it takes to qualify for tax exemption can save wasted effort, time and money.

The state will require a specific number of incorporators in order to file. As founder, you will be one of the incorporators and you will need to choose others to meet minimum requirements. The incorporators do not have to be future board members. In Michigan, when I incorporated, a minimum of three people was required. I chose my husband and a business associate/friend in addition to myself. A filing fee will be required (typically under $100). I recommend that you file electronically which will greatly expedite the process.

The corporate filing office will return a certified copy of the articles to you. This document will become part of the official records of your organization. You will have occasion, time and again (opening a checking account, submitting the IRS application, accepting a grant award, etc.), to produce evidence of incorporation as a nonprofit. Make several copies and keep the original in a safe place.

Step Three. Write a Mission Statement. Your mission statement is a succinct summary of your guiding purpose. It states why you do what you do and inspires others to support you. The mission statement also defines the scope of the nonprofit so that all programs, service and activities undertaken must somehow fulfill and relate back to the organization's stated mission. There are numerous free, online tutorials on how to write a mission statement, with samples of good mission statements provided. Googling "nonprofit mission statements" should yield a wealth of material to study. A good mission statement will serve you well in terms of recruiting board members and donors, so it's worth putting some time into it. After crafting your mission statement, run it by twenty people for feedback. Do others understand your mission as you intend?

See also "Crafting a Mission Statement" in *The Doula Business Guide Workbook, 3rd Edition.*

Step Four. Create corporate bylaws. Bylaws are the rules that govern the internal operations of a corporation. Bylaws articulate procedures for holding meetings, voting on issues, electing directors and officers, amending the bylaws, etc. Sample bylaws are readily available in the Mancuso materials referenced above. Start with the standard template language; read through them carefully and make any desired changes (e.g., frequency of board meetings, number of directors). If you can get an expert to review them, so much the better, but don't sweat this part too much. Formally adopting the organization's bylaws should be on the agenda for the first meeting of the board of directors. Bylaws can be reviewed periodically and amended as the organization evolves, as they should reflect actual organizational policies and practices. Legally, you are supposed to be operating as the bylaws dictate, though the bylaw police are not likely to come knocking on your door.

Step Five. Appoint the initial members of the board of directors. In some states you must choose your initial directors before filing the articles. A minimum number of directors will be required by the state (e.g., Michigan requires three) but you can have more than the minimum. The terms of service for board members and commitment required are determined by the bylaws, so you can define those parameters when you are drafting your bylaws. Initially, most founders put together a willing group of close professional contacts or friends with a view to simply fulfilling mandated requirements. If at all possible, try to recruit people who will be an asset when it comes to fundraising or who bring other skills that you need (see more on this subject below).

Step Six. Draft plans for programs and a budget. The IRS wants to know what you will do and how you plan do it, so the application requires a preliminary three-year budget. Don't get too hung up on this; just take your best, most reasonable guess at income and expenses. To be sustainable, you will need income from revenue-generating programs, grants and donations or fundraising activities.

Sample Three-Year Budget Plan

Submitted with a successful 501c3 nonprofit application for a web-based volunteer doula program

Income	2011	2012	2013
Online doula registry listings	$500	$1,000	$1,500
Sale of online continuing education programs	$500	$1,000	$1,500
Fundraising	$1,000	$2,000	$2,000
Grants	$12,000	$25,000	$25,000
Projected Annual Total	**$14,000**	**$29,000**	**$30,000**
Expenses	**2011**	**2012**	**2013**
Office Supplies, Postage	$1,000	$1,000	$1,000
Website Hosting	$200	$200	$200
Website Development & Tech Support	$8,000	$2,500	$2,500
CEU applications	$300	$300	$300
Doula Training Scholarships	$2,000	$5,000	$5,000
Outreach/Marketing	$2,500	$2,500	$2,500
Payroll		$15,000	$16,000
Occupancy		$2,500	$2,500
Projected Annual Total	**$14,000**	**$29,000**	**$30,000**

Set some organizational goals here. Then try to estimate your operating expenses. Board members may be able to provide feedback and assist in making adjustments on the numbers at the first board meeting.

Step Seven. Hold the first meeting of the board of directors. The first meeting is organizational in nature and is prescribed by state law. The purpose of the first meeting of the board of directors is to conduct the initial business of the corporation and take care of other formalities (see below). State law will prescribe a process for calling the first meeting; for example, in Michigan, any board member may call the first meeting with not less than three days' notice to each director. A majority of directors constitutes a quorum for the first meeting of the board. The notice should include an agenda for the first meeting and a copy of the articles and proposed bylaws. At the beginning of the meeting a recording secretary should be appointed who agrees to be responsible for taking notes and producing minutes of the meeting. The following agenda, at a minimum, defines the actions that should be taken at the meeting:

- Accept the articles of incorporation as filed.
- Adopt the proposed bylaws with any necessary amendments. (After this meeting the organization should operate as prescribed by the bylaws or else amend the bylaws.)
- Elect officers, according to the bylaw. Most states require a president, secretary and treasurer and sometimes a vice president as well. Two or more offices may be held by the same person, if allowed by the bylaws, but an officer cannot execute a legal document (e.g., bank loan) in more than one capacity.
- The directors should authorize the newly elected officers to take actions necessary to start the business of the nonprofit, for example setting up a bank account and making any necessary financial transactions.
- Authorize someone to prepare the IRS Form 1023 to apply for tax exemption, or review and approve a draft already prepared by the founder.

After the meeting is completed, minutes of the meeting should be created, approved by the board and filed in a corporate records book (a simple three-ring binder works). This is required by law.

Step Eight. Apply for federal 501c3 tax-exemption status. The application can be filled out by the founder prior to the first meeting of the board, so the order of these steps is somewhat changeable. You will need the following forms and publications, available online at IRS.gov (don't be daunted; one step at a time!):

1. Form 8718, User Fee for Exempt Organization Determination Letter Request
2. Package 1023, Application for Recognition of Exemption; the IRS has released a new interactive Form 1023 (i1023) which can be used to apply for tax-exempt status under Section 501c3.
3. Publication 557, Tax-Exempt Status for Your Organization (instructions for completion with online help and prompts)

Help may also be available through your state's nonprofit association. Most states have a professional membership association whose purpose is to help nonprofits be successful. They often offer seminars and conferences, newsletters, group discounts on insurance and so on. Do an online search and see what's available. There may even be a group in your community whose mission is to help you get started!

> **Tip:** Find a donor to cover the IRS application fee. If the application is approved, it will be retroactive to the application date and the donation will be tax deductible. Note that this approach involves some risk for the donor.

The fee for submitting the application, with no guarantee of approval, is $400–750. After the IRS reviews your application, it will send you a letter indicating that it has approved your nonprofit status, or it might request more information. The IRS can also deny your application outright. If this happens, see a lawyer who specializes in nonprofits.

Step Nine. Apply for state tax exemptions. This step may not be required as each state is different. Contact your state tax agency to find out what steps you must take to receive the full benefits of federal tax-exempt status in your state.

Step Ten. Obtain any state-mandated licenses and permits. Many businesses are required to obtain state or local licenses and permits before commencing business. Check with your state department of consumer affairs (or similar state licensing agency) for information concerning licensing requirements. A local business license, tax registration certificate, solicitation license (for fundraising) or sales tax permit may be required. Pleading ignorance regarding what is required, by the way, is not an acceptable excuse.

Step Eleven. Apply for property tax exemption. Before securing office space, check with your local tax assessor for exemption from local taxes on property held by the organization and used in its activities. This application should be made before taxes are assessed since obtaining retroactive exemptions may prove difficult.

Step Twelve. Complete mandated employer registration. Once the organization is ready to hire employees, register with the appropriate state and local government agencies for required withholding for income and unemployment taxes (though payments into the unemployment fund may be deferrable until a claim is made). You may also need to purchase worker's compensation insurance. You may want to use an accountant to help you with this piece. Some accountants offer payroll services and take care of all the details and reports for you. In the end, their fees may be well worth the benefit of freeing an overburdened ED from one more set of tasks to focus on leading the organization.

Step Thirteen. Nonprofit bulk-mail rates. As a nonprofit, you will qualify for reduced rates on bulk mail at the post office. An application will need to be submitted to your local postmaster, along with an application fee plus an annual fee paid. As I recall, this totaled about $200. When I first went to set it up, I was taken aback when the postal agent handed me a rather thick manual containing "the policies" related to bulk mailings that I needed to familiarize myself with. (There was an optional day-long class that one could attend in lieu of reading the book!) After going through the process once, which required separating the list by zip codes and complying with mandated bundling requirements, I determined that the hassle and cost factor was something of a wash, especially for our organization doing only one mailing per year. In addition, with bulk mailings, you will not get your returns, so there is no way to update your list with this approach. As each year passes, your list will become more and more out of date but you will have no way of knowing which addresses are still good and which aren't. Furthermore, it can take up to three weeks for your mail to reach its destination as it is a very low priority and, shockingly, some pieces may simply go permanently missing. These days, most nonprofits rely on electronic newsletters to communicate with their base.

About "The Board"

Choosing members for your board of directors is, hands down, the single most important decision you will make as you establish a nonprofit. A common phenomenon, manifesting through the lifecycle of nonprofits, has been noted by experts. Referred to as "stages in board development," a progression from a "founder board" to a "working board" to a "governing board" characterizes the mature and successful nonprofit. You will likely progress through these stages regardless of whether it is a conscious process. Let's take a step back so you can see the big picture.

Founder boards are typically a group of friends and associates recruited by the founder to fulfill state requirements and complete the IRS application process. The founder may promise initial board recruits that "they won't have to do anything" other than attend a meeting or two and lend their name to the required legal forms. Such a board is more like a cheering squad than an actual, functioning board. It will rubber stamp pretty much anything the founder wants to do—such is the nature of the founder board. A working board model is one that many nonprofits function under, with board members undertaking much of the day-to-day work of the organization, similar to staff members, albeit unpaid staff. "Governing boards," on the other hand, focus on providing oversight for the big picture. In this model, the board is primarily engaged in ensuring that the nonprofit has the necessary funds to fulfill its mission, but leaves program implementation and day-to-day management of the organization to the ED and staff.

While the founder board guarantees that a great deal of autonomy and independent decision making is left to the founder, the working board helps get the job done via volunteer labor while the governing board provides real leadership that adds legitimacy to the organization. It's a bit of a conundrum, but in the end, growth of the organization will be constrained by a nonfunctioning board. Even worse, micro-managing boards—those that overstep their bounds and get involved in the daily management decisions of the organization—are to be avoided like the plague. Can you see how members of a working board may have a tendency to move in the direction of micro-management? After all, the lines between staff and board are already blurred and hard-working board members can become very invested in their own views of what is best for the organization. Make sure your board understands its proper role. It will help a lot if at least some board members have served on the boards of other nonprofits because they will have an appreciation for some of the pitfalls.

Growth in functioning of the board is a process. Having an idea of what an optimal board looks like will help as you go about the process of recruitment. Following are some considerations regarding composition of the board.

- Board members must believe in your mission; preferably, they should be passionate about it.
- Ensure that your constituency—the population being served—is represented on the board. Funders care about this; if you claim that your programs are designed to meet unmet needs in the Latina population, then you really should have a representative of the target community on your board to be credible.
- Diversify your board in terms of ethnicity, age, gender and race if possible.
- Identify needed skills or areas of expertise that will be required. Most nonprofits will benefit from having an accountant or financial specialist on the board. A lawyer or someone well versed in nonprofit law will come

in handy. You need fundraisers as well as people who travel in circles with people who have money. Marketing, technology and grant writing expertise are needed. People who are connected in the community and able to mobilize resources are an asset. You need leadership too—someone whom you trust to steer and inspire the board as an entity, preferably making it fun along the way.

- Some individuals may have a conflict of interest in that they have connections with other organizations offering overlapping or competing programs or services. Or they may be in a position to benefit financially from their relationship with the nonprofit. Conflicts of interest do not necessarily preclude participation—indeed they are common. They do, however, require an awareness regarding what constitutes a conflict and a willingness to acknowledge and address it. Board members, for example, should recuse themselves from voting on matters before the board where a conflict exists such that they (or a family member) may benefit financially from a specific course of action.
- Personality issues on a board can become a problem. Avoid folks who are lame (lots of talk, no action; repeatedly come late and unprepared to meetings; have poor follow through on tasks, etc.); difficult, overbearing or humorless; or ones who seek to exert power over others. You need a functional team here.
- Keep in mind that, as founder, you want to ensure that the balance of power on the board is always in your favor; that those with whom you might have conflicts never out-number you. I realize that might not be a very politically correct thing to say, but I'm fairly confident that it is a statement with which 99 percent of founder EDs would agree.
- Much of the available literature about boards presents a fairly paternalistic and, in my view, archaic system, employing Robert's Rules of Order (e.g., motions, seconding of motions, decision by vote of the majority and a top-down power structure). The manner in which the board is to function is delineated in the organizational bylaws. I encourage founders to think outside the box here and come up with a system designed to achieve consensus on most issues, if possible. See the organizational chart of the Women's Center of Southeastern Michigan (reproduced on page 156) for a sample nonpatriarchal structure. It may all seem theoretical and not critical to getting the work done, but the structure itself sends an important message to potential board members and sets the tone overall for the organization. So, it does matter.

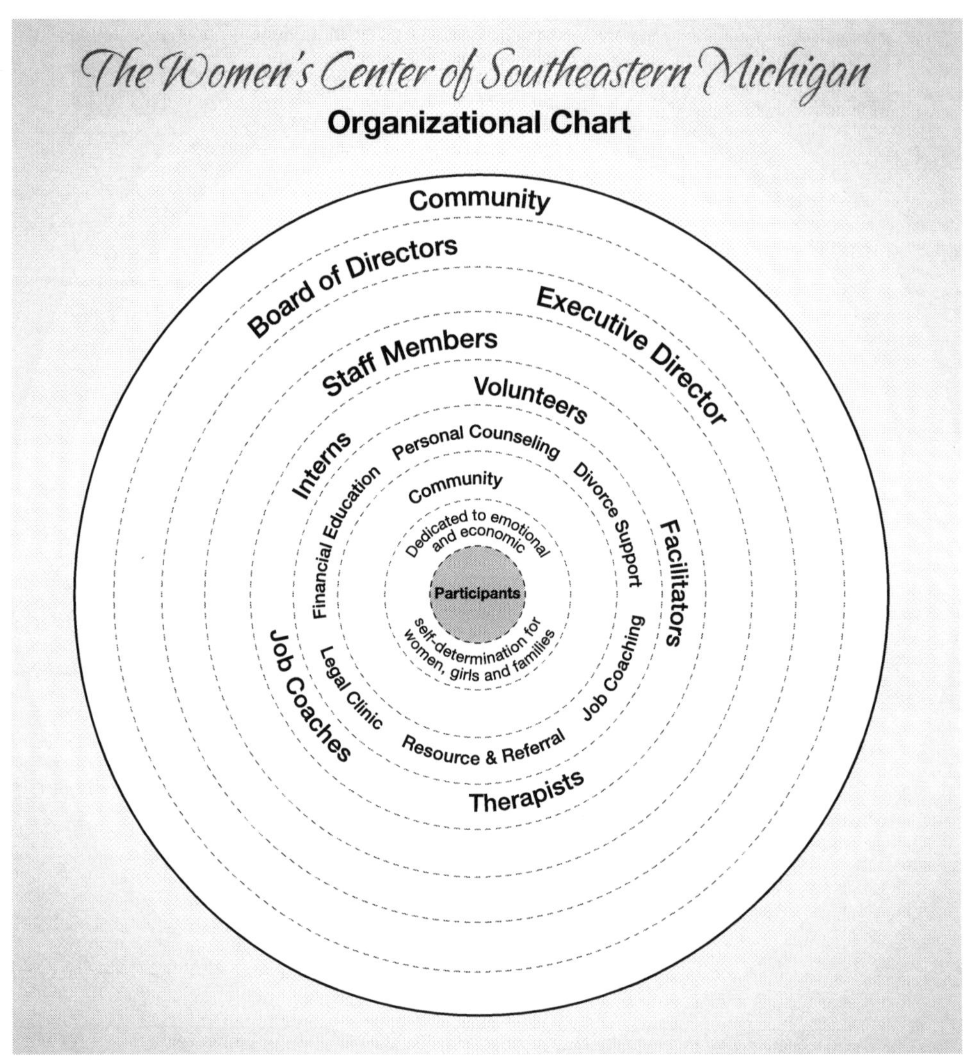

- ***Write it into the bylaws that the ED will be a voting board member.*** This should be a no-brainer, but questions or debate may arise on this point. Just know that there is well-established precedent for it and the reasons for ensuring that the ED have a vote are compelling. I found it completely unacceptable not even to be able to vote on major decisions affecting the future of the Center (my baby!), especially given the fact that, on occasion, I had board members who were not even clear in their minds what our programs were. The ED can recuse herself from voting on issues, such as her salary, where a clear conflict of interest exists.

When recruiting, keep in mind that if you must twist arms to get someone on the board as a favor to you, you will most likely get little actual work from this board member. Potential board members should be excited, enthusiastic and committed to putting hours in, raising funds and/or leveraging connections. Otherwise they are dead weight and can become a liability for the organization. Perhaps you are considering an individual because her/his name and status in the community may lend greater credibility to your work? Be careful about the message you are sending to the rest of the board by doing this. Consider forming an "advisory board" for this purpose. The advisory board is composed of folks who believe in the mission and are willing to put their reputation on the line to advance the mission, as well as grant an occasional favor or help make key connections in the greater community.

Directors' Legal Responsibilities and Duties

Members of the board of directors should familiarize themselves with legal compliance regulations for operation of a nonprofit charitable organization. While steps can be taken to protect board members from personal liability (see Chapter 7), directors are not protected if they fail to exercise "due diligence."

Infrastructure and the House of Cards

A nonprofit infrastructure needs to be in place in order to conduct business, but attention to the details of infrastructure development must not be given precedence over fundraising. The house of cards falls apart if you can't meet payroll or have to start dipping into restricted funds (grant funds approved for specific program-related expenses only) in order to cover indirect costs (ED salary, occupancy, etc.). The bare-bones infrastructure basics include:

- Setting up an accounting system to record the receipt and expenditure of money in accordance with the bylaws and with reporting requirements that will be imposed on the organization by funders (mandated grant reports) and governmental agencies (e.g., IRS Form 990, mandated payroll-related state and federal forms, etc.). Absolutely get yourself set up with a bookkeeping software program such as QuickBooks. Had I taken a community college class on nonprofit accounting, it would have saved me countless hours and headaches, but I never felt I had the time, so I was always winging it, with less than satisfactory results.

Questions to Ask Before Agreeing to Serve on a Nonprofit Board of Directors

The following question was asked on a Facebook forum of savvy professionals, many of whom have served on boards: "What do you wish you would have asked or wanted someone to tell you BEFORE you agreed to serve on a board?" I have organized the responses according to the primary themes that emerged from the responses.

Board culture

- Is it a governing board or a working board?
- What are the interpersonal dynamics between board members (especially if it is a working board)?
- How does the board manage conflict?
- Are there written policies and procedures for board governance?
- If I'm a minority, how can I be assured I'm not a token for the sake of diversity?

Expectations

- What are the hourly time commitments per week/per month?
- Are there expectations for participation on committees, beyond the general board commitment?
- Are board members expected to make a financial contribution?

Meetings

- Is there a time limit on meetings?
- Does the board follow Roberts' Rules?
- Is there a specific process and format for making proposals?
- Are meetings productive or is there in-fighting?

Is there a formal orientation?

- What's the process like getting up to speed on issues for a new member?
- Can board members describe the impact of the organization? Can they articulate the vision? Why does it matter?

- What issues are the board currently dealing with?
- Are there any ongoing issues that have been or will continue to be problematic for the board?
- Are there clear boundaries and good position statements on what board members are supposed to do?
- Is there clarity regarding the board's nonprofit status and what is allowed in terms of grassroots and direct lobbying, electioneering, etc.?

Fiduciary responsibility:

- Review financial statements, at the very least, a balance sheet.
- Know how to understand a financial statement!
- Never forget your fiduciary responsibility as a board member.
- Ask to see the annual tax return (a public record and should be available to every board member).

Recommendations

Responses from the group reflected a hard-won understanding that it is difficult to find people who see the overall vision of the boards they serve on and understand that it's a job and will require time and dedication.

- Under no circumstances are board members allowed to shirk their duties just because this is a volunteer position. If the position is too much, resign or let people know that you need help, but don't just get embarrassed and stop working. This is a job; expect it to be a job.
- Directors' & Officers' Insurance isn't nearly as important as actually knowing what documents are being signed in the name of the board.
- If this is a membership organization, never forget you're there to serve the membership.
- Most importantly, people need to take initiative and actually do something, complete projects and even sometimes pay up to cover costs (be an example by donating!).

- Establishing procedures for recruitment of board members, orientation of new board members and succession in board leadership. This, like fundraising, is an ongoing process; you are never done with it. You will have turnover on your board.
- Creating a system for preserving corporate documents such as articles of incorporation, bylaws and amendments, and the minutes of board meetings, committee meetings and the meeting of the incorporators. These corporate documents and minutes are a permanent part of the organization's history and are required by law. A simple three-ring binder works, in addition to electronic records.

Cloning the Executive Director

Okay, you can't actually clone yourself, but there will be days, weeks, even months when you wish you could. EDs need help! And if the organization cannot find a way to get help for the ED, then burnout is unavoidable. The downward spiral of trying to do it all and feeling as though one doesn't even have the time required to tell or teach another how to take over certain tasks—the belief that help would be more trouble than it's worth—ensures limitations on personal job satisfaction as well as growth of the organization. And yet, there is more than a grain of truth regarding the challenges presented as helpers come on the scene.

An effective ED must learn to integrate help. In hindsight, I believe I was a poor manager in this regard. For me, there were a number of things in play. I wanted people to like me (to a fault). I was reluctant to confront bad or lame behavior, allowing uncomfortable situations to go unchecked and I had no system in place to hold people accountable. In short, I really didn't have the people-management experience that I needed. A few years later, with the benefit of hindsight and no need to be defensive, I can frankly say that I may not have been cut out for the ED gig. Certainly, at a minimum, I could have benefited from some training in nonprofit management. Hopefully, you can learn from my mistakes. Here are a few tips for addressing the challenge of integrating help:

- Start by noting how you spend your time each day. Just track it for a couple of weeks—time spent answering email, talking on the phone, doing administrative chores, fundraising, overseeing or doing the nitty-gritty of program development, bookkeeping, marketing and so on.
- Note which tasks take up an inordinate amount of time, due to lack of needed skills (in my case, running budget reports).

- Next determine which chores could most easily be passed on to others. For example, the ED should not be engaged in copying and collating course materials, assembling mailings, doing data entry or cleaning bathrooms. Write down procedures for accomplishing the tasks that you are doing that can be passed on to someone else—a recipe for completing the task at hand. Keep it simple. It's hard to pass off a task that has no systematic process attached to it. If the "system" is Patty, then no system exists. *Creating systems will make integrating help easier.*
- Expectations for staff, volunteers or interns should be clearly stated, specific tasks assigned and timelines for completion of tasks delineated, followed by systematic accountability.
- Ditch people who waste your time and are more trouble than they are worth.

Sources of Help

Board Members. While board members can be a source of help, beware of getting them involved in doing the work of the organization lest the distinction between their oversight function and detailed micromanaging gets blurred. Encouraging board members to spearhead fundraising efforts, however, is appropriate and necessary.

Student Interns. Get approved as a site for college or university interns to complete practicum requirements. Folks in the process of getting their master's degree in social work or public health are likely candidates. Often these placements can be quite substantial, lasting over two school terms or more, so you may be able to find interns who become a significant asset. You will likely need someone with an MSW credential on staff who can serve in a supervisory role for the intern, but this person need not be onsite at your organization. For example, I have used MSW student interns who have given me up to 20 hours per week. I am not an MSW myself, so a local former doula who is credentialed and works as a professional social worker in a local NICU agreed to provide the required supervision. I'm the onsite supervisor but the intern also has the option of shadowing the MSW mentor at the hospital. It has worked out well.

At one point, I tried accepting interns who needed a five-hours-per-week service placement for one school term. In my mind, this meant help for four months (September through December). In reality, the "help" started the last week of September which is when the students were required to commit for class credit. After negotiating schedules and job duties (eating up more time), the interns got to work. Next thing I know, no one is coming next week because it's "fall break." A couple more weeks of work and we're facing mid-term exams and a "study week" followed by Thanksgiving, finals and an early break for the holidays. I kept thinking, "fall break?—uh … Real World here." No fall break in my world. So, as I learned, working with students means you are entering the alternate universe of academia.

The other challenge is that the students are looking for a "learning experience." Now, it would be hard to argue that stuffing envelopes, copying course packs or data entry has educational value—unless the value is to drive home just how boring repetitive, mindless tasks can be and how one should aspire to do more in life! But honestly, completion of these mundane tasks is precisely what may be most helpful for you. So, while interns can indeed bring skills, youthful energy and passion to the organization, they have specific needs and motivations for being there and it is all a bit of a balancing act. Just like any relationship in life, there is a give and take and it is essential that you get your needs met. The decision to take on an intern or two should be approached thoughtfully and carefully. What, precisely, do you need this person to do for you? And consider investing your time in someone who is going to be around longer than three months.

Work/Study Students. If you are a 501c3 nonprofit with a nearby university, your organization should qualify as a site for federal work/study students. The government picks up approximately 50 percent of the wages with this program, so it may be possible to get data entry help and other administrative assistance at a relatively low hourly rate. Be aware in this scenario that the student will have a predetermined award amount each term. You will need to figure backwards from the award amount to come up with the per-hour pay rate and weekly work schedule if you are looking for consistent help. That way, you can spread the help more evenly throughout the school term (there's that alternate universe again). There is an approval process to become a work/study site with the university and this can take a few weeks. You will be required to pay the student up front and then be reimbursed. As the employer, you will be responsible for payroll taxes and related reports. Consider hiring a freshman rather than a senior in the hope that you might find someone who wants to stick around for more than one school term or year. One benefit to this source of help is that, as an employee, the person can be held accountable for what you need.

Volunteers. Ensure that all volunteers are assigned specific tasks and given direction, feedback and appreciation. Beware of folks who waste your time and choose quality over quantity. Ideally, it would be great to have someone in charge of volunteers whose job it is to direct and support them. There's a science to attracting and maintaining an effective and enthusiastic volunteer pool.

The concept of self-interest is central to understanding the motivations of individuals who volunteer their time for a nonprofit organization. Not all motivations are purely altruistic in nature, but that's okay. There is always some perceived benefit to the volunteer, even if it is to fulfill an unhealthy need. Here are some non-mutually-exclusive possible motivations:

- To pay back or pay forward—a desire to help someone because you were helped when you were similarly in need (e.g., teen mothers helping other teen moms, or respite care for an exhausted caregiver)
- To develop a résumé and work experience profile
- To hone skills or learn new ones
- To claim power and exercise control over others (rarely a conscious motive)
- To make professional connections and further your career
- To have fun
- To be needed (also rarely conscious)
- To be in community with others around a shared purpose
- To achieve recognition
- To advance professionally
- To feel appreciated for your efforts
- To make the world a better place
- To seek redemption through charity
- To experience a sense of purpose
- To simply help others

By understanding what motivates people to become involved as volunteers, community partners or board members, we can best direct their energies. Have a list of possible volunteer opportunities within your organization that includes a range of time commitments and activities so that it will be easy to plug them in. Once a new volunteer or board recruitment has been identified, it is important not to waste time. If they step forward as a volunteer, they want to do it *now.* If they spend their first three months in association with your organization floundering, then you are at risk of losing them altogether. And, since a fair amount of effort can be put into recruiting volunteers and board members, it is critical to leverage their motivations and skills efficiently and to optimize their contributions. For example, the person who needs her involvement to be fun will feel tortured by long, boring meetings. Find out what constitutes "fun" for her, and put her in charge of a fun project. Set deadlines with all volunteers and hold them accountable.

In hindsight, one of my biggest challenges and sources of frustration was the problem of accountability for volunteers. There can be no serious threat of dismissal, such as being fired from the job if performance is less than expected. Yes, board members can be voted out of office and other volunteers dismissed if they become more of a liability than an asset, but the reality is that this rarely happens unless there is a gross offense (a process for dismissal of board members should be defined in the bylaws). Typically, if volunteers are willing to contribute in any way, large or small, we must be grateful for whatever they are able to accomplish, no matter how far short of needs, hopes, expectations or self-proclaimed intentions that may be. So, if they do what they say they are going to do, great. If they exceed expectations, fabulous. If they flake out completely, so be it. When someone is donating time, demanding accountability is inherently problematic.

While acknowledging that it is inherently problematic, however, I will say this—the leadership of the organization does need to hold key volunteers accountable, while making every effort to help folks succeed in being an asset to the organization. Oversight and reporting systems are needed. Volunteers or board members should not be allowed to waste everyone's time nor drop the ball on key initiatives while expecting others to smile and say "thank you."

Fundraising: The Bottom Line

Money is your bottom line. Embrace this notion. Ongoing fundraising is a simple fact of life in the nonprofit sector. Few (if any) grants will provide unrestricted funds designed to cover overhead costs such as rent or salaries for full-time employees in the organization. Persistent cultivation of community supporters is essential to survival. Ideally, the fundraising becomes systematic.

> **Fundraising is urgent.** Talking about the best ways to fundraise is not the same as fundraising. Just do it!

Likely there are existing programs in your community that you can plug into such as grocery scrip programs, annual charity marathons/walks, media drives, etc. A great job for a volunteer would be to get you set up as a participant through these established fundraising venues. It's not a ton of money, but hey, everything helps. Cultivate donors, including big ones capable of substantial support. Think of potential donors as partners who are vested in the success of your mission. In other words, they are not doing you a favor; they believe that your work is needed and worthy of support. It's not about you, so don't take it personally if a prospect doesn't come through. Leave an open door for them to help later.

The need for focused leadership on your team to drive fundraising efforts cannot be overemphasized. Establish a fundraising committee and identify the most responsible and skilled board member you have to head it up. Plug volunteers and interns into fundraising efforts. While the ED should also be a member of the fundraising committee, it should not be the ED's job to track all the tasks and who is doing what. That is the committee chair's job. Be careful to only undertake projects that are worth the time invested for the return. For example, a garage sale involving days of work and numerous volunteer hours for a return of $500 might better be replaced by an event with greater fundraising potential or, even better, securing one donor gift in the same amount.

The good news is that you have an easy case to make. Helping moms and babies and families? Improving birth outcomes? Reducing disparities in health outcomes? Serving the growing number of elderly people who are struggling and in need of help? Saving healthcare dollars? Not a hard sell.

Story of Center for the Childbearing Year

The evolution of Center for the Childbearing Year, the nonprofit organization that I founded and led as ED for ten years, is a story of both failure and triumph. It contains some hard lessons learned that I trust will help readers seeking to implement a similar vision.

I founded the organization because I needed to make a living and I had a vision for how I could continue my career in the birth field after retiring from my homebirth midwifery practice. A key driving factor was that I had a private donor in the wings who offered to provide $10,000 in seed money to launch the dream. I also had revenue-producing educational programs in place that included childbirth preparation classes and doula trainings, and I possessed the experience and skills to promote and teach those classes. In addition, I had started a grassroots, community-based, volunteer doula program known as *Doulas Care.* Briefly, *Doulas Care* matched doulas (newly trained by me) with pregnant women in the community who needed some extra help but couldn't afford to hire a doula. In turn, the new doulas had a ready-made opportunity for gaining hands-on experience at births and fulfilling professional certification requirements.

Milestones in the History of the Center

1998

- Patty retires from midwifery practice and begins the transition to full-time educator; thus, the revenue-producing programs preexist the nonprofit business model and are managed by Patty under a sole proprietorship.
- The *Doulas Care* program is launched by Patty as a grassroots initiative.
- The administrative work is done from Patty's home and classes are taught at a variety of venues in the city of Ann Arbor.

1999

- A private donor advances $10,000 in seed money, thereby covering the IRS application fee to become a 501c3, as well as invest in equipment and updated teaching supplies.
- The organization is incorporated, and nonprofit status is applied for and granted by the IRS.

2000

- A limited nonprofit infrastructure is put into place.
- A suitable permanent teaching/office space becomes available and the Center finds a home.
- Two other businesses (a homebirth midwifery practice and a birth photographer) move into adjacent space, thereby forming a collective of independent businesses around the theme of the childbearing year.

2001

- The first grant for *Doulas Care* is awarded in the amount of $5,000 from the Michigan Women's Foundation.

2002

- A close collaborative partnership begins with a university faculty member who proves to be a key player in our development and growth.
- A $36,000 grant from the W.K. Kellogg Foundation is awarded to establish an evaluation component for the *Doulas Care program.*

2003

- A $25,000 grant from March of Dimes is awarded to hire a volunteer coordinator to handle daily administration of the growing *Doulas Care* program. This is the beginning of a multi-year relationship with March of Dimes.
- A $189,000 two-year grant from W. K. Kellogg Foundation is awarded in support of *Doulas Care.*
- *Doulas Care* is awarded the *DONA International Founders' Award for Excellence in a Doula Program.*

2004–2005

- Demand for all programs continues to grow.
- Ongoing success with securing grant funding from a variety of sources is experienced.

2006

- Kellogg funding ends.
- The Center is approved as a site placement for interns in social work and public health and full-time interns begin to work at the Center.
- The board president resigns after efforts to resolve ongoing conflicts with the ED fail and a new board president steps in.

2007

- The Center hires a work/study student as a part-time administrative assistant for the ED (first paid assistant not associated with the doula program).
- An unresolved budget crisis signals the approaching demise of the organization.
- Board membership and accountability (with notable exceptions) is at an all-time low.
- Due to lack of unrestricted funds, the nonprofit can no longer afford to meet the ED's salary for the last quarter. Patty agrees to finish out the year in order to meet obligations to funders and constituents.
- A deal is brokered by the board president between two stakeholders, with Patty seeking to revert revenue-producing educational programs to her control and the partner stakeholder seeking to continue the doula program. In lieu of salary owed, Patty is granted some of the assets of the nonprofit organization, including the name, the website and control over the

revenue-producing educational programs. Since the physical space which is the (rented) home of the Center was secured through Patty's personal relationships, she maintains control over it. The 501c3 entity changes its name to *Doulas Care,* thereby cutting *Center for the Childbearing Year* loose as an independent for-profit organization. It is believed that this unique solution will allow both program arms of the organization to move forward in a seamless transition for constituents.

2008

- The transition process starts at the beginning of the year.
- *Center for the Childbearing Year* incorporates as an LLC.
- *Doulas Care* comes under new leadership with a volunteer ED and new board.
- *Doulas Care* maintains an administrative office onsite at the Center, paying rent as a tenant to Patty. Patty also agrees to continue hosting *Doulas Care* on the Center's website for a period of one year.
- The Center continues to support *Doulas Care* through the doula training scholarship program, funneling newly-trained doulas into the volunteer doula program.
- A few loose ends remain and are resolved as the year unfolds.

2009

- The separation of the two businesses is completed.
- *Doulas Care* moves offsite to a new location and launches an independent website.

Key Successes of the Nonprofit

- Achieved across-the-board excellence in program development.
- Gained ongoing grant funding for the doula program.
- Established collaborative partnerships with key community stakeholders.
- Recruited a diverse group of committed, enthusiastic and generous community-based volunteer doulas.
- Developed programs that resonated with the target population.
- Created excellent word of mouth in the community about the organization.
- Created an increasing public demand for programs and services.

Key Failures of the Nonprofit

- *Fundraising to cover indirect program costs was inadequate.* Few grants are designated for unrestricted purposes, meaning that funds will only cover expenses associated specifically with programs or initiatives. In hindsight, the big Kellogg grant may have played a role in the ultimate decline of the nonprofit. It enabled us to invest in equipment, expand staffing and services, and grow the doula program. So far, so good. It may also have contributed to an aura of complacency, a feeling that we had "made it" and that fundraising was not urgent. The hope was always that Kellogg would continue to be a funder, but this turned out not to be the case. And when that funding went away, we lost a disproportionate percentage of our operating budget. The take-away lesson here is to diversify funding streams and ensure systematic fundraising. If you are overly dependent on one funder, you are vulnerable.
- *Financial oversight and fiscal leadership were lacking.* The board of directors and I were well aware that expertise in this area was needed. In the last few months, an accountant who was a former ED herself volunteered to lend a hand in an advisory role. I began to glimpse how incredibly helpful it would have been to have that level of skilled mentoring years earlier. My advice to readers is to: (1) procure help in the beginning to get your systems set up properly for nonprofit fiscal management, (2) recruit at least one board member who can teach the rest of the board what financial oversight actually means, (3) ensure that the ED is trained in the use of Excel spreadsheets and QuickBooks and (4) move to an accrual, rather than cash form of bookkeeping once grants start coming in that are based on anything other than a calendar year (or set it up that way from the start!).
- *Board recruitment, development and succession/continuity planning (i.e., identification of qualified individuals to replace current board officers when their terms expired) were an ongoing challenge.* I think we tried here. It was just very difficult and time consuming. You will need some depth in your board, approximately seven or so people. When board members inevitably experience life challenges, such as a spouse's sudden unemployment, their priorities understandably shift. Volunteer work for the local nonprofit agen cy may become a luxury they can no longer accommodate. It's just how it goes. Board members come and go.
- *The capacity to publish outcomes for the doula program was impaired due to two factors: (1) reliance on a volunteer evaluator and (2) the ongoing challenge of getting volunteer doulas to complete and submit required forms.*

When program managers are able to make a strong case—based on outcome data measured against a baseline—that a program is benefitting the target population as intended, then re-funding and fundraising are enabled. Reporting mere numbers served, with implied benefit, is not the same as demonstrating that a program is actually having a positive effect on outcomes. In hindsight, evaluation was too urgent of an organizational need to be left in the hands of a volunteer. My recommendation is to secure skilled help while ensuring that every grant builds in evaluation as a line item in the budget (see Chapter 6). Up to 15 percent of your grant budget is standard. Set a firm timeline for publication of evaluation reports, probably to coincide with upcoming grant report deadlines. (See Chapter 5 for more on steps taken to increase compliance with reporting requirements by the volunteer doulas.)

- *Prevention of ED burnout by hiring help was a case of too little, too late.* It took me too long to get the hang of this. Once our wonderful work/study administrative assistant came on board and competently took over many of the mundane, repetitive tasks that had been claiming my time, I was well past burnout.
- *Dysfunctional leadership and personality dynamics exacted a toll.* Yikes. This is a Pandora's Box and I dare not open it here. Suffice it to say, I had my part in it and bear no ill will towards anyone involved. Sometimes, we are trying to force a square peg into a round hole and we just have to stop. The take-away? You can't go wrong with honest, open communication and clear accountability. Take it as a given that you can't please everyone and be willing to let someone walk if that is what needs to happen.

The "Essentially Flawed Concept"

In 2006, when burnout was high and tensions between me and a couple of board members were peaking, I sought counsel from a founder ED friend of mine who heads a family services agency in another state with a budget over $1 million, a staff of 50 and a ten-year head start. As I poured out the details of the power struggle I was embroiled in, my friend offered two clarifying insights.

(1) She stated simply that the whole concept of nonprofit corporations and how they are run is "essentially flawed." The idea that a volunteer board of directors—who often have (shockingly) little to no knowledge about programmatic details or how the organization is managed on a day-to-day basis and are often lacking in the necessary oversight skills—should nevertheless have full decision-making

authority, is ludicrous. This was a light-bulb moment for me. No wonder I was having a hard time! The whole concept was *essentially flawed.*

(2) Next I asked my friend, who proposed the budget, including the ED salary and benefit package, in her organization? Her response was that *she* handled all of that. Interesting, but not the case in my organization. "Did the board always just go along with what she wanted?" I asked. "No" she answered. Me: "Doesn't that make you crazy, then?" "Yes" she replied, "but I let go of it." Instantly a mirror was held up for me. Admittedly, letting go is not one of my strong points. (Could one simply choose to "let it go"? What a concept!) She had a similarly easygoing attitude toward soliciting potential donors. If they said "no," she lightheartedly said "Well, thanks for your time and keep us in mind when your ship comes in." She didn't view it as a gut-wrenching, excruciating personal rejection.

So, what's my take-away message here? (1) There is a delicate balance of power to be achieved in running a nonprofit organization, with inherent challenges and (2) certain personality types may be more graceful and effective at navigating the power dynamic than others. When all is said and done, I am much happier in the role of business entrepreneur and risk taker than I am in a leadership position with nonprofit constraints. But that's just me.

Reality Check

"Best Practices" and "transparency" are the current buzzwords for nonprofits, so find out what these terms mean—what is expected to qualify as a well-run, reputable organization. The bottom line here is that people with money to give (whether they are individuals or large foundations) are not likely to give it to a clueless, floundering organization, under questionable leadership, with little to no transparency and big hearts. No one is inspired to rescue a sinking ship. It doesn't all have to be in place overnight, but ignorance of what is required or expected is not an excuse for poor management.

Put idealism aside for a minute and try to go into this process with your eyes open. Given the considerable challenges involved, it behooves you to explore whether or not there is an existing nonprofit in your community who might be willing to partner with you and serve as the fiduciary agent for your proposed program. Under the umbrella of another organization (you will have to be a good mission match), you may be able to achieve your goals without having to create a whole new organization and complex infrastructure. In this scenario, you are free to focus all of your efforts on development of your program and cultivating funding sources to sustain it (a plenty big job in and of itself). If your program attracts supporters and constituents and becomes sustainable on its own merit, you can always leave the fiduciary relationship and become independent. Be sure to make this explicit in your contract right from the start (see more on fiduciary relationships in Chapter 6).

If you are determined to proceed and implement your vision as the founder of a nonprofit corporation, bless you! Helping others is a worthy endeavor. May you draw the very best people to support your cause and be granted the wisdom to lead them effectively and joyfully.

Past experience as a board member for a nonprofit organization would be highly beneficial and provide insight into the gig. If you don't have it, find others who do. Your local community college or state nonprofit association may offer classes (often online) in nonprofit startup and management. These will be well worth the investment of time involved. A great idea is to make a connection with one or two other EDs—whether in your community or outside of it—and actively solicit advice. Be respectful of her/his time (all EDs are overcommitted) and offer to meet over coffee or lunch on their turf. This peer support will be very helpful! If you can find a founder ED to consult, so much the better. There is no one who will better understand your position and challenges or is better positioned to be an ally.

I invite all readers seriously considering taking this step to subject themselves to ruthless self-examination. What evidence do you have that you are a good leader, capable of being an effective boss, leading a team of volunteers and working effectively with a board of directors? What are your strengths and weaknesses? What needed skills do you lack and how are you going to address this? And last, but definitely not least, who will lead your fundraising efforts?

The Story Continues . . .

After hearing my story and warnings, you may be surprised to learn that, a few years later, I chose to form a second nonprofit doula program and serve as its volunteer executive director. I see now that the process of writing the first edition of this book was cathartic. The last couple years of running the first nonprofit, and especially the negotiations and fallout at the end, were traumatic. For me, writing is a way to process my experience. Once I had done that, I was free to put it behind me and move into a more forward-thinking mode.

For many years, I served on the Program Services Committee for the March of Dimes Michigan Chapter. Among other things, this committee is responsible for administrating the Community Grants process, evaluating grant proposals and distributing funds. As a sometimes grant recipient, I was not unique on the committee in having a conflict of interest. Acknowledgment of this conflict means that I must recuse myself from all committee discussions and votes that would give me an unfair or biased advantage—literally stepping out of the room when a grant proposal that I submit is under consideration by the committee.

It so happened that in early 2011, one of our grantees returned the bulk of their $25,000 Community Grant stating that they were unable to fulfill the terms of the grant. From a funder perspective, having a grant returned is a problem because the funder must spend down the entire grant line in the annual timeframe or lose it. If "lost," the funds go back to March of Dimes national and are no longer targeted for our state. The committee decided to release a unique, quick turn-around Request for Proposals (RFP) and I saw an opportunity.

The idea for a web-based alternative to *Doulas Care* (which I knew to be floundering for lack of funding and leadership) was born from this emerging opportunity. I quickly formed a new nonprofit organization, fast-tracked the 501c3 application (the IRS has a special process for this) and drafted a proposal for March of Dimes funding. I was able to do all of this in about one week (choosing to forego the ten months of procrastination experienced the first time around). Ain't experience grand?

I decided to keep everything as simple as possible. With a web-based program, I would not require administrative staff. Funds were used to design and launch the website, provide scholarships for low-income women to become doulas and create outreach materials to be used for grassroots growth. I would serve as a volunteer executive director. If opportunities arose in the future (e.g., grants), I would be free to act or not. The website, which was designed to be self-serve, would remain a resource for Michigan families regardless of whether money and time continued to be invested.

In forming *Michigan Doula Connection*, I sought out board members who would be willing to serve on a "founder board" and I kept the number of board members at the legally required minimum. The only real qualification to serve on "my" board was the willingness to say, "Yes Patty." How's that for clarity and simplicity? This is a 180-degree turn from my first time around as a founder ED. For five years, the website worked as intended and keeping it going felt manageable. However, once the custom-designed database and search mechanism began to experience technical failures (and the firm that had designed the database went out of business), I was forced to close it down. Note that a key difference between these two nonprofit models is that my income was never dependent on *Michigan Doula Connection* and I remained the captain of my own ship. ◆

CHAPTER 5

Doula Programs

AS THE EVIDENCE IN SUPPORT OF DOULAS CONTINUES TO MOUNT, the demand for doula programs will grow. More hospitals are looking to start birth doula programs as a cesarean-reduction strategy and to enhance patient satisfaction scores in a competitive marketplace. Additionally, the appalling state of race-based disparities in birth outcomes for both moms and babies is generating a demand for initiatives aimed at reducing risks and improving outcomes that are likely to find widespread support. Recently, New York state expanded their Medicaid program to cover a pilot doula program for this purpose.

While birth and postpartum programs have been around for a couple of decades, end-of-life doula programs are now emerging in response to a growing demand for holistic approaches in hospice and palliative care from a rapidly aging population. As more hospices are implementing end-of-life doula programs, the National Hospice and Palliative Care Organization (NHPCO) formed an End-of-Life Doula Advisory Council in 2018 to promote awareness and understanding of the end-of-life doula's role among hospice providers and consumers. Entrepreneurial end-of-life doulas and hospice providers can learn much from the pioneering work done by birth and postpartum doula program visionaries. Whether seeking to establish community-based, hospital-based or hospice-based programs, we are not at ground zero.

In this chapter, we will explore a variety of doula program models and parameters, common challenges, and strategies for addressing those challenges. Ultimately, there is significant overlap in how the benefits and risks of one model versus another apply to both the mother–baby realm and end of life. In this discussion, we will focus primarily on birth (and postpartum) doula programs, as much more information is available to analyze the pros and cons of pivotal features. Hopefully, this discussion will help get the wheels turning and pave the way for end-of-life visionaries to create and adapt new hospice doula program models for comprehensive and compassionate support of the dying and their families.

Doula Status	Type of Program
Doulas are employed by the program	Community based
Program refers to independent doula contractors	Hospital based
Doulas are volunteers	Hospice sponsored

The table above shows the primary program types. They can be cross-mixed and matched so that, for example, a community-based program might employ doulas or rely solely upon volunteer doulas. Or a hospital-based program might hire doulas, use independent contractors or depend on volunteers. And so on. There is also the potential for hybrid models, for example, programs that use both volunteers and doulas for hire (whether staff or contractors). Choosing the right model for your purposes (and budget) involves a complex set of considerations.

Preliminary Considerations

There is a great deal of overlap between the models if you think in terms of community need, service gaps and the benefits of doulas. Choice of a model is likely to be determined more by your service setting and available resources for establishing a program—the opportunities at hand—than by inherent superiority of one model over another. For those seeking to establish a doula program, some preliminary considerations are in order. Consider the following questions.

Whom are you intending to serve?

Is your program aimed at a specific population? Think in terms of demographics—age, location, race, income level and other relevant factors. Who, specifically, are you trying to help? Here are some possibilities:

- All mothers having their first baby at Hospital X
- All nurse-midwife clients at Hospital X
- Pregnant African-American women in City X
- Pregnant clinic patients on Medicaid at Hospital X
- Pregnant teen mothers in County X
- Pregnant women with a history of premature birth
- Low-income pregnant women in tri-county area X

- New immigrant population in County X
- Individuals with a new terminal diagnosis
- Folks who are receiving palliative care
- Individuals who are already in hospice

What is the goal or focus of your program?
You will need to have a clear mission and articulate your purpose. Once your program is up and running successfully, how will the people served be better off? How will your community or hospital be different? Here are some possibilities:

- Improve birth outcomes for moms and babies
- Reduce primary cesarean rate
- Reduce postpartum depression
- Integrate doulas into maternity care team
- Maintain/enhance patient satisfaction scores
- Save Medicaid dollars
- Build community support for the dying

What is the best setting for your program?

- **Community-based.** These programs need to be under the umbrella of a nonprofit organization or government sponsored. The nonprofit can be one that is founded for this purpose, or perhaps an existing family-focused nonprofit in your community would be willing to sponsor (serve as a fiduciary agent for) a doula program. As a nonprofit, your program must have a public service mission. A primary feature of the community-based model is that the doulas are members of the community served. They speak the same language and are familiar with and respectful of the cultural norms of the families served.
- **Hospital-based.** A successful initiative for launching a hospital-based program will have a champion/advocate in the administrative hierarchy. The services of a consultant may be engaged to navigate the process, including bringing more key players on board within the system. Get your ducks in a row regarding the problem you are trying to solve and evidence-based benefits of doulas (e.g., cesarean reduction, increase in volume of OB patients, improvement in satisfaction scores and patients willing to recommend the hospital, etc.).

- **Hospice-based.** Currently, most end-of-life doula programs are in-hospice volunteer programs serving, primarily, folks who are actively dying. There is much room for innovation here as families have often overwhelming needs at this time.

Program Variables

Regardless of the setting, all doula program implementers will need to consider the pros and cons of key variables in program structure and delivery of services. These are discussed below.

Volunteer vs. Living Wage Doulas

The use of volunteers is becoming increasingly controversial in the doula community as many leaders in the field feel that the practice undervalues the doula's role, resulting in reduced sustainability for career doulas. The refrain, *"Please, no more volunteer doula programs"* has echoed through social media forums with escalating passion in recent years. Clearly, if volunteer programs are to continue, great care must be taken to value the work of the doulas. This is best accomplished if the volunteer program is set up to support career development for the doulas. The best models will include training, mentoring and support to complete professional certification requirements and a pathway to employment. (See our description of the *Doulas Care Program* below for more details). In addition, as more end-of-life doulas are engaging the work, many are grappling with whether or not to provide volunteer services, as they are reluctant to set a precedent that end-of-life doulas are unpaid volunteers.

The primary benefit of a volunteer program is saving money for the sponsoring organization. But we must ask, "Can we get the job done using volunteer labor?" It depends on your goals. Volunteer programs are not without significant drawbacks including the following:

- The program is likely to be predominantly populated by inexperienced, uncertified doulas—often matched with the highest-need population. Hmmm …
- Volunteer accountability can be a challenge. When someone is donating their time, their sense of commitment may be more fluid. Reliability and compliance with program requirements can become problematic.
- Turnover will be ongoing so that your pool of volunteers may fall short from time to time. It may prove difficult to get the quantity of doulas needed for reliable coverage.

- Conflicts are likely for volunteers needing to hold down a full-time job while being on-call for births (thereby potentially facing lost wages when attending a birth).
- Hospital programs using an ever-changing pool of inexperienced volunteers rather than professional career doulas compound the challenge of acceptance and integration of the doula into the maternity care team.
- Pushback from independent doulas who feel that the doula's role is being de-valued may ripple through the community, adversely affecting referrals to the program and subsequent growth.

The advantages of using doulas who are paid market value for their services need not be enumerated here. It is obviously a benefit to all stakeholders in the equation and program stability is the likely result.

Certified vs. Non-Certified Doulas

Certified doulas have demonstrated a commitment to meeting professional standards. Unless training and mentoring of the doulas is a core ingredient of your program concept, it may make more sense to use certified doulas, or at least to require that program doulas be in the process of completing certification requirements. In the hospital or hospice setting, where acceptance of the doula's role by medical care providers may be tentative (or worse), certified doulas, arguably, will be better able to demonstrate value in their role. Both nonprofit boards and hospital administrators may also want to consider this variable from a risk-management perspective. (See Chapter 7 for more information on risk management.)

Continuity Doulas vs. Shift Doulas

The research on birth doulas suggests that labor support is most effective when it is continuous, provided by someone outside the woman's social network, and is the sole responsibility of the support person. What is not clear from the research is whether this continuous support must come from the same doula to be effective. Will a doula team or rotation of doulas through shifts achieve the same results? According to doula researcher Amy Gilliland (see Resources), we don't know definitively the answer to this question.

Continuity is integral to considerations of whether prenatal meetings or postpartum home visits are included as part of your program's service package. Private practice birth doulas typically include one to two prenatal visits and one postpartum visit as part of their care. When working in teams, both doulas participate in prenatal visits and the doula who was at the birth attends the postpartum visit.

This is continuity of care. A trusting relationship is created between the doula and her clients. The doula holds the thread of the mother's story. She knows her client's hopes and dreams, fears and challenges. The mother does not have to start over with each new care provider who arrives on the scene at an overwhelming and vulnerable time. Given the fragmentation of care in our current system, programs that build continuity into the doula's role can fill this gap, helping communication to flow smoothly between all parties and potentially catching problems that otherwise fall through the gaps (e.g., a severely depressed mom at two weeks postpartum).

When part of a larger team with rotating on-call schedules, doulas are not able to connect and build a relationship with clients prenatally. Clients may be provided with an opportunity to "meet the doulas" prior to delivery. This might include a short informational session, birth center tour and chance to mingle. If the doula program is intended to be a preventive intervention (e.g., lowering risks in a high-risk population), then the failure to provide continuity of care through prenatal mentoring is a lost opportunity to optimize the doula's role. Whether postpartum visits are included in the service package varies from program to program but may be less common in hospital-based programs.

In some hospital programs where doulas work shifts, the doula may be willing/able to stay to complete support services for a laboring client who has not birthed by the end of her shift. This is obviously best from the mother's point of view, though it may not be possible for the doula with child care concerns or other pressing conflicts. If shift doulas are required to attend more than one woman in labor at the same time, then the doulas' ability to achieve the evidence-based benefits demonstrated by the "continuous presence" of the doula in labor is put in jeopardy.

Dial-a-Doula

University of Michigan Hospital, Ann Arbor, MI

In this very simple, scaled down hospital-based volunteer program, trained volunteers sign up for 12-hour on-call shifts. There is no prenatal or postpartum contact and referrals are made primarily by the nurse-midwife practice. The on-call doula is called in when a woman arrives in labor whom the midwives believe could benefit from doula support. The doula can stay through her shift to continue providing support until the baby is born if she chooses, or the next person on-call can be called in. The program is administered by a volunteer, keeping program costs at a minimum. (In many programs, the position of an unpaid program coordinator is shared between two people.)

Matching Process for Doulas and Clients

Where continuity of care is built into a birth doula program, a process for matching or assigning doulas and clients during the prenatal period must be determined. Here are a few options:

- Clients are interviewed by program coordinator and a doula is carefully assigned (no client choice; best suited to volunteer programs).
- Clients are interviewed by a program coordinator who narrows down the doula pool to doulas who are available and appear to be a good match for the client. Client then has an opportunity to briefly interview two or three doulas.
- Doula profiles are published online and clients have a choice to narrow their own selection of doulas, followed by an opportunity to interview. This option, which most closely aligns with how independent doulas work, is well suited for hospital programs that use independent contractor doulas.

> ***CenteringPregnancy Programs***
>
> Yet another adaptation is the possibility of incorporating doulas into the group prenatal model pioneered by *CenteringPregnancy.* This evidence-based proprietary program might be offered to clinic patients or otherwise integrated into care by select health care providers with whom the doulas could collaborate.

Primacy of the doula–client relationship

The community-based doula program model emphasizes the primacy of the doula–client relationship, thereby sidestepping a potential drawback of some hospital-based doula programs. While all doulas should endeavor to work collaboratively with medical team members, the doula's first loyalty is to her client. However, in hospital-based models wherein the doula is an employee/representative of the hospital, the employer–employee relationship *may* trump the doula–client bond. Hospital program implementers are advised to take steps to protect the integrity of the doula's role as a mediator and client advocate. She is not there to promote compliance with hospital policy or care provider recommendations but, rather, to empower the client to make informed choices and to realize her own best vision for her birth.

Doula Scope of Practice (SOP)

All doula programs must adopt a formal SOP for participating doulas. I recommend the DONA International SOP as having set the standard for the doula profession.

However, other training organizations will have articulated their own versions of SOP, typically overlapping with DONA's more than not. Program managers may want to craft a SOP statement for their model and practice setting that is consistent with the core principles articulated in the DONA SOP. End-of-life doula program administrators should consider adopting the SOP articulated by the National End-of-Life Doula Alliance [NEDAlliance.com].

Two Community-Based Doula Program Models

Doulas Care Program

I started this award-winning program in 1998 and oversaw its development through 2007. At that time, oversight passed to a partner who had been instrumental in growing the program. Doulas Care served an average of 250 families per year in 11 counties throughout southeastern Michigan. The program closed in 2014 due to lack of funding and lapse in leadership. Since it is the model with which I am most familiar and believe there is much that can be adapted for other program models, I am sharing details below about how the program worked.

Doulas Care was conceived, from the beginning, as a win–win proposition. Women who had recently completed doula training and were eager to get to births were matched with low-income expectant mothers who desired doula support. New trainees were thereby provided with a ready opportunity to gain hands-on experience at birth and complete professional certification requirements, while moms who might otherwise face birth alone, or with inadequate support, were matched with a trained volunteer doula from their own community. Since many of the volunteers were themselves low income, a doula training scholarship program offered the opportunity to become a professionally trained and certified doula, providing a career development pathway for the volunteers. Hence the win–win core of the program.

The community-based model of care was fundamental. Our first successful grant proposal funded scholarships for low-income women from targeted communities to take professional doula training. As a payback for training, scholarship recipients agreed to provide free doula services to a minimum of five women in their community, thereby also completing professional certification requirements. Our success, over the years, in building a culturally diverse volunteer base and clientele was phenomenal. In many cases, recruits were women who had served informally in the role of doula for cousins, sisters, daughters and friends without ever calling themselves a "doula." They were the go-to women in their communities, the recognized wise women. A doula program helps these birth sisters professionalize their time-honored role, while grounding their support in evidence-based principles. By staying true to the community-based heart of the program, we can avoid the pitfalls of culturally inappropriate, authoritative care—the "we know what's best for you" approach.

The use of often inexperienced, volunteer doulas was a core element of the *Doulas Care Program* model. In terms of the advantages of using volunteers, clearly there is cost savings compared to models wherein doulas are paid. Willing volunteers are abundant and many funders will prioritize support for initiatives that promote community volunteerism. I never cease to be amazed at the ease with which *Doulas Care* was able to attract a substantial volunteer base. Annually, we averaged about 100 culturally diverse volunteers from various socioeconomic strata, ranging in age from 18 to 63. Students from local colleges and universities enrolled in nursing, midwifery, pre-med, public health and social work programs valued the opportunity to work with women in a community setting. Then there were the empty nesters and retirees who felt that it was finally "time for me" and believed that doula work was something they felt called to do. Recently unemployed women and others interested in starting a second career and intending to become self-employed professional doulas, comprised another contingent of volunteers. Social workers, outreach workers and educators already engaged in providing services to pregnant women sought to enhance the quality of their interactions and support on the job. And then there was the core group of childbearing women—those in the trenches, raising families themselves, who felt a strong empathy for other mothers. Often, these were women who were disappointed in their own birth and early parenting

Doulas Care Success Stories

Several scholarship recipients who trained with the program and completed the certification process went on to gainful employment. Four were hired by public health departments to be home visitors, one was hired by *The Doula Project* in Chicago, and one by an *Early Head Start* program to be a parent educator. A few started independent doula practices. One story involved a single mother of five hired to be a home visitor with Michigan State Extension Services. She was delighted to be earning health insurance for the first time in her children's lives, having supported her family doing night-time nanny work for years!

experiences, having lacked essential education and support, and sensing in their gut that there had to be a better way. Others simply felt that becoming a mother was the best experience in their lives and it broke their hearts to contemplate the prospect of a woman giving birth alone and frightened. Collectively, the doulas were motivated to help women's entrance into motherhood be as healthy, informed, positive and empowering as possible. I cannot imagine a more motivated, engaged and committed group of volunteers.

Challenges unique to the volunteer model include the difficulty of holding volunteers accountable for their actions. The "flake" factor will inevitably come into play. On occasion, volunteers accepted a client and neglected to make contact in a timely manner, failed to deliver services or alert the program coordinator when backup was needed, or neglected to turn in client forms. For a few, the scholarship payback proved to be a hardship. Volunteers who were single mothers and/or held down jobs with inflexible work hours, or lacked reliable transportation or childcare, found the challenges insurmountable. A low-income doula with a family to support will find it extremely difficult to be faced with the reality of missing a day's wages in order to attend a volunteer birth, a dilemma only overcome by paying the doulas a living wage for their work. Some of the accountability challenges may be addressed through the following strategies:

- Deliver a consistent message that the volunteers are part of a *program,* not just winging it on their own. Brand the program and give the volunteers an identity as participating doulas, providing nametags and logo-bearing t-shirts or sweatshirts, for example. Take every opportunity to build a sense of community among the doulas via ongoing educational opportunities, support groups, an e-newsletter, Facebook group, etc.
- Emphasize the importance of follow-through by explaining that many of the women being served by the program have experienced abandonment in their lives. If they reach out for help, are given the promise of a "special friend/mentor" and then experience rejection, the net effect of the doula program on their lives is a negative. (This is the Guilt Trip strategy.)
- Refrain from pressuring volunteers to accept clients. We made it easy for the volunteers to decline a referral. They were simply asked to respond promptly "yes" or "no." No excuses or reasons required. Some volunteers participated on a very limited basis (one or two clients per year), while others were very active, taking up to ten clients per year.
- Develop a strong administrative support component for the program. A system should be put in place that prompts the volunteer coordinator

to check in with the doulas periodically, as well as with the clients, so that problems can be identified sooner, rather than later, and promptly addressed.

- Disqualify for participation any doula with a poor track record who is not willing or able to self-correct.
- Devote a portion of your budget to doula stipends to cover the out-of-pocket costs of being a volunteer (including lost wages for missed days at work, childcare, transportation, supplies, etc.).

Services Provided

Birth Doula Services. Participating birth doulas provide a minimum of three prenatal visits, attendance at the birth, three postpartum visits and phone consultations as needed up to six weeks postpartum.

Postpartum Doula Services. Postpartum doulas provide a minimum of two three-hour visits per week for a period of two weeks. In many cases, additional hours are provided with the overall goal of engendering confidence in the mother and gradually weaning her from dependence on doula support. In special circumstances, such as families with multiples, premature or sick babies, or moms suffering from postpartum mood disorders, care may be extended up to three months. Sometimes a team of doulas provide additional hours of care in high-needs circumstances. In these cases, a lead doula ensures continuity and coordinates care so that essential information is communicated through shift changes and issues requiring follow-up don't fall through the cracks.

Initially only birth doulas were involved in the program. As community acceptance and recognition grew, a clear demand emerged to help meet the needs of newly postpartum women and their families as well. Our first call from a hospital social worker seeking support services for a postpartum mother involved a breastfeeding mother of three children under the age of five who three months earlier had been left partially paralyzed after giving birth with an epidural. The woman was about to undergo spinal surgery to repair the damage she had suffered. She had been told by medical personnel that she would need to wean her baby unless she secured around-the-clock in-hospital care throughout her post-op recovery period. Nurses would care for her, they said, but were not available to provide the infant care that she would be unable to manage on her own. Her husband was unable to do it, needing both to work and provide overnight care for the couple's two small children. An email call for support went out to the volunteer birth doulas: Would anyone be willing to take a shift so that this mom could continue to breastfeed her baby? Would they! The mother received the needed support and our volunteer postpartum doula program was born. After discharge from the hospital, the client continued to receive support as her doula helped reorganize her home, making needed items accessible from her wheelchair. She did, eventually, regain her ability to walk and became an unbridled fan of doulas and enthusiastic spokeswoman for the program.

Special Services. Some client needs led us to stretch the doula role to include "logistical" support. The volunteer coordinator endeavored to determine the scope of client needs during an initial phone interview. Enhanced doula services were provided to women with special needs including:

- Transportation to and from prenatal/postnatal care visits, to the hospital in labor, and home from the hospital after discharge
- Accompanying a single mom to a series of childbirth preparation classes as her partner and providing transportation
- Support in accessing community resources to get basic needs met for housing, food and clothing
- Bilingual doulas for non-English speakers

Program Operations

Population Served. The program was designed to serve low-income pregnant women at medical or social risk throughout 11 counties that comprise southeastern Michigan. Each client was screened to determine income eligibility using federal poverty guidelines. To qualify, household income had to be at 185 percent of poverty guidelines or less. Approximately 80 percent of women seeking doula support services were Medicaid eligible. Since African-American babies are three times more likely to die before reaching their first birthday than Caucasian babies, outreach efforts were increasingly directed toward reducing disparities for this high-risk population. Additional risk factors included:

- teen mothers
- women struggling with depression/anxiety
- previous low-birth-weight or preterm babies
- previous experience of postpartum depression/mood disorder
- previous cesarean birth

- history of addiction
- living at or below the poverty level
- lower weight gain during pregnancy
- late entry into prenatal care
- recent immigrants
- socially isolated women lacking family and social support

Reasons to Decline Services to a Client

- Failure to meet income guidelines
- Volunteer abuse demonstrated through repeated missed appointments and unreturned phone calls
- Unabated lying or manipulative behaviors
- Inappropriate expectations of the doula (e.g., free babysitter, free housecleaner, chauffeur, etc.)

Outreach. Client brochures were distributed to service providers in target communities through direct mailing and exhibiting at community baby fairs, health fairs and similar venues. Participating providers who served as referral sources included midwives, physicians, public health personnel, hospital-based social workers, community clinics, childbirth educators, other community nonprofits and so on. Women who could potentially benefit from doula support were given a brochure and encouraged to enroll in the program.

The process of connecting with referral sources was accomplished by building one relationship at a time. Presentations to service providers during monthly staff meeting proved to be a good recruitment strategy. We asked for ten minutes to share information on doulas and the program and offered to bring refreshments. There is no better way to build community than with food! In addition to program brochures in both English and Spanish, we brought calendars and mugs with the program's name, logo and website imprinted. The gifts left behind reinforced the program's existence and ensured that contact information could be easily accessed.

Volunteer Recruitment. As an approved DONA International doula training center, volunteer recruitment was not especially challenging for our program. Women from all demographics and persuasions are drawn to support their sisters at birth and immediately afterwards and the DONA brand is well known. For the most part, they came to us. Several volunteers were women who had themselves been served by the program. Ask if folks will pass an announcement along to their email lists. Post flyers in the community and then brainstorm additional possibilities. Local universities and colleges provide another fertile pool of potential volunteers. Reach out and identify sympathetic instructors in nursing, public health, premed, social work, child development and women studies programs. Offer to give a presentation on the status of maternal–infant health in the United States, show a short video, introduce the doula solution and program, and leave time for Q&A. Make a compelling case and you will not only engender a steady stream of enthusiastic doula volunteers, you will initiate life-altering insights for the next generation of birthing women. You will be planting seeds of passion, I guarantee.

Making the Match. So, how did the process work? Shortly after a doula training weekend, a Volunteer Orientation was scheduled. Eligible volunteers must be at least 18 years old, residents of counties served by the program and have completed formal doula training. The volunteers were given time to complete an in-depth questionnaire and the following information was entered into a volunteer database:

- Name
- Contact information (phone, email)
- Address
- Age
- Ethnicity
- Religion, if any
- Languages spoken, including fluency level
- Number of children
- Number of births attended
- Profession/work history
- Related training/skills
- Experience working with families during the childbearing year
- Experience with newborns
- Areas of interest/expertise (e.g., substance abuse, teen pregnancy, depression, multiples)
- Limits on travel radius
- Preferred hospitals or care providers
- Areas of discomfort regarding clients served (e.g., smokers, pet allergies)

- Preference for working with a particular demographic (e.g., lesbian moms, Muslim couples, teen moms); we found that some volunteers wanted to limit their services to one specific target population
- Anticipated availability or conflicts for the coming year
- Comfort level in providing services (prenatally, at birth, postpartum)
- Special concerns
- Willingness or capacity to go beyond the minimum service package
- Willingness to serve as a backup doula
- Interest in helping with outreach efforts

One lesson learned early on was to require clients to call the program directly for services. On occasion, a health care provider or a social worker called on behalf of a client, often with the client sitting in her office. We learned that poor follow-through on the part of the prospective client was a common outcome in this scenario and we subsequently required that clients demonstrate a desire for a doula. Essentially, we were giving them a hoop to jump through in order to qualify for services. This cut down on the disappointment of a volunteer showing up for an appointment and the client being a no-show. The only exception allowed was for clients who could not speak English, though eventually a bilingual volunteer coordinator was hired to return these calls and enroll women in the program.

When a woman called seeking doula services, a scripted phone interview was conducted. If the caller qualified for services, the following information was collected and entered into the database:

- Name
- Contact information (phone, email)
- Address
- Age
- Ethnicity
- Religion, if any
- Self-identification of income level (lower, middle, higher)
- Type of insurance (Medicaid, state-financed programs, private insurance, uninsured)
- Baby's due date
- Planned place of birth

- Care provider type (OB/GYN, family practice doctor, CNM, direct-entry midwife, other)
- Care provider's name and location
- Partner involvement? (name and relationship)
- First child? If no, then following questions were asked:
  - » Number of living children; their ages?
  - » Vaginal or cesarean births?
  - » Any history of preterm labor, low-birth-weight baby, complications?
  - » Any other significant medical history?
  - » Planned VBAC?
- Month or week of pregnancy that prenatal care began
- Plans regarding feeding the baby
- Living situation; support at home?
- Depression Screening Questions (Note: these were added later, as part of a grant proposal aimed at providing screening and support for depressed mothers. If the mother answered "yes" to any of the three questions, then she would be encouraged to complete the full Edinburgh Postnatal Depression Scale.)
  - » Have you or anyone in your family had periods of sadness and depression?
  - » Have you had symptoms of sadness or depression during this pregnancy or after the birth of a previous child?
  - » Are you feeling anxious, worried or sad now?
- Race/ethnicity
- Employment status; if employed ...
  - » Currently on medical leave (why?)
  - » After baby, will take maternity leave
  - » Plan on returning to work after the baby (how soon?)
  - » Will quit job but planning to return to the workforce (how soon?)
- Occupation or profession
- Highest level of education completed
- How did she hear about the program?

- What prompted her to contact the program?
- Any concerns/issues to share in terms of what she wants from a doula?

This interview averaged about 15 to 20 minutes in length. The level of detail requested helps program administrators identify key information about the population being served by the program which is essential when making the case to funders for support.

After completing the interview, the volunteer coordinator consulted the doula database to make the match. Care is taken to make appropriate matches, according to doula–client preferences and needs. For example, a highly anxious 38-year-old primip would not be matched with an 18-year-old doula who has never had a baby nor attended a single birth. Next an email was sent out to the potential volunteer containing only information on location, due date, whether it's a first baby and special needs identified (if any). Doulas were asked to respond within 48 hours. If the first doula solicited for the match declines, then the coordinator moves on to her next best option. In cases where time is short (e.g., "My due date was yesterday"), the coordinator occasionally emailed the entire group to solicit a volunteer. Potluck is not perfect, but it seemed to work out surprisingly well.

Once the match is made, the doula is emailed the client's name, contact information and a few more details from the phone interview. The ball is now in the doula's court to contact the client and she is urged to make contact as soon as possible. We found that some doulas would wait for a period of two weeks or more before making contact, often due to pending scheduling concerns. Clients were disappointed by these delays and perceived it as "she doesn't want to be my doula." So, we began to emphasize the importance of making prompt contact, even if the doula was not available to meet the client immediately. The client was also informed that a doula had been chosen for her and that her doula would be contacting her soon.

While an occasional prospective client asked to "interview several doulas," we deemed this to not be acceptable treatment of our volunteers. Why should a volunteer be set up to face potential rejection? It struck me as abusive. In the volunteer model, doulas are assigned. If the match turns out to not be a good one and a happy rapport does not develop between the two parties, then we were always willing to attempt a rematch. Rarely, women dropped out of the program if they were dissatisfied with the assigned volunteer, despite our willingness to find a different doula or other attempts to address any issues.

Program Staffing

As a true grassroots effort, initially I trained the doulas, did the community outreach, took client calls and coordinated the match. On occasion, I served as the doula as well! Over time, as funding streams were developed and demand for the program grew, a part-time volunteer coordinator was hired to take calls from women seeking services. Additional positions were added organically, based on emerging needs and available funds. This is how the staffing worked once we matured as a program:

Executive Director provides guidance for program design and oversees staff and operations; writes grants, manages grant budgets and files grant reports. Estimated 50 percent of ED's time.

Grant Writer/Director of Evaluation assists in program design and grant writing; oversees all program evaluation components; publishes program evaluation reports. Part-time, project oriented and deadline driven.

Volunteer Coordinator matches doulas with clients seeking services and provides follow-up support. We used a software program called ACT! for doula–client tracking. 25 hours per week.

Education/Outreach Coordinator coordinates all outreach efforts for the program; develops continuing education programs to meet the needs of the doulas; supervises service-learning interns. 15 hours per week.

Latina Outreach Coordinator coordinates referrals for Spanish-speaking clients and bilingual volunteers; promotes the program within the Latina community, including outreach to both providers and parents. 5 hours per week.

Social Work Consultant provides consultation to the volunteer coordinator and the doulas to help support new families dealing with challenges beyond typical doula expertise. This role need not be separate from the volunteer coordinator if that person is an MSW. Having an MSW associated with the program qualified us to become a placement site for MSW student interns which was a big benefit. 5 hours per week.

Student Interns. As the program grew in scope, the need for additional help emerged. Hence, the development of a student intern program. We were lucky to be in a town that is also home to a large university. Likely candidates are graduate students in Social Work and Public Health. We also drew interested students from Women's Studies and the School of Nursing who needed to complete service-learning requirements. Master's level student interns brought more value because they were often seeking more substantial placements lasting from several months to a year. While they preferred a site that paid interns a stipend, our organization was never able to offer one and we were nevertheless able to attract quality help. If we were a good fit for the students' career objectives, then they found a way to finance it. We did offer complimentary attendance at all our professional trainings as compensation. Because interns are seeking to enhance skills or gain exposure to educational opportunities, we endeavored to build those components into their placement experience, individualizing expectations as much as was reasonable while still getting our needs met.

Sometimes the effort required to integrate help can feel overwhelming. Given how over-the-top busy I was, I felt daunted at the notion of recruiting, interviewing, training and supervising student interns, only to have to turn around a few months later and start all over again with the next batch (hence the Education/Outreach Coordinator position came into being). My best advice here is to start small with one or two interns. Provide them with a specific project and define what the "deliverable" (end-product of their work) will be. Give them enough structure to succeed and weed out applicants who will need a lot of hand holding to get the job done. If part of what you need help with is simple clerical tasks involving mailings, copying and collating, then be sure to say up front that they will be expected to pitch in and help with these tasks. Minimum commitment of five hours per week.

Work–Study Students. As a nonprofit organization, we qualified to participate in the local university's work/study program (see Chapter 4 for more information). This allowed us to hire part-time administrative help and data-entry personnel at half the cost. Estimated 5 hours per week.

Training and Support for Volunteers

Core Doula Training. Birth and postpartum doulas serving with the program were primarily trained by an approved DONA International trainer and curriculum. The 23- and 30-hour trainings included the pre-requisite classes and fulfilled certification requirements. Doulas trained by other organizations were also welcomed into the program and were simply required to provide proof of having completed professional doula training and agree to abide by the specified scope of practice. While low-income women were eligible to apply for training scholarships, at least half of the volunteers in the program paid for their doula training (which helped to underwrite costs).

Volunteer Orientation. Early program evaluation results, including data gleaned from focus groups with the volunteer doulas, revealed that many volunteers felt unprepared to meet the unique needs of the population served by the program. For the most part, the doulas were "birth junkies" trained to explore the development of a birth plan with the expectant mother and provide hands-on support at the birth. In some instances, however, the doulas were matched with homeless women whose primary concern was whether Children's Protective Services would take

Volunteer Orientation Agenda

Part I: The Nuts and Bolts: Policies, Procedures and Benefits for Volunteers

- Introductions and meet the staff
- Brainstorm: Who are we serving?
- Program Overview
- Scope of Practice
- Expectations, policies and procedures
- Volunteer benefits and supports
- How the referral process works
- Use of forms with clients
- Use of the Edinburgh Postpartum Depression Scale
- Meet the Doula (bring in a current volunteer to speak about her experience)
- Completion of Volunteer Survey
- Signing of Volunteer Contract

Part II: Outreach Worker Training

- General risk assessment during the childbearing year
- Postpartum mood disorders and the doula
- Domestic violence awareness and the doula
- Multicultural awareness
- Values clarification
- Community resources and referrals

their baby away if they were unable to find affordable housing before the birth. Clearly, birth plans take a back seat when survival issues are on the table! Furthermore, helping doulas to establish good boundaries with their clients emerged as THE primary issue with which the doulas needed help. In response to these challenges, a two-part orientation program was developed. Part I was designed to enroll the volunteers in the program and explain administrative policies and procedures. Part II expands the role of the doula as a community outreach worker and provides training in perinatal risk factors and related topics (see sidebar).

Continuing Education. To address the ongoing training needs of doula volunteers, continuing education programs were offered at regular intervals throughout the year, typically using expert speakers in the community who donated their time. Topics included breastfeeding support, bereavement support, boundary setting, nutrition, effects of sexual abuse on childbearing and trauma-informed care, and more. We obtained continuing education contact hours for these sessions and opened them to professionals in the community for a fee, thereby creating a revenue stream (and more friends!) for the program.

Supervision. It can be helpful to have peers to debrief with after a particularly challenging birth. Our partners, after all, have a limited capacity for listening to birth stories. My very indulgent husband claims to know WAY more about birth than his natural curiosity would lead him to acquire—"TMI" as they say. A support group for doulas is a great solution, serving as a venue for group problem solving, learning from each other's mistakes and identifying common themes for future training. It is essential that group members vigorously protect client confidentiality in presenting cases, reiterating and enforcing the rules at every session.

Other volunteer supports included the ongoing availability of the volunteer coordinator who systematically checked in with the doulas. The ability to offer on-call emergency support or weekend coverage to the doulas was never within our program capacity, but the doulas were encouraged to call and discuss any concerns. Hands down, the most common challenges experienced by volunteers revolved around the issue of doula–client boundaries. Some clients were flaky, missing appointments or neglecting to return phone calls prenatally and then expecting the doula to be available at the last minute to attend the birth. Others would call at inappropriate times of the day or night, expecting unlimited time and support from the doula. Still others would make inappropriate requests of the doula such as asking her to babysit or wanting the doula to provide transportation so she could go out nightclubbing! Part of the coordinator's job was not merely to reinforce

Summary of Volunteer Benefits

- Scholarship-funded, comprehensive doula training for low-income women
- Community outreach worker training and manual of resources
- Monthly doula support group
- Quarterly volunteer newsletter
- Online resources
- Regular continuing educational opportunities, with contact hours approved (designed in response to needs identified by the doulas themselves)
- Phone counseling as needed
- Lending library containing multiple copies of all the books required for certification
- Program-branded items (personalized name badge, t-shirt, doula supply bag)
- Assistance in paying certification fees
- Doula stipends
- Ability to quickly fulfill the experiential, hands-on component of doula certification requirements
- Ability to put new skills into practice soon after training
- Excellent service-learning opportunity for school credit
- Encouragement (and training!) to build independent doula businesses
- Excellent venue for community service
- Résumé builder with program administrators serving as references for job and school opportunities down the road
- Increase competitive edge for students applying to midwifery or other advanced-degree programs
- A community of doulas forming an extended support network
- Satisfaction of making a significant difference for new families
- Professional backup and troubleshooting support for tricky or high-risk situations
- Annual Doula Appreciation Night
- Great food at all events
- Regular praise and thanks!

the importance of setting professional boundaries, but to role play with the doula how to do so effectively, if needed.

> One woman, employed as a home visitor with the public health department, told me, ***"You know you have a boundary problem when your client asks you to co-sign their car loan."*** Indeed. Yikes!

We began to implement systematic boundary setting on behalf of the doulas. The basic idea was to frame a consistent message to clients regarding reasonable expectations of their doula via program brochures, phone interview and a welcome letter. Before ever meeting their doula, clients were given the same message in multiple ways. Then, the onus was on the doula to enforce the boundaries. (See Chapter 7 for more on this topic.)

Honestly, a whole range of issues came up. There was the client whose postpartum doula reported witnessing that the family did not have a working toilet in the home on more than one occasion (we identified resources to pay the water bill). There was the teen mother being discriminated against by hospital personnel who were refusing access to her newborn for reasons that were unclear (we got the hospital's Patient Advocate involved and a quick resolution followed). There was the postpartum doula trying unsuccessfully to avoid being swept into a Black Hole of Need after being assigned to assist a family with newborn triplets and a father hospitalized with severe depression (we encouraged her to set firm boundaries on what she *could* do, got a doula team in place, and validated that the doula's contributions were valuable). And there was the doula whose client met her at the front door when she came to visit and insisted that they conduct the prenatal meeting as a walk around the block for an hour, while her husband stayed home (What's going on? Hostile dad? Abusive relationship?). Just a few red flags …

Doula Stipends. Stipend amounts ranged from $25 to $100, depending on available funding. They were never intended to represent the value of the doula's work but rather to reimburse some of the out-of-pocket expenses of being a volunteer (such as gas, parking fees, child care or lost wages from missed work days).

Certification Support. Some funders were particularly aligned with the career development aspect of the program and covered not only the cost of training but also certification fees. Only scholarship recipients who had fulfilled all requirements of their contract were eligible for this benefit.

Feed and Appreciate the Doulas! Volunteer appreciation is key. During orientation programs, support groups and trainings, the doulas were fed well. Our interns would persuade caterers to donate a meal or otherwise hunt down contributions. We hosted a Volunteer Appreciation Night each year. Lights were strung up, small gifts donated, massage therapists provided free massages, and festive food was served. It was the staff's turn to nurture the nurturers!

Tracking the Data/Evaluation Pitfalls

Evaluation is an essential component of program development. No matter how modestly you start out, be sure and track what you are doing from the very beginning. At a minimum, gather the demographics on clients served and track services provided. To be attractive to funders and draw supporters to the program, it will also be necessary to gather data on OUTCOMES. See Chapter 6 for an in-depth discussion of outcomes, program evaluation and specifics on what to track. Funders require that grant objectives be framed in terms of *measurable outcomes.* Simply reporting on numbers served and how those numbers break down in terms of your target population (documenting *the process*) is not the same as demonstrating the true value of your program.

You will need to develop forms for the doulas to use with their clients and implore, demand or bribe the doulas to comply. The consistent failure of a percentage of our volunteer doulas to turn in forms on clients was an ongoing challenge and frustration for program managers. Here are a few strategies:

- Present the forms as a requirement for participation in the program at the very first volunteer orientation session.
- Role play how to use the forms with clients.
- Emphasize that program sustainability depends upon gathering this data.
- Make volunteer stipends dependent upon form submission at the completion of client services; give them a deadline (e.g., within four weeks of completing services) in order to qualify for the stipend.
- Enable doulas to enter information directly into an online system.
- Track doula compliance and follow up with doulas who have forms outstanding (a good task for student interns).
- Stop referrals to doulas who consistently refuse to comply and notify them of this action.

Clients should be included in the evaluation process. Mothers were mailed an evaluation form, along with a self-addressed, stamped envelope, at the completion of services. Ideally, clients should also be given the option to enter their feedback directly into an online system. The client evaluation form asks the same set of questions as the doula forms, but from the mother's perspective. Include questions regarding the mother's feelings about having a doula (would she do so again?) and whether she felt her doula was responsive and capable. If mothers do not complete the forms, a staff member can call and attempt to complete it with them over the phone. When language or literacy barriers proved to be obstacles, our bilingual coordinator visited the woman and completed forms in person.

Finally, we must then take the data, run the reports and publish the results. Key areas to highlight are specific measures of improved health outcomes for moms and babies. Findings from this report will:

- constitute the content of periodic mandated grant reports,
- be included in your organization's annual report,
- be published on your website and
- provide the basis for ongoing fundraising efforts.

Overall, a positive evaluation report helps to make the argument for continuation of the doula program. It is the only way of knowing whether you have accomplished your goals and objectives. It reveals your weaknesses, allowing you to do better. Sing your own praises! Better still, let your numbers and results sing for you. Solicit testimonials from both clients and doulas. Take pictures of your program in action, of the doulas supporting clients (have a photo contest!). Put the very best pictures and testimonials to work for you to raise money for the program. While some potential funders/donors may only skim the details of a proposal, they can be engaged emotionally with a compelling story and picture. And remember, while program managers might get away with neglecting to crunch the numbers and publish a report for one grant cycle, or even two, they are quite likely to see funding streams go dry if they cannot demonstrate *proof of benefit over time.* So, keep program evaluation front and center.

Organic Program Growth

It's great to dream big. I would be the last person to suggest that anyone think small. That said, keep your ideas focused and allow the program to grow in stages, organically, recognizing opportunities as you go. There will be serendipities that occur, unexpected help from various quarters and funding trends that emerge. With your vision in mind, you will get there one step at a time. Be patient with this process and don't overwhelm yourself by trying to roll the whole thing out at once. Allow it to unfold and adapt as you go.

For example, you might want to start your grassroots program in your home county, providing only birth or only postpartum doula services. Train the doulas. Get your systems in place. Make connections with care providers and referral sources. Organize your fundraising efforts and identify potential grant opportunities. Believe me, that right there is a big bite for the first year. In your second year, you will want to do some program evaluation and refinement, all the while looking for funders who are the right match for you. Over time, you can add components such as expanding into neighboring counties with high-needs populations, addressing funder-driven issues such as postpartum depression or breastfeeding, or targeting specific ethnic groups suffering from disparities in birth outcomes (see Chapter 6, Working with Multiple Funders).

HealthConnect One Program

Not all community-based doula programs are volunteer based, as evidenced by the model created by HealthConnect One (HC One) [HealthConnectOne.org] wherein the doulas are hired by the program to provide services to a specific target population. There are five essential components to their model:

1. Employ women who are trusted members of the target community.
2. Extend and intensify the role of doula with families from early pregnancy through the first months postpartum.
3. Collaborate with community stakeholders/institutions and use a diverse team approach.
4. Facilitate experiential learning using popular education techniques and the HC One training curriculum.
5. Value the doulas' work with salary, supervision and support.

Since 1986, HC One has worked closely with over 70 sites in 28 states to replicate their community-based doula and breastfeeding peer counselor programs. Replication involves a formal partnership whereby HC One guides agencies through distinctive phases of planning and program development, providing consultation and technical support at each stage. Each site serves a unique at-risk population, from non-English-speaking immigrants, to women in addiction treatment, to teen mothers and so on. Model replication costs for the first year of services are $100,000 followed by an estimated $75,000 per year to keep the program running.

HC One outcomes include the following effects (for more details and published reports, see their website). Whether you are seeking to replicate this model or one of your own creation, these are the themes that have emerged where doulas have demonstrated benefit. Keep them in mind as you begin to search for potential funding sources for your program.

- fewer preterm births
- increased breastfeeding rates
- increased birth weight
- fewer medical interventions in the birth process
- fewer cesarean deliveries
- more positive birth experiences
- increased mother–child interaction
- improved parenting skills
- lowering the cost of health care
- lowering teen pregnancy rates
- decreasing incidence of child abuse and neglect through increased family attachment
- improving school readiness through increased family attachment
- career development for unskilled women who become doulas
- reducing health disparities
- decreasing discrimination by bridging gaps between clients and medical care providers

Funding Community-Based Doula Programs

First Steps: Procure Seed Money. If you are in the initial stages of considering establishing a community-based doula program, or perhaps even founding your own nonprofit, the first step is to identify enthusiastic supporters in your community who will provide seed money for your project. One or two major private donors would be a great start. A few more who can be ongoing "special friends of the program" is even better. Your target goal will depend on the model you intend to implement and the help/talent you have available.

If you feel absolutely daunted by this prospect and are not willing to go out now and raise money for this idea; if you are not committed to becoming a fundraiser;

if you think you can do this in a vacuum, by yourself, without help; if you're a dreamer, not a doer—then do yourself a favor and give it up before you start. However, if the vision in your mind and the fire in your belly compel you forward, and you succeed in raising the necessary seed money, then you will have a promising foundation upon which to build your program!

Grants. The community-based volunteer doula program model is likely to be primarily (though it should not be wholly) a grant-funded program. As a public health intervention, it is both innovative and proactive. It is also evidence based. With its focus on prevention, the model is not a hard sell to the right funder. Numerous foundations identify priority areas for support that are a natural fit with doula programs, such as women's health, women's career development, prematurity and infant mortality, infant mental health, community volunteerism, family health initiatives and more. Learn to write a competitive grant proposal to the right funder and you will get funded! See Chapter 6 for a grant writing primer.

Fundraising. First the bad news: fundraising never stops! This is simply a fact of life in the nonprofit sector. Few grants will cover overhead costs such as rent, utilities or salaries for full-time employees in the organization. In grant-speak, these are "indirect" program costs. Viability as an organization depends upon the ability to generate non-grant-dependent funding streams to cover indirect costs. Therefore, persistent cultivation of community supporters is essential to survival of the program. Recruit some fundraisers to your board of directors; be careful not to just load the board up with birth junkies (we love them, but we need money!).

Now the good news: the case for doulas is strong. Everybody gets it that a new mother coming home with twins is going to need some extra help or she will likely fall prey to severe sleep deprivation, depression or complications such as hemorrhage or infection. If she is just a few days post-surgery and has a toddler to boot, the situation becomes dire. Throw into the mix that she is a single mother or the non-English-speaking wife of a foreign graduate student lacking in family or community support, and you have hospital social workers frantically scrambling for resources. You see what I mean? It does not take a great leap of imagination to establish that gaps in essential services exist, thereby making the case for financial support. Doulas do make a difference! And fundraising can never be put on the back burner.

Revenue-Generating Ideas. A charitable doula program can be underwritten by offering programs that generate a revenue stream such as childbirth preparation and other programs for parents, as demonstrated by the model established by Center for the Childbearing Year. The Center also offered fee-based birth and postpartum doula trainings. Eventually, we added a sliding-scale fee-for-service component to the volunteer program for women who called but did not qualify for free services. What other strategies can you and your board of directors dream up?

Community Partnerships. Do your homework! Your idea to serve underserved childbearing families does not exist in a vacuum. A community-based doula program can certainly fill an unmet need, but you must think in terms of collaboration with established programs rather than competing with them. As you begin the process of information gathering, you are, in effect, building community partnerships and identifying "friends" of the proposed doula program. Identify the limitations of existing programs. Your program will be well received if it is perceived to be filling a gap.

Where are the gaps? When I started *Doulas Care,* there were a handful of programs in the community working to support at-risk pregnant women. A collaborative group had formed to address racial disparities in birth outcomes, in particular the high rate of premature birth among African-American women in Ypsilanti, Michigan. This group had put together a *Sister-to-Sister Program.* The *Sister-to-Sister Program* did not use the word "doula," but was based on the concept of individualized support and mentoring. The population served by the program was a very targeted (and limited) demographic. Opportunities for collaboration between the two programs included shared training needs and cross referrals when one program could better serve a given woman.

The local public health department also had maternal–infant health advocates on staff who worked with the same *Doulas Care* target audience. Often the advocates attended births, as translators, for non-English-speaking clients. The addition of bilingual birth doulas to our volunteer base, offering of doula training scholarships for the public health advocates and cross-referral options were well-received collaborative efforts.

Another gap in services emerged in discussions with the Visiting Nurses Association affiliated with a local hospital. The nurses were limited to one postpartum home visit per patient lasting approximately one hour and focused on medical concerns of mom and baby. Limited breastfeeding support and infant-care education were included. Clearly, the nurses were trying to fill a significant vacuum in postpartum mother–baby care in the community. There is a tiny bit of overlap between the two roles, but there is much room for collaboration as the nurses' time is so limited and they are not really providing the much-needed emotional and hands-on household help consistent with the postpartum doula's role.

I think you can get the idea. An essential pathway to establishing credibility for your program is to do so in collaboration with other agencies by filling in "service gaps" and "meeting unmet needs." These are not only buzzwords of the grant makers, but building community partnerships on these principles will generate referrals to your program and assure the needed letters of support to potential funders.

Hospital-Based Doula Programs

Here too, there are many variations and models. Hospital programs can be volunteer based, employ the doulas or use independent contractor doulas. They might provide birth doula services only or postpartum services or both. Doulas might rotate on-call shifts for birth-only services or provide continuity of care including prenatal and postpartum care. Hospital programs can be revenue producing or charitable or both, with grants and donors underwriting a sliding-scale fee structure and free services for very low-income families. These are all decisions which must be made.

Where to Start?

Support by upper management is essential—a deal-breaker even. Identify your primary advocate here. In many hospitals, doula programs are under the umbrella of the childbirth education department. Use a multi-disciplinary team to undertake a preliminary exploration of the viability of a doula program at the hospital. Team members can include a labor and delivery nurse supervisor, a midwife, a couple of OBs, a manager from the childbirth education department, the family birth center director, a NICU nurse or parent advocate, a representative from the marketing department, an administrator, and so on. The team can engage in a preliminary discussion on goals and vision for the doula program, the type of model that might work best, potential stumbling blocks and identification of other key players to bring into the conversation. For the program to work, there needs to be buy-in from the bottom up and the top down so good communication and team building are essential. Advocates will need to talk with everyone who is going to be affected. Emphasize the benefits of doulas who are acting within scope of practice.

As an early step in the process, research the hospital's mission, values and vision. If the target hospital is part of a large system of hospitals owned by one entity, then scrutinize the parent company's website to learn more. Building your case

Benefits to the Hospital

- Win–Win: Doula programs provide a low-cost opportunity to *improve maternal-infant health outcomes and address disparities,* while saving health care dollars.
- Doulas represent an *integrated, holistic approach* consistent with St. Mary's goals and values.
- Doulas provide a cost-effective opportunity to improve the overall quality of the family's labor, birth and postpartum experience, with benefits extending well beyond the service period.
- Doula programs provide a *comprehensive blanket of maternity services* that enhances *continuity of patient care,* while meeting and *exceeding customer needs and expectations.*
- A doula program will create enhanced marketing opportunities in a competitive environment, securing *"customers for life"* who are loyal to St. Mary's Hospital.
- A doula program can help St. Mary's Hospital expand its *community benefit ministry to meet unmet needs in vulnerable populations.*
- The program presents an opportunity to demonstrate national leadership in providing effective, compassionate, comprehensive and innovative maternal–infant health services. This is truly superior care that will move St. Mary's Hospital toward realization of their 2020 Vision.
- A doula program presents an opportunity to realize St. Mary's *mission of "caring excellence."*

involves demonstrating how a doula program can help the organization "walk the talk" of their stated mission and goals. See the sidebar for sample language adapted for St. Mary's Hospital (fictional name) that is part of a chain of Catholic-owned hospitals. Italicized words represent concepts and language taken from the parent corporation's website.

Variables Unique to Hospital Doula Programs

Doulas as Employees vs. Independent Contractors (ICs)

The main difference here is that ICs do not qualify for hospital benefits and are responsible for their own taxes (see Chapter 1 for more information), resulting in cost savings for the hospital. The primary downside of ICs may be a less stable pool of doulas. ICs are, by definition, likely to have some clients referred by the hospital (with the hospital taking a cut of the fee) and others who are private-pay clients (doula keeps the full fee). ICs, who have primary accountability to their clients, set their own fees, are interviewed by prospective clients, offer prenatal and postpartum meetings, and provide labor support, much like private practice doulas. The main difference is the hospital is referring to their own vetted team of doulas and processing fees for services. At the Swedish Hospital Doula Program in Seattle, WA, the hospital retains a small portion of the IC doula's fee for program administration and another portion is used to provide low-income families with doulas at no cost. Another program that uses ICs offers a 70/30 percent doula/program split with clients paying market rates.

Fee-Based Models

Again, variable approaches abound. Most programs have a set fee that the hospital collects from the family for doula services. Many offer considerations for low-income families with the hospital subsidizing Medicaid-dependent or military families. A couple of programs offer a two-tiered system, charging a lower fee for "apprentice doulas" (trained, non-certified, inexperienced, with mentoring) and market price for experienced, certified doulas. Doulas may be paid for shift work, like nurses and other hospital personnel, or per birth. The latter per-birth option ensures that the laboring mother gets the all-important continuous support.

Coverage

When an on-call shift system is in place, doulas are assigned to 8–, 12– or 24–hour shifts. Doulas are paid established fees for on-call and per birth. In some staff programs, doulas are expected to be at the hospital during their shift to be available to any woman at any time. When not helping a laboring mama, the doula might help with a variety of needs on the unit, from breastfeeding support to holding babies (though take care not to dilute the doula's role with other responsibilities; her primary focus should be on the client). On the other hand, if demand exceeds available help, the hospital might put into place additional resources to ensure coverage such as a call/text list of doulas.

Some Possibilities ...

On-Call Birth Doula Services Model. The program coordinator creates a rotating call schedule for the doulas. Doulas are assigned on-call shifts and respond when a client comes into the hospital in labor and requests a doula. The doula is paid at a lower rate for on-call time if her services are not needed and at the established reimbursement rate if she attends the birth. On-call doulas also respond to "Warm-Line" calls (see below). The doula provides a continuous presence during labor and birth and does one postpartum follow-up visit. Benefits of this model include greater flexibility of scheduling for the doula, possibly reducing doula burn out. Under this model, clients might be offered the following services:

- **A Prenatal Planning & Information Packet.** Contains valuable information about the doula services and non-drug pain management, as well as instructions and a template for creating a birth plan.
- **Monthly Meet-the-Doulas Open House.** An opportunity each month is provided for expectant parents to meet the doula staff, interact with them, take a tour of the birth center and get their questions answered.
- **Prenatal Doula Warm Line.** For nonemergency questions, clients leave a message a doula returns the call within 24 hours.
- **24-Hour On-Call Doula Coverage.** A team of doulas will be on-call 24 hours a day, available whenever labor starts. The on-call doula will meet the woman and her partner at the hospital and provide continuous labor support, staying for an hour or two after the baby is born.
- **Postpartum Visit.** One postpartum follow-up home visit is provided by the same doula who attends the birth.
- **Postpartum Doula Warm Line.** For nonemergency questions up to six weeks postpartum, clients may leave a message on the doula warm line and receive a return call within 24 hours.

Continuity of Care Model. Clients are assigned a birth doula and a backup doula and begin to build a trusting relationship during the prenatal period. The doula provides a continuous presence during labor and birth and does one postpartum follow-up visit. Benefits of this model include extension of care into the prenatal period. Drawbacks include a less flexible 24/7 on-call period of two weeks before and up to two weeks after the woman's due date. Doula burnout is a risk. One strategy to avoid burnout is to assign a team of doulas who rotate on-call duties; both go to prenatal visit(s); person who does the birth provides the postpartum follow-up visit.

Hybrid Models. There any number of variations within variations. It gets complicated. Hybrids, such as the two-tiered systems mentioned earlier (apprentice doulas and certified doulas), have evolved from simpler models that needed tweaking. It makes sense to me that creating an ongoing training program of select doulas who

Summary Table of Variables Based on Doula Status			
Comparison Parameter	**Employees**	**Independent Contractors**	**Volunteers**
Doula training	Required; hospital may or may not provide	Already trained and practicing in community	Provided by hospital
Doula certification	Required	Required	Not required; working towards certification; program provides means and mentoring for completing requirements
Continuity of care (prenatal)	Variable; yes, if doula or doula team is pre-assigned and prenatal visit(s) are included	Yes	No; doulas meet clients in labor; may have met at a "Meet the Doulas" event
Continuity of care (birth)	Variable; continuity is lost with rotating shifts of doulas or if doula is required to care for more than one client at a time	Yes, but doulas may call in team member/backup doula if birth goes long	Variable; on-call doula may stay to complete birth when shift is over or let next on-call doula take over
Continuity of care (postpartum)	Variable; some programs do not include postpartum follow-up visits or calls	Yes; one postpartum home visit and phone support up to 6 weeks post-birth are common	Variable; some programs do not include postpartum follow-up visits or calls
Client choice in selection of doula	Variable; matches made by program coordinator; or clients may interview several doulas and choose; no choice if doulas work shifts	Variable; matches made by program coordinator; or clients may interview several doulas and choose	Usually no choice; client gets the doula who is on-call

Comparison Parameter	Employees	Independent Contractors	Volunteers
Doula pay	Salary and benefits paid by hospital	IC doula paid by hospital; receives a percentage of client fees; no benefits	No salary; may receive free training, mentoring, small stipend
Client fees paid to hospital	Client charged a fee for doula services; may have sliding scale or fee waivers for low-income	Client charged a fee for doula services; hospital may subsidize a charitable component for low-income families	No fee for services; fundraising and grants to cover administrative program expenses
Quality of doula care	High; uses trained, experienced and certified doulas	High; uses trained, experienced and certified doulas	Variable; uses least experienced, uncertified doulas
Doula turnover/ burn-out potential	Low, especially if doulas have regular time off-call and benefits; hybrid models allow hospital to have a doula pipeline so volunteers who have completed requirements and are fully trained and vetted, can move into paid positions as needed	Medium; retention improves if doulas make a competitive wage and have regular time off-call	High; may be difficult to keep program staffed sufficiently to meet the need
Doula mentoring and support	Mentoring and group problem solving can be built into the program; continuing educational sessions offered regularly; supervision by program manager who is a doula	Variable	Mentoring can be systematically built in, especially with hybrid models in which more experienced doulas are available; continuing educational sessions offered regularly; support provided to complete certification requirements

Swedish Hospital Doula Program Model, Seattle, WA

Fee-based program offers two tiers of support:

- Apprentice doula services valued at $500. Swedish apprentice doulas have completed doula training and are working toward completion of certification requirements. They are hand-selected by Swedish from the graduates of their doula training course and receive mentorship from Swedish certified doulas.
- Certified doula services valued at $800–$2500, depending on experience.

Service package:

- One or two in-person prenatal meetings
- Phone and email support throughout pregnancy
- Attendance at labor and delivery
- One in-home visit after baby is born
- Phone or email support to troubleshoot questions until baby is one month old

Doula Selection

Prospective clients are encouraged to call the doula program office and complete a phone interview with the program coordinator. The coordinator will then make recommendations of doulas who have availability for the woman's due date. Next, the client is encouraged to review the doulas' profiles on the Swedish website to determine which ones she wants to interview. The doulas offer free 30–45 minute in-person interviews.

In the 2016 Swedish Doula Program Annual Report, 98 percent of providers said the doulas had a positive impact on the patient experience and 98 percent said they wanted to work with a doula again. (See Resources for a copy of the Report.)

come up through the ranks and are ready to step in as needed might contribute significantly to the stability of the program over time.

Cesarean Support Package. With this option, the doula arrives two hours prior to the scheduled C-section and offers emotional support and comfort measures as parents await surgery. She answers questions and addresses any concerns. Immediately postop, she gives comfort measures and support for the initiation of breastfeeding and skin-to-skin contact between mother and baby. She provides one postpartum home visit to assist with maternal recovery, breastfeeding and newborn care concerns.

Doula Training

All doulas participating in the program should receive high-quality, professional doula training that reinforces the doula's scope of practice. Hospitals may want to sponsor regular fee-based trainings, open to the public, to increase awareness of the program and help with doula recruitment. Encourage the labor and delivery nurses to take doula training as well (offer continuing ed contact hours as an inducement). Training will enhance nurses' labor support skills and understanding of the doula's role, fostering camaraderie between the two parties and hopefully heading off turf battles.

As in the community-based model presented earlier, an orientation program should be designed to ensure smooth integration of doulas into the maternity care team. The orientation should cover: requirements for staff/volunteers (e.g., TB test, immunizations); any hospital-specific trainings (e.g., HIPAA compliance); and doula program logistics. Finally, offer ongoing continuing education programs to enhance skills and address emerging needs of the doulas.

Budget Items

- Personnel (program coordination and management, doula salaries, and benefits for full-time employees)
- Consultant fees (for program design and implementation)
- Core doula training workshop (cost may or may not be covered by the hospital; can be fee based)
- Continuing education of doulas and maternity staff (could be integrated into existing structure of nursing continuing education programs within the hospital)
- Advertising and outreach
- Space for trainings and meetings
- Space for coordinator(s) to work
- Supplies (office supplies, birth kits)
- Parking passes and meal vouchers for volunteer doulas

Hospital Culture and the Doula

Perhaps the biggest challenge to be overcome when implementing a hospital doula program is the potential for conflict with hospital staff. If care providers have experienced negative interactions with community doulas in the past, especially those acting outside of scope of practice, then there can be significant anti-doula pushback. Rather than an ally, the doula may be perceived as an adversary or unwanted intruder. Here are some strategies for addressing challenges in this area.

- Present a clear and concise view of the doula's role, including scope of practice and established benefits on birth outcomes.
- Solicit staff input and feedback at key stages of program implementation and at the end of the pilot program period.
- Develop policies, procedures and practice guidelines that will enable doulas, nurses, physicians, midwives and anesthesiologists to work as a team.
- Employ a doula coordinator who serves as a liaison between the doulas and hospital staff.
- Provide in-service education programs that stress team roles.
- Present on doulas at Grand Rounds.
- Establish a clear-cut communication pathway for team members to hold doulas accountable to scope of practice, professional standards and hospital guidelines regarding provision of services. *Doulas should be held accountable by the program administrator rather than directly by caregivers.*
- Brand the doula program so participating doulas are readily recognizable as hospital-affiliated doulas (e.g., logo, t-shirt, nametag, etc.) and have a sense of identity and belonging within the system.
- Solicit feedback from participating doulas.
- Provide administrative support to help the doulas troubleshoot any challenges they are encountering.

Pitfalls and Best Practices

In her article, "Keeping clients' needs first as a hospital-based doula" published in the *International Doula* magazine (see Resources), Laurie Levy sums up the following pitfalls and best practices of hospital-based doula programs:

- Use of volunteers—can these programs thrive long-term with highly-skilled doulas when doulas are not paid?
- Limiting the doula scope of practice or requiring doulas to work outside of it

Nurses and Doulas

With the increase in the use of inductions, epidurals and cesareans, as well as charting requirements, labor and delivery nurses find themselves increasingly consumed by clinical/technical duties. Many bemoan the fact that their job no longer allows time for emotional support and comfort measures or that they have very little training in non-medical labor support techniques. Some may remember when they did get to be the warm fuzzy person in the room and feel envious of the doula–client connection or sad when they are left out of pictures after the baby is born. And yet, as the following chart shows, the nurse's role is quite distinct from the doula's role. Each has her place, but there is some overlap. Nurses need to appreciate how the doulas can be an ally for the family, while doulas need to tread lightly. Everyone on the team wants to feel valued.

	Role of the Nurse	Role of the Doula
Meets client prenatally	No	Usually yes, but some programs may not allow for this
Performs clinical tasks	Yes	No
Consults with doctor/midwife	Yes; advocates for patient by communicating patient's desires to provider	No; advocates for patient by helping them identify questions and communicate with staff
Presence	Intermittent; may have more than one patient at a time; may undergo shift changes during the labor	Continuous support
Comfort measures, reassurance	Intermittent as able; has clinical duties, tasks; may have limited training and knowledge in this area; high rate of epidural use diminishes perceived need for comfort measures	Continuous support; trained in labor support skills, support for physiologic birthing practices; central to the doula's role
Supports the birthing mother's partner	Information only	Yes, including emotional support, guidance in supporting the mother, support for family birth plan, and support for informed decision making
Documentation	Yes, responsible for time-consuming charting	No charting; may keep own records
Postpartum follow-up	None	Usually one postpartum home visit

- Requiring doulas to do unrelated work (delivering lab samples, filing charts, stocking supplies) thereby taking away from her primary focus on the client
- Doulas attend only women who are unmedicated (out of pain does not mean out of distress)
- Limit to one type of provider (e.g., midwives)
- In the case of a woman being transfer from an affiliated birth center to the main hospital, the doula does not follow the client, thereby losing emotional support at a major stress point in her experience.
- Encourage staff to stay open to and welcoming of private-practice doulas as well.

Program elements that work best for all stakeholders include:

- Patient drives all decisions.
- Doulas are present for the entire labor, including administration of epidurals and cesarean births.
- Doula functions in an evidence-based way, offering continuous care, and her advocacy role is maintained.
- Doulas are accountable to a program manager who is a doula, rather than directly to care providers.
- A variety of tools such as role playing, suggested scripts for challenging situations and support meetings are shared to help doulas choose language and actions that support clients with appropriate advocacy.
- Foster a culture of openness. Develop forums to facilitate open communication with all stakeholders, pre-program and ongoing, to discuss any issues.
- Develop methods to systematically track and evaluate care processes and outcomes.

It is critical that, as doulas endeavor to be accepted into the hospital mainstream, our role not be compromised or co-opted. While doulas participating in hospital-based programs must be accountable to the hospital, they nevertheless must retain the autonomy to remain true to the essence of their role. Their primary purpose is not to ensure a compliant patient for hospital care providers. Rather, it is to provide multi-dimensional support for the mother and her family and, in cases where conflict or misunderstanding between the two parties emerges, act as a mediator to enhance communication. This should never devolve into client coercion on the part of the doula.

Sustainability of Hospital-Based Programs

Program managers will always be juggling how to pay the doulas and fund administrative costs while keeping services affordable for customers. Creative experimentation seems to be in order.

Following are a few options to explore to ensure that the doula program is not a drain on hospital resources and can continue to serve families for years to come.

- Make the program self-sustaining by incorporating a fee-for-services component.
- Consider the best way to make the program inclusive to patients of all income levels.
- Secure grant funding for a charitable component.
- Explore available institutional support. How much is the hospital willing to target for the initiative? Does the hospital have a charitable foundation? Is the hospital willing to absorb the cost of implementing a doula program?
- Identify a graduate student in need of a project who might provide administrative support (e.g., design a survey, help create an evaluation process, etc.).
- Work with hospital's marketing team to highlight the doula program and its benefits for moms, babies and families.

End-of-Life Doula Programs

Currently, end-of-life doula programs appear to be hospice-affiliated volunteer programs only. Some are like the *Eleventh Hour* or *No One Dies Alone* programs that many hospices have incorporated, where emphasis is placed solely on support for the active phase of dying—the final days and hours. An end-of-life doula program, in that context, involves a rotating team of trained volunteers providing round-the-clock support. But private-practice end-of-life doulas are offering a variety of services beyond vigiling support—services that benefit individuals and families from initial diagnosis, through the dying and afterwards. Families have many unmet needs further upstream of the active dying phase and, in this respect, there is room for innovative programs including for-profit and nonprofit, pre-hospice and in-hospice. I predict that the next five years will see a variety of end-of-life doula program models emerge. There are just too many benefits for all stakeholders and the demand will grow.

Benefits to Hospice

- Helps meet the 5 percent volunteer requirement of Medicare Conditions of Practice (CoPs) (mandated for all hospice organizations)
- Increase volunteer commitment and retention
- Complements the holistic, wrap-around services available to families
- Increase length of stay through earlier referrals (= increased revenue)
- Increase patient and family satisfaction scores (= increase in referrals = increased revenue)
- Gain a competitive market advantage

Benefits to Patients

- Companionship, presence, emotional support
- Support for informed decision making
- Help with life review, legacy projects
- Vigil planning for what patients want to see, hear and feel around them in the last days
- Comfort measures (e.g., visualization, massage, ritual)
- Support for the person's wishes

Benefits to Families

- Easing caregiver burnout; respite care
- Logistical and household support
- Education on the end-of-life process
- Being present during the dying process
- Bereavement resources

Summary

Doula programs are here to stay! Like the independent doula business models discussed in Chapters 1 and 2, programs "evolve." A successful program involves many stakeholders. Assemble your team of key players, choose a model, hash out the details and give it your best shot. I have provided you with a framework for creating a program and the questions you should be asking. Some guesswork will assuredly be involved as you launch your pilot program. Evaluate and adapt as needed. In the initial phases, as you gather information and consider your options, just do your best to discern the model components that are the best match for your goals and the resources at hand. What does your intuition tell you? ◆

CHAPTER 6

Making the Case for Funding Doula Programs

FIRST, THE GOOD NEWS: funders like doula programs. And now the bad news—actually, there isn't any, unless you're simply not willing to set some goals and be held accountable for achieving those goals. I'm going to assume that if you are reading this chapter, then you are (a) someone who gets things done, (b) relatively new to grant writing and (c) eager for guidance because time is of the essence.

In my role as a nonprofit executive director and founder of two community-based volunteer doula programs, I have achieved an 85 percent funding rate on grants that I have written and/or collaborated on. As a member of the March of Dimes Michigan Program Services Committee, I participated in the chapter's community grants annual review process over ten years. It was a great education to sit on the other side of the grantmaking table and witness the proposal vetting and grants-distribution process in action. Every year the most basic, common mistakes are repeated by petitioners who are subsequently disqualified. In this chapter, I will cover the basics of grant writing and include a variety of tips and strategies for developing ongoing partnerships with funders. Let's get your program funded!

Identify Funders with a Mission Match

It's important to understand the mission of the organization that you are petitioning and ensure that your proposal aligns with their mission. Many grant proposals are denied simply because they are submitted to the wrong funder. Pay special attention to the funding priorities identified by the funder. Look at their funding history over the past five years (this information should be available on their website). If your project is not congruent with a prospective funder's priorities, look for a better match. If you are a good match, be convincing as to how your project dovetails with their posted guidelines.

Read *carefully* a prospective funder's guidelines or Request for Proposals (RFP), eligibility requirements and evaluation criteria. In many instances, it's a good idea to inquire by phone or brief letter to see if a granting agency has any interest in your project. Some funders may even require you to call first. Foundation staff can often provide guidance that will make a major difference in the final form and focus of your proposal. Pay careful attention regarding what to emphasize and what to tone down and be prepared to take notes on your conversation.

Local giving is important. If your local community foundation can't give you money, it may be able to help with training and assistance.

Fight the temptation to "chase the money." Ideally, the grant-seeking process unfolds in this order: (1) define program goals, (2) identify resources needed to accomplish the goals and (3) find a likely funder. "Chasing the money" reverses the order of the process, with the prospective grantee learning about a pool of available funds and then shaping goals and needed resources to the funder's specifications. In some cases it can work, but the pitfall is that it can cause you to compromise the integrity of your program. In the end, you may be funded for doing something other than what you really wanted to do and find yourself embroiled in time-consuming tasks that take you in a whole other direction.

A memorable example pops to mind. I had assembled all of the materials necessary to submit a proposal for funding of our volunteer doula program to the state of Michigan's Children's Trust Fund. The fund is intended to prevent child abuse and neglect. It is paid for by state income taxes when citizens elect to designate an additional dollar or two for this purpose on their annual tax returns. I was undaunted by the idea of connecting the dots between doulas and child abuse prevention. We in the doula world understand that an overwhelmed and frustrated new mother, or one who is suffering with postpartum depression, may be at greater risk of neglecting or harming her children, especially if she is under-resourced. It doesn't take a great leap of imagination to suppose that a caring mentor, offering hands-on support and referrals, might make a difference.

No, it was the fine print in the RFP that proved to be the biggest deterrent, specifically requirements that would, in effect, turn our volunteer doulas into spies for the Department of Children's Protective Services. Now, don't get me wrong. I'm a strong advocate for the innocent and absolutely in favor of reporting child abuse and neglect to the authorities. But the extent of the reporting requirements for this particular RFP (including personally invasive questionnaires that the doulas would be required to administer with each family served) would undoubtedly compromise the doula's capacity to build trust with the families and would undermine the very essence of her role of nonjudgmental support. From a programmatic point of view, whole new systems would need to be put in place to meet the requirements of this funder. That was not so unusual nor necessarily a deal breaker, but the fact that I couldn't stand the thought of doing it was! And if I was so strongly repulsed at the thought of it, I'm guessing we would have lost a few excellent volunteers along the way as well. The volunteers in the doula program are an awesome group of dedicated women who would likely prefer to keep moms and babies together through their loving ministrations and *preventive* efforts. It appeared that the Children's Trust Fund was more focused on identification of potential abusers. All things considered, we were not a good fit.

> **The funder needs a worthy project** and you need money. It's a partnership and, for it to work, the needs of both partners must be met.

Rather than forcing the fit, find a funder that is the right size and shape for you. Trust me, there are plenty of foundations with agendas favoring preventive health care initiatives, healthy families and so on. Find one that will be excited about what you are already doing or will provide seed money for what you want to do. No doubt, if you are like most nonprofits, you are trying to do a lot with a little, in terms of overall resources. Why spread yourself thinner by adding program components that take you off track?

Foundations are made up of people. Each foundation has a theme, a mission, an overarching purpose. Sometimes the theme is geographic, such as in community grants programs, or the theme may be demographic, such as funds designated for African-American women of childbearing age, low-income elderly and so on. In other cases, the funding priority may be issue-specific, such as breastfeeding promotion, prematurity prevention, increasing the practice of advance care planning, or reducing isolation among the elderly in your community. Look for a funder with whom you have a clear overlap of purpose and priorities.

How to Search

Let's start with a few general tips:

- Find out which foundations have given grants in your region. Foundations often shift their funding focus and timing is everything. Watch for time-sensitive opportunities and get on mailing lists for RFP notification.
- Start a multi-year calendar to track the grant cycles of your most likely funders, noting key dates for RFP releases and grant submissions.
- Some foundations require a financial audit of your organization, while others require only a copy of last year's IRS Form 990. As you conduct your research, pay attention to this requirement. The cost of an audit (several thousand dollars) may be prohibitive for small nonprofits, thereby limiting eligibility. You need to know this upfront and, for starters, prioritize your opportunities accordingly. If you appear to be a good match with a foundation that requires audited financial statements, call and ask whether they are flexible on this point (some will waive it and accept the 990). Considering the long-term, an important sustainability strategy is to begin preparing now for your first audit. Try to get an accountant familiar with nonprofits involved with your organization (perhaps a volunteer?). If you get it set up correctly from the start and have all the systems in place for tracking grants, then you can be proactive regarding the types of issues that would get red flagged during an audit.
- Start collecting samples of successful grant proposals to use as boilerplate models. I have included two short grant proposals at the end of this chapter.

There's no easy way around the investment of time necessary to identify your best opportunities. That said, it is time well spent. The funding directories that enable you to compile a comprehensive list of foundation and corporate funding sources are as handy as the nearest Foundation Center cooperating library [FoundationCenter.org] where you can use them for free. You can also find and add state and federal grant-funding opportunities to your search package. Make printouts of pertinent opportunities and file for later reference. You can also subscribe to an online funding directory service (see Resources).

Corporate Letter Requests

A quick and easy two- to three-page letter requesting grant monies, donated equipment or services, or technical assistance can be written in less than one hour. The

Funding Sources

- Contact your local Community Foundation; these foundations often offer smaller grants, under $10,000; don't ignore "capacity building" grants.
- Look for private foundations that have targeted your region or state; amounts variable (e.g., W. K. Kellogg Foundation, headquartered in Battle Creek, Michigan, prioritizes a certain percentage of their grant making budget for programs serving the residents of Michigan).
- Look for large corporations with grant-making divisions who are headquartered or have subsidiary locations in your state (e.g., in southeastern Michigan, Ford Motor Company, Blue Cross Blue Shield Foundation of Michigan, etc.). If the corporation is within a 100-mile radius of your service population, so much the better.
- Identify the Regional Association of Grantmakers (RAGS) in your area. RAGS are nonprofit membership associations of private and community foundations, corporations, individuals and others committed to strengthening philanthropy in the geographic areas in which they operate.
- Don't neglect the small, private, local organizations that raise money for the community (Kiwanis, Salvation Army, etc.).
- Government grants (state or federal) can be very large amounts. Accountability requirements can overwhelm a small organization such that a strong organizational infrastructure (solid bookkeeping system and experienced staff) will need to be in place.

hard part is identifying the hundreds of businesses and industries that will consider such a letter request. However, if you hone your search skills, you should be able to retrieve (from free online sites) the names, addresses and contact persons for potential sources on the local, regional and national scene (see Resources). This is a great job for a student intern or board member who wants to help with fundraising.

Letter Proposals for Corporations and Foundations

One of the easiest, yet underused, writing formats is the letter proposal. Write two- to three-page corporate letter requests to send to small businesses, corporate giving programs at large businesses and small foundations (those without staff). In comparison to a five-page (or longer) full proposal, the letter proposal is a mini-proposal, more concise and with fewer attachments. It is most successful when you keep the amount requested under $25,000 and ask for a direct grant (monetary award with no strings attached) or a product donation (such as food for an event). Letter proposals will be reviewed by a trustee of the board of directors, a corporate giving manager, a community relations director or a foundation program officer.

What do the reviewers look for in a successful request? Businesses and foundations want to know how your request meets their area of interest or why you chose them as the recipient of your corporate letter request. You will need to do your homework to align their mission or corporate philosophy with your organization's mission.

Grant expert Beverly Browning (see Resources) reports that she has used the following formula for ten years, with a predictable 30 percent funding rate. I adapted her ten-step formula to incorporate language requesting funding for a postpartum doula program, but I think you can get the idea and play with it a bit to suit your initiative. What have you got to lose?

1. Opening salutation (obtain the correct name of the contact person, title and full mailing address).
2. Introductory sentences; write three bulleted sentences that are compelling and grab the attention of your reader.
   » *For Dawn, new motherhood means juggling caring for her two-year-old son and newborn twins alone as she recovers from an emergency surgical delivery.*
   » *For Mary, new motherhood means going through the motions of caring for her baby while feeling an utter lack of connection. She is depressed, can't sleep and feels hopeless. She thinks about ending it all.*
   » *Every day, social workers at our local hospitals are attempting to identify support for new mothers in need and the most they can offer is a one-hour visit from a nurse.*
3. Introduce your organization: include who you are, where you are located, the organization's mission and information on your constituency; keep this to one paragraph.
4. State your organization's problem: write two to three paragraphs on your needs, issues or problems that need solving.
5. Beg the issue: write several sentences that emit gloom and doom about the problem:
   » *Infant mental health research has established that untreated depression in the mother causes depression and developmental delays in the infant—a likely setup for lifelong emotional and relationship problems.*

6. Connect funder money to your need: write one to two paragraphs to tell your reader how their funding can help solve the problem.
7. Ask. Tell the reader how much money or the kinds of product donations you need and what a gift to your organization will mean to the constituency you serve, such as in the following:
   » *A donation of $5,000 will enable Support for Moms to provide 250 hours of postpartum doula care for families in need. Your gift may make the difference between keeping families whole and together or seeing children who fail to thrive. Every child deserves a chance!*
8. Write a sentence thanking the funder in advance, on behalf of the constituency to be served.
9. Complementary closing and signature
10. Add one final thought-provoking sentence, such as:
    » *P.S. Your partnership will help families at risk receive loving doula care, "mothering the mothers" so that they, in turn, will become better mothers.*

Attach the following documents to letter requests:

- IRS 501(c)(3) letter of nonprofit determination
- Most recent financial statement (audited, if available) or IRS Form 990 from previous year
- Board of director's roster (with affiliations)
- Informational brochure or annual report

Working with Multiple Funders

While it is considered inappropriate to submit the same grant to multiple funders at the same time, one option is to change the grant slightly so multiple funded grants dovetail together instead of creating duplication. For example, look at the grant cycles of various funders. Some may run from January through December, while others may do an annual grant process beginning in April, June or September. Ideally, you would have more than one funder for your program and the cycles would not end at the same time. Another strategy is to have a slightly different thematic focus in each grant. For example, one grant might target pregnant women in a particularly underserved geographic area that the funder is also targeting, while another might be aimed at identifying women at risk of postpartum depression and tweaking doula services to address that need. Keep your proposals focused and don't be too far reaching. It's great to leave some avenues open (e.g., targeting immigrant populations or expanding to a neighboring county) because it allows you to grow the program organically, building on your success. In addition, funders appreciate a new angle if they are going to be a long-term funder. They typically don't want to just keep funding the same program over and over, but they might fund a targeted expansion.

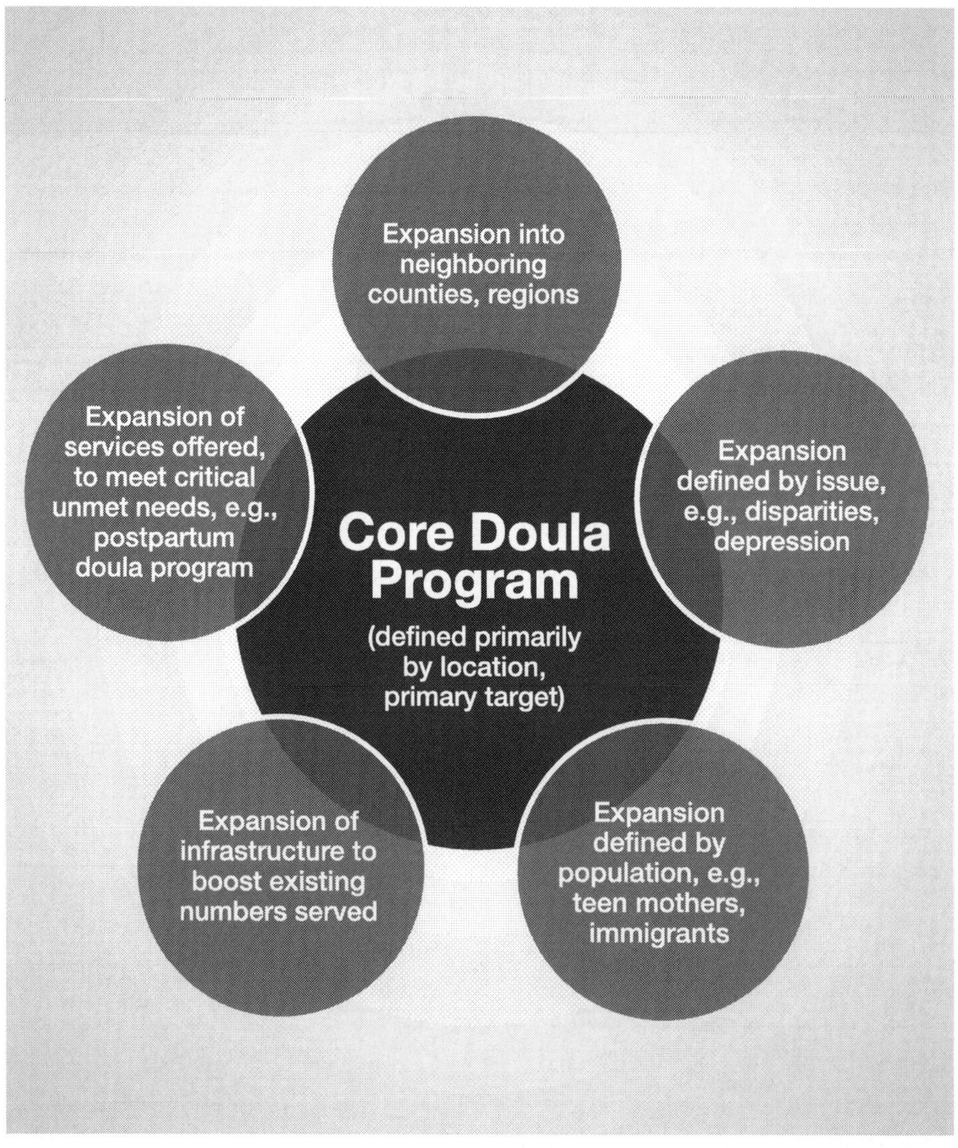

Cultivating the Grantor–Grantee Relationship

In a nutshell, it's all about relationships and establishing a track record. Since some funders are more geared toward providing seed money for startups, a track record is not required in those cases. Over time, however, you *are* establishing a track record, for better or for worse. Once things take a negative turn, it will be hard to come back into the good graces of grant makers. If, for example, you violate the terms of your contract (a legal document) and make unauthorized changes to the grant budget, that's a problem. If you do not turn in your required reports on time, or fail altogether to account for the grant funds, that's a problem. If you fail to respond to the grantor's request to conduct a site visit, that's a problem too. And there are many more variations on this theme, but they all add up to one thing—the grantee refuses or neglects to meet the basic accountability requirements of the funder.

Communicate!

Respond promptly and affirmatively to emails, phone calls and requests from the funder. Hostile and defensive interactions with the funder won't cut it.

From the funder's perspective, in any of the above scenarios, you are making them look bad because they, in turn, are accountable to their constituents and donors who have given money in trust for a specific purpose. It is the trustee's job to get the biggest bang for their bucks and make a difference for the targeted purpose. Grant funds are never an endless amount of cash and the task of dividing it up is not taken lightly. For every ten organizations that are funded, another forty (or more) are not.

Accountability is not the same as success or failure in reaching goals. A grantee who openly comes back to a funder with a budget change request or an unanticipated obstacle related to implementation of program objectives will generally be looked upon favorably by the grantor. They will often agree to reasonable budget adjustments, provide a needed extension to the grant period or otherwise provide problem-solving assistance. One funder told his audience that when the foundation he represents receives bare-bones progress reports from grantees claiming complete success with all program goals and objectives, he sees a red flag. Funders don't want to be sweet talked and lied to. They are reality based, seeking to partner with real programs achieving real results. When a grantee is honest about problems encountered and challenges faced, that feedback is transferrable to subsequent grantees so they don't make the same mistakes. It's all about helping people.

The proper attitude is one of appreciation and endeavoring to be worthy of the grant support provided. Take every opportunity to acknowledge the funder, on your website, at public events, in your Annual Report and so on. If a reporter interviews you about your program, be sure to emphasize your funding source and then send along to the funder copies of any publicity for the program that you have garnered (unless the funder has specifically requested anonymity). Take pictures of your program in action. Include testimonials from constituents served about positive effects in their lives. Funders can use these pictures and testimonials in their annual reports and on their websites. Keep it pithy. Capture any feedback that packs an emotional wallop. Testimonials will help sell ongoing support for your program and are much more powerful than statistical reports about numbers served. You need to keep building a case for why doulas matter.

Avoid lame excuses of the dog-ate-my-homework variety. Honestly, no one cares, and who has time for that? The grantee is responsible for:

- Tracking the RFP releases of a funder
- Meeting all deadlines for letters of intent or proposal submission
- Following the RFP requirements precisely
- Responding to the funder's requests for photo ops, issuing of press releases, use of their logo on materials developed with grant funds, cooperating with site visit requests, etc.
- Submitting complete, periodic reports on the funder's mandated timeline (which will be specified in the grant contract)
- Recognizing that there is no such thing as throwing the ball back in the funder's court regarding any of the above

Follow the Required Format of the RFP and Avoid Common Mistakes!

Read the RFP carefully! Let me say it again. *Read the RFP carefully!* The RFP is a highly refined document. It states precisely what the grantor wants to see. If you are the "idea" person/grant writer and looking after the details is not your strong suit, then make sure someone's got your back on the details. If the RFP states that the funder wants four copies of a proposal by 5:00 PM on a specific date, don't send one copy or turn in your proposal after the deadline. If it says they don't accept electronic submissions, believe them. On the other hand, if it specifies online submission, don't send a hard copy. Seems like a no-brainer, right? Nevertheless,

I have witnessed many applications go straight into the reject pile for precisely these reasons.

Format your proposal as requested. If the funder limits the proposal to four pages with one-inch margins and 12-point type, you must work within these limitations. And here's a hint—don't worry too much about space limitations on your first draft. Get the ideas down. Later, you can come back to it with a fresh eye and refine and edit it to communicate key ideas more efficiently. Some funders may allow appendix materials, which permit more in-depth background information, program brochures, etc., to be included.

Good time management in meeting grant deadlines can mean the difference between winning or losing literally thousands of dollars.

If the funder specifies items they do not fund such as equipment, capital improvements, salaries for existing full-time employees or indirect costs, do not include these items in your budget. Predictably they will be disallowed and the attention you draw with their inclusion may cause the funder to question your ability to accomplish stated goals without funding for the disallowed items. Semantics matter. A disallowed budget item (e.g., "marketing") can be reframed ("community outreach" or "education on the role of the doula") without setting off alarms. On the other hand, it is impossible to disguise a laptop computer as anything other than "equipment." If a funder states that equipment is disallowed, then don't request funding for a laptop computer in your proposal.

Pay attention to the minimum and maximum amounts set for grant requests. I participated recently in a round of grant reviews and witnessed two Letters of Intent out of 53 go straight into the recycle bin because applicants asked for less than the minimum award amount defined in the RFP. Likely, the applicants thought they were demonstrating frugality and a lack of greed with this move (unless it was simply a matter of utter cluelessness on all levels), but the funder is constrained by the RFP and the rules are the rules. When a prospective grantee can't follow clearly-articulated guidelines in the RFP, it brings up the question of credibility. Why should the funder trust you with thousands of dollars when you can't follow simple directions?

Components of a Proposal

The first thing you need to do is assess the value of your idea and your ability to implement it. Is it needed? Does it solve an important problem? Is it timely, unique and innovative? Can you or your organization realistically follow through on what you are proposing? Funders generally base their decision to finance a project on five criteria:

- significance of the problem,
- importance of the solution to the problem,
- quality of the people involved,
- stature/reputation of the sponsoring institution, and
- reasonableness of the budget.

How does your idea measure up to these criteria? The following questions will assist you in thinking through your goals and overall concept.

- *What problem are we addressing?* This is your statement of need. Convey a sense of urgency and make it compelling.
- *Who will be helped by this initiative?* This is your target population. Be specific.
- *How are we proposing to address the problem?* Paint a clear picture of your program. Can the reader see it in action in their mind?
- *How will things be different? Will the problem be solved or improved when you are done?* How will you know that you are succeeding? What will you measure to determine the effects of your program and what may need to change or be adjusted?
- *What do you need to try to solve the problem?* This must correspond with the approach you have described above.

If you can tie yourself to a major regional or national issue and position your proposal as a model to be replicated once you've proved your idea works, you can increase interest in your project. A specific strategy for broadly sharing your solution—such as presenting results at a major professional conference—can then be included in your proposal. That said, refrain from overly ambitious claims. A red flag for grant reviewers is the indication you've planned to accomplish more than your budget makes realistically attainable. It is better to limit your proposal to smaller, more assuredly attainable goals than to back yourself into a corner and promise more than you can deliver. Many organizations find that they badly underestimate funding for staff and particularly tech support. Be realistic and conservative.

Below I break down a proposal into commonly used segments. Remember that each funder will have its own guidelines, so requirements may not always match exactly what I have listed here. Always follow the funder's guidelines.

Cover Letter

Cover letters should be no more than one page and written as a means of introducing yourself. A brief description of your organization and background, the purpose of funding and the amount of your request should appear in the first paragraph. Make a connection with their funding priorities and your program goals. Indicate that you look forward to partnering with them for the greater benefit of families (or something to that effect). Be sure to include a contact name, phone number and address.

Executive Summary/Abstract

This is the most important section of the entire proposal. The abstract distills the whole proposal into its essence. It is the first thing that reviewers see, and it may be the only section that some members of the grants distribution committee read. In the space allotted, it should state your project's purpose, how it will be implemented and include an outcome statement. The outcome statement is a powerful summary of what you hope to accomplish, describing how the target population will be better off due to your efforts. State the organization making the request and link the organization's background to the proposal's purpose. Include your total budget amount, other funds that are committed (if any), and the amount of your request. Ninety percent of funding decisions by private donors and foundations will be made by the time the funder finishes reading this page. It must be concise (limit to one page), compelling and clear!

Demonstrate Compelling Community Need for the Proposed Initiative

Most funders want to know that your proposed program or initiative is not duplicating services already offered to the target community. Your program may be a great, innovative idea, but it will not exist in a vacuum. Begin to get other key stakeholders in the community involved. Build collaborative relationships and keep the focus on the need for the proposed project. How does your proposal fill a gap in services or reach an underserved population? A proposal will often sink or swim based on the need for the project.

An Insider's Peek at the March of Dimes Grant-Review Process

- Letters of intent are submitted in response to the annual RFP. These are screened for compliance with RFP guidelines and put into a reject pile if they are noncompliant. Past grantees who are not in good standing, but who nevertheless submit a letter of intent for continued funding, also go in the reject pile.
- The committee—volunteers composed of maternal-infant health professionals from the medical community, public health sector and community-based organizations throughout the state—meets to review the letters and decide which agencies will be invited to submit full proposals. Through this process, a few more letters are added to the reject pile for a variety of reasons, though lack of clarity is frequently cited. Committee members are essentially asking themselves, "Do I want to hear more about this idea? Does it pique my interest?"
- Once the list of invited agencies is finalized, notification is sent to all applicants regarding their status. Those invited to submit full proposals have approximately three months to meet the next deadline.
- Completed proposals are then sent out to committee members for review. Each proposal is reviewed and scored by three members, using a score sheet provided by March of Dimes.
- Next, the proposals are ranked in order of the composite scores returned by the reviewers, from highest to lowest.
- The committee meets and reviews each proposal, starting with the top-ranked proposals and moving to the bottom of the list. Committee members have the composite scores and reviewer comments/questions in front of them and may consult the actual proposal if there are questions, though typically only the abstract is reviewed at this level. Individual reviewers, who may not all be present for the joint review process, often serve as de facto advocates for a well-written proposal that they liked or can kill one that they found problematic. On occasion, there is a strong recommendation against funding by a reviewer.
- All reviewers identify any potential conflict of interest and will step out of the room during discussions related to proposals from agencies with which they have a vested interest, close contacts or personal history.
- By the end of the process, some proposals will be accepted, and some rejected, and award amounts designated.

- About three months later, after award amounts have been finalized by the national office, notification is sent out to all applicants, followed by contracts and then checks to grantees.
- March of Dimes splits the award into two checks, the second one being released after the required interim report has been reviewed. The second check is dependent upon the grantee having made reasonable progress on the grant objectives and use of funds.
- At the close of the grant cycle, a final report is due in which the grantee is asked to report on the results of implementing their objectives and account for expenditure of all grant funds.
- March of Dimes will consider re-funding a program for up to three consecutive years, though typically something new would need to be added each year.
- The Community Grants Program makes awards in the amounts of $10,000–$25,000, but this amount may vary from state to state.
- Most years, a smaller pool of funds is set aside to support small, short-range projects, up to $3,000 or so, through the coming year.

Timelines

The RFP is released in the spring for funding in the next calendar year. Therefore, if an applicant misses the RFP deadline for submitting a Letter of Intent, their next opportunity will be to submit the following year for funding the year after that. Hence the need for planning and a "grants opportunities" calendar. Each funder is different. For example, my local community foundation has two grant cycles each year.

Who are the community stakeholders for birth/postpartum doula programs? Think in terms of anyone who might be in the position to refer women and families who can benefit from your program. This includes clinics serving low-income families, midwifery and OB practices, social workers employed in the high-risk clinics of local hospitals, your local department of public health maternal–infant health programs, WIC office, First Steps programs, Visiting Nurses, local childbirth educators, practicing doulas (who might be approached or interviewed by women who can't afford their fees), other community agencies serving low-income families or sponsoring programs targeting women, and so on. In your conversations with these professionals, ask if they believe that a doula program would provide a needed service in the community and whether they would be willing to refer women to the program.

For end-of-life doula programs, community stakeholders include hospices, palliative care providers, programs to serve the elderly, gerontology medical practices, neighborhood health clinics in low-income communities, and pretty much anyone who is offering services to the same target population.

While carving out your niche and establishing cooperative relationships between community stakeholders, you are also establishing your status in the community and are building support for the program. Formalize key relationships by asking for letters of support that testify to the community's need for your program and stakeholders' eagerness to make referrals, provide office or meeting space, and so on. You cannot wait until two days before a proposal is due (or even a week, for that matter) to begin collecting your letters of support.

Document the need, whenever possible, quantifying it with current data. It will likely be helpful to gather a few statistics to make your case, such as: the total number of births in your target county each year; number of premature babies; perinatal mortality statistics (both local and national, for comparative purposes); incidence rates of postpartum depression, cesarean delivery, teen pregnancy or single mothers giving birth; demographics of immigrant populations and health care access issues; breastfeeding initiation, duration and exclusivity rates; and so on.

For end-of-life initiatives, helpful data might include the growing numbers of elderly in the community and projected population trajectories; how many of these are living in poverty; existing hospice options; availability of respite care and adult day care; overall data on hospice enrollment numbers and timing of entry into hospice; and more. You need to place yourself in the information flow. As these numbers come to your attention through professional journal articles, email newsletters and local news stories, capture and file them for future reference. National statistics can be used to provide a baseline for comparative purposes and allow you to zero in on a high-risk population or geographic area with a disproportionate number of poor outcomes. Whenever you find a website that contains a variety of demographics or one that cites current research results on topics related to your program (see Resources), add it to your web browser's "favorites" list. Create separate bookmark folders labeled by subject and then add sites to the appropriate folder for easy retrieval later.

As you develop the statement of the problem you intend to address, use a funnel approach:

- Start with the generalized problem as it occurs in your community.
- Move to the conditions that make this a problem.
- Outline current resources that address this problem and identify gaps in those resources.
- Identify how your proposal will fill these gaps.

Sample Need Documentation

- Percentage of women suffering from postpartum depression nationally and lack of treatment options locally
- Racial disparities in birth outcomes
- Number of folks dying at home under hospice care versus the overall number of hospice-eligible patients dying in the hospital

Describe the Target Population

Describe in detail the population that you intend to serve. What are the demographics? Include ethnicity, gender, age, location, new immigrant populations and so on. Describe any special needs (translation services, transportation, lack of access to existing services, low literacy levels). Be as specific as possible (e.g., low-income women living in the following zip codes who have been identified as high-risk for premature delivery). Make a reasonable estimate of how many people constitute the potential target population (e.g., estimated total number of pregnant non-English-speaking Latina women in the county). If your program is designed to address specific risks, then enumerate those as well.

For most maternal–infant health initiatives, both the mother and the unborn or newborn child are being served, so include both in your overall numbers. If both families and care providers comprise the population served by the program, then describe both groups and estimate the numbers to the best of your ability. This was the case for our volunteer program, which was designed with the dual purpose of filling gaps in services for pregnant and newly postpartum women and their families AND as a career advancement pathway (via doula training scholarships and certification) for the volunteer doulas who were from the communities being served.

Sample Target Population Description

Doulas Care is a community-based volunteer doula program that serves low-income pregnant women who are at medical or social risk, in counties throughout southeastern Michigan, with the majority coming from Washtenaw County. Many women are referred to the program because they are socially isolated and struggle with depression. In addition to adolescents, referrals encompass women with the following risk factors: previous low-birth-weight or preterm babies, previous experience of postpartum depression, previous cesarean birth, a history of illicit substance use, living at or below the poverty level, lower weight gain during pregnancy, late entry into prenatal care, and recent immigrants and other women lacking family and social support. Since African-American babies in the counties served are three times more likely to die before reaching their first birthday than Caucasian babies, outreach efforts are increasingly directed toward reaching this higher-risk population in an effort to reduce disparities.

- The average age of our clients is 29 with a range from 15 to 50; 10% are teen mothers.
- 60% report being low income; 82% say they have financial concerns; and 55% say they do not have enough money to cover their basic needs.
- 55% are unemployed.
- 25% have a high school degree or less.
- Only 29% are married; 65% are single mothers with over 25% of these having no involvement or support from the father of the baby.
- 52% are experiencing their first pregnancy and are new to parenting.
- 22% percent are African American.
- 10% are non-English-speaking Latina women.
- We provide services and education to families in eleven counties in southeastern Michigan, including: Washtenaw (50%); Wayne (30%); Oakland (10%); and Macomb, Lapeer, Genesee, Livingston, Ingham, Jackson, Lenawee, and Monroe (10 %). The total number of referrals in 2012 was 150; total in 2013 was 219.

Note that our sample description is for an existing program that has accumulated data. This level of detail is not too much. For start-ups, it is understood that you will not have this level of information and detail but be as specific as you can regarding your intentions. Available data can also be summarized in a graph (which funders will appreciate; remember, most reviewers won't read your entire proposal, but they will read the abstract, look at pictures and captions, and perhaps glance at a summary table or graph).

Proposed Solution to the Problem: Goals and Program Design

Goals are conceptual and overarching. They explain why you do what you do. When articulating goals, begin by rewriting the needs statement as an outcome. Consider whether your goals are realistic or are there too many goals for a one-year grant period? The more skillfully you can tie in your goals with the funder's stated funding priorities, the better. Specifically, what are you trying to achieve? Following are some sample goals.

Sample Goals for Maternal–Infant Health Initiatives

- Improve birth outcomes for at-risk moms and babies in Monroe County.
- Increase breastfeeding initiation, duration and exclusivity rates among Austin-area African-American mothers.
- Provide early identification and support for depressed new moms throughout the state.
- Develop career pathways for low-income women in five counties in South Carolina.
- Reduce disparities by decreasing the number of preterm births and low-birth-weight infants born to African-American mothers in the following zip codes ____.
- Reduce disparities by assisting the region's pregnant new immigrant population to access available health care and other needed social services.

> **Goal of the grant** = the end toward which effort is directed
>
> **Grant objective** = the steps or benchmarks to reach the goal

When writing the description of your program, aim to strike a balance between so much detail that the reader gets lost and making folks guess what it is you do. Be sure to give enough detail related to any items that end up in your budget so that the reader understands why this is important (e.g., if you are asking for funds for outreach, you need to make it clear in the program description how you

Funders are looking for evidenced-based solutions.

identify and recruit program participants). Include a simple statement that introduces your program: "We are a community-based doula program that matches low-income, at-risk pregnant women and their families with a volunteer doula." You may want or need to provide background information about your issue as many readers may not know what a doula is. Describe the services offered and how they are/will be delivered. Describe anything else that is central to your program. Try to accomplish all of this in one or two paragraphs.

State Objectives in Measurable Terms and Anticipated Outcomes

Grant seekers often confuse objectives with goals. Objectives describe how you are going to reach your goals. Once the grant is over, exactly what will have been produced, how will it be disseminated and exactly how many people will have benefited? How do you intend to measure tangible outcomes or milestones to prove that the projected benefits occurred? Articulation of these measurable, anticipated outcomes is a key area of your proposal. Don't overshoot here in an effort to impress. If you overshoot and fail, then you look bad and raise doubts about your organization. In the end, if you go above and beyond your goals, so much the better. Ultimately, the objectives will relate to line items in your budget, so think in terms of what you need funding for as you form the objectives. It has to all tie together and make sense to someone who doesn't know anything about you or your program.

To win grants, programs need to focus on outcomes, not problems.

There are two different kinds of objectives: process objectives and outcome objectives.

Process Objective or Evaluation

Process evaluation focuses on how a program was implemented and operates. It identifies the procedures undertaken and the decisions made in developing the program. It addresses whether the program was implemented and is providing activities as intended. Documenting the program's development and operation allows an assessment of the reasons for successful or unsuccessful performance and provides information for potential replication. Here is a sample format for writing process objectives:

By ____________, ____________of ____________ will ____________.
(By when?) (How many?) (Who?) (Do something)

Some examples of process objectives are:

- By March 2020, 100 pregnant women will receive counseling services related to the smoking cessation program.
- By September 2020, 200 women will be screened for WIC eligibility and assisted with filling out applications.
- By March of 2020, 200 women will receive counseling and information on the importance of taking a multivitamin containing folic acid every day.
- By December 2020, 200 people over the age of 65 will have completed Advance Directives facilitated by a trained end-of-life doula.

Outcome Objective or Evaluation

Outcome evaluation is a type of evaluation used to identify the *results of a program's effort.* It seeks to answer the question, "What difference did the program make?" It yields evidence about the effects of a program after a specified period of operation. Outcome evaluation measures health, knowledge or behavioral change for the target population. It measures (1) the proportion of the target audience expected to show a change in a specific indicator or (2) the amount of change expected in the indicator. Outcome objectives may follow one of two formats:

By ____________, ____________of ____________ will ____________.
(By when?) (Percent change) (Who?) (Indicator)

By __________, ____________ will ________________ of ____________.
(By when?) (Who?) (Percent or % change) (Indicator)

Some examples of outcome objectives are:

- By December 2020, at least 40% of pregnant women enrolled in the smoking cessation program will quit smoking.
- By December 2020, the proportion of women eligible for WIC who are enrolled will increase to at least 70% in three areas (2018 baseline: 45%).
- By December 2020, 50% of women who receive counseling and information about folic acid will state that they take a multivitamin every day.
- By December 2020, 70% of participants over the age of 65 who received Advance Care Planning facilitation by an end-of-life doula, will have completed an Advance Directive.

Sample Funded Objectives for a Doula Program

- Increase program capacity and outreach coordination by hiring a paid volunteer coordinator so that program referrals grow by 30% by the end of the grant period.
- Increase the number of volunteer doulas by recruiting 12 low-income women in Detroit with an interest in serving as a volunteer doula for a minimum of five women and provide them with doula training scholarships.

Occasionally, after stating an objective, you might need to add a line or two of justification for the objective (e.g., demand for services has outstripped the existing infrastructure; hence need to expand role of the volunteer coordinator).

The Implementation Plan, Including Timelines

Next, think in terms of specific steps required for each objective. These are your methods or activities—a precise description of actions you will take. While the implementation plan may be incorporated into the grant narrative, some funders provide a table format that includes not just the steps that will be taken, but who will be responsible for each step and a timeframe for when it will be accomplished. As you can see, we are moving from the general to the specific. On timelines, once again, don't back yourself into a corner. If your timelines are not reasonable, then the entire proposal becomes suspect. Specifically, many proposals do not take into account the time needed to hire and train new staff or recruit participants for a new initiative.

Defining Success: Proposed Evaluation of the Project

Evaluation is how you prove your success at the end of the grant period. *Evaluation is the key to winning your next grant.* You will need to identify both the criteria and process for evaluation.

When framing your objectives, think about what measurement tools you could use to evaluate the objectives. In other words, how are you going to keep track of what you are doing? If your objectives are quantifiable and your activities are specific, then your measure of success will be the extent to which you were able to do what you said you were going to do. In the evaluation section of your proposal, simply spell it out for the funders. What are the benchmarks and what is the data-collection process associated with it? If your evaluation tools are already developed and the funder allows appendices to be attached to the proposal, then

Sample Flow from the General to the Specific

Goal: *Offer training opportunities on postpartum depression (PPD) for professionals who work with pregnant and newly postpartum women and their families.*

Objective A: *Develop two two-hour-long programs to be offered in 2019 through our established quarterly lecture series for professionals who work with women and families during the childbearing year.* (Note that this is a process objective.) Programs will be scheduled for February, April, June, and August by the volunteer coordinator. This lecture series is preapproved for 2.4 continuing education contact hours for nurses and has an existing email notification list serve of over 1,100 professionals throughout the region. A recent training on meeting the unique needs of teen mothers, offered in August 2018, attracted 35 professionals, indicating a growing regional reputation for this lecture series.

Activities for Objective A: (1) Engage ___ as an expert speaker on PPD and develop program content in partnership with her. ___ is a clinical social worker and certified childbirth educator who specializes in treating women suffering from PPD. (2) Expand the audience for this series by pursuing continuing education credits for social workers as well as nurses. (3) Replicate the presentation on PPD at two other sites in southeastern Michigan to reach a wider audience of professionals. [We met this objective by presenting at the Healthy Mothers Healthy Babies Michigan Conference and at the Michigan Infant Mental Health Association Annual Conference.] (4) Develop promotional materials, including flyers and brochures, and feature on our website and in our e-newsletter.

Objective B: *Continue to identify and procure the latest publications, DVDs and other cutting-edge educational resources on PPD for our Lending Library.*

Activities for Objective B: (1) Purchase materials. (2) Create an annotated bibliography of available materials and integrate bibliography into the new *Directory of Resources.* (3) Ensure doulas and other care providers are informed about available resources.

Objective C: *Develop our newly upgraded website as a vehicle for online information and resources on PPD and promote the website as a community service for providers and consumers throughout Michigan.* The website will include resources for families with limited incomes who experience the greatest difficulty accessing mental health services.

Activities for Objective C: (1) Develop a dedicated PPD resources page on our website that includes: (a) a directory of PPD resources, (b) relevant articles updated on a regular basis and (c) the annotated bibliography of educational materials mentioned above. (2) Notify entire email database, including professionals and consumers, of the web-based resources.

you can provide samples, but it is okay to say which systems you will put in place pending funding. Use the results from the specified evaluation process to report back to the funder on your progress/success as required in the grant contract.

Beyond measurements of objectives, what do funders like to see in the program evaluation design?

- More than one kind of evaluation tool (e.g., surveys, observations, pre- and post-test scores, focus groups)
- Involvement of an external evaluator (especially true for government grants); not absolutely necessary, but it builds credibility if there is some objectivity in the process. If it appears that everything in the proposal rests on one person who is wearing multiples hats (grant writer, program visionary, ED, program director, evaluation director, etc.), then that is dubious.
- Involvement of your constituents (doulas and clients served) in the evaluation process
- A plan for dissemination of program results to all stakeholders
- Intention to share information with other professionals or agencies who are engaged in addressing similar problems/issues/needs (e.g., publication in a professional journal, presenting on results in the form of posters or lectures at professional conferences, etc.)
- Designation of up to 15 percent of the project's total budget for the evaluation process is acceptable.

If an evaluation review shows that you are not on track with your objectives, don't panic. It's as important to know what doesn't work as it is to know what works well. Funders understand that this happens, and they will look favorably upon agencies that report problems and then work through solutions to challenges faced. Communicate with your funder. They have experience that you don't and may be able to offer suggestions. Plus, they want you to succeed.

Doula Program Evaluation

You will need to develop a database for systematic tracking of program results. If possible, get someone with database expertise to set up a system for you, the sooner the better. Ideally, the person will be available to you for a year or more to help troubleshoot any problems. Be sure that person documents exact procedures for making changes to the system once it is up and running. Accept that it won't be perfect and that you will need to add items and tweak it as you go. A direct-entry system that bypasses paper forms would be ideal for two reasons: (1) in my experience, doula volunteers are notoriously horrible at turning in forms and (2) anything you can do to reduce administrative overhead, such as having to pay someone to enter data into the system, is good. You may not be able to dispense with paper forms altogether but keep it simple and try to systematically capture the information. The system should help you with the following:

1. Collect demographic information to document the population served. Include place of residency, age, marital status, ethnicity, number of people in the home and whether the client is Medicaid-eligible. (If a high percentage of clients served are Medicaid-eligible, then we have established by default that the program is serving low-income families.)
2. Document core services provided for each client including number and length of home visits and services provided.
3. Document educational topics covered. The doulas can be provided with a list of core topics. The content of the list may change over time, based upon the focus of different funding opportunities. For birth and postpartum doula initiatives, the list might include: one-to-one education on folic acid during pregnancy, nutritional recommendations for pregnant and breastfeeding mothers, benefits of breastfeeding, shaken-baby syndrome, safe sleep recommendations, postpartum mood disorders, and so on. For end-of-life doula initiatives, topics might include: an introduction to palliative care, hospice eligibility guidelines, signs of caregiver stress and fatigue, respite strategies for caregivers, importance of advance care planning, after death care options and so on.
4. Document outcomes. Birth outcomes for moms and babies might be measured by: Apgar scores; infant's gestational age; birth weight; complications experienced by mom or baby (provide a checklist); medical interventions employed during labor, birth and immediate postpartum (again, use a checklist); and initiation of breastfeeding.
5. For the postpartum period, track maternal outcomes (incidence of post-discharge hemorrhage, infection, depression, re-hospitalization, duration and exclusivity of breastfeeding), infant outcomes (infection, re-hospitalization, jaundice, failure to thrive, feeding problems), and special needs.
6. For end-of-life initiatives, outcomes might include: increasing awareness and use of palliative care, completion of advance directives, reduction in caregiver stress, and earlier entry into hospice programs. (For the unaware, there is evidence that when people enter hospice earlier in their life-limiting illness, rather than waiting till the last week of life, they live longer and have a better quality of life.)

7. Track any special needs that emerge and how these were addressed. This section may need to be a combination of medical and social needs categories (e.g., hospitalization during pregnancy; toxemia; substance abuse issues; mental health problems; and referrals for assistance with food, shelter, domestic violence, immigration issues, etc.).
8. Track all referrals made to community agencies, programs and care providers. If a doula helped a homeless client access shelter, encouraged enrollment in WIC or made a referral for smoking cessation, suspected postpartum depression, substance abuse treatment, or elder neglect/abuse, capture this in your system. It demonstrates to funders that you are working in community with others and helping people access available services.
9. Ask one or two open-ended narrative questions of the doulas as well (e.g., "How were you able to make a positive difference for this family?" or "What did you learn from this experience?"). What you are aiming to gather here is testimonials regarding the program.
10. On the client evaluation side, you will also want to capture "soft" data via an open-ended question designed to gather testimonials from clients about their doulas. Ask "How did your doula make a difference for you?" or "Would you use a doula again?"

For the most part, you want checkboxes or quantifiable data, rather than open-ended narrative questions. For checklists, add a category of "none" so that you have an indication that the doula completed that section of the form and include an "other" option with space for a brief explanation.

There is additional information that you will want to track from a programmatic viewpoint such as doula performance and follow through (from both client and doula perspectives). And the doulas should be systematically surveyed regarding their experiences, challenges and ongoing training needs (see Chapter 5).

Budget and Budget Narrative

Funders want to see how their money will make a difference. This is the case you need to make. Typically, prospective grantees must complete a budget form accompanied by a narrative justification. If, for example, you need $1500 to run a volunteer doula orientation training, do the breakdown for how you arrived at that amount. Include specific costs (multiplied by estimated number of participants) for a volunteer manual, food for the day-long training, stipend for attendance (we used $25 Meijer gift cards), volunteer supplies (customized program t-shirts, doula bag and nametag), and speakers' fees. Avoid gross overestimation or underestimation of expenses. Following are a few strategies for avoiding common mistakes in the budget and budget narrative sections of your proposal:

- *Do not include items in the budget that the funder has stated they will not fund!* If they say they don't fund research, marketing, equipment, overhead, conference attendance, or whatever, then just don't push that button.
- *Avoid simple math errors.* Putting together a grant proposal is akin to assembling a jigsaw puzzle. Budget numbers will shift until all the pieces fall into place. Check your numbers and check them again. It may take a fresh set of eyes to catch any inconsistencies. If you present sloppy math from the get-go, how does the funder know that your math challenges will suddenly self-correct once you have thousands of dollars to account for?
- *Avoid wasteful spending.* Limit your costs to what is reasonable (e.g., if you need to send staff members to a training, is it possible for them to ride together and perhaps share a hotel room, rather than budgeting for individual transportation and private rooms?). Funders will appreciate efforts to use funds judiciously.
- *Don't include anything in your budget that is not explained or referenced in the proposal.* Funders want a justification for your budget; more detail is better than less. This is very important.
- *Don't pad your budget.* Competent reviewers will know the cost of goods and services and will understand prevailing wages and benefit packages. See if your state nonprofit organization has collected data on average salaries for nonprofit personnel in your state and use that as a baseline for establishing compensation levels.
- *Diversify your budget.* If it appears that you are just trying to fund salaries for existing staff, then the whole proposal is suspect as a new initiative.
- *Avoid underfunding essential staff positions.* For example, your grant activities include a ton of work that staff is responsible for, but the responsible staff member holds a 10 hour per week position). If you can demonstrate that the staff member's position is partially funded from other sources or that the individual is making an in-kind donation of their time, you can get around this. But make it clear. Who is paying for what?
- *Report all sources of support for the program, including in-kind donations.* In the sample orientation budget discussed above, if you can demonstrate that you will seek donations for food or printing services, or you have

secured expert speakers who are volunteering their time, this demonstrates resourcefulness and community support for the project. Funders like to see that the entire effort is not solely dependent upon a single source of support, that they are one component of a winning team rather than rescuing a sinking boat. Assigning an estimated value to in-kind services and including them in the overall cost for the project makes the big picture transparent to the funder.

Common Budget Categories

- Salaries and wages (state the percentage of full-time equivalent employment that the position represents—.5 FTE for 20 hours per week—and show the calculation for the number of hours times the hourly rate of pay)
- Payroll taxes (add approximately 10 percent to above amount or have an accountant crunch the numbers precisely for you)
- Fringe benefits (if you offer these, then calculate precise amount)
- Contract services/professional fees (for outsourced services or workers, including consultants, trainers, tech support, third-party evaluators, etc.)
- Office space or occupancy costs (rent, utilities, maintenance, phone, fax, internet access)
- Equipment (computers, laptops, printers, etc.)
- Supplies (office supplies, postage, educational materials, food for trainings)
- Staff/board development (professional development training, conferences)
- Travel-related expenses (airfare, mileage reimbursement, hotel, meals on the road, airport shuttles)
- Program evaluation (up to 15 percent)
- Incentives for client participation in, for example, focus groups or educational sessions ($25 Meijer gift cards work well; less has been shown to be insufficient as an incentive, even among very poor populations)

For volunteer doula programs, we might regularly include:

- Scholarships for doula training
- Volunteer orientation program
- Stipends for doulas (to cover out-of-pocket expenses)
- Outreach (brochures, mileage reimbursement, giveaways, display materials, fees for exhibitor's tables)

Budget Terminology

Direct costs are the total for all the line items.

Indirect costs include operational expenses not directly connected with the proposed project. These may or may not be allowed by the funder. You always want to include, whenever possible, whatever the allowable percentage is for indirect costs if you can. Just ask the funder if the RFP does not make it clear one way or the other.

In-kind contributions are what the grant applicant and its community partners are contributing to the project but not requesting from the funder. Don't overlook these.

Matching funds are what the grant applicant matches in the project budget from cash reserves or projected income, or funds that will be provided by another funder, pending approval of the proposal. Some grantors, particularly government agencies, require a specific percent of matching funds per dollar granted.

Restricted funds are monies designated for a specific purpose and that purpose only, for example, most grant budgets.

Unrestricted funds are monies given or earned with no strings attached. The organization is free to set spending priorities for all unrestricted funds.

Budget Progress Reports

Be sure to explain under-spending of grant funds if you are required to turn in a mid-term report and less than half the funds are spent. The funder might reasonably wonder whether you are on track with your objectives and program activities if the funds have not been spent. Tell them what your challenges have been and explain your plan for addressing these challenges. Remember, the funder is your ally! Your success is their success.

Organizational History and Accomplishments

Funders will be curious about your organization's history, credibility, capacity and stability. For the history, impart straightforward information such as (1) when the organization was founded, (2) who founded it, (3) where was it founded, (4) why it was started (original purpose or mission) and (5) services it provides, who benefits from the services and how you fulfill your mission today. The funder is looking for experience, reputation (especially of founder), location, mission match, and services and benefits.

On the credibility side, funders are interested in knowing if you have a history of setting goals and reaching them and whether you are new or experienced in the service area. You can highlight progress made by the board of directors, list any awards given (including ones for non-profit management), discuss notable successes of clients helped, landmark goals reached or model programs replicated. Celebrate your successes! In a nutshell, indicate why you are the person or organization best qualified to solve the problem. Emphasize what makes your proposal or organization unique. Describe the qualifications of the personnel who will be responsible for overseeing the project and implementing grant objectives. Describe any essential collaborative or fiduciary relationships. If consultants are going to be employed, describe their qualifications as well.

> **The funder doesn't know** your organization. Help them "see" a picture of who you are in their minds.

This section is a perfect example of a piece of a proposal that, once developed, can easily be plugged into other grants in a boilerplate fashion. In other words, it's recyclable! Many sections of a grant proposal, for example description of your target population, can be recycled. They may require some tweaking for each funder to emphasize different aspects and priorities, but you don't have to start from scratch each time you write a grant.

Anticipate Potential Barriers

Not all funders will specifically require you to address the question of barriers. It is helpful, nevertheless, to attempt to anticipate potential problems or barriers. How will you overcome them? For example, what will be involved with reaching out to an immigrant population? How will you recruit volunteer doulas from a community that is unfamiliar with the concept of doulas? If the doulas are low income themselves, what obstacles might they have to overcome to participate with the program? How will you keep program volunteers motivated? Will there be any resistance to program participation in the target population?

Sustainability Strategies

Sustainability is a hot topic. Too many grant projects disappear after the funding is gone. None of us want to go to such great effort, build a client base and develop a steady source of referrals only to have it all disappear into thin air. How are you going to ensure ongoing benefits once the funding runs out? This is one of the biggest questions in the mind of the grant reviewer. More and more funders are requiring applicants to specifically address their plans to build in sustainability for the program. Don't be too daunted by this! There are no guarantees; take your best shot. In general, a common theme of sustainability strategies is that revenue-producing programs, or aspects of the charitable program that can be turned into revenue producers, will underwrite at least part of the cost of the charitable program. Is there a way that you can build this in? (See Chapter 5, page 215.)

Appendices

The appendices, if allowed, are supporting documents that provide more detail about your program and proposal. They may include:

- program brochure
- evaluation tool(s)
- letters of support
- outreach literature samples
- job description for new position(s)
- proof of past accomplishments with the program, such as certificate of award

For the most part, reviewers are unlikely to scrutinize these documents (except for the letters of support); however, if they have questions about your program or proposal, the appendices provide an opportunity to find the answers. This can be especially helpful when space limitations in the RFP make it challenging to provide desirable background information. For example, in doula program proposals to some funders, I felt that it was necessary first to define and explain the role of the doula. Including as appendices the DONA International position statement on the role of the doula, along with the standards of practice and code of ethics for doulas, helped to build credibility.

Proposal Writing Tips

- Make sure your writing style is crisp, concise and quickly makes your point.
- Avoid generalities; be specific about the problem you are addressing, who will be helped by your initiative and how.

- Be consistent in style and format throughout your proposal. Your proposal should read as though it were written by a single person (even if that is not the case).
- At the same time, put some heart into it. Engage the reader. Judicious use of pictures or quotes can help you stand out and can be incorporated if space limitations allow.
- Present your strongest arguments and most compelling documentation first.
- Anticipate the reviewers' questions in articulating your rationale.
- Support your proposal with concrete and specific documentation, but don't overdo it. You don't want the reader to get lost in statistics. To establish credibility, make sure all your references are correct and your data as current as possible.
- Proofread carefully and use a spell checker before submitting the proposal. Overall, make sure your proposal is complete, free of errors, grammatically correct and attractively presented.
- Visual aids such as charts, graphs and tables make data more accessible and are appreciated.
- The first time you use an acronym, write out what it stands for and put the acronym in parentheses, e.g., Center for the Childbearing Year (CCY). After that, you can just use the acronym.
- Seek out reviewers to read your proposal and comment on it. Potential reviewers include colleagues and experienced grant writers. Most importantly, find someone who is not familiar with your project, an industry outsider, to read your proposal. This person will help you identify presumptions you may be making; if they "get it," then it is likely your reviewers will too. You also want someone to do a technical review, matching the proposal to the RFP and ensuring that all conditions have been met.
- Less is more! Reviewing stacks of proposals is a difficult job. Grant reviewers are often busy volunteers who quickly learn to scan proposal abstracts to get a quick overview of what you expect to do, with whom, when, how and toward what measurable outcomes. If you are short and to the point, and you've answered the key questions, your grant will be viewed as comprehensible and fundable. If you bog down the reviewer with too much ambling detail, they'll have a hard time understanding your proposal and it is likely to end up in the reject pile. Good proposals are easy to understand.

- More and more funders are going to online submissions. These can be tricky. Assume that you will run into time-consuming technical glitches and then be relieved if they don't manifest. You should not count on tech support being available when you need it, especially on deadline day, so don't cut it too close to the wire with online submissions. One recommendation is to write up the entire proposal in a Word document; get all your reviewers' feedback; incorporate necessary changes and then cut and paste completed sections into the online system.
- If mailing your proposal, allow plenty of time (or FedEx overnight if you like living on the edge).
- A catchy name for the project or program can make a big difference. First impressions and a memorable theme are important! Remember, you are selling an idea.

Doula Program Funding Strategies

Here are some strategies that worked for our community-based volunteer birth and postpartum doula program.

Scholarships for doula training should be a line item on nearly every grant proposal. By providing scholarships, the program can ensure a community-based approach that involves doulas serving families from their own community. The executive director became an approved doula trainer (we chose DONA International). We used funds from one grant to pay for the ED to gain these credentials as part of an overall "sustainability strategy." (I qualified for acceptance into the trainer program because of my longstanding experience as a childbirth educator and practicing doula.) Once credentialing was complete, the DONA doula trainings allowed us to offer a revenue-producing program capable of attracting folks who were able to pay for doula training. It also allowed us to write scholarships for doula training into grant budgets.

Now, here's a secret—pay close attention to how this worked for our organization. The entire scholarship package was valued at approximately $500 per person. We could then fill our trainings with folks who paid for training, as well as those funded by scholarships. The scholarship funds, in effect, went toward covering indirect costs for the organization. How? As a line item in the budget, scholarships funds were "spent" every time a scholarship was awarded. But this expenditure was not the same as most other expenditures in the nonprofit's budget, such as the purchase of supplies, whereby money goes outside of the organization. As a paper transfer, it simply freed up those funds for indirect program costs. In nonprofit lingo, the scholarships (once awarded) became unrestricted funds. The benefit here was that these funds were then available to help cover the ED's salary, rent and so on.

Frame the role of the doula as a community outreach worker and add specialized training for at-risk pregnant women. Seek funding for "enhanced training" beyond the core doula curriculum that covers risk-related topics such as prematurity prevention, substance abuse during pregnancy, domestic violence awareness and so on (see Chapter 5 for more on this topic).

Emphasize the value of the one-on-one mentoring aspect of the doula role. This personalized continuity of care provided is a unique program benefit.

Promote community volunteerism. Volunteer doula programs should highlight the opportunity for community service provided by the program.

Making the Case for End-of-Life Doulas

Qualitative and quantitative research is needed on how doulas affect patient and family care at the end of life. The evidence base for end-of-life doulas does not exist today. Yet, intuitively, the concept resonates widely. There isn't one person with whom I have shared my latest pursuit who hasn't been curious and affirming about the idea. Advocates seeking to make the case for end-of-life doulas might want to reference the Institute of Medicine's 2015 Landmark Report, *Dying in America: Improving Quality and Honoring Individual Preferences Near the End of Life.* The report makes five recommendations for healthcare providers across the spectrum to improve end-of-life care in America. End-of-life doulas are in alignment with all five recommendations, as represented in the table below.

Recommendations / What is needed	How doulas are aligned
Deliver comprehensive patient-centered and family-oriented care.	• Doulas provide compassionate patient- and family-centered care.
Initiate high-quality conversations about Advance Care Planning (ACP).	• Doulas have a thorough understanding of ACP concepts. • Doulas promote ACP and may become trained ACP facilitators.
Stronger knowledge and skills in palliative care across disciplines	• Doulas are familiar with palliative care philosophy, including the bio-psycho-social model of care and the patient and family as the unit of care. • Doulas are team players, collaborating with palliative care and hospice professionals to ensure all needs are met. • Doulas share information and promote exploration of palliative care options.
Policies and payment systems to support high-quality end-of-life care	• Doulas are cost-effective, trained caregivers. • Third-party insurance reimbursement for end-of-life doula services would help fulfill unmet needs and ensure all families had access to doula care.
Public education and engagement to encourage ACP and informed choice based on the needs and values of individuals	• In accordance with the doula model of care, doulas promote informed decision making. • Doulas help individuals and families plan ahead. • Doulas provide individualized care based on the client's needs and values.

Heads-Up on Fiduciary Relationships

Fiduciary relationships were described briefly in Chapter 4. For our purposes, their primary use is to fund a doula program (or related initiative) without having to set up a freestanding nonprofit organization. Ideally, the doula program would be an independent entity under the umbrella of the fiduciary who qualifies for all the tax benefits of a nonprofit organization including grant funding. In this scenario, grant checks must pass through the fiduciary to the doula program. Most fiduciaries will have a set percentage (10 percent, perhaps more) that they will retain for their efforts. If an argument can be made that the fiduciary agency is providing some real value on the grant (beyond passing checks), then a reasonable argument can be made in the grant for that 10 percent; otherwise it may work against you, from the funder's perspective, as a line item in the budget.

One foundation that was interested in our doula program informed us that we wouldn't qualify for the big ($200,000 plus) grants through their organization because the foundation had a rule that the size of a grant could not equal more than 25 percent of the grantee's annual budget. In other words, we would need to have an annual budget of $400,000 to qualify for a $200,000 two-year grant. In response, we forged a fiduciary relationship with the department of nursing of a local university, thereby overcoming the restriction on grant size, and subsequently won an $189,000 two-year grant from the W. K. Kellogg Foundation.

While the Kellogg grant was a huge success for the program, the fiduciary relationship presented its own set of challenges. The primary one was that we were now dependent on two large bureaucracies to process checks. The foundation was shockingly slow to issue checks. If a grant period technically started, by contract, on March 1, we might not have money in hand until as late as November! I was always baffled by the assumption that we could or would nevertheless proceed with implementation of all project objectives, despite the lack of actual funds. The next obstacle was getting the university to process invoices to transfer funds to our organization. This was an ongoing source of irritation as there were multiple steps in the process and multiple stages and departments involved in releasing the funds and this complexity provided the opportunity for mistakes to be made, ensuring a very slow process. Our main contact person to troubleshoot all of this was chronically over-committed and often unavailable to make solving these issues her new part-time job. So, we waited. And waited.

Recommendations: Be Proactive!

- Formalize the fiduciary relationship with a letter of agreement *before* proceeding with development of the grant proposal(s). As in all partnerships (see Chapter 1), spell out who will be responsible for what and in what specified timeframe.
- Sit down with a representative of the fiduciary agency and ask them to describe how the transfer process works and what you can do to ensure that it works as smoothly as possible.
- Try to keep the transfers to a minimum, ideally moving the entire available amount in one transaction (though there may be reasons they can't do this).
- Get fund transfer timelines in place and identify your key contact person for follow-up and problem-solving support. Meet this person, nurture the relationship throughout the grant period and express gratitude for this individual's efforts. You want your fiduciary representative to be an advocate for your program and to feel invested in your success.
- Given the number of items that are outside of your control, the need to have some depth in your funding sources is made even clearer. Even with a "big" grant landed, you can never stop fundraising. You may need to bridge gaps between grants, as well as gaps between the start of a grant period and the release of funds.

Sample Funded Proposal: Ann Arbor Thrift Shop

This organization is a small, local charity run by women. It took me approximately two hours to write this proposal, adapting language from previous proposals and plugging it into this funder's RFP format, which was very small in scope and did not require outcome objectives or an evaluation component. The ladies loved it and were especially impressed with the win-win concept of helping the volunteers as well as the mothers being served. I think incorporating the one success story along these lines really drove it home and got them engaged emotionally.

Cover Letter

Please find attached our proposal for funding from the Ann Arbor Thrift Shop. We are seeking funding to expand our capacity to serve more families in the city of Ann Arbor through our innovative *Doulas Care Program.* This program offers a unique service that is gaining a growing reputation among care providers in the city who work with childbearing adolescents and other populations of women with at-risk pregnancies. We welcome this opportunity to acquaint you with our program and make a difference for moms and babies. Thank you for your consideration.

Proposal

Project Description

We are requesting funding support to increase the number of women served by our community-based volunteer doula program known as *Doulas Care.* This program matches low-income pregnant women with a trained doula who provides emotional, educational and logistical support during pregnancy, birth and the first six weeks postpartum. At a minimum, doulas provide three prenatal visits, attend the labor and birth, and provide three postpartum home visits for each woman enrolled in the program. In cases where extended postpartum services are needed, doula teams provide in-home support from six weeks up to three months postpartum.

Doulas reduce isolation, provide needed social and household support and help women access medical care and community resources. Doulas are often said to "mother the new mother," mentoring and encouraging her as she transitions into her new role. For isolated new mothers suffering from depression, recovering from surgery or caring for twins without family support, doulas can make a significant difference. Currently, every woman enrolled in the program is screened for depression and receives referrals for follow-up services if determined to be at risk.

The *Doulas Care Program* has been in existence since 1999. An estimated 280 families will have been enrolled this year. Currently, the program has approximately 75 volunteer doulas in 11 counties throughout Southeastern Michigan, but more doulas are needed in the city of Ann Arbor. The doulas come from the communities they serve and, in some cases, are themselves low-income women or former teen mothers. A few bilingual doulas are available to serve Latino, Arabic and French-speaking families.

Who Will Be Served by the Funding?

We will target low-income Ann Arbor women who are currently pregnant or newly postpartum and their families, including teen mothers, immigrant mothers and others with limited resources and high needs. Specifically, funds will be used to provide 10 doula training scholarships for low-income women who want to become doulas and participate as volunteers in the program. In exchange for training, scholarship recipients agree to provide support to a minimum of five families each, which means that at least 50 Ann Arbor families can be served with this initiative.

The volunteers are themselves served by the *Doulas Care Program* because the doula training offered at CCY carries professional certification through DONA International, the largest certifying organization for doulas in the world. The community volunteer work provides newly trained doulas with an opportunity to get hands-on experience in the field and complete the certification process. Many women are using doula training and experience as a pathway into nursing, midwifery, social work or public health careers, while others go on to establish independent doula businesses. Others just want to be long-term volunteers and help moms and babies. One former scholarship recipient/volunteer was a single mother of four who had supported her family for years with night-time nanny work. After obtaining doula certification, she was able to get a job with Michigan State Extension Services as a home visitor—a job that carries full medical benefits for her family, something she had never been able to provide before. In summary, the program serves both families and doulas, a true win-win proposition.

How Will Those Served Benefit from This Funding?

The use of doulas is an innovative, low-cost option for addressing complex health problems during the childbearing year such as reducing the number of low-birth-weight babies, improving access to prenatal health care and social services, and preventing postpartum depression. By combining social support with risk identification, doulas bridge gaps between the health care system and individual pregnant women. The doula acts as a trained navigator addressing the unique needs of the woman she is serving while encouraging and enabling access to existing community resources. Through this effort, we hope to reduce health disparities in the communities at greatest risk and improve maternal and infant health outcomes. Additionally, research has established that women supported by doulas are more affectionate toward their babies at six months postpartum than women who did not receive doula support.

How Will This Funding Benefit the Ann Arbor Community?

Doulas Care fulfills CCY's mission of "promoting healthy families." We believe that beginnings are important and are doing our best to ensure that more families get off to the best possible start in life. The community benefits because a child's optimal physical and mental health cannot be nurtured by an overwhelmed, depressed mother who is suffering in isolation. Doulas provide concrete household help, transportation to doctors' visits when needed, and education regarding infant calming and coping skills. They also help families access appropriate community services. Through early intervention and prevention, we hope to get families the help they need before child neglect and abuse manifest. If the mother is mothered, she becomes a better nurturer.

Please Provide Specific Examples of Your Organization's Past Accomplishments

The *Doulas Care Program* received the DONA International Founders' Award for Excellence in a Doula Group. This award was presented at the DONA International Annual Conference in New Orleans on July 24, 2004 to Executive Director Patty Brennan. Accomplishments include a steady growth rate for the *Doulas Care Program.* Specifically, in its first two years, *Doulas Care* served 8 families. In 2001, 38 families were served; in 2002, 81; in 2003, 118; in 2004, 151; in 2005, 220; and in 2006, we project a total of 280 families served. The consistent growth of this program demonstrates: (1) that there is a need in the community for the unique services offered, (2) that a referral network is well established and (3) that senior staff possess program development and delivery expertise.

How Will the Thrift Shop Be Recognized for Its Support?

1. Upon receipt of verification of support from the Thrift Shop, CCY will issue a press release announcing the grant award.
2. Notice will be placed on the front page of our website for the first month.
3. Ongoing acknowledgment throughout the grant period will be posted in multiple spots on the website.
4. Support will be acknowledged in our annual report which is also published on our website.
5. Support will be acknowledged on a display board that is used at all community outreach events attended by CCY to promote our programs.

Proposed Budget

10 Doula Training Scholarships @ $500 each = $5,000

Sample Funded Proposal: Ann Arbor Community Foundation

The following proposal to our local community foundation was in response to an RFP for nonprofit organizational "capacity-building" grants. The proposal demonstrates creative adaptability to available opportunities. This grant went in under the "arts" arm of the foundation, which was unique for us.

Purpose of Grant

To create a touring photographic exhibition entitled *Doulas in Community* designed to increase public awareness about the value of doulas as providers of social and educational support for pregnant and newly postpartum women and their families.

Grant Summary

For this project, we will partner with local photographer/artist/anthropologist Harriette Hartigan, who will serve as the photo documentarian for the Center for the Childbearing Year's (CCY) community-based volunteer doula program known as *Doulas Care.* Harriette is an internationally renowned photographer whose compelling work bearing witness to women's and families' experiences of pregnancy, childbirth and breastfeeding has been widely published. Through this project, we intend to tell a story in pictures with accompanying brief narrative or quotes from the subjects. The product will be the creation of an exhibit, suitable for public display, portraying the work of the doula as she provides support to women and their families. The exhibition is designed to travel throughout the region, finding its home in a series of public venues, to inform people about doulas.

The word "doula" comes from a Greek word meaning "one who provides service." In all cultures throughout time, women have always supported each other through the transition into motherhood, both at the time of delivery and throughout the early weeks postpartum. The emerging role of the doula mentor represents the professionalization of the role of the female support provider. Doulas are strictly nonmedical, nonclinical care providers who provide emotional, social and informational support. Social and emotional support are understood to be key factors in ameliorating the damage caused by depression and in addressing a host of medical and social risk factors. A growing body of evidence demonstrates that doulas have a positive effect on maternal–infant birth outcomes and on women's feelings of self-esteem and competence in their mothering role.

In the *Doulas Care Program,* pregnant women are matched with a volunteer doula, trained by CCY, who provides a minimum of three prenatal visits, labor and birth support, and three postpartum visits. Women who are at risk of postpartum depression, or who have special needs postpartum, are given extended doula care up to three months postpartum. The program is filling a gap in services for the population served, as social support is scarce. Most home-visitor programs are limited to one or two hour-long visits by a nurse or social worker. The doula provides continuity throughout all phases of the experience by developing a mentoring relationship with the mother. Doulas are trained in risk identification and their role involves helping families access existing community resources and services. All services provided by the program are free to qualifying low-income families.

Program Outcome Statement

We intend to produce a compelling and educational community outreach tool that can be displayed in an ongoing series of public venues throughout our service area to grow the capacity of CCY's charitable *Doulas Care Program.*

Target Population

The target population includes the following: (1) Potential *Doulas Care* clients who are low-income, high-risk pregnant or newly postpartum women and their families in Washtenaw county (risk factors include teen pregnancy, single mothers lacking social support, women struggling with depression or who have a history of postpartum depression, mothers of newborn twins or triplets, women with a history of having given birth to a preterm or low-birth-weight baby, and socially and linguistically isolated new immigrants); (2) all women of childbearing age who might be interested in having a doula in the future if they become pregnant; (3) anyone who works with or knows pregnant women who could benefit from doula support and can serve as a referral source to the program (this target group includes professionals such as nurses, doctors, social workers and public health personnel as well as sisters, friends and grandmas); (4) women of all ages who may want to become doulas (potential volunteers include low-income community women who are supported with doula training scholarships to become doulas and complete professional certification requirements, thereby benefiting themselves from the program through enhanced employability; volunteers also include college students who are pursuing careers in nursing, midwifery, medicine, social work and public health);

(5) potential funders and donors who may provide support to the program but may not know about doulas.

Numbers served: Last year, 249 referrals were made to the *Doulas Care Program*. That number translates to 249 mother-baby pairs or a minimum of 498 people served (not including other family members who also benefit from the doula's support). Approximately 80 percent of our clients are on Medicaid. In addition, 28 low-income women were provided with doula training scholarships and then joined the volunteer program in 2006. This number includes a culturally diverse group of women, many of whom are bilingual. This program experiences steady and significant growth each year, from 38 women served in 2001 to 249 in 2006.

Program Components and Activities

A. Create Program Content

1. Engage local photographer/artist/anthropologist Harriette Hartigan to be the photo documentarian for the *Doulas Care Program*. Harriette participated in the formulation of this proposal and is ready to begin the project upon notification of funding support.
2. Schedule photo sessions that will document how the *Doulas Care Program* benefits both the families served and the volunteer doulas. Photos of doula training and support groups will be taken on site at CCY. Photos of doulas and their clients will be taken in client homes and hospitals where the clients are giving birth. Our projected timeframe for the May 2007–April 2008 grant cycle is as follows:
    - » Complete photographic sessions to include: (a) doula training; (b) volunteer orientation; (c) a doula support group meeting; (d) profile of three volunteer doulas; and (e) profile of three to five clients served—doulas in action serving diverse clientele. (May 1–October 1)
    - » Choose the photographs that will comprise the exhibit and prepare them for exhibition. (October 1–November 1)
3. Complete the narrative that will accompany the pictures (November 1).
4. Complete translation of the narratives into Spanish (December 1).

B. Line up Exhibit Venues (secure first two venues by November 1; the remainder will be ongoing)

1. Contact every public library in Washtenaw County and explore the possibility of hosting the exhibit (ideally, the exhibit would stay up for one month at each venue).
2. Use the CCY database to inform constituents of the availability of the exhibit and solicit suggestions for other possible venues.
3. Explore university and college venues, especially community colleges.
4. Pursue community churches as possible venues.
5. Plan to exhibit at conferences in the state for wider public exposure. These can include annual conferences sponsored by the Healthy Mothers Healthy Babies Coalition, Michigan Infant Mental Health Association, BirthNetwork, Michigan Midwives Association and so on.

C. Promote the Exhibit.

1. Endeavor to get a newspaper feature for the premier (November–December 2007).
2. Send out a press release for each new venue (ongoing).
3. Promote on our website (ongoing).
4. Host a duplicate exhibit on permanent display at CCY (by November–December 2007; ongoing thereafter).

Goals and Measurements

Goal 1. Make doula work visible. Since so much of doula work is done in people's home or behind closed doors on the Labor and Delivery unit, the nurturing and skilled support that doulas provide is largely invisible to the larger society. We will show doulas in action. The measure of success will be completion of an exhibit of at least twelve photos with accompanying narrative. [This is a *process* objective.]

Goal 2. Increase public awareness about the role of doulas. While we have witnessed a growing awareness of the doula role since the program's inception in 1999, there are still many people who have never heard the term "doula" before. This is particularly true when we first attempt to expand services to underserved populations such as Latinas or residents of Ypsilanti, Willow Run or Jackson. The measure of success will be that, prior to the end of the grant period, we will have displayed the exhibit in at least four public venues. [Another *process* objective]

Community Impact Statement

The proposed project is intended to develop or engage a critical mass to increase the capacity of our *Doulas Care Program.* To measure this impact, we will poll each person who (1) enrolls in the program as a client or (2) joins the program as a volunteer to determine how they first learned about doulas. We will also track reactions to the exhibit by providing feedback cards and program brochures at all venues where the exhibit is on display. We will track the number of brochures that are disseminated at each venue. We expect donation revenue to CCY to increase, but it will likely not be possible to say with certainty whether this is a direct result of grant funding. However, we will track the number of fundraising events that make use of the exhibit and the funds earned at these events. We can also make note of any donor who specifically mentions the exhibit and compare the total annual donation revenue with the previous year's amount. We estimate the impact on overall program capacity will be at least a 20 percent increase in referrals to the program, volunteer base and targeted donations manifesting well beyond the grant period. However, this goal is not likely to be reached by the end of the grant period, but rather by the end of 2008 (once the exhibition has had a full year of touring).

Sustainability

The concept of sustainability is at the heart of this proposal. Once we have completed production of the photo gallery, we will have a powerful tool to captivate and emotionally engage the viewer and mobilize support for the program. We believe the exhibition will realize its potential as an educational outreach and fundraising tool for years to come.

Funding for the *Doulas Care Program* is provided by the W. K. Kellogg Foundation, Blue Cross Blue Shield of Michigan, the James A. and Faith Knight Foundation and Medicaid Match funds. Past funders have included March of Dimes, the Michigan Women's Foundation, Pfizer Corporation, Ypsilanti Area Beyer Memorial Health Foundation, Ypsilanti Area Community Foundation and the Ann Arbor Thrift Shop. Our successful track record of steady growth, as well as the ability to secure both private and public funds, indicates the evident value of the *Doulas Care Program* and the resonant chord we are striking in the communities served.

The CCY board of directors is currently engaged in a strategic planning process with the goal of creating a plan for increasing program and donation revenue in an effort to ensure sustainability of the organization over time. Several initiatives are under consideration. We expect to have a plan in place by late spring. *Doulas in*

Community will certainly prove to be a significant asset in implementation of that plan. Thank you for your consideration of our proposal.

Budget

- Photographic services, 60 hours @ $100 per hour = $6,000 (includes mileage, supplies)
- Production of prints for exhibition = $2,000 (in-kind donation amount)
- Estimated travel costs incurred when setting up and taking down the exhibition = $300
- Evaluation costs = $200

Total Project Cost = $8,500; Award Request = $6500

What if Your Proposal Doesn't Get Funded?

Always send the funder a thank you note or some type of follow-up letter, even if your request is declined. Most funders will be happy to sit down with you and point you in the right direction to writing a more competitive proposal for the next grant cycle. Remember, the proper attitude is one of partnership. Funders want good proposals to fund. Their default position is to want to work with you. That's great news!

Even if your first grant proposal doesn't get funded, the planning and writing process allows you to resubmit your idea elsewhere. As you construct and refine the language for various pieces of each proposal and accumulate community partners and letters of support for the program, you make the next proposal submission less daunting.

Honing Your Skills

Find a Mentor/Grant Consultant

An experienced grant writer can help you plan your grant strategy and be available to answer questions and provide feedback as you develop the proposal. Successive proposals will each get a little easier. A little hand holding goes a long way—eventually, you will be a confident proposal developer. I had absolutely no experience when I first started but I did have a mentor.

Foundation and Corporate Training Opportunities

Your local community foundation may offer one-day workshops designed for groups interested in submitting proposals. These technical assistance workshops are free and open to the public, so keep an eye out for opportunities in your area. Corporate funders may also offer technical training. It's a great opportunity to meet the people involved and gain an insider's perspective on how grants are awarded. They will teach you, very specifically, what they want.

Government Technical Assistance Workshops

Many government agencies provide annual technical assistance workshops for specific grant competitions. To be notified via email of these workshops, you'll need to contact the individual state or federal funding agencies. These sessions are free and tailored to individual grant-making programs.

Local Colleges and Universities

I have taken two online grant-writing training classes through my local community college (Washtenaw Community College), both of which were offered by Beverly Browning (see Resources) and were excellent. Check to see if anything is being offered in your community or connect to the WCC online classroom.

Local Library

Before investing in subscriptions to any of the following resources, you may want to check them out at your local library first.

- Catalogue of Federal Domestic Assistance (CFDA)
- Chronicle of Philanthropy
- The Federal Register
- The Foundation Directory
- Foundation Grants Index
- Foundation News and Commentary
- Guide to U.S. Foundations
- Non-Profit Times
- Philanthropy News Digest

Nonprofit Management Organizations

Most states will have a member organization. Often these groups will sponsor trainings or include sessions on grant-writing basics at their annual conference. Some cities may also have a nonprofit management institute or group whose mission is to help you succeed in getting funded. Do a Google search to see what's available near you.

Online Programs and Websites

There are tons of websites that provide free information on grant writing with lots of sample grant proposals and templates that can be adapted for your purposes (see Resources). On my website [LifespanDoulas.com] you will find an in-depth webinar on "Writing a Winning Grant Proposal" (by yours truly) available for purchase. It is available as a download to watch on your computer. The program contains three distinct sections: (1) an overview of the grant-writing process, (2) a work-group session to generate specific goals and outcome objectives for a range of maternal-infant health initiatives, along with on-the-spot assessment of the goals and objectives generated and (3) a panel of March of Dimes Michigan grants distribution committee members speaking about their perspectives and common problems seen with submitted proposals, as well as doing an audience Q&A. This program was sponsored by March of Dimes Michigan as a preconference workshop for the Healthy Mothers Healthy Babies Annual Conference. The package contains a PDF download as well that includes the March of Dimes proposal score sheet used by grant reviewers, a super bonus. ◆

CHAPTER 7

Risk Management for Doulas and Doula Programs

WE KNOW THAT WE ARE LIVING in highly litigious times. Obstetricians are the single most frequently sued medical specialists. When parents relinquish all personal power and decision-making capacity to a higher authority, they are understandably prone to assign blame in the sad circumstance of a poor birth outcome. Trial lawyers then set about the task of determining who has the deepest pockets. Everyone who was present in the room or had a hand in the mother's birth care is a candidate for being sued, including the birth doula. In addition, postpartum doulas, end-of-life doulas and doula program administrators face a unique set of risks. How can doulas safely navigate the malpractice quagmire? In this chapter, we will identify a variety of strategies designed to limit risk exposure for both doulas in private practice and organizations running doula programs. While insurance can be one piece of the puzzle, emphasis is placed on preventive strategies, managing the liability associated with unhappy customers or poor outcomes, and the development of a comprehensive plan.

There are four ways to manage risk: elimination, retention, reduction and transference. Let's consider each approach in turn. As a strategy, elimination of risk involves discontinuing the product or service—simple enough and a good starting point for our discussion. If one chooses to offer doula services to families, either as an individual or as a program provider, then complete elimination of risk is off the table. Retention is a conscious choice to accept some risk and proceed to deliver services. The strategy of reduction, then, involves placing limits on an accepted risk. In Chapter 2, the option of protecting personal and family assets by establishing a limited liability corporation was discussed in detail. This is one approach to risk reduction. And finally, transference is the purchase of insurance so that someone else (the insurance company) bears the financial risk of a potential lawsuit.

Often, when we think in terms of limiting liability, insurance is the first approach that comes to mind, whether it is car insurance, health insurance, home insurance or malpractice coverage. We tend to think of insurance as protecting us against lawsuits when, in fact, anyone can sue anyone else at any time for just about anything. Keep in mind that professional liability insurance does not prevent the filing of a lawsuit any more than health insurance prevents the need for health care. What these policies can (and should) do is pay for a legal defense against the charges and cover the cost of a settlement should the court rule in favor of the plaintiff. In other words, insurance can limit the financial risk of engaging in doula work. And, while it is important to limit financial risk, clearly the emotional, psychological and energetic toll of a lawsuit is likely to be devastating well beyond financial considerations. I think it is safe to assume that we would all prefer to avoid any scenario that involves defending ourselves in court. So, while it may be advisable to purchase insurance protection if available, we must nevertheless focus our attention on strategies that can limit risk or prevent the filing of a lawsuit in the first place.

Scope of Practice

The number of organizations certifying doulas have multiplied rapidly in recent years. Any organization worth affiliating with should have published position papers defining the doula's role, scope of practice and professional code of conduct. Before dismissing scope of practice as being too restrictive, doulas should appreciate that it protects the doula every bit as much as the consumer. If doulas work diligently to practice within their scope, endeavoring at the same time to communicate clearly with their clients regarding what they can and cannot do, their risk exposure will be significantly reduced. Doula program administrators should be highlighting and emphasizing compliance with a defined scope of practice for all doulas participating in their program.

The nonclinical, nonmedicalized role of the doula is paramount. DONA International standards of practice clearly state that:

> *Doulas do not perform clinical or medical tasks such as taking blood pressure or temperature, fetal heart tone checks, vaginal examinations or postpartum clinical care ... Additionally, as doulas do not "prescribe" treatment, any suggestions or information provided within the role of the doula must be done with the proviso that the doula advise her client to check with her primary care provider before*

> *using any application … Clients and doulas must recognize that the advocacy role does not include the doula speaking instead of the client or making decisions for the client.*

Lifespan Doulas has articulated a scope of practice for end-of-life doulas which has been adopted by the National End-of-Life Doula Alliance [NEDA.com]. The following limitations are delineated:

- As non-medical care providers, end-of-life doulas do not perform clinical tasks (e.g., monitor vital signs, administer medication).
- Doulas refrain from giving medical advice or from persuading clients to follow a specific course of action or treatment.
- Doulas refrain from imposing their own values and beliefs on the client.
- Doulas do not undermine their clients' confidence in their caregiver(s). However, in cases where clients are initiating a discussion about a caregiver's advice or expressing dissatisfaction with a caregiver's practice or attitudes, the doula uses good listening skills to support clients to consider their options.
- Doulas do not usurp the role of other professionals and caregivers such as the hospice nurse, social worker, chaplain, home health aide, etc., but rather work as a member of the support team.
- Doulas do not facilitate medical aid-in-dying but may be present per client request.
- Doulas cannot take payment for hands-on care of the body of the deceased.

The more a doula takes on in terms of advice and decision making for her client, assuming an authoritative position, the higher the risk of blame being directed to the doula in the case of a poor outcome or broken relationship. And the simple truth is that doulas are not sufficiently trained, nor getting paid enough to take on the liability associated with assuming a more authoritative or medicalized role. In this section, we explore the practices, beliefs and ethical issues that the doula scope of practice is designed to address. We will unpack the underlying themes to better understand why they needed to be articulated in the first place.

Client Self-Determination

What can doulas do, specifically, to foster *self-determination on the part of clients?*

Doulas can teach clients about the process of informed consent and shared decision making. Encourage them to dialogue with their care providers and consider their options. Suggest that your client write down questions to ask their care provider at the next office visit. Role play with the client until she feels confident about asserting her needs. By employing these strategies, doulas are teaching their clients self-advocacy skills. Now she is prepared to be her own advocate rather than depending on the doula to be her voice and security blanket. For complicated issues that clients may be grappling with, the doula can employ good listening skills, providing a sounding board for them to work through their own problem rather than attempting to solve it for them.

> **Informed Consent**
>
> **Is it an emergency? If not . . . Use your BRAIN.**
>
> **B**enefits? How will the recommended test/treatment positively affect me?
>
> **R**isks? How could it negatively affect me?
>
> **A**lternatives? Is there anything else I can try first? Other options?
>
> **I**ntuition? What is my intuition telling me? What does my gut say?
>
> **N**othing? What will happen if I choose to do nothing?

Encourage families to write letters to hospital or program administrators if they are especially happy or unhappy with certain aspects of their care. This is a good way for the consumer's advocacy voice to be heard and it provides the means to safely discharge anger (if any) at the source. If there is any truth to the notion that depression is anger turned inward, then this is an important step toward mental health. Families can make note of the names of care providers who were especially kind and respectful or inappropriate and controlling. Encourage clients to let administrators know how much they appreciated having the option of a water birth. Or that they chose this hospital because midwives were on staff or this hospice because of the end-of-life doula program. On the other hand, if parents find an institution to be unresponsive to their needs, they should absolutely let the people in charge know why they will be taking their health insurance somewhere else in the future!

Hospitals are in a highly competitive market. The one time in life when 99 percent of Americans are likely to interface with their local hospital is when having a baby. In most cases, if this is a positive experience, the customer will return to that same hospital for care throughout their lifespan. Thus, hospitals are motivated to win and keep maternity care customers. Our clients alone have the power of the dollar. It's the doula's job to encourage clients to claim their power.

Give some examples of doula actions or attitudes that do not foster self-determination but rather encourage the client to be dependent upon the doula.

Examples of inappropriate doula behaviors include: A client claims that she feels intimidated by her doctor and is "not good at speaking up for herself" and the doula consents to speak for her. A doula reinforces the client's notion that the doula's presence can ensure success with a "conscious death" or any pre-determined outcome. The doula tells the client what to do. The doula imposes her own agenda on the family. And so on.

Client Confidentiality and Privacy

Confidentiality and privacy are probably the most often violated tenets of the Code of Ethics/Conduct. How can doulas protect the privacy and identity of clients while still seeking support from other doulas after a difficult client scenario or needing to problem solve an issue?

This question acknowledges that doulas have a strong need to talk with each other about their experiences. If we can find a way to do so respectfully, maintaining client confidentiality, then there is much we can learn from each other. Beyond merely refraining from using client, family member and caregiver names, doulas should carefully avoid reference to any demographic information about their clients that might identify them. Details such as what they do professionally, where they live, and their religion or socio-economic status should all be kept private.

Be thoughtful and purposeful in storytelling and avoid any tendency to simply blab.

Consider whether your need to talk about a client scenario is due to a need for specific resources, problem-solving or feedback (e.g., is there anything else I could have tried?), or if it is more personal to you (e.g., a boundary issue with a client, someone who is pushing your buttons or a need to vent). If personal, then you might go outside of the local doula community to a friend, counselor or doula friend from out of state. If you are simply seeking resources for a client and want to go on a Facebook doula group, just ask for the help you are seeking; you don't need to go into the details of the client scenario: "Does anyone have a recommendation for a good chiropractor in East Detroit?" rather than "My client, who is having her third baby in October, was told by her doctor that . . . bla, bla, bla . . ." We're on a need-to-know basis here.

Discuss how the internet may lead doulas into violation of a client's privacy.

Keep in mind that the internet is a public forum. Blogging about a client's story and sharing on social networking sites, even without identifying the client by name, is risky. The clients may very well read what you wrote and recognize themselves in the story. And, while you are both witnessing the same events unfold, the folks at the center of the story will have a different view of the experience than the doula. It's their story; let it be their choice whether to share it. Even something as innocuous as posting on Facebook "I'm off to a vigil (or a birth)" could be harmful if a friend or family member of the client is aware these folks are your clients. It will lead them to know what's going on when your client might prefer to control the release of all information and announcements. In that case, you have just "outed" them.

Doulas should also refrain from posting client photos on the internet or using them in their own promotional materials, unless they have obtained written permission to do so. Written permission ensures that there can be no misunderstanding on this score. Each person depicted in the photograph must give their permission.

Duty to Complete Services

List factors that could challenge or prevent the doula's ability to reliably complete services to a client. What qualifies as a legitimate excuse and what doesn't? How should the doula handle an important family event of her own that was not scheduled when the client first hired her?

Factors that can challenge a doula's capacity for fulfilling her end of the contract include illness of self or close family member, two births/vigils at once, funeral to attend, car breakdown, lack of child care, or blizzard/road conditions that make driving extremely hazardous. Some of these factors are legitimate and some not so much. As doulas, it is our responsibility to have reliable transportation available. If we have small children, we need to have multiple layers to our babysitting support—primary go-to person, backup for the primary, and backup for the backup's backup. You get the idea. The same goes for our backup doulas. We want to be careful to avoid the entire category of "lame excuses." We all know one when we hear one.

I have driven (very slowly and with an unhappy husband) to births during blizzards. I have attended births on my children's birthdays and Christmas. I have turned down trip opportunities and missed professional conferences. However, under no circumstances was I going to miss my parents' 50th wedding anniversary celebration or my son's promotion to Black Belt, nor was I going to leave my father's hospital bedside as he lay dying. I can't give you a comprehensive list of what qualifies and what doesn't. If we require more built-in flexibility to accommodate our lifestyle, then perhaps teaming up with another doula—so that the client understands from the outset that she may get one or the other team member—may be the way to go. Each doula will need to make that call. We must, however, take our commitment to "be there" very seriously.

The Issue of Refunds

Under what circumstances should a birth doula refund the client's fee?

Clearly, if the doula misses a pre-paid birth due to her own fault or issues, then she should refund the full fee to the client. Yes, this includes refunding even time spent in prenatal visits, in my opinion. The client's primary reason for hiring a doula is that she wants support at *her birth.* Prenatal visits are a necessary part of the service package so that the doula can get to know her client and help her identify how she would like to be supported *at her birth.* If we miss the birth, we are just about the most worthless doula ever, from the client's perspective. In the following circumstances, the birth doula does *not* owe the client a refund:

- Mom calls the doula late or births precipitously; doula got there in a reasonable response time but misses the actual birth. *(BUT: Doulas must take care to communicate clearly, in writing, how and when clients should notify them that labor has begun. In other words, be proactive about this risk.)*
- Mom changes her mind after the refund date has passed. *(BUT: The refund date must be written into a client contract. Usually, the date is coincident with the onset of the "on-call" period, approximately two–three weeks prior to the due date.)*
- Mom is unhappy with her birth; perhaps a planned unmedicated labor or VBAC delivery ended in a cesarean. *(BUT: Doulas must take care to respond appropriately during prenatal visits if the mother attempts to shed responsibility for her birth. Doulas must always reflect back to the mother that she is the one who has the power and that we can only support her in her strengths. If the doula allows her client to put her on a pedestal in the role of savior, then the doula must be prepared to fall off the pedestal.)*

If the doula misses the birth through no fault of her own, a reasonable response would be to offer additional postpartum support services in compensation. The message is that you care about your client and you want her to feel that she received good value for her investment with you. Good value translates to happy customers, referrals and return business.

The "BUTs" listed demonstrate the central importance of good communication skills and boundaries on the part of the doula. These are learned skills and, in some cases, we have to learn the hard way. In the case of an angry client, justified or not, doulas may want to consider refunding the fee as a means of damage control. A slight risk here could be that returning the fee might be interpreted as validating the client's complaint. If the doula strongly feels that the client is being unreasonable and that the doula bears no responsibility for whatever occurred, then the doula may want to hold her ground. Running the scenario by a trusted mentor, as part of your decision or response, is a recommended reality check. Overall, keep in mind that the very best way to market your doula practice is by creating excellent word of mouth about your services. We all recognize the truth in the saying that a happy customer tells five people, while an unhappy customer tells 30. Sometimes, we just need to cut our losses.

> **Inclusion of a refund policy** in your contract can head off a lot of problems. Overall, the contract sets a professional tone for the relationship, delineating reasonable expectations for both parties.

The issue of stillbirth often comes up when discussing the topic of refunds in a doula training. In the case of the death of a baby, many class participants feel it is the right thing to do to refund the client for fees paid, feeling that such an act of compassion will be appreciated by the family. Or will it? If the doula attended the birth and did her best, then what would be the basis for refunding the birth fee? Does the doctor or midwife still get paid? Of course they do. Is it your fault that the baby died? For doulas acting within scope of practice, this is not possible. Your role is one of support only and doesn't include making life-and-death judgment calls. Consider whether an offer to refund your fee somehow implies responsibility on your part—in which case, it would be a tacit admission of fault and possibly increase your liability. Consider also whether or not the family might not feel offended by such an offer as it may indicate a lack of validation for their experience. Did you not deliver on your service contract? A birth took place here and you did your job. Doulas are not responsible for the outcomes of births they attend.

Some families are proactive and hire a postpartum doula before the birth takes place, while others are more reactive, responding to unanticipated needs after the birth. Postpartum or end-of-life doulas who are reserving time in their schedule for a family typically charge a retainer fee to do so. This may be a set amount or it may be a percentage of the anticipated total charges. Under what circumstances does the postpartum or end-of-life doula owe her client a refund of the retainer fee?

Clearly, if the doula cancels the contract for any reason, then the client is owed a total refund. A policy must be in place for potential cancellation on the part of the client. If your retainer fee is nonrefundable, then state so, in no uncertain terms, at the time it is collected. If a portion of the retainer fee is refundable, then a refund deadline must be set. In the case of client cancellation after the deadline has passed, the doula does not owe a refund. It is not fair for the doula to be subject to the whims of clients' shifting financial priorities or the arrival of unanticipated help. Consider the doula's position that perhaps she has turned away other business during the anticipated timeframe set aside, by contract, for the client. Bottom line, if you are collecting money up front for future services, you need a written refund policy and explicit timeframe.

Information versus Advice

Consider the difference between "advice" and "information." What are some strategies for avoiding advice giving?

Information and resources can always be shared, but "advice" is another matter. Advice entails giving your opinion in support of a specific course of action. Advice usually contains or implies the words "you should." The individual giving advice is stepping into an authoritative role and consequently must recognize the added liability that this entails.

Careful reframing of the issue at hand is in order. If the doula keeps in mind the fundamental idea that the individual is central to her own experience and acknowledges her as the source of power in her own life, then the doula's role will remain one of effective support. She will not put herself in the compromising position of authority over her

Reframing "I think you should . . ." statements

You may want to consider . . .

Have you thought about . . . ?

Would you like more information about . . .?

What do you think is best?

client, nor engage in a power play with family members or care providers on her client's behalf. Her job is to help her client access her own inner strengths and manifest them. She does not "empower" her per se, because the power is not hers to give. She provides evidence-based information, assists clients in a review of available options, and then backs off and trusts her clients to behave as adults capable of making the decisions that are right for them.

Another technique is for doulas to use reflective listening skills to help clients problem solve their own issues, rather than trying to "fix" them. Motivational interviewing is an evidence-based communication skill that employs reflective listening techniques. It recognizes the ambivalence that is often at the heart of a struggle and offers more nuanced options (beyond parroting back what the client just said) to support the client's movement through ambivalence. If you have an opportunity to receive training and practice in motivational interviewing, I highly recommend it. Time spent on acquiring/improving communication skills will never be wasted.

In addition, doulas can encourage and enable clients to seek other sources of information rather than becoming singularly dependent on the doula. Put together a reading list, ask your local library to stock the books on your list, assemble information on local resources and internet resources, and so on.

Encourage clients to write down any questions and concerns they want to discuss with their care providers. Pregnant teen mothers I have worked with were routinely encouraged to write down three questions for each prenatal visit. This puts them in the driver's seat and forces the caregiver to slow down and address the whole person with her fears, hopes, past traumas and concerns. In other words, it is empowering. Medical prenatal visits should not exclusively be about assigning numbers to body functions (blood pressure, fundal height, fetal heart tones).

To stay within their scope, doulas should refer clients with questions about medical issues to their medical care provider and squelch the desire to "save" clients from their own healthcare providers! Finally, refrain from falling into answering the trap question, "What would you do?" Your answer is irrelevant because you are not her and you do not need to live with the consequences of any choice she makes. Just put that ball back in your client's court as it betrays an underlying need to relinquish the responsibility associated with heavy choices. "I have no idea what I would do. It's tough to make these decisions. What's most important to you at this time?"

Mediation versus Advocacy

Consider the difference between "advocacy" and "mediation."

Both advocacy and mediation presume an adversarial situation. Doulas should avoid putting themselves in the middle of an adversarial relationship and speaking for their clients. Rather, teach your clients to become their own best advocates. When an important decision is pending and the family wants the doula's input, ensure that they do not put you on the spot in the presence of the care provider with the question, "What do you think?" Ideally they have learned how to ask the key questions regarding benefits, risks and alternatives directly of their care provider, though they may need prompting to do so. On occasion, some medical care providers are not forthcoming with complete answers to these questions and the client would benefit from your input. Prepare them to request privacy or more time "to think it over" if this is the case. Once care providers step out of the room, you can assist your client(s) by listening carefully to their concerns, helping them track their follow-up questions, filling in information if needed, and thereby supporting informed decision-making. In this scenario, the doula is behaving as a mediator between two parties. It may also be appropriate for the doula to prompt her client with a question, in the presence of the care provider, such as, "Would you like more information about the benefits and risks of ___?"

> **Advocacy:** the act of pleading for, supporting or recommending; active espousal
>
> **Mediation:** to settle disputes, or bring about an agreement, as an intermediary between parties, by means of compromise, reconciliation, removal of misunderstanding, etc.

On the other hand, birth doulas may need to step into the advocate role for a vulnerable client for whom the doula is the primary support person. For example, if a mother is at a point in labor when she is not able to speak up for herself and there is no partner present, then it is appropriate for the doula to remind care providers of key elements of her birth plan.

Doulas can embrace both the role of activist and doula, but not at the same time. Consider which hat you are wearing at any moment. Are you wearing your doula hat or your political advocacy hat for systems change, improved end-of-life care, or more responsive patient care? Clearly, the room where a birth or death is unfolding is not the time nor place for political advocacy. Rather, it is the time to focus on that one family in your care and assist them to achieve the best possible

When advocacy becomes necessary…

Early in my career, I was the doula for a single, African-American, teen mother on Medicaid. From our very first meeting, she told me, in no uncertain terms, that she "did not want to be cut." She had heard about episiotomies from friends and she wanted no part of that. This theme reemerged time and again in the course of caring for her. It appeared to be her bottom line—if they cut her, she would be unhappy with her birth. Period. At her birth, she was as vocal and directive with all attendants as she had been with me prenatally. Basically, she told everyone who entered her room this important piece of information regarding her birth plan. "Don't cut me." Shockingly, as the baby's head began to crown, the attending physician loaded up a syringe with lidocaine. His intentions were clear and I felt that I had no choice but to be her voice in this instance. I remember saying "You did hear her say that *she does not give her consent* to an episiotomy, right?" (By the way, those are the magic words that should stop any care provider dead in his or her tracks.) He responded, looking me in the eye, "You know she's going to tear if I don't do this." And I responded, "Well, isn't that her right to choose?" He put down the syringe and she birthed her baby over an intact perineum.

If we can avoid this type of confrontation with care providers, then we most certainly should not engage directly. However, in this instance, I suspected that the blatant disregard for her wishes was an act of discrimination due to her age, socioeconomic status and/or race. I could not let it stand, nor allow him to violate her unnecessarily. Teen mothers have rights too. There may be other scenarios in which the timeframe for the doula's advocacy is not so urgent. In these cases, if discrimination is suspected or other unacceptable staff behaviors are manifesting, the hospital's **Patient Advocate** can be called in to mediate the situation. The Patient Advocate is a person who works for the hospital and whose job it is to help patients resolve any disputes or miscommunication they may be experiencing with hospital staff members.

A few years ago, I received a weekend call from one of the volunteer doulas in our community-based program. She had attended a single, teen mother's birth on the previous day. Upon follow-up, she learned that the mother had been separated from her baby for reasons that were unclear. When the mother repeatedly asked for her baby, she was told to stop coming down to the nurses' station. Both the doula and the mother were at a loss to explain the reasons for the prolonged separation and the staff was not forthcoming, to say the least. Hearing only one side of the story, I could not make sense of it. I suggested that the doula advise her client to request mediation by the hospital's Patient Advocate. Within an hour of doing so, the mother had her baby in her arms. Clearly, whatever was going on was not due to a medical need for the baby to receive care separate from the mother and the Patient Advocate effectively resolved the situation. Had the doula gone in and made a scene on the client's behalf or alleged charges of discrimination, we cannot predict exactly what would have happened, but we can suspect that staff members may have responded defensively and dug in their heels. Perhaps the doula would have found herself virtually blacklisted so that, when attempting to provide care for future clients in that setting, she would experience significant resistance to her presence or efforts. All things considered, calling in the Patient Advocate was the right move.

experience in the given circumstances. What the doula is sometimes called to witness may no doubt fuel her passion as an advocate, but that work is for another time and in another place.

Ethics of Selling Products

Doulas should be wary of engaging in multi-level marketing schemes (aka pyramid selling, network marketing and referral marketing) or other referral kickback arrangements, especially if the doula's relationship with the company and her financial self-interest is not 100 percent transparent to the client. Honestly, selling any kind of products to your clients can be a bit dicey.

I remember seeking out chiropractic care for the first time. After an assessment and a couple of adjustments, my new doctor recommended that I purchase an ergonomically designed office chair (from him), a new special pillow (from him), and some supplements (again, from him). These were all purported to help me with my pain issues. They also represented a considerable investment of money. The effect of his recommendations? I became immediately suspicious of the entire practice set up and fired him. I didn't go to him to buy products; I went to get professional help. Had he made these same recommendations but not been enriching himself in the process, all would have been well. But making money on these recommendations? Not okay.

This does not mean that you should never sell products. I have sold a blend of herbs to be used in a postpartum healing bath for many years now. The reason? The herbs are hard to find at the last minute, after a birth, when the mama needs them. They are sold locally but the markup is considerable, retailing in the range of $40–45 per pound. Through a wholesale account that I set up, I can purchase the same herbs for $12–25 per pound. So, I keep them on hand for local customers at a slight markup (well under the retail price), more as a service than an income generator. There may be other products that fall into this category—things your clients want or need that are not otherwise readily available locally. At one point, I also set up a wholesale account for high-quality food-grown prenatal vitamins. If people in my childbirth classes wanted to make a cooperative purchase, I placed an order so they could get the wholesale price. I didn't make any money on these. I just felt uncomfortable recommending a very expensive, albeit high-quality, product and this made it much more affordable for my clients. In case you are unaware, the difference between wholesale and retail price represents a savings of 40 percent. Just be careful how you proceed. Pushing products is not a good pathway to building a trusting relationship. However, helping to meet needs is okay.

Referrals can be another tricky ethical area. If the doula is approached by another business owner who suggests a referrals reward arrangement, a little skepticism is called for. Remember our discussion earlier regarding community resources and referrals? Making referrals is an essential component of the doula's role. Referrals should be unbiased and offer choices to the client. Steering everyone to one business, whereby the doula receives a fee for the referral, is not in keeping with the doula spirit. And if you do pursue such an arrangement, be sure to make it transparent to the consumer.

How Doulas Treat Each Other

How will you view and treat other doulas in your community?

Other doulas are your backup, your support network. We have thoroughly established how much we need each other. When we are feeling unsettled about our competition, with every latest addition to the marketplace and every new doula setting up practice throwing us for a loop, we need to examine our own beliefs about abundance and scarcity. A scarcity mindset reinforces the concept that if I have my little slice of the market and someone else moves to town and takes her slice, then my slice will necessarily be diminished. This belief can become a self-fulfilling prophecy, thereby providing us with a ready excuse for failing or quitting if that is what we want to do. However, there is another option—bake a bigger pie! If more doulas are practicing, then more families will hear about how wonderful doulas are and want to hire us. The choice is simple—we can choose to drown in our isolation and parsimoniousness or we can embrace the new doula in town and invite her to join us in a "Meet the Doulas" event at the local library, perhaps securing a new backup doula (and friend!) in the process.

When fears and scarcity get the best of you, work through the "Examining Our Beliefs about Money Exercise" and the "Scarcity Versus Abundance Worksheet" in *The Doula Business Guide Workbook, 3rd Edition.*

The truth is we are all protected when families have choices. Not only is it best for them, it's good for the doulas and the care providers as well. If there is only one midwife in town, clients are more likely to tell that midwife what she wants to hear than they would if there were a handful of midwives, all working in different practice settings, from whom to choose. When consumers can shop around a bit and find the care provider who is the best match for their beliefs and needs, then we all benefit because the relationship will be based on a truthful exchange of information. The more we cling to the notion that our sister/brother doulas are our competitors, the more we will grasp at clients whom we might be better off not attempting to serve. Be yourself and have a little faith. Let the clients sort themselves out and trust that choice is good for everyone.

Beyond the need for backup, all doulas can benefit from having a support network—someone to debrief with after an emotional or disappointing experience, help problem solve an issue or just listen. Let's face it, it's unbearably hard when we are called to witness systemic inadequacies, paternalism, incompetence, manipulation or abuse. A doula with heart can really let it get the best of her. Likewise, end-of-life doulas may find themselves navigating dysfunctional family dynamics, contentious bickering, complicated relationships, unsupportive caregivers, systemic limitations and more. No one will better understand the challenges faced than another doula. Partners, even very supportive ones, have a limited capacity for listening to endless client stories. But our doula homies always have time!

What can be done about "that doula*"?*

If there is a doula in your community who is behaving inappropriately and working outside of the professional scope of practice, there is not a great deal you can do directly to intervene or make her stop. Certainly, you can speak with her about your concerns. There are two sides to every story and things may not have gone down as you have heard. Nevertheless, anyone calling herself a "doula" is, by default, representing the whole doula profession. You have a self-interest in holding her accountable. If the person in question is claiming to possess doula credentials, double-check with the credentialing organization. There will be consequences for claiming to be certified if you are not or for violating scope of practice if you are certified. In addition, any organization that certifies doulas should also have a procedure for filing a grievance against a certified doula.

If the doula is "out there" in a public way, creating bad press for doulas, performing clinical tasks, giving medical advice, or otherwise creating an adversarial atmosphere with medical care providers resulting in a hostile environment for which other doulas (and their clients) must pay the price, here are some damage-control ideas.

- Write an educational piece about doulas for your local news that emphasizes standards of care for professional doulas. One such piece that I wrote, in response to an outrageous, front-page local news story that reflected very poorly on the doula profession, ended up on the wall in the labor and delivery nurses' lounge at our local hospital. I endeavored to write my response as an educational piece intended to clarify the true role of the doula.
- In the case of a hostile OB department, ask to meet with the labor and delivery head nurse, introduce yourself and/or your doula group, and provide her with a copy of your professional standards of practice and code of conduct. Establish an open dialogue so that issues may be vetted and concerns addressed. Be curious about the nature of the problems the staff has experienced with doulas. Listen. (It doesn't hurt to bring a plate of cookies to this meeting!)
- Introduce yourself to all professionals who enter the client's room in your presence. Convey that you are a team player (you will catch MANY more flies with honey than with vinegar). Always remember that you are on someone else's turf.

How to Make an Effective Referral

Making referrals and sharing community resources for clients in need is crucial. Doulas need never cross the line to giving medical advice if they have a reliable list of practitioners in the community to whom they can refer. Doulas make referrals for requests that are: (1) outside of their scope of practice, (2) outside of the doula's professional and personal boundaries, or (3) beyond the doula's expertise. If we are in over our heads, it's smart to know when to ask for help.

Referrals versus Recommendations

Doulas should remain mindful of the difference between a referral and a recommendation. A recommendation puts our personal stamp of approval on the referral source. A recommendation is often accompanied by a testimonial regarding past successes with using this particular source and is stronger than a referral, which is generic and impersonal. It is not necessarily wrong to make a recommendation. If one particular lactation consultant in town is routinely more effective at helping moms and babies, then I would, without hesitation, recommend her. Whenever possible, I nevertheless supply a couple of other names to the client so as to provide her with choices.

Referral: to direct to a source for help or information

Recommendation: to represent as worthy of confidence, acceptance, use; commend, mention favorably

An attorney I consulted advised caution in the use of referrals stating that people have been sued for referrals that resulted in a poor outcome. His recommended protection involved listing at least three options in each referral category. While this strategy may not always be possible (not every community has three acupuncturists, for example), it is a good general principle to keep in mind. Another precaution is to include a disclaimer on directories or referral lists. For example, I publish a statewide directory of practitioners on my website. My disclaimer reads as follows:

> *All service providers listed are independent from Lifespan Doulas, LLC and have paid to be listed in this directory. Inclusion of a practitioner or service on this list is not an endorsement of any one individual. Users are encouraged to investigate service providers by checking references and credentials.*

In addition to the disclaimer, I have published *A Consumer's Guide to Hiring a Doula: Getting the Help You Need* to help families navigate unfamiliar terrain. The guide contains considerations and questions to ask prospective birth, postpartum and end-of-life doulas to aid the family in making informed decisions and discerning which doula might be the best fit for them.

After making referrals or recommendations, it is incumbent on the doula to follow up on the client's experience. Did they get the help they needed? Was it a positive experience? If you find the answers to these two questions to be anything other than affirmative, it might be time to revisit your referral list. Certainly, repeated negative feedback should constitute cause for removing a provider from your list. But if you don't ask, how will you know?

Signs that a mental health referral may be appropriate

- Repetitive storytelling; there is no change in detail, focus or affect
- Recall of an event (e.g., previous loss, birth experience or sexual assault) as if it were yesterday or with intense affect
- Fear and anxiety that are high and/or unchanging
- Ambivalence, confusion or indecision that are intense or persistent
- Lots of anger and blaming of others
- Woman is shut down with a blunt affect
- Depression with a decrease in the ability for self-care, trouble fulfilling roles, feelings of hopelessness
- Unrelenting guilt or shame
- Failure of her plan for improving mood or functioning
- Absence of support or very little support in her everyday life
- Multiple overwhelming problems

How to make a referral for mental health services

Especially when it comes to mental health issues, it can be touchy or uncomfortable to make a referral. An effective referral is one that is likely to be acted on. Here are a few suggestions.

- Reflect what you see happening in the person's life. ("I've noticed that we talk about the same thing each appointment and things don't seem to be getting better for you." Or, "You seem to be overwhelmed by many challenges right now.")
- Share how you are feeling. ("I can really feel how much pain you are in and I'm not sure how to help." Or, "I'm really worried about you.")
- Relate your own experience, if true. ("When I had a similar problem, it really helped me to talk it out with someone objective.")

Here are some ways to frame your questions and concern:

- "Have you ever consulted with/considered consulting with a counselor or therapist?"
- "The healthiest person in the family is the one who seeks help."
- "It doesn't mean you're crazy."

- "Sometimes, we need an objective person to bounce ideas off of, someone who isn't invested in the outcome or the decisions we make."
- "Why suffer longer than you have to?"
- "This problem usually doesn't get better without professional help" (e.g., substance abuse, family violence, posttraumatic stress disorder, complicated grief with intense emotions lasting longer than a year, postpartum depression).
- Use the analogy of a broken leg; it wouldn't be a sign of weakness to see a doctor (but minimize allusions to "illness").

If the person is reluctant to see a counselor, help her to establish a plan to determine when asking for help would be appropriate. How will she know when things are better ("I will feel better, like getting out of bed every morning")?

- Set a time limit, two to six weeks, depending on the severity of the problem (postpartum depression lasting beyond eight weeks is cause for a referral).
- What is her plan for improving the situation? ("I will take a 30-minute walk every day." "I'll ask my mother to come over once a week for two hours so I can have some time to myself." "I'll ask for help when I need it.")
- Make an agreement that, if at the end of the predetermined time limit, the feelings or situation has not improved, the person will contact a therapist, doctor, etc.
- Work with dad or other family members to overcome reluctance to seeking help so that they are not the barrier to a woman seeking help. ("Would it help if I talked with your partner?")
- Have a source of referrals handy. ("I know someone good. Would you like me to introduce you?")
- Remember that sometimes people who need help withdraw from others. Don't let this stop you from following up. ("I'm just calling to see how you are doing.")

Developed by Melisa Schuster, a clinical social worker and certified childbirth educator who specializes in working with women suffering from postpartum mood disorders in Ann Arbor, MI [MelisaSchuster.com]. Reprinted with permission of the author.

Creating Effective Client Contracts

Now that we have had the opportunity to discuss some of the issues that can arise between doulas and their clients, the importance of creating clarity at the beginning of the relationship emerges as an essential strategy for limiting risk. Good communication of mutual expectations is key. We must be willing to let a potential client go and find services elsewhere if we discover early on that we are not a good match for her/his needs. This is, of course, easier said than done. Imagine working hard to generate referrals to your doula business. You paid for your training and certification. You purchased some books, perhaps a few supplies. Perhaps you have a partner on the sidelines wondering when your "business" is actually going to generate money coming in rather than money going out. Sound familiar? No doubt, you will feel highly motivated to bridge any gaps between potential clients and your doula services. And, yes, you can go for it. In my years of really active doula work, I loved the diversity of my clientele and how some clients challenged me and stretched me and forced me to grow. However, when red flags start waving, one after the other, we must pay attention, slow down and respond appropriately. We are not chameleons, no matter how much we want to support the family in their choices. We cannot turn ourselves into someone we are not, violate our ethics or stretch our scope of practice to please them, nor should we. In every instance of a failed relationship or poor outcome, in hindsight, it is easy to spot those red flags. Very few storms emerge from a clear blue sky. The trick is to act on them at the time that they emerge, not play ostrich, burying our heads in the sand and hoping for the best.

> **Be Transparent**
>
> You can make it up as you go along, but you can't change the parameters or expectations with existing clients. A "no-surprises" approach is best.

All doulas should develop a client contract as a tool for clear communication. It is okay to use a template contract, such as those available on the market (see Resources) or provided in your doula training manual. However, I would encourage each doula to put her own personality into her contract. Make it your own and think of it as a living, evolving reflection of your services, your philosophy and your business.

Language that attempts to indemnify the doula is not likely to be enforceable in court, should the doula ever find herself in that situation. In other words, one cannot simply state, "I am not responsible if you are harmed in any way" and then proceed under the assumption that this proclamation constitutes protection against liability. However, language in the contract that establishes a good faith effort at clear communication of mutual expectations and responsibilities will work to the doula's favor. Therefore, I would not recommend including inflammatory indemnification language in a doula contract. It is unpleasant and it raises legal action into the realm of the possible at the very beginning of your relationship. My stance is that legal action against me is not an option and I will do everything in my power to ensure that it does not occur. The essential components of a client contract include:

- Explanation of the doula's role
- Scope of services offered
- Limitations on services offered
- Use of backup doula(s)
- Identification of parties entering into contractual agreement
- Responsibilities of each party
- Timeframe for provision of services
- Fees charged and terms and timeframe of payment
- Refund policy
- Dated signature lines for both parties and *be sure to include the partner or key decision-makers!*

Sample Birth Doula Contract

Services Offered

I see my role as providing support to you through your pregnancy, birth and immediate postpartum experience. My goal is that you feel well cared for, that you are supported in your choices, and that you make the transition into becoming a mama as smoothly and joyfully as possible. I am especially careful that my role is not to take the place of your partner or others whom you have invited to your birth, but rather to facilitate everyone's optimal involvement. The following services are included in my fee:

- Initial consultation/interview in your home (no obligation)
- Two prenatal visits in your home, lasting approximately 90 minutes each

- On-call availability beginning two weeks before and up to two weeks after your estimated due date [fill in date]
- Continuous support during your labor and birth in the hospital or birth center of your choice, or for your homebirth
- Support at home in early labor, if desired and appropriate
- Support after your baby is born during the immediate recovery phase (approximately 2 hours)
- One postpartum home visit, typically on the third or fourth day (can be earlier if needed or preferred)
- Phone consultations as needed, up to six weeks postpartum

Limitations on Services

As your doula, I am committed to supporting you and your partner to make informed choices regarding your experience and care. I will not make decisions for you nor directly interfere with your health care providers on your behalf. My role is to provide nonmedicalized care focused on emotional, informational and physical support, including hands-on comfort measures, during labor and birth. I do not perform clinical tasks such as monitoring fetal heart tones or checking dilation while at home in early labor.

Backup

I promise to be available for two weeks on either side of your due date, except for any dates I provide to you up front at our initial interview. Should you birth outside of the on-call timeframe, I may very well still be available, but if I am not, a backup doula will be on call for me. This way, you can be assured that you are covered and will always receive excellent care. Please understand that illness, a family emergency or two births happening at once might also cause me to activate my backup doula. In the case of using backup, I will continue to provide as much of the care as possible, including the postpartum visit.

Fee and Timeframe for Payment

My fee is [fill in amount]. If you decide to hire me, a nonrefundable retainer of [fill in amount; perhaps 50 percent of the total fee] will be due at contract signing. The balance owed is due at the second prenatal visit, which is typically scheduled three to four weeks before your expected due date.

Refund Policy

A partial refund of your birth fee will be given if you change your mind regarding my services, for any reason, and you give me notice at least two weeks prior to your due date. In this case, I will refund half of your total birth fee upon request. A refund of your birth fee will not be given under the following circumstances:

- I miss your birth because you fail to contact me in time or your labor is precipitous.
- You change your mind regarding having a doula present, for any reason, within two weeks of your due date.
- Your labor results in a cesarean birth or otherwise departs from your ideal birth plan. Please understand that my presence at your birth is not a guarantee of success for any specific desired outcome. I can only support your strengths and help you to make informed decisions; the rest is up to you and your medical care providers.

You are responsible for:

- Keeping me posted on how you are doing and updating me on any significant developments related to your pregnancy. Please call me, at a minimum, within a day or two following each prenatal visit with your care provider.
- Calling me if you suspect that you are in early labor. If it is in the middle of the night, and you are still able to sleep between contractions, then you do not need to call, but I need to be put on notice by 7 a.m. the next morning. The more notice I have of your impending need, the better prepared I can be to leave at a moment's notice.
- Communicating honestly about your needs. While I believe I am intuitive and empathic, I am not a mind reader and truly appreciate frank direction if there is anything I can do to adapt to your needs.
- Fulfilling your part of this agreement in terms of payment of fees and established timelines for doing so. If you anticipate a problem regarding a scheduled payment, please give me as much advance notice as possible so that we can problem solve the issue together.

I promise to:

- Return your nonurgent phone calls within 24 hours (unless it is a weekend, in which case I will return your call on Monday).
- Maintain availability to respond promptly to all urgent calls.

- Notify you when my backup doula is taking call for me, for any reason.
- Provide all services as described in this agreement.
- Do my very best to support you to have the experience you are hoping for.

Agreement

This agreement is between [Your Name] and [Clients' Name(s)] for the purpose of providing non-medical birth doula services. We have read this Letter of Agreement and agree that it accurately reflects the discussion had by all parties. In signing this Agreement, clients are promising to pay for the services described above. I promise to provide the services as described and look forward to helping your family.

[Insert signature lines and dates for all parties.]

Sample Postpartum Doula Contract

What is the Postpartum Doula's Role?

As a postpartum doula, I provide an extra set of hands and information as needed to help you parent your newborn and adjust to changing family roles with confidence and knowledge. I will listen and offer emotional support to the mother and her family. I will take the edge off for exhausted parents and help with other challenges by flexibly supporting your family according to your priorities each day.

My Services Include:

- Nurturing for the mother's postpartum recovery
- Opportunities for rest and family bonding
- Support and inclusion of partners
- Parenting information, including newborn care and feeding support
- Attention for older siblings
- Light housework (e.g., grocery shopping, laundry, dishwashing)
- Basic meal preparation
- Taking care of guests
- Connections to community resources

Limitations to Doula Practice

- The support I provide is nonmedical. I do not diagnose medical conditions in the mother or baby. I do not weigh babies, administer medicine or take temperatures.
- I can assist you in learning to care for your baby's needs and building your confidence as new parents. Unlike a baby nurse, I do not take over care of the baby, except to free the mother for a nap, shower, time with older children, etc.
- I can assist with the care of older siblings though their care will never be completely in my hands. A responsible adult must be present to supervise care of older children.
- I do not do heavy housecleaning or yard work.
- If you are breastfeeding, I will offer basic support. I have experience as a breastfeeding mother and have completed training in breastfeeding support. If breastfeeding issues develop which are beyond my scope of practice, I can refer you to a certified lactation consultant.
- I do not transport clients or family members, but I will accompany the mother for errands or appointments, if desired.

Client Responsibilities

- Communicate honestly regarding medical or emotional conditions that may affect your postpartum experience.
- If you wish to terminate my postpartum doula services before contracted hours have been completed, it is expected that all unpaid contracted hours will be paid in full.
- Contact me within 48 hours, by phone or email, regarding any hospital admittance or delivery of baby.

Billing, Hours and Scheduling

- My hourly fee for doula services is $28, with a three-hour minimum per day.
- Hours will be billed at the end of each week of services and payment is due at that time.
- Reimbursement for groceries or supplies is due the same day, unless otherwise arranged.

- For billing purposes, an hour begins when I arrive at your home; if errands are run on the way to your house, the billing hour begins at the first stop.
- Should you decide that you would like me to work additional days or hours, additional time will be subject to availability and mutual agreement.
- Once we schedule set hours and days together, I will do everything in my power not to change them. However, should I be sick or have an emergency, I will make every attempt, based on your preference, to either arrange for a backup doula or to reschedule services at a time that is convenient for you.
- If I arrive at your home to provide doula services as scheduled but am not needed for some reason, I will be paid in full for the time previously agreed upon. Services must be canceled/re-scheduled 48 hours in advance. Upon being canceled for the second time, I can choose to terminate further services and expect that all unpaid, contracted hours will be paid in full.

Agreement

- This agreement is between [Your Name] and [Clients' Name(s)] for the purpose of providing nonmedical postpartum doula care services after the arrival of your baby, expected around the date of [insert date].
- We have read this Letter of Agreement and agree that it accurately reflects the discussion had by all parties. Based on our discussion, we agree to the following schedule/number of hours: ___.
- A non-refundable deposit of [insert amount] is due upon signing this Agreement. The deposit will be applied to the final hours of contracted services.
- In signing this Agreement, we are promising to pay for the services described above. I promise to provide the services according to the schedule set forth above. I look forward to helping your family.
- [Insert signature lines and dates for all parties.]

Sample End-of-Life Doula Contract

Role and Services of the End-of-Life Doula (EOLD)

- General description (e.g., family-centered care, emotional support, information and support for informed decision-making, referrals and community resources as needed, non-judgmental support based on client's values and preferences, respectful collaboration with other care providers, etc.)

- List of services and their scope. Be as specific as possible, including definitions. For example, respite may mean one thing to you and something else to the client.
- Any limitations to services, including both scope of practice limits and personal/professional limits.

How Services are Delivered

- Do you work with other doula partners or as part of a team? Specify.
- If in solo practice, what is your policy regarding backup for the times you cannot be available to the family? Under what conditions might you not be available to fulfill your commitment to the family?
- Do you offer consultations? Work shifts? Provide overnight respite care? Take emergency calls? Agree to be "on-call" for the family? Spell out exactly what they can expect from you.

Responsibilities of the Client

- Primary responsibility is to pay you according to the terms of the Agreement. List how and when payments should be made.
- Notification regarding need for services (if not starting immediately). How do they activate your support? How much lead time do you need? Do you want regular updates? How should they contact you (text, phone, email)?
- Think about other needs/expectations you may have. For example, if you offer vigil support, is there a room where you can retreat to rest?
- What do you require for self-care when staying with a family? Will you eat their food or bring your own? Do you interact with pets or do you request that they be taken care of by someone else or restricted from the room you are in?

Timeframe for Services

- When do services begin/end? How long will visits be?
- Do you include a closure session with the family after the death?
- What about ongoing bereavement support?

Fees and Terms of Payment

- How much do you charge for services? When is payment due? Are you offering a package of services at a set fee? Billing for services rendered week to week? Collecting a retainer fee to be "on-call"? Spell it out.
- Refund policy. If a retainer is collected to remain available to the family, most doulas will consider this retainer non-refundable. Be clear if it is non-refundable or state circumstances under which it might be partially or fully refunded.

How to Handle Conflicts or Complaints

- Most doulas prefer that if the family is not satisfied for some reason, they contact the doula directly as soon as possible. Explain this preference. Mentioning this in the Agreement helps open the lines of communication in the hope of preventing problems becoming insurmountable.
- Consider mentioning that if you find that you are not compatible, or cannot meet their needs, you will provide them with a referral to someone else. This prevents abandonment.

Contact Information

- Doula's preferred method of contact; you may want to include instructions for the middle of the night (if they are welcome to call you then)—do you take your phone to bed with you or is there a better way to reach you at 3 a.m.?
- All key family members/caregivers, indicating which method(s) of contact they prefer
- Emergency contact numbers and circumstances under which they should be contacted

Signatures

- Key decision-makers, responsible parties on the client side
- Doula and doula partner(s), if any
- Dates

Have two copies of the Agreement available for signing; one is for you to keep and the other should be given to the client.

Small Claims Court and the Doula

There are two likely scenarios for doulas to become entangled with small claims court. The first involves a client suing the doula for a refund of fees paid to her. The second involves a doula suing the client for money owed. The maximum dollar amount that can be recouped in small claims court is set by state law and ranges from $2,500 to $25,000 with most states between $5,000 and $10,000. Each state also has a statute of limitations for filing suit. The number of years is variable depending upon whether there was a written or oral contract and whether or not bodily harm or property damage is alleged. Hence, doulas should retain client records for at least the state-specified period of time.

In the first instance, we have a broken relationship, an unhappy client, for whatever reason. If our contract is good and we have the client's signature on the contract, then certainly that document affords some protection to the doula, provided that the doula is not at fault. It will demonstrate to the judge that a contract for services existed between these two parties as well as the terms of the contract. Doulas should also document all prenatal and postpartum visits and phone calls in their client records. A brief summary of topics covered and doula response is sufficient, including dates. Do not rely on memory for this information.

The small claims process will unfold something like this: You will be served notice that a lawsuit has been filed against you. Notice is typically delivered via registered mail, requiring your signature. If you refuse to pick up or accept the registered mail, then the petitioner must arrange to have you served in person, at additional cost to them. The notice may contain a date for mediation with a court-appointed lawyer or a court date. The notice will state that a default judgment will be rendered in favor of the petitioner if the defendant fails to show.

If the case goes directly to court, the judge will likely ask if the two parties have attempted to settle this dispute without court intervention and will provide an opportunity for you to step out in the hallway and negotiate a solution. If either party refuses to negotiate or an agreement still cannot be reached, then the judge will hear each side of the story and make a decision. In most cases, the losing side will also be held responsible for court costs.

In the second instance, the doula is the petitioner. My primary recommendation here is that you not put yourself in this position. Work with clients you trust. If you are a birth doula, make sure that your full fee is paid two to four weeks in advance of the woman's estimated due date. If you are a postpartum doula, get your last week of anticipated services paid in advance, as a security deposit. End-of-life

Why you need a "demand letter"*

Most people who know they owe you money expect you won't pursue them, but things often change if you write a firm letter, called a demand letter, laying out the reasons why the other party owes you money and stating that if you fail to get satisfaction you plan to go to small claims court. For the first time, the other party must confront the likelihood that you won't go away but plan to have your day in court. He or she must face the fact that time and energy will need to be expended to publicly defend his or her position.

How to Write a Demand Letter

- Review the history of the dispute. At first this may seem a bit odd—after all, your opponent knows the story. However, if you end up in court, the letter can be presented to the judge, who doesn't know the facts of your dispute.
- Be polite. Avoid personally attacking your adversary (even one who deserves it). The more disparaging you are, the more you invite the other person to respond in a similarly angry vein. Instead, you want the other person to adopt a businesslike analysis. (What are my risks of losing? How much time will a defense take? Do I want the dispute to be made public?) With luck, the other party will decide it makes sense to compromise.
- Ask for a specific resolution. For example, ask for a specific amount of money to be paid by a set date.
- Make it look professional. A demand letter should not be handwritten. Keep a copy for your records. If you have a lawyer in the family who can draft the letter for you, so much the better.
- Threaten the alternative of court. Conclude by stating that you will file a lawsuit if your demand is not met.

** The material in this section was adapted from Nolo.com, a great resource for anyone facing small claims court.*

doulas should get retainers for holding space in their schedule and collect fees as they go. Deal with all money issues in a straightforward and non-apologetic manner and confront bad behavior (see Chapter 2). If a client passes you a bad check, for example, presume that it is a mistake and give her a chance to make it right. However, if the check bounces a second time and the client will not make this right with you, then a crime has been committed and should be reported to the police rather than seeking redress through small claims court.

If, despite your best efforts, a client refuses to pay for services rendered, you can hold her accountable through the small claims court system if you choose. Start with a demand letter (see sidebar) and hope for the best. Prior to committing to a court process, consider the following questions.

Does your client have the money? Can they pay you? If they don't have the money, they are likely to be a "no-show" in court, your claim will be uncontested, and the court will render a default judgment against them.

Do you have the information and will necessary to enforce collection of monies owed in the instance of a default judgment? A default judgment does not equal payment. There is an old saying, "you can't get money from a stone." The state will assist you in collecting a judgment in the following ways: (1) seize state income tax returns; (2) garnish wages; (3) issue a writ of execution enabling a court officer to seize property to satisfy a money judgment; and (4) if all else fails, issue an arrest warrant. Consequently, doulas will need to know their client's current address and social security number(s), or state driver's license number(s), or state license plate number(s). If you do not have this information, you do not have a reasonable expectation of getting paid. You will need to make a decision from the outset regarding how serious you want to be in pursuit of payment. Do you want your ex-client at risk of being arrested, possibly with her children in the car, if she is pulled over on a traffic violation? Just how angry or in need of cash are you?

Are you willing to throw good money after bad? You will need to come out of pocket to file a claim in small claims court. Typically, this cost will be under $100. If your client makes it difficult for you to serve notice of the lawsuit, then you will need to come further out of pocket to accomplish this step.

Are you within the legal claim amount limits and timeframe for a small claims case in your state? You certainly don't want your claim thrown out on a technicality. Read all the rules.

Are you filing your claim in the correct jurisdiction? The correct jurisdiction is defined by state law, but is likely to be the county within which services were contracted for and provided. This might be a little confusing if you live (or have your office) in a different county from where your client lives, or if some services were provided in their home located in one county, but they birthed at a hospital located in a different county. Which is correct? You will need to do your homework from the outset or run the risk of having your claim thrown out on a technicality.

Is it in the client's best interest to let it go? This question may surprise you, as your peremptory response may be "who cares?" But there are people out there who really need to be held accountable for their behavior. It is not okay to not pay your doula for services rendered in good faith. It is not okay to take advantage of people. It is not okay for someone's modus operandi to be that they play the rest of us for suckers. It's not only a problem for the next victim in their path; it's self-destructive for any human being to live this way. They may require you to set a boundary and say "this is not okay." It may be the first step toward helping them heal.

Is it in your best interest to pursue payment or would it be better to let it go? There are many ways to deal with anger. We can forgive. We can trust in karma, in the notion that "what goes around, comes around." We can express it and get it over with—tell someone how we feel, write a letter and send it or write a letter and burn it. What we should not do is let our anger eat away at us, leading to professional burnout and physical illness. So, one way or another, find a healthy outlet to deal with it and move on.

Risk Reduction Strategies for Doula Programs

I started a community-based volunteer birth and postpartum doula program as a grassroots effort. The program was up and running and served eight women in its first two years. During this time, I was pursuing the 501c3 nonprofit status and recruiting a board of directors. At that point, expansion of the doula program was put on the back burner while board members considered the issue of liability exposure.

The ensuing search for suitable insurance for our doula program proved elusive. At the time, one group offered insurance to individual, certified doulas. This option was not consistent with our program needs. Our volunteer base was developed on the concept that newly trained doulas seeking to fulfill certification requirements would be eager to provide support to families who otherwise could not afford to pay for doula services. The program was designed, from its inception, to serve both the doulas and the families and was framed, in part, as career development for women. We could not require certification as a prerequisite for insurance when the essence of what we were doing was creating a pathway to professional certification. After exhausting our search, we chose to forego "errors and omissions" insurance and focused instead on risk-reduction strategies. The following strategies were identified.

Incorporate indemnification language into the Articles of Incorporation.

Include an indemnification clause in the Articles of Incorporation for the nonprofit. Articles can be amended by vote of the board of directors and filed with the state, if you are adding this language after the fact. Since each state has its own laws governing nonprofits, you will need to identify and reference your state's law. It may be a good idea to consult an attorney familiar with nonprofit law in your state. There is no language that can guarantee complete indemnification for a board member or officer of the corporation as each will retain a fiduciary responsibility (as described in Chapter 4). Consider leaving this issue and related tasks to the board itself to resolve. After all, it is in their self-interest to gain the additional protection and it is an appropriate task for a board member to undertake.

Articulate and mandate scope of practice.

Adopt a formal professional scope of practice that clearly defines the doula's role and limits to her role, including all program-specific requirements, and ensure that all participating doulas adhere to it. You can adopt an existing scope of practice document from a reputable professional doula organization and then adapt it to meet program needs (such as the recommendations included in this section). Then create a contract between the doula and the agency/program that summarizes all requirements, and have the doulas sign it.

Prohibit labor support at home.

Prohibit participating doulas from providing in-home labor support and require them to meet laboring clients at the hospital or birth center. An exception to this policy can be made in the case of a planned homebirth, but only if the midwife is present in the home at all times that the doula is present; doulas are not to be used as "labor sitters" by the midwives nor should they ever agree to attend an "unassisted" homebirth. It is important to note that professional doulas often do provide very beneficial in-home reassurance and support to mothers in early labor. For the anxious first-time mother who might head off to the hospital in very early labor, only to be sent home again, the doula's presence can help keep her calm, confident and rested at home. However, program directors need to consider whether it is reasonable to accept the risk that an inexperienced doula might be put in the position of catching a baby at home and I recommend against accepting this risk.

In the case of an unassisted homebirth, doulas should be especially non-obliging. Either a birth is unassisted or it is not. Engaging a doula's services provides a false sense of security that somehow expert help is available if needed. Doulas are strictly non-clinical in their skills, specializing in emotional support and comfort measures, and are not qualified to be primary attendants or handle emergencies. The motive on the consumer's side is likely to save money on the homebirth midwife's fees, so they hire a doula instead. This is not safe for the doula, whether she is participating in a program or in her own practice.

Program administrators may want to consider making an exception for the client who needs transportation assistance to the birth center or hospital. Given the high-risk population many doula programs are targeting, removing "access to care" barriers through transportation assistance may advisedly be a retained risk.

Doulas are not babysitters.

Participating doulas are prohibited from providing services in a home where no other responsible adult is present at the time services are rendered.

Place restrictions on age.

Set a minimum age of 18 years as a requirement for participating doulas. In my experience, there were a few younger women who desperately wanted to work with our program and did not meet this requirement, but we welcomed them into trainings and managed to get them involved in other ways until they could qualify.

Do a criminal background check.

Call your local police department to see what is involved in doing a criminal background check for participating doulas. It is certainly a reasonable precaution to take when sending doulas into people's homes.

Develop a policy regarding transportation of clients.

All doula programs need to consider and discuss with their insurance provider the implications of doulas using their own vehicles (a) to transport clients and (b) to provide services such as home visits or running errands on a client's behalf. One strategy to limit transportation-related risk for doulas is for the doula to drive the client's car for errands or transportation to and from doctor visits. In this instance, doulas can be required to check the client's proof of registration and insurance before driving the client's car. And doulas should ensure that all passengers are properly restrained, according to law.

Develop a policy regarding child car safety seats.

Restrict doulas from installing child safety seats in clients' cars unless a safety technician is immediately available, prior to use, who can check that the seat is correctly installed (e.g., doula installs the seat in the hospital parking lot and the hospital's technician is available) OR certify the doulas in child car safety seat installation.

Require enhanced doula training.

Basic doula trainings are generally short, typically a three-day or four-day workshop. In that condensed format, there is sufficient time to cover the basics of the doula's role—essentially all the Doula Training 101 core topics. But there is insufficient time to cover a range of issues, critical to program success, for doulas working in the community, especially with at-risk populations. (See Chapter 5 for more information.) Consider offering additional training, beyond the core doula training curricula, that addresses medical and social risk topics such as:

- Instruction in infection risks and universal precautions
- Substance abuse risks, behaviors and appropriate doula responses
- Domestic violence awareness for doulas
- Child/elder abuse and neglect and the doula's role
- Client confidentiality and HIPAA laws
- Cultural competency
- Establishing and maintaining professional boundaries
- Personal safety strategies and self-defense for home visitors
- Community resources and accessing help

Provide administrative support for volunteers.

If the program coordinator is not an MSW professional, an experienced social worker should be secured as a consultant on an as-needed basis. Her job is to help resolve any high-risk situations that the doulas might find themselves in and identify community resources for special client needs. The program coordinator assists the doulas in setting and maintaining good professional boundaries, consults with the social worker as appropriate and identifies emerging training needs.

Host a doula support group.

A monthly doula support group can be offered as a venue for doulas to come and share tips and resources, problem solve client scenarios and learn from each other's mistakes. Look for ways to build a sense of community among the doulas and the program. In our program, we worked to ensure that the doulas understood that, while they had a great deal of autonomy in their one-on-one relationship with the client, they nevertheless were part of a program and were accountable to the program.

Support the doulas with administrative boundary setting.

It is important to establish clear and systematic expectations for both volunteers and clients. Deliver a consistent message to clients regarding available services, limits to services and the timeframe for services. This can be accomplished through: (a) a descriptive brochure (written at a third-grade level of literacy and also translated into Spanish, etc.) that clients receive from their care provider or other referring agency; (b) a verbal explanation during the initial phone enrollment interview with the program coordinator; and (c) a reiteration in writing, sent out in the form of a Welcome Letter and Client Contract (see more below). Volunteers should be informed of the steps staff members are taking to set boundaries on their behalf. And volunteers should deliver on what has been promised.

Create a Client Contract.

Develop a contract that specifies:

- services provided
- limits to services
- timeframe of services,
- expectations of the client
- level of experience for volunteer doulas

Require clients to sign the contract as a condition of receiving services. In the case of language barriers or low literacy, the doula can review the contract with the client to ensure understanding. Some clients, in particular recent immigrants of questionable legal status, may be reluctant to sign forms of any kind. In such cases, program administrators may choose to waive this requirement and simply make an effort to ensure that the client understands the terms of the relationship.

Use a client confidentiality release form.

Notify clients that doulas will be collecting demographic information on clients served and data about services rendered and any known outcomes. All programs need to collect such data to: (1) establish that they are reaching the intended population and (2) demonstrate their outcomes to make a case for continued funding. The information should be kept confidential, but permission of the client needs to be given. See the section on HIPAA below for specific language recommendations.

Use a photographic release form.

Have doulas and clients sign a release for their images to be used on the website, in program literature, in program reports and so on. Photographs will help "sell" the doula program to providers, clients and funders. A good photo will engage the viewer emotionally in the work of the doula. It tells our story in a more compelling way than any bulleted list of benefits can accomplish. Encourage doulas and clients to share their photos. However, if you don't have the signed release, then you don't have permission to publish their image. The following language should suffice:

> I give [insert organization's name] right and permission to copyright and/or publish, or use photographs of me, or in which I may be included in whole or in part, for art, education, advertising, media production or any other lawful purpose whatsoever. I waive any right to inspect and/or approve the finished product in whatever way it may be used, including digital alterations. (Include signature line, printed name, date and witness.)

Design and implement a program evaluation process.

Program administrators will need to gather feedback from both the doulas and their clients and closely monitor that feedback. If a pattern emerges with a "problem" doula, it should be promptly reviewed with the doula and resolved. Doulas with repeated negative feedback, demonstrated poor judgment, scope of practice violations, or reliability issues will need to be barred from participating with the program.

Identify high-risk incidents as they occur.

A clear-cut support system for the doulas should be established and response to potentially high-risk incidents made a priority. Doula program administrators should put a mechanism in place enabling doulas to notify them, as soon as possible, in the following instances:

- Any time there is a poor birth outcome
- Any incident in the home involving personal injury when the doula is present
- Any incident involving emergency hospitalization of the client(s) if the doula is present or in any way involved
- Any incident involving anger or rage on the part of the client or a close family member
- Any incident in which the doula is witness to illegal behavior
- Any incident in which the doula feels that her personal safety is at risk
- Any incident in which the client's response seems unreasonable or out of proportion to the stimulus
- Any incident in which the hospital's Patient Advocate is called to intervene
- Anytime the doula feels scared or lost in trying to manage a client scenario

If you have an insurance policy, check with your provider regarding their reporting policies for high-risk incidents as well. The policy may include specific mandates.

Poor Birth Outcomes and the Doula

I remember when I first told my father, a lawyer, that the dream closest to my heart was to become a homebirth midwife. First, he asked me if I was sure that I wouldn't like to become a nurse (like my sister). He even offered to pay for me to go back to school and get a nursing degree. I tried to explain that midwifery wasn't the same as nursing, but I don't think he really understood. Next he asked, "What about liability?" I responded with the direct-entry midwife's party line: "My liability insurance was the time spent in prenatal care with my client, the *relationship* cultivated . . . studies show that lawsuits occur in direct inverse proportion to the amount of time the care provider spends with the client—the more time spent, the less likely one is to be sued." And my dad said (wisely), "Well, that's all fine and good, but people have a way of turning on you when things don't go as planned." Indeed.

Nevertheless, relationship does matter. And cultivating a caring, responsible relationship with clients, *one based on solid communication of mutual expectations and grounded in the doula scope of practice,* I believe, is the doula's best available protection against being sued. There are some situations that might arise however, per my dad's wisdom, regarding the danger that emerges when things don't go as planned. I would like to address them here.

No one plans on the death of a baby. Such a tragic outcome is always a shock and it is devastating. Doulas need to muster their courage and strength of character if or when they are called to witness such a loss. From both a humanistic and risk management perspective, my strongest recommendation is to provide good follow-up care with the family who has experienced a loss. Do not be afraid to continue to bear witness to their grief. You cannot fix this. And it is not your fault. Provide an extra postpartum visit (or two) with the family. Use reflective listening skills to allow the parents to process anything they may need to about the birth. Avoid blaming the care provider or the hospital or suggesting that something they did was wrong or neglectful. Some babies are going to die; they weren't all meant to be here. When did we all start believing that we had a right to a healthy baby and that technology could deliver on that right? Read a book on perinatal grief support and take advantage of continuing education opportunities in your community that address this topic. It's very helpful to have had some training on how to support the grieving family. The bottom line is that you continue to provide compassionate care. The parents don't want to feel dropped like a hot potato because they have experienced a loss.

Not all poor birth outcomes are as devastating as the loss of a baby or a baby born with compromising birth defects. In the course of their careers, doulas are likely to be involved in births where the mother/couple are disappointed in their experience. Perhaps they were hoping for a natural birth or a VBAC and medications or surgery were used. Some mothers enter a state of shock or grief after a birth that didn't live up to their expectations. Again, the wise doula will provide caring postpartum follow-up with these clients. If the client blames the doula for her role at the birth or is disappointed in her services, the smart move is to let the client express her feelings on the subject directly. It's only human to move into a defensive attitude, but doulas must allow the mother and her partner to express their anger and disappointment. Keep an open heart. Listen to their version of events and validate their feelings. (Feelings are feelings; they are not right or wrong.) Understand that anger is part of grief. There may be an opportunity, once the parents have felt heard, for clarification on this point or that. Perhaps a misunderstanding occurred or the doula might have information or a piece of the story that the parents are missing. Doulas must be willing to step up and take responsibility for their part in the case of a failed doula–client relationship. Doula program administrators can provide a safe sounding board and guidance for doulas in this difficult situation.

In cases where the parents are so angry that they want nothing to do with the doula or organization and are avoiding contact altogether, avoid pestering them. Two attempts to contact them (leaving messages) is sufficient effort. We need to understand that some mothers do not want to "process" their births in the early days or weeks postpartum. They not only have to set about the business of recovering from physical and possibly emotional and psychological trauma, they have a newborn baby to care for. It can be completely overwhelming. Many women will put their story on the back shelf for now and simply attend to the business at hand. Often, a subsequent pregnancy is the trigger that brings the story to the forefront once again and it is only then that they are ready to address it. This can be years later. We can leave an open door for them, an invitation that if, at some time in the future, they would like to discuss what happened at their birth, we are available to do so. It may also be appropriate to refund a portion of the birth fee that represents the postpartum care they are refusing (perhaps $50–$70, depending on the total package fee). The invitation and the refund are mailed to them with a short, nondefensive and straightforward note that indicates you get they are upset, you are sorry they are disappointed in the care received, and that you are available to speak with them about it if they choose. And that's it. Wish them well and let it go.

You are the common denominator in all of your failed relationships (ouch!).

Lawsuits are less about money and more about justice than is commonly realized. Unresolved, unexpressed anger seeks an outlet. Consider relieving the pressure a bit, like a pressure cooker, and letting some steam out. If the client feels listened to and if the doula has the opportunity to clarify misunderstandings or express regret, then everyone can move on.

Finally, doulas must engage in a process of self-examination after such an experience. This is not the same thing as "feeling guilty." It is a rational process. Broken relationships always have two players. You had your part in it, *to be sure.* Were there subtle (or not so subtle) messages that you gave the client in the course of prenatal care that encouraged her to have unrealistic expectations of you? Were there times something was "off" between you, but you let it slide? Were you burned out? Was your client a difficult personality and you simply didn't know how to manage her or the relationship? Moving forward, how can you prevent repeating your mistakes? Doula program administrators can provide systematic support in these difficult situations in the form of talking the case over with a sister doula, mentor, counselor, doula support group and so on. The law of attraction states that, if we fail to learn from our mistakes and disappointments, then we will continue to attract the same lessons until we "get it." Sounds like a prescription for burnout to me!

Evaluation of Doula Services

Continuing briefly on the theme of disappointed customers, it is wise to offer all clients some type of evaluation process or tool at completion of services. Many folks are unlikely to be directly confrontative, but if we indicate that we value their feedback, we are giving ourselves the opportunity to do some damage control, learn from our mistakes and evolve our services. If your client is unhappy, wouldn't you want to know the nature of the complaint(s) against you?

HIPAA Laws and Doulas

While doulas are not HIPAA-mandated, they should inform clients if they intend to collect data about them, the services provided or outcomes—and gain permission to do so. To complete a professional certification process, most doulas will be required to document hands-on support services provided and share this information with the certifying organization. The Confidentiality Release Form developed

Client Confidentiality Release Form

Developed by DONA International

I, [insert client's name], give permission for my doula, [insert doula's name], to take notes about me, including personal information I choose to disclose to her, and information regarding the labor and birth of my child. I understand that this information may be used for the purpose of doula certification or recertification and will be shared with the certification committee of DONA. I realize that this information will be shared with the doula that is providing backup support. I also understand that this information will anonymously be used for the DONA data collection for statistical purposes, and that my doula may use this information to provide me with a summary for my own personal use.

DONA recommends that all doulas procure a signed release form from their clients before taking any notes about them or their labor. After signing, provide the client with a copy of the signed form.

by DONA International contains language aimed at full disclosure of the doula's intentions and the client's rights. Doula programs may adapt this form for their purposes, such as the need to collect data in order to report back to funders of the program. Provide two copies for the client to sign and leave one copy with her.

Child/Elder Abuse and Neglect and the Doula: Are Doulas Mandated Reporters?

Child/elder protection laws are enacted to protect the health and welfare of vulnerable people, especially in instances where parents or other immediate family members are unwilling or unable to do so. To this end, statutes identify certain professions whose members are legally required to report abuse or neglect or suspected abuse or neglect. Those listed are the only professionals identified as having a legal obligation to report abuse. The standard statutory interpretation is that when a list is affirmatively delineated, that list is complete and omissions from it are intentional. Therefore, if doulas are not specifically mentioned, then they are, by definition, not considered to be mandated reporters. Statutes vary from state to state so you will need to research the wording of your state's law. Though doulas are not likely to be identified as mandated reporters, there is no prohibition against doulas making a report. Indeed, the Child Protection Act in Michigan states:

> *In addition to those persons required to report child abuse or neglect … any person, including a child, who has reasonable cause to suspect child abuse or neglect may report the matter to the department or a law enforcement agency. (Michigan Law, MCL 722.624).*

So, while a doula is not legally liable for failing to report suspected abuse or neglect, she certainly may—and hopefully will—report it.

Domestic Violence Awareness

I am including this information here because I believe that domestic violence presents a special set of boundary challenges for doulas and therefore, risk. If we promote awareness of the signs that a problem exists—along with appropriate ways for the doula (or, indeed, any observer) to respond if she suspects that her client (sister, friend) is in an abusive relationship—then doulas will be better enabled to protect their own safety as well as be more effective safety advocates for the families they serve.

Statistics on Domestic Violence

- One-fifth to one-third of all women are abused by partners three or more times per year.
- 15% of women showing up at hospital emergency rooms are abused.
- 20–25% of pregnant women are in battering relationships.

Factors contributing to an increase in battering during pregnancy:

- Pregnancy is essentially not under control; it does not submit to power and control relationship dynamics.
- The batterer may feel jealous of the mother-child relationship that is unfolding.
- The batterer may not want the child.
- Many relationships are put under additional financial strain with the impending birth of a child.

Domestic violence is defined as "a pattern of coercive behaviors that one partner uses against another in an intimate relationship to gain and maintain power and control over his/her partner." Domestic violence always involves a physical assault or a credible threat of physical assault. It is not spontaneous or random; it is about exerting power and control. That is why the victim is most vulnerable when she decides to leave the relationship.

Tactics of Batterers

A range of tactics are used by batterers to exert power and control over their victims.

- **Intimidation:** Using certain gestures or looks to incite fear; destroying things that have sentimental value; abusing pets; playing with or displaying weapons in her presence; breaking or smashing walls, dishes, etc.
- **Emotional Abuse:** Needing to know where she is and who she talks with at all times; making her feel like she is worthless, crazy, stupid; calling her vulgar and insulting names; humiliating her in public or in front of family and friends; using jealousy to justify his actions.
- **Isolation:** Telling her where and when she can go out and controlling who she has contact with (also falls under emotional abuse); limiting her outside activities; not allowing her to learn English; not letting her

apply for her driver's license; taking away her passport; speaking for her during appointments.

- **Minimizing, Denying and Blaming:** Making light of the abuse; not taking her concerns about his behavior seriously; denying the abuse happened; blaming her for his actions ("if only you would have done ___, this would not have happened").
- **Using Children:** Making her feel guilty about her children; using children to relay messages; not letting children learn survivor's language; using visitation with kids to harass survivor; threatening to take children away or have them removed; saying she is a bad mother, etc.
- **Economic:** Not letting her find and/or keep work; making her ask for money for food and rent; taking her money; not including her in big financial decisions; not letting her learn English to improve her skills.
- **Coercion/Threats:** Threatening to harm or kill her; threatening to leave her; to commit suicide if she leaves; to harm her family, either in this or her home country if she leaves; to harm her children or to take them away from her; to report her to authorities for a made-up crime or immigration issues; making her drop criminal charges against him; making her do illegal things.

Two "power and control wheels"—one for domestic violence and one especially adapted for immigrants—summarize these tactics. Both wheels were developed by the National Center on Domestic and Sexual Violence, who also provide many variations on the wheels for special populations, including Hispanic translations, on their website at NCDSV.org.

Survivor. We use the term "survivor" to help empower victims to see themselves as strong individuals who are using their own resourcefulness to keep themselves and their children safe.

Batterer. We refer to survivors' partners as "batterers" to reflect the true nature of their actions. The legal system often refers to someone who has been charged with domestic violence or assault as "the defendant" or "assailant."

Power and Control Wheel

Physical and sexual assaults, or threats to commit them, are the most apparent forms of domestic violence and are usually the actions that allow others to become aware of the problem. However, regular use of other abusive behaviors by the batterer, when reinforced by one or more acts of physical violence, make up a larger system of abuse. Although physical assaults may occur only once or occasionally, they instill threat of future violent attacks and allow the abuser to take control of the woman's life and circumstances.

The Power & Control diagram is a particularly helpful tool in understanding the overall pattern of abusive and violent behaviors, which are used by a batterer to establish and maintain control over his partner. Very often, one or more violent incidents are accompanied by an array of these other types of abuse. They are less easily identified, yet firmly establish a pattern of intimidation and control in the relationship.

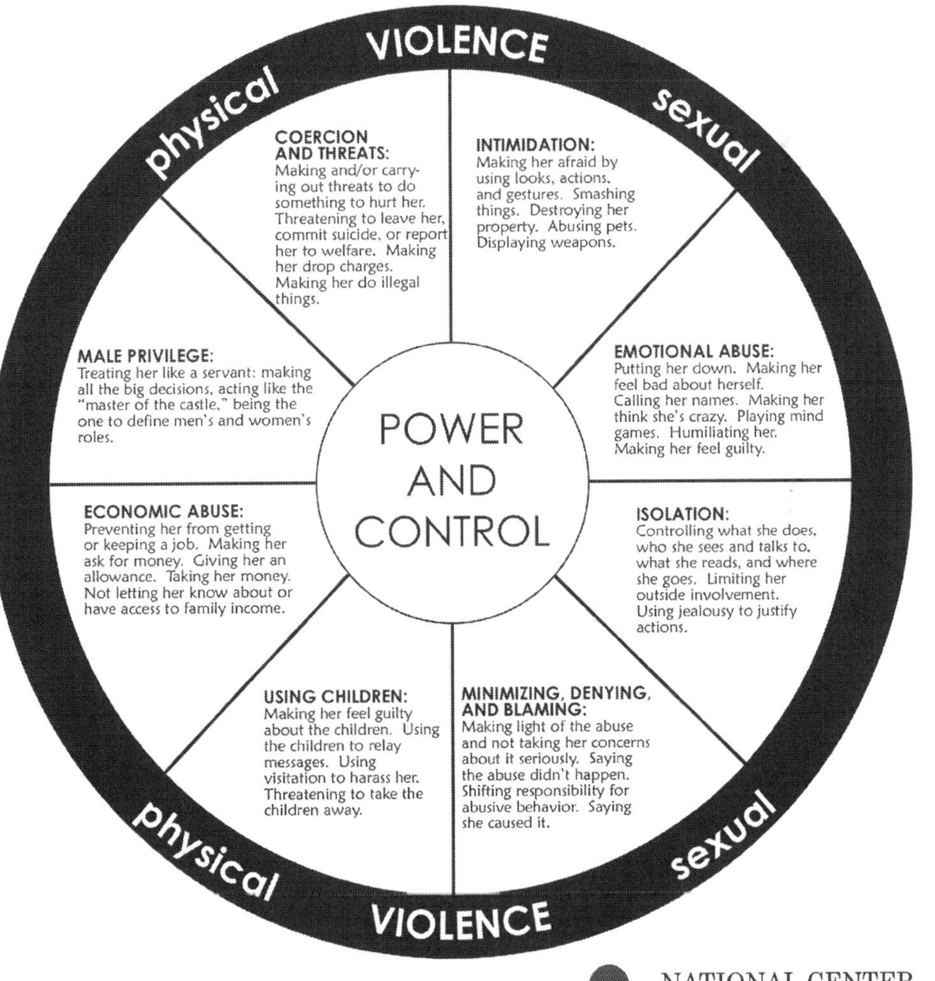

VIOLENCE

physical

sexual

COERCION AND THREATS: Making and/or carrying out threats to do something to hurt her. Threatening to leave her, commit suicide, or report her to welfare. Making her drop charges. Making her do illegal things.

INTIMIDATION: Making her afraid by using looks, actions, and gestures. Smashing things. Destroying her property. Abusing pets. Displaying weapons.

MALE PRIVILEGE: Treating her like a servant: making all the big decisions, acting like the "master of the castle," being the one to define men's and women's roles.

EMOTIONAL ABUSE: Putting her down. Making her feel bad about herself. Calling her names. Making her think she's crazy. Playing mind games. Humiliating her. Making her feel guilty.

POWER AND CONTROL

ECONOMIC ABUSE: Preventing her from getting or keeping a job. Making her ask for money. Giving her an allowance. Taking her money. Not letting her know about or have access to family income.

ISOLATION: Controlling what she does, who she sees and talks to, what she reads, and where she goes. Limiting her outside involvement. Using jealousy to justify actions.

USING CHILDREN: Making her feel guilty about the children. Using the children to relay messages. Using visitation to harass her. Threatening to take the children away.

MINIMIZING, DENYING, AND BLAMING: Making light of the abuse and not taking her concerns about it seriously. Saying the abuse didn't happen. Shifting responsibility for abusive behavior. Saying she caused it.

physical

sexual

VIOLENCE

Developed by:
Domestic Abuse Intervention Project
202 East Superior Street
Duluth, MN 55802
218.722.4134

Produced and distributed by:

NATIONAL CENTER
on Domestic and Sexual Violence
training · consulting · advocacy
4612 Shoal Creek Blvd. · Austin, Texas 78756
512.407.9020 (phone and fax) · www.ncdsv.org

Immigrant Power and Control Wheel

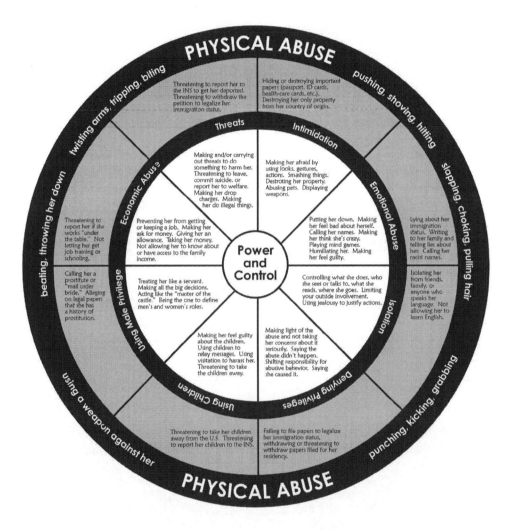

PHYSICAL ABUSE

twisting arms, tripping, biting

pushing, shoving, hitting

slapping, choking, pulling hair

punching, kicking, grabbing

using a weapon against her

beating, throwing her down

Threatening to report her to the INS to get her deported. Threatening to withdraw the petition to legalize her immigration status.

Hiding or destroying important papers (passport, ID cards, health-care cards, etc.). Destroying her only property from her country of origin.

Lying about her immigration status. Writing to her family and telling lies about her. Calling her racist names.

Isolating her from friends, family, or anyone who speaks her language. Not allowing her to learn English.

Failing to file papers to legalize her immigration status, withdrawing or threatening to withdraw papers filed for her residency.

Threatening to take her children away from the U.S. Threatening to report her children to the INS.

Calling her a prostitute or "mail order bride." Alleging on legal papers that she has a history of prostitution.

Threatening to report her if she works "under the table." Not letting her get job training or schooling.

Threats

Making and/or carrying out threats to do something to harm her. Threatening to leave, commit suicide, or report her to welfare. Making her drop charges. Making her do illegal things.

Intimidation

Making her afraid by using looks, gestures, actions. Smashing things. Destroting her property. Abusing pets. Displaying weapons.

Emotional Abuse

Putting her down. Making her feel bad about herself. Calling her names. Making her think she's crazy. Playing mind games. Humiliating her. Making her feel guilty.

Isolation

Controlling what she does, who she sees or talks to, what she reads, where she goes. Limiting your outside involvement. Using jealousy to justify actions.

Denying Privileges

Making light of the abuse and not taking her concerns about it seriously. Saying the abuse didn't happen. Shifting responsibility for abusive behavior. Saying she caused it.

Using Children

Making her feel guilty about the children. Using children to relay messages. Using visitation to harass her. Threatening to take the children away.

Using Male Privilege

Treating her like a servant. Making all the big decisions. Acting like the "master of the castle." Being the one to define men's and women's roles.

Economic Abuse

Preventing her from getting or keeping a job. Making her ask for money. Giving her an allowance. Taking her money. Not allowing her to know about or have access to the family income.

Power and Control

PHYSICAL ABUSE

Adapted from original wheel by:
Domestic Abuse Intervention Project
202 East Superior Street
Duluth, MN 55802
218.722.4134

Produced and distributed by:

NATIONAL CENTER
on Domestic and Sexual Violence
training · consulting · advocacy
7800 Shoal Creek, Ste 120-N · Austin, Texas 78757
tel: 512.407.9020 · fax: 512.407.9022 · www.ncdsv.org

Doula Observations

Following are some of the signs of an abusive relationship that doulas might observe in the course of providing care:

- Pattern of injuries with incompatible explanation (e.g., objects that leave an imprint, but she says that she fell)
- Repetitive psychosomatic complaints
- Prone to "accidents"
- Depression and suicide attempts
- Multiple injuries in various stages of healing
- Any injury during pregnancy
- Inter-relationship between the couple; their demeanor is "off"
- Woman may be evasive, ashamed, avoid eye contact
- Woman defers to her husband; he does all the talking, makes all the decisions
- He's overly concerned and demonstrative; sits too close to her; has his arm around her
- He never leaves the doula alone with the woman
- He ensures that the doula does not have independent access to her client; the woman doesn't have her own phone, is completely dependent upon him, etc.

Barriers to Leaving the Relationship

A woman may have very good reasons for staying in relationship with a batterer. She may love him and want the relationship to work out. She may rightly fear he will follow through on his threats to harm her, himself, her children or her family if she leaves him. The most serious assaults occur when a survivor has left her batterer, called "separation violence." This makes sense if we think about it. If the batterer's agenda is about exerting absolute power and control, then the woman who has decided to leave is the biggest possible threat to that agenda. When he feels he is losing control, he is quite likely to escalate his efforts to regain it.

Additionally, she may be afraid of losing her children through custody battles or she might believe that she cannot parent her children alone and that they need their father/father figure. She might be financially dependent on her abuser and not have sufficient job skills to support herself and her children. Cultural

Signs of a Lethal Situation

- Threats to kill survivor, himself, the children or a member of the family
- Threats to use weapons to harm or kill the survivor
- Survivor states she has told him she is leaving
- Separation (survivor has left the batterer)
- Stalking behavior (numerous messages/calls to her, following her, letting her know he knows where she is at all hours and who she sees, calling her work or school to make sure she is there, etc.)
- Survivor tells you he is obsessed with her
- Depression or recent losses (jobs, death of loved one, accidents, etc.)
- History of assaulting her while he is intoxicated
- Mutilating or killing a pet
- Recent dramatic change in behavior

and/or religious beliefs might dictate that she stay in the relationship. The woman's self-esteem may have been so badly damaged from years of abuse that she believes him when he tells her she deserved or caused the abuse. She might feel too ashamed to tell anyone. The daily exhaustion from dealing with his abuse might leave her feeling unable to make a major change.

Immigrant survivors have another whole range of reasons for staying. She might fear that if she reports him to the authorities, he will report her status and she will be at risk of deportation. She may not know where to access services. She might believe that agencies will not be able to help her because of language barriers and/or staff who are unfamiliar with her cultural beliefs. Or she may have a general distrust of government in any form.

Doula Responses

Things to avoid saying to someone you suspect might be living with domestic violence:

- *Are you a victim of domestic violence?* Most survivors will respond negatively to this question. It is better to ask, *"Have you ever been hit, punched, kicked, pushed, strangled, threatened or otherwise hurt by your partner?"*

- *What did you do to make him hurt you? What were you doing right before he attacked you?* These kinds of questions imply she is to blame for the assaults. She is never to blame, nor does she deserve the abuse.
- *Why haven't you left him? Why did you go back to him?* Because of all the reasons for her to stay, she might be reluctant to leave, or she may have left and returned. We know that leaving a relationship, for anyone, is a process. ***On average, a survivor will leave her batterer seven times before the relationship is over.***

Strategies that work well to facilitate disclosure and discussion of domestic violence in a survivor's life include the following:

- *Listen to her.* This may be the first time she has talked to anyone. She might not talk again about the violence she is experiencing. Just listen to her without judging or telling her what to do.
- *Empowerment vs. intervention.* Avoid telling her what to do next or trying to solve her situation. She is the authority on her life and knows how to survive in her situation. Telling her what she should do only results in one more person having control over her life.

If the woman does disclose that she is being abused, let her know:

- Battering is a common problem that happens to many, many people.
- She is NOT alone.
- The abuse is not her fault; she doesn't deserve to be treated like this.
- "I am concerned about your safety and the safety of your children."
- "I am here for you if you want to talk, regardless of whether you are ready to leave the relationship."
- Listen, provide empathy, try to understand, validate.

The goal is to provide knowledge and support to the woman so she will do something about her situation. Listening allows her to identify what is happening and hopefully experience enough safety to take the next step. She needs to know her options. Leave the door open for her. When she is ready to take the next step, she needs a safety plan. Ask her what she has done in the past that worked (remember, she is a survivor). It is time to get a professional involved, such as a safety shelter! *Do not feel that you need to be the one that rescues her.* Doulas must guard against the desire to rescue the woman. If we see ourselves as rescuers, we continue to victimize her. *Rescuers need victims to rescue.* Be honest with yourself if you notice you are experiencing any of the following classic signs of rescuing behavior:

- Obsessive worrying
- Desire to take her children home with you
- Lending her money
- We're on pedestal and now she's angry that we let her down
- We hear what we want to hear; she lies to us
- Making excuses for her
- Daydreams of revenge on her assailant
- Feeling that she's not grateful enough for all you do (Can she do more for herself?)

In her book *Doula Programs,* Polly Perez discusses the difference between being responsible "to" others rather than "for" others (see Resources):

When you feel responsible *to* others:

- You show empathy, encourage, share, confront, level, are sensitive, listen.
- You feel relaxed, free, aware, high self-esteem.
- You are concerned with relating person to person, feelings and the person.
- You are a helper/guide.
- You expect the person to be responsible for themselves and their actions.
- You can trust and let go.

When you feel responsible *for* others:

- You fix, protect, rescue, control, carry their feelings and fail to listen.
- You feel tired anxious, fearful, liable.
- You are concerned with the solution, answers, circumstances, details and being right.
- You are a manipulator.
- You expect the person to live up to your expectations.

Boundaries, Personal Safety and Self-Defense for Doulas

Thanks are due to Jackie Kelleher for bringing these concepts together in her presentation under the same title at the 2005 DONA International Conference in New Orleans.

My family has been involved in martial arts for the past 32 years. My eldest son is a fifth-degree black belt master and professional instructor of Tai Kwon Do. His younger brother earned his third-degree black belt in Tai Kwon Do. Their proud mom (yours truly), after cheering from the sidelines for fifteen years, earned a black belt at age fifty-one. From karate, I progressed to practicing the more martial, Chen-style form of Tai Chi and Chinese sword forms. So, it is only natural that I want to share a bit of what I have learned from these years of exposure to the martial arts.

Self-defense is not a skill set that women can learn from reading a book. Nevertheless, the concepts presented here are a progression. Presumably, before one finds oneself in a situation where self-defense techniques are called for, either a bad decision was made or common-sense preventive tactics were missing altogether. Of course, hindsight is 20/20. But it truly is! That means we can learn from situations where crimes were committed against women. We can dissect them, after the fact, to uncover the behaviors and choices that put the woman at risk of an assault. The resulting personal safety strategies that emerge involve—among other measures—the ability to establish and maintain good personal boundaries. We've talked about the importance of professional boundaries from various angles. In this section, the concept of boundaries takes on yet another level of significance.

Boundaries

The lack of clear personal and professional boundaries can leave us vulnerable to people who may try to take advantage of us, even to the point of assault. This is because we are sending the wrong signals. Now, let me say at the outset here that I am not "blaming the victim" with my argument. Yes, there is evil in the world and there are people who behave abominably. If we become their victim we did not ask for that, nor did we deserve to be violated. However, that is not the same thing as saying whether or not we could have prevented what happened. And this is the part that most interests me.

> **Boundary** = something that indicates a border or limit

Crimes against women are rarely spontaneous or random acts of violence. In a high percentage of cases, the assailant is someone familiar to the victim. In cases of stranger attacks, criminals interviewed in prison admit to "shopping for a victim" or looking for an "easy target." Even in cases of sexual harassment in the workplace, an escalation of inappropriate behaviors from the perpetrator is typically evident. Rarely does a coworker start his intimidation with inappropriate touch or a physical assault. No, it is more likely to begin with, perhaps, standing too close in the break room, telling a smutty joke, asking about your personal life or commenting on your appearance in a way that makes you feel uncomfortable. You may be shocked when this same individual suddenly grabs your breast one day (or worse!), but in another sense, you are not shocked. The guy has "creeped you out" from the start. You were never comfortable with his comments, his presence or his behaviors.

The question is, what did you do about it? Did you draw a line in the sand and establish from the get-go that the joke is not funny, that your personal life is off limits or that he is standing too close and needs to back away? Or did you try to be nice? Were you concerned about hurting his feelings? Did you try a number of strategies for coping with his inappropriateness other than direct confrontation and calling him out or reporting him to a supervisor? "Strategies" such as complaining to a friend or coworker? Was avoidance your primary strategy? You are in the company of many other good, sweet women whose cultural conditioning to be "nice" overrides their survival instincts if you chose to pursue any path other than laying down the line. So, it may take some training, some "unconditioning" for women to overcome entrenched, learned tendencies that put us at risk.

In order to enforce our boundaries, we need to have defined them in the first place. Often we don't realize a boundary has been crossed until someone does it. Or we don't know our own boundaries until we are solidly on the uncomfortable side of where the limit should be. That's normal. We can always reset a boundary.

There are all kinds of boundaries. How many clients can you comfortably serve in a month? How far are you willing to drive to a client? How much time will you spend on the phone with a client? Will you disclose details about your personal and family life with your clients? How much detail is too much? When can clients call you for nonurgent matters? How far will you go to accommodate someone who is disrespectful of your time and keeps you waiting without notice for 15 minutes, a half-hour, one hour? How will you respond when a client doesn't hold up her end of a contract, for example neglecting to pay you on time? Where's the limit? At what point do you mean what you say? That's the boundary.

Every parent of a toddler or teenager understands the importance of setting limits. It seems to be human nature to push the limits. The truth is people feel more comfortable, more secure, if the limits are clear. If there are none or the limit changes constantly without rhyme or reason, then it's something of a jungle out there. The individual—whether toddler, teenager, client or coworker—is placed in a moment-to-moment survival mode. He or she will do what they can to get his or her needs met. That person will adapt the best he or she can to a relationship or world without limits. If one of your limits is that you absolutely will not buy candy for your toddler at the checkout line in the grocery and the first time your toddler pitches a hysterical fit in line, you refuse to give in and there are unpleasant consequences for that behavior (and I don't mean spanking), then the boundary is maintained. The process is unpleasant, but it is unlikely to repeat. Give in to the fit and you have essentially agreed that the boundary does not really exist, that you do not mean what you say, and the whole episode will repeat itself every time you go grocery shopping. The completely unreasonable and totally self-centered toddler is in charge.

What are your personal boundaries? Do a personal inventory. What behaviors do you find unacceptable from your kids, your partner, your mom, your friends, your coworkers, your clients? What about boundaries with strangers? Do you have boundaries around being touched or hugged by people you are not close to? People who "get in your face"? Is there a comfortable space zone around your person that you prefer to keep so that if someone is standing uncomfortably close, your instinct is to take a step back to maintain the zone? Awareness of our boundaries is a liberating first step.

What can you do when a boundary is crossed? First, allow yourself to acknowledge what you are feeling. Name it. "I'm feeling angry, threatened, irritated …" Trust your instincts. Feel the tension in your body. You feel this way for a reason. Don't judge yourself and don't rationalize it. If someone is testing your boundaries, you did not cause them to do this. It is not your fault when someone behaves inappropriately. Once you become aware that a boundary has been crossed, restate the boundary firmly and hold to it, no exceptions (otherwise it is not a boundary; it is a murky imaginary line). If you let the person testing your boundaries get away with it, it is an invitation to do it again (and again and again).

Personal Safety

Job #1: Don't be there.
Job #2: Plan ahead.
Job #3: Use all of your senses.
Job #4: Fail the victim interview.
Job #5: Trust your gut.

Once our boundaries are in place, regular employment of safety strategies will hopefully prevent the need for self-defense techniques. The first rule of personal safety is to not place yourself in a situation or place that has a high-risk potential for making you the target of a crime—avoiding back alleys at 2 a.m., dangerous neighborhoods, sketchy bars and the like. If late-night travel is a necessary part of your job, women can minimize their risk exposure with some advance planning.

- Have sufficient gas in your tank whenever you are on-call; fuel up on your home turf rather than on someone else's.
- Keep your vehicle in good repair.
- Have reliable directions and know where you are going; double check directions with your client, especially during the road repair season.
- Have a fully charged cell phone with you in case of emergency; keep a charger in your car.
- Avoid highway rest stops; choose a well-lit restaurant or gas station if it becomes absolutely necessary to stop (use the bathroom before you head out!).
- If the neighborhood is bad, have your client's partner escort you; call from your car when you arrive; ask that they observe your departure until you are safely on your way.
- Park in well-lit areas. You may even want to walk a little further to stay in a well-lit area, compared to parking closer to a building entrance but off to the side in a dark corner.
- When using parking garages at hospitals in the late night or early morning hours, ask a security guard to escort you to and from your vehicle.
- If approaching your car alone at night, have keys in hand. Most key fobs have a built-in system whereby pushing "unlock" once opens the driver's side and pushing it twice unlocks both sides; use this safety feature to unlock only the driver's side. You can also hit the alarm button if necessary.
- Lock all doors as soon as you enter the vehicle and drive away promptly. Many women make themselves a target as they sit for several minutes,

tending to business, talking on the phone, distracted and possibly observed. Drive to a safe place before checking phone messages, etc.

It is essential that women pay attention to their surroundings and remain fully in the present moment, especially when out in public. All of our senses are important in staying safe and aware because we process information on an unconscious level much faster than we process it consciously. Animals can perceive danger through a sense of smell, among other signals. Only humans would be so stupid as to eliminate a primary capacity to receive information from their environment, such as jogging with an iPod or talking on a cell phone walking down the street! Why is it that we are always doing at least two things at once?

Trust the hairs on the back of your neck, a sense of tension in your body, a feeling. This is your autonomic nervous system at work, acting on clues picked up unconsciously that something is off. A precious escape window may close if you begin to question what you are feeling or attempt to process it intellectually. Trust those protective instincts! Run, go back in the building, drop your packages, hit the alarm on your car. Better safe than sorry. Most victims, in hindsight, admit to disregarding a warning signal.

We have already identified one of the main barriers to acting on instinct: fear of being rude. What a powerful conditioning it is for women to be so concerned about the feelings of others, to be nice, to "act like a lady." Furthermore, we may have a fear of appearing foolish, of creating a scene. How do these fears actually stack up against the very real potential threat that someone wants to rape, assault or murder you? Keep it in perspective!

Women's Self-Defense

What if, in spite of your best preventive efforts, someone has chosen to threaten you or put you in a compromising position? Now what? The truth is that very few women, even those trained in self-defense techniques, will be successful at overcoming a stronger and bigger opponent who has decided to exert power over them. If no weapons are present, our very best strategy is to flee! If we must fight, the goal is to discourage our attacker, to not be an easy victim and to disable the opponent sufficiently to create space to flee. What weapons do we have at our immediate disposal?

Use your voice. In a loud, commanding voice, yell "NO!" "Back off!" "Step away from me now!" "Leave me alone!" If anyone is within earshot, they cannot mistake the nature of the exchange that they are overhearing. Birth attendants

Victim Body Language

- Stoop-shouldered, "poor me" attitude
- Chin pulled in
- Averts eye contact, turns back on potential predator
- Hands held behind back conveys a submissive, open attitude
- Compromised by drugs or alcohol, foggy behavior
- Emotionally distraught, crying in public; radiates vulnerability
- Distracted, multi-tasking in public
- Non-purposeful walking, not paying attention to surroundings
- Impaired hearing due to talking on a cell phone or listening to an iPod while out in public, jogging, etc.
- Encumbered with bags, packages and babies; stupid shoes, overly confining clothes; purses can be an invitation

Nonvictim Body Language

- Stand tall, sternum lifted
- Chin jutted forward
- Uncompromising eye contact (= "I see you")
- Hands on hips is aggressive, confrontational
- Hands crossed in front is defensive, not open
- Arm out/"Stop!" is authoritative
- All senses fully operational in the present moment
- Emotions under control; radiates confidence and self-esteem
- Purposeful walking
- Unencumbered (when unavoidably encumbered, extra vigilance is called for)

well understand the difference between sounds coming from the throat versus the diaphragm. We are often instructing women that high-pitched screaming indicates fear, while a low-pitched vocalization, coming from the diaphragm, accesses our power. Use your diaphragm. Screaming "help!" only further plays into the victim picture. As birth attendants, doulas are familiar with the fact that many women feel inhibited about making the low, loud and powerful sounds often accompanying birth. So that is another bit of conditioning to overcome.

Your legs are stronger than your upper body. The blow that a woman could deliver with her fist is unlikely to be effective. The famous knee to the groin, however, can definitely disable an opponent sufficiently for the woman to flee. If grabbed from behind, a foot stomp (smash the top of his foot as hard as you can with your foot) may be effective in getting your assailant to let go of his hold. Use what you've got. These are the most vulnerable target areas: groin, eyes, throat pit, solar plexus, knee and top of the foot.

If a weapon is involved … all bets are off. But your survival instincts will kick in. Some women have reported cooperating with an assailant because their gut told them that was the best survival strategy. Remember the story from 2005 of Ashley Smith, the woman who was taken hostage in her own home for seven hours by escaped prisoner Brian Nichols who murdered four people in the course of his escape? She made him pancakes "with real maple syrup" and read him passages from *A Purpose Driven Life.* She spoke about her daughter, about the idea of redemption. Eventually, he allowed her to leave the apartment to pick up her daughter from school and was subsequently recaptured. How did she know what to do, what would work to keep her alive in that situation? I think she followed her instincts and was given grace. There is no formula.

The Ladies Go Black Belt

On my first day in Karate class, I met two women my age who were also just beginning. The three of us became fast friends, attending noon class twice a week for nearly four years and often going for lunch together after class. On the eve of our first promotion, from white belt to yellow belt, we made a common confession. Each of us had only been pretending to do the "ki hap" in class. The "ki hap" is that yell in martial arts that focuses mind and energy. It is delivered with a blow or a kick. It comes from the diaphragm, with a forceful exhalation, and sounds similar to the sound a weightlifter makes on exertion, putting a little extra "oomph" behind the accompanying force. Now, we were facing a test that called for correct performance of the form, *with accompanying ki haps,* which we had all been too self-conscious to perform to date. We decided to have a practice session focused on the ki haps and completed our test as the most forceful (and loud!) bunch of late-forties women in the history of the school. Interesting, though, isn't it—the power of our cultural conditioning that women just don't make that sound?

The value of training and support. The real value of training in martial arts or taking women's self-defense classes lies in the increased safety awareness that such classes impart, as well as instilling a willingness to fight, to not be a victim. Some of us will naturally be more skillful boundary setters than others and, therefore, less likely victims. If you are experiencing repeated issues with boundaries, abusive relationships and victimization, seek personal counseling. Such support can help you to identify and reprogram the beliefs and behaviors that make you an easy target.

LLC Formation

Choosing a Limited Liability Corporation business structure enables the business owner to protect personal assets in the event of a lawsuit. Should the court decide in favor of the plaintiff, only your business assets will be at risk. Formation of an LLC is a straightforward and inexpensive process. However, the protection provided is not absolute. Take care to ensure that you are also running the business as an LLC. In particular, refrain from co-mingling of company and personal funds (e.g., don't pay your mortgage with a business check). Instead, write yourself a paycheck from the business account and deposit the funds to your personal checking account first, and then write your mortgage check with a personal check. See Chapter 2 for more information about LLCs.

Transfer of Risk—Insurance Considerations

The nonprofit organization that I headed purchased three types of insurance in addition to employee health insurance: (1) directors' and officers' insurance, (2) general liability or "slip and fall" insurance and (3) an automobile rider as an addendum to the general liability insurance policy. At the time, we were unable to find affordable malpractice or "errors and omissions" insurance and, after much debate, chose to proceed without it.

Directors' and Officers' ("D&O") Insurance

For only two years, the nonprofit purchased D&O insurance. In hindsight, I believe this to have been a poor use of limited funds (currently estimated between $5,000–$10,000 per year). Of course, it is easy for me to say that, given that no one sued us. Had the worst happened, no doubt we all would have been less burdened due to the insurance coverage. But let me play devil's advocate for a minute.

The two primary reasons lawsuits are filed against nonprofits are (1) employee claims of discrimination, often in hiring practices and (2) misuse of public funds or fraud (e.g., mismanagement of grant funds). Many nonprofits engage in program activities designed to serve a high-risk clientele, including home visitor programs, but this does not necessarily raise liability risk, especially if the organization implements systematic risk-reduction measures. So, why did we buy the expensive D&O policy?

The argument went something like this. We were transitioning away from what is known as a "founder" board (Patty's birth-community friends who "rubber stamp" whatever Patty wants to do) to a "governing" board and attempting to raise the bar for participation on our board of directors. A need for good fundraising leadership, as well as fiscal management, had been identified as being crucial to the organization's survival and growth. An assumption was made that we would not attract community members outside of the birth-junkie circle (where an appalling lack of accountants and fundraisers or "big money" people was evident) unless we could offer insurance protection. *In fact, no potential board recruit ever claimed that insurance was an issue and few ever asked about it.*

In hindsight, we were building a proverbial house of cards. Even with D&O insurance in place, we were unsuccessful in recruiting board members who possessed the much-needed skills and commitment. It occurs to me now that it would have been much better to skip the insurance, continue to build the board and make it a board problem for members to finance their own insurance, if desired. Anyone savvy enough to make it an issue should be capable of fundraising to cover the cost. If potential board members are not willing to commit to fundraising, then their overall value to the nonprofit is reduced to the level of rubber-stamp cheerleaders (aka "founder board") anyway, and so the whole argument for insurance as a board recruitment strategy falls apart.

If a decision is nevertheless made to purchase D&O insurance, check with your statewide nonprofit association to see what they can offer in the way of competitive pricing. See also our Resources section for additional nonprofit risk management resources.

General Liability ("Slip and Fall") Insurance

General liability insurance covers property loss in case of fire, theft and the like. Like homeowner's insurance, it also provides liability coverage in the case of accidents that might happen on your residential or business property, such as a client slipping on an icy driveway as she/he enters or leaves the building. Cost will depend on the amount of assets, property location and other variables. These policies are more affordable and likely to strike a reasonable balance between risk protection and cost. Shop around a bit and get quotes from at least two companies.

Doulas in private practice with a home office where they meet with clients may be covered under their homeowner's policy. Be aware that if you come clean with your insurance agent regarding your home office, your premiums may go up, significantly shifting the risk-cost ratio. Therefore, it may be advisable to get an anonymous cost quote first, on a theoretical basis ("How would it affect a homeowner's premium if . . . ?").

Whether or not general liability insurance has been purchased, agencics and business owners with property to protect should take all reasonable precautions to prevent losses or accidents. Steps such as prompt removal of snow and ice, maintaining night-time lighting at the entranceway to the building, and care regarding building security and employee access are no-brainers. Ensure that the building is secure with deadbolt locks, install and maintain smoke detectors and fire extinguishers, collect keys as folks leave for other pursuits and track who has key access. In our building, four different businesses have access. With turnover of staff, midwifery apprentices, student interns and work/study students, it seems prudent to change out locks every couple of years or so and issue new keys to current users only. Risk is increased anytime someone who has a key is leaving under less than friendly circumstances and we have been quick to take preventive action in these cases and have the locks on the building changed.

Automobile Rider

Finally, our insurer recommended that we purchase a "rider" on the general liability policy to include coverage for volunteer doulas who may be transporting clients in their own vehicles. At less than $100 per year total cost, this was an affordable option. Our agent explained that, if an accident occurred, the insurance companies involved for both parties are likely to fight it out. The drivers' business and destination at the time of the accident will become part of the facts in the case. Once it becomes known that one party to the accident was providing services in her role as a volunteer/employee of a local nonprofit, the nonprofit becomes liable. Again, the balance between risk and the cost of protection seemed more than reasonable and we opted to purchase the rider. Private practice doulas will need to make a decision whether they are willing to transport clients in their vehicle and, if so, consider purchasing extra coverage.

Malpractice ("Errors and Omissions") Insurance

Malpractice insurance protects doulas in two important ways: It can (1) cover the costs associated with a legal defense and (2) cover the cost of a settlement if the court rules in favor of the plaintiff. Depending on the policy, other protections may be available, such as coverage for medical costs or lost wages in relation to a covered incident. Malpractice insurance cannot: (1) prevent the development of unpleasant or dishonest relationships; (2) prevent dangerous situations from developing; (3) prevent accidents from happening; (4) prevent the filing of a lawsuit; or (5) prevent the emotional, psychological and energetic cost of a lawsuit. The good news is that there is much within the doula's power to prevent each of these, as discussed throughout this chapter.

Several companies offer affordable professional liability (or "errors and omissions") insurance for doulas (see Resources). You will need to shop around to find the right fit for your needs and budget. Some of the companies listed specialize in insuring groups and might be better suited for agency or studio owners or folks offering classes and training. Others have affordable options for private-practice doulas (between $135–200 per year). If you can't find "doula" or "end-of-life doula" as a covered category on a company's website, call and ask for help. If you have a professional affiliation (e.g., DONA International, Lamaze), you may find that your membership or certification qualifies you for a reduced, fixed rate. Ask for a copy of the policy and read it carefully. Pay special attention to sections regarding "exclusions" such as homebirths. No doubt the insurance landscape will continue to change as the doula profession evolves and becomes more mainstream. Keep checking.

> **When addressing liability issues** with nonprofit boards for community-based doula programs or risk-management departments of hospitals for hospital-based doula programs, it may be helpful to frame the question as *"What will it take for you to feel comfortable with ... [incorporating a doula program to serve our clientele?] [doulas working in the OB department?]."* By steering decision makers away from a "yes" or "no" approach to the issue, you are setting a framework for problem solving with the presumption that a solution will emerge.

The argument that having insurance may constitute a reason to be sued must be considered. Lawyers do seek to identify, among all parties involved, which party has the deepest pockets and therefore capable of paying out a settlement amount if one is awarded.

Individuals with few assets and no insurance, or those doing business as a limited liability corporation with few corporate assets, are consequently unattractive targets for a lawsuit. Lawyers don't get paid when defendants claim bankruptcy.

When speaking with insurance companies, keep in mind that it is their business to sell insurance. To accomplish this end, they will play on every possible fear of what might happen, everything that could go wrong. Such is their world. The parallels between the medicalization of birth (playing on women's fears of everything that *could* go wrong and basically viewing birth as an emergency waiting to happen) and the risk scenarios presented by insurance agents and nonprofit lawyers are enough to make all of us throw up our hands in despair and give way to paralyzing fear. *I am not going to recommend fear as a reasonable approach to risk.* Life is risky. Every time we get in a car, we are accepting risk. We are all going to die. In the meantime, we need to live. We can choose to take all reasonable precautions and proceed in a faithful and conscious manner. Or, we can choose another profession. It's a simple choice in the end. ◆

CHAPTER 8

Going the Distance

BURNOUT HAS BEEN REACHED WHEN your client calls you to tell you she is in labor and you hang up the phone and burst into tears. Burnout is when you feel like a hamster in a wheel, running and running, faster and faster, and getting nowhere. Burnout is when you feel like an actress and you are just going through the motions of your work, pretending, but all the passion is gone. Burnout is when you are irritable with everyone around you. Burnout is when all the joy is gone and you feel stuck. Burnout is no fun!

The Art of Being "On Call"

My goodness, this can be a challenge! There is an art to being on call, but we must start by acknowledging that it is not only difficult for us; it is also very challenging for our partners, children, friends and extended family. Because we can never say, absolutely, that we will be there, anywhere, and disappointments are inevitable.

One luxury not enjoyed by those of us on call is procrastination. For moms, it is especially challenging. If there isn't a bite of ready-made food in the house or an acceptably clean set of clothes on hand, then who is going to whip it together for the kids when you are at a birth in the morning? The empty gas tank, the essential car repair, the empty wallet or urgent bank deposit—none of it can be left until some nebulous future moment. When we are on call, it is our job to be ready. So, we must garner some discipline and have our *#@! together.

On the other hand, as you do your best, managing to leave everyone in reasonable condition on the home front as you head off to a birth or death vigil, then you need to trust that your support system is in place and let it go. And here is some advice: (1) Do not call home during a birth or vigil to see how they are managing in your absence. Seriously, you don't want to know. What can you do about it? And if it's not pretty, it will adversely affect your ability to help the family who needs you. (2) Do not call home as soon as the baby is born or your client dies to say that you will be home "in two hours." I can't tell you how many times I backed myself into this stressful corner and came home to a distraught husband because it was actually three hours, not two. You see, once he got word that relief was at hand, he set his coping mechanism for two hours. Every minute past two hours was pure torture from his perspective. A better strategy was to call when I was actually on my way. Until then, my time belongs to the family I am serving.

One day I had an epiphany upon coming home, after a long birth and sleepless night, to a house in chaos, overflowing wastebaskets, dirty dishes, irritable husband and children wanting attention. Understandably, I was feeling "what's so hard about this? I do it every day!" And then it happened. I realized he was doing

Strategies for making it through a long birth

- Eat something substantial to ground and sustain yourself before heading off to a birth.
- Wear smart shoes.
- Doula yourself with positive words and images (babies always come out; this too shall pass; I can do it).
- Go ahead and admit (to yourself) that you're tired, but don't make a tragedy out of it ("I'm tired, but it's not a big deal").
- Bring food for yourself, splash water on your face, brush your teeth and comb your hair, put some deodorant and a fresh shirt on.
- Pack a self-care bag with your doula supplies so that you can do all of the above.
- Remember that your client doesn't have a choice whether or not to continue.
- If you are the woman's only support person, consider calling in another helper if needed.
- If you have already gone through your second wind and third wind, you might not have a fourth comeback in you. At this point, we all need to consider whether we can still be an asset for this family or whether it is time to activate our backup doula for some relief. I have been most likely to be in this situation when I have had back-to-back births, with no time for sleep in between, and then the second labor goes on for 24 hours or more (a rare occurrence to say the least). Be sure to include your policies around activating your backup doula in your client contract.

his best. Seriously, I wished he could manage it better, but he was willing and he was trying and I needed to recognize that it was hard for him too.

In working with my children's teachers and school commitments, I decided to let the teachers know, at the beginning of each school year, that I would not be volunteering to help chaperone school trips or events. I could not even be counted on to deliver a fresh plate of cookies at a specified time. However, I also informed her that I would be her go-to backup person if a scheduled chaperone was unable to show. On the spur of the moment, I would help if I could. I gave myself permission to do this, felt justified in doing so and never felt guilty about it.

A childcare support system, with multiple layers of backup, is necessary for doula mamas on call. Contingency plans must be in place. I will always remember fondly the handful of times that my friend Mickey's husband Scott dropped pajama-clad, sleepy-eyed children and pillows off at my house at 7 a.m. as he headed off to work while Mickey was at a birth. Mickey, a sister homebirth midwife and homeschooling mother of two, lived a couple blocks away and our kids were the same ages. There is no one who can better understand than someone in the same boat! But Mickey and I were only one piece of each other's multilayered childcare backup plans.

The art of being on call is a balancing act that involves having trustworthy support systems (childcare, backup doulas) in place so that when you are not actually being called to support a family, you can be absent needless worry and allow your nervous system to fully relax. If we bring excess tension to the on-call aspect of our work, and if we limit ourselves from enjoying our lives between births or death vigils due to the impending claim on our time, it will translate as adrenal depletion and nervous system exhaustion. Keep yourself in the present moment and put a lid on any tendency to over commit (whether it's taking on too many clients or volunteering at your children's schools). You have important work to do that benefits families and the greater society; you are making your own unique contribution. There is no need for excuses or guilt, and it is a sign of wisdom to know your limits.

Boundary Setting Revisited

Within the context of the volunteer doula program that I managed, the issue of boundary challenges between doulas and their clients was a persistent theme. A surprising percentage of calls from the doulas to the volunteer coordinator involved uncomfortable doula–client scenarios that were, in essence, a boundary problem. Nothing will burn you out quicker than poor boundaries with high-needs clients.

It will also make you a rather ineffective doula. The reverse is also true: the ability to establish and maintain boundaries will enhance your ability to provide quality doula care resulting in a more fulfilling experience for both parties. The boundary challenges that doulas face are multifaceted. Which ones do you struggle with?

- balancing the doula's desire to serve in the face of overwhelming client needs
- acknowledging one's own needs
- setting firm boundaries
- enforcing boundaries without offending others
- bringing closure to the relationship

Specifically, some of the issues that emerged were:

- Client blames the doula when birth goes against expectations, results in cesarean, etc.
- Client calls doula at all times of the evening or weekends for nonurgent reasons
- Challenge of keeping the relationship on a professional basis when client wants to think of the doula as her "friend"
- Managing meeting times and schedules with clients; balancing that with family needs
- Identifying the need to connect with community resources and other sources of help for clients in need
- Client tells you what you want to hear or is not always honest
- Client is extraordinarily demanding, expecting inappropriate services (such as housecleaning, babysitting, etc.)
- Client drains you; absence of boundaries
- Client refuses to advocate for herself
- Client wants the doula to tell her what to do

In order to address boundary challenges, the doula will need to observe herself and attempt to identify patterns in her relationships. Doulas experiencing repeated strong boundary challenges with clients are quite likely experiencing boundary issues in other areas of their lives as well. Following are some themes that have emerged as challenges for the doulas with herself.

- Trying to "fix" things
- Lacking time for her client, her family and herself translates as "no time for myself"
- Lacking confidence in her role leads to not upholding professional doula standards
- Difficulty discerning what the client is really asking for; learning to read between the lines
- Trying to advocate for women who can't or won't advocate for themselves
- Questioning ability to make strong, clear boundaries between doula work and personal life
- Managing difficult personalities ("My last doula was terrible, but you're perfect" accompanied by repeated manipulative behaviors)
- Fatigue, exhaustion, muscle pain, sleep deprivation
- Balancing other work and doula work
- Burnout (staying patient, repeating the basics, feeling underappreciated)
- Financial stress; getting clients to pay; dealing with people who can't pay, making it very tight financially for the doula, leading to feelings of bitterness
- Becoming too concerned, involved; feeling guilty if things don't go well
- Difficulty juggling, multitasking
- Lack of professional recognition, respect and acceptance from medical professionals
- Limited separation between home and work

American psychiatrist William Glasser wrote about the key needs shared by all human beings. These include being loved, giving love, being of value to self and being of value to others. Consider how clients might cross a boundary to get their need met to be of value to you. One possibility is to offer personal services to the doula in the form of bartering. Can you think of any others?

Why are the doula-client boundaries so blurred and sticky? Could it be that the intimate and nurturing nature of the relationship is inherently fraught with boundary issues? Cell phones, email, text-messaging, instant messaging and online social networking can all lead to expectations of immediate and endless availability. An occasional client may tend to idealize her doula, harboring uncommunicated expectations of constant support, expecting the doula to be interested in every detail of her personal life, keep her healthy, be her best friend and so on.

Signs of a Boundary Problem

- Doula-client relationship is problematic.
- Doula has uncomfortable, awkward, even queasy feeling toward a client.
- Doula is exhausted, irritated, annoyed by a client's behavior.
- Doula feels fear of confronting a client.
- Doula finds herself complaining to others on a regular basis about a client.
- Doula wants to rescue a client (see signs of rescuing in Chapter 7, page 316).
- Doula is losing sleep over a client.
- Doula is still involved with a client long after services have ended.

Remember, actions speak louder than words. If your first phone "chat" with a prospective client lasts an hour and a half, you are sending a message that you have no boundaries regarding your time on the phone. Do not be surprised if this client expects lots of long phone chats with you throughout the course of your care. If you do not nip a 10 p.m. nonurgent call in the bud ("I'm sorry, this is rather late for me to take nonurgent business-related calls; can I give you a call back in the morning around 9:00?"), then get ready for the next call to be at 10:15 p.m. (or worse).

A special area of risk for boundary issues is when someone you know asks you to be their doula. Be careful here: boundaries still need to be in place. There is a danger that both sides will make too many presumptions and the end result may be a damaged relationship. Treat the friend, family member or coworker as a client deserving special affection. Have a clear understanding of mutual expectations. Nonjudgment and staying within your scope of practice are every bit as important, perhaps even more important in this situation. One way of keeping it all in check is to be self-aware. *Do you care more about a specific outcome than the person being supported does?* This is not support; it is an agenda and it is inappropriate. It is so NOT about you.

> Set a boundary that you will not care MORE about your client's experience than they do. Whether it be a natural birth, success at breastfeeding, or a conscious death . . . the doula is committed to supporting the client's agenda, not imposing her own.

I heard a professional therapist speak on the well-defined boundaries for psychotherapists in a therapeutic relationship. In a therapeutic relationship, the therapist's needs cannot be met by her clients. With friends, however, the therapist's needs get met too. She made a distinction between being friends and being friendly. Doulas would do well to consider, beyond the defined scope of practice, what the boundaries are in relationship with clients. Are you expecting clients to meet your needs? Who is doing most of the talking when you meet?

Doulas who have unresolved issues about their own birth and breastfeeding experiences will need to examine their beliefs and motives and continue to process past challenges, disappointments and trauma. Likewise, end-of-life doulas who have experienced a recent loss will need time to process their own experiences. This must be done on your own time, not the clients' time, nor through the lens of your clients' experience. It's not about us.

The very tools that will help traumatized clients to heal are the ones that doulas can employ for their own healing. In her book *Transformation through Birth,* Claudia Panuthos suggests several techniques for healing past trauma. She suggests

What factors might tempt a doula to step outside of professional boundaries?

- Doula views the client as a victim and wants to rescue her.
- Doula views herself as hero, savior; has an exaggerated sense of self-importance.
- Doula comes under the power of clients who are difficult personalities and master manipulators.
- Doula is in a co-dependent relationship with her client; getting her buttons pushed (we all have our buttons!).
- Doula over-identifies with an issue that client is facing; projects too strongly from her own experience.
- Doula fails to grasp implications of her own and client's behavior *in* the moment.
- Doula avoids confrontation at all costs.
- Doula generally lacks good personal boundaries in her relationships.
- Doula is passionate about obstetric abuses or feels powerless in the face of medical abuses.
- Doula has a strong desire to "fix" things, people.
- Doula cares more about a specific outcome than the client does.

that we engage in an ongoing process of becoming conscious of our beliefs. What is your view of your body? What were your mother's experiences and beliefs? How have you manifested these beliefs in your experiences? Which beliefs have limited you in some way? Which beliefs would you like to transform? Limiting beliefs, when brought up to the conscious level, can be examined, stripped of their power and converted into positive self-messages. The book's title implies that birth has the power to transform us.

In the book *Birthing from Within* by Pam England and Rob Horowitz, additional techniques designed to help individuals explore the psychological and emotional aspects of birth are given. The artwork exercises can be helpful for doulas as well. Draw your own most powerful image of birth or death. Process it. (And, if you are artistically impaired like I am, don't worry about that; it's not a contest and you're not going to be judged.) What images come to mind?

Blaming (bad things happened because other people did things to us or didn't meet our expectations) is a symptom of unresolved issues and should be a red flag for doulas.

If we discover that we have a limiting belief that birth is dangerous, for example, we likely have very good reasons for that belief, whether it is based on our own experience or planted by someone else. Identification of that belief at the conscious level is the first step to converting the belief, but it does not magically go away because we have named it. However, it does give us the ability to ask for help in dealing with it, to allow others the opportunity to support us and to move forward in life, creating new experiences that counterbalance that limitation. If the past trauma is so deep as to constitute a state of posttraumatic stress and the person (doula or client) appears to be "stuck," then counseling is recommended. See "Signs that a Mental Health Referral May be Appropriate" (page 284).

Saying goodbye or bringing closure to the doula–client relationship presents another realm of boundary challenges. Don't skip this step! Realistically, can you be friends with all of your clients on an ongoing basis? Do you want to? Does the relationship transfer easily from you nurturing them in exchange for payment for services rendered to a 50/50 give-and-take relationship? Or are you expected to just continue your nurturing, but now you are not getting paid? Here are some suggestions for meeting this challenge successfully:

- Lay the foundation for closure at the first appointment, stating an end date for services (e.g., "phone availability through six weeks postpartum").

- Provide an opportunity for clients to evaluate your care.
- Thank clients for the privilege of having been able to share this special time in their lives.
- Some doulas like to bring a small gift to the last visit (a t-shirt, an herbal bath, a baby foot printer, a small hand-made memorial, etc.).
- Let the family know that you would love to serve them again in the future if they have need and that you appreciate any referrals to your services.
- If you host any type of forum (e.g., grief support group, ongoing classes on parenting topics, blog, summer reunion picnic, Facebook group), be very specific about what former clients are invited to do.
- Say the word—"goodbye."

Nurturing Yourself as Well as You Nurture Others

When flying in an airplane, we are instructed that if oxygen masks appear in front of us, we must put our own mask on first and only then help others for whom we are responsible. This is a great metaphor for the correct priority that self-care should be given in our lives.

Can you be as kind and gentle to yourself as you are with a newborn baby, a laboring mama or someone who is dying? Why do you deserve less? None of us can serve as a good role model for others if we are always running on an empty tank ourselves. Nourishment, R&R, laughter and play are all as important as any other piece of the picture, perhaps more! Because if we are sick, then we can't function and do any of it well.

What are some self-nurturing activities that doulas can engage in? As a doula, you're adept at helping others identify these strategies, right?

- Take a vacation!
- Take an undisturbed nap.
- Engage a babysitter and indulge yourself for an afternoon.
- Enjoy a chick flick.
- Lie on the couch and read a novel.
- Immerse yourself in an Epsom salts bath with a splash of pure essential oil of lavender or chamomile; light candles; lock the door and disappear.

- Dance!
- Make love.
- Have coffee or tea with a friend.
- Pray.
- Go for a walk with a friend.
- Take a yoga class; do some recuperative/restorative yoga poses.
- Choose flower essences for psychic and emotional support (check out Olive, Oak and others from the Bach Flower Essences collection).
- Talk with another doula.
- Join a doula support group.
- Start a doula support group.
- Get a massage.
- Use your imagination!

In the end, let's trust our own timelines for coming into this work that so many of us experience as a calling. Does it make any sense at all for us to sacrifice the well-being of our own families so that we can help other families? If you just can't seem to make it work on the home front, perhaps there is another time for you to engage this work. Or, perhaps there is another path to service of comparable value. You may not necessarily need to turn your back on the whole doula gig but, rather, take a little detour along the way. Sometimes the detours present an opportunity for serendipities to occur and new realms of opportunity to open. It seems to me that when the timing has been right at different pivotal junctures in my life, doors magically open and the universe seems to say "yes!" And when something isn't such a good fit, the doors all close, forcing me in a new (often more fulfilling) direction. The lesson for me has been to trust the purposefulness of how my path unfolds.

I Don't Have Time to Read a Book on Time Management!

Many executive directors, program managers and entrepreneurs find themselves caught in this Catch-22. We are so busy working IN our businesses that we don't have time to work ON our businesses. We are so busy trying to keep up that we literally don't have time to tell or show someone else what they could do to help us lighten the load. We are wearing too many hats and not all of them play to our strengths. We will struggle with budgeting, or database management, or employee management, bumbling through with a payload of stress and wasted time, but the thought of studying how to create Excel spreadsheets, implement time-management strategies or deal with difficult people feels like just another add-on to an endless list of to-dos. We can't see the forest because we are lost in the trees.

I have learned the hard way that this is a self-defeating approach to the problem of not enough hours in the day. Some thought has to be invested in the big picture, the long haul. Whether you are a doula juggling multiple demands on several fronts or a program manager, founder or visionary seeking to keep a doula program funded and operational, time management strategies are your friend. Feeling sorry for yourself, blaming others for your exhaustion or getting increasingly more frantic won't help you "go the distance."

See our "Pie of Time Exercise," additional "Time Management Strategies," and our "Time Tracker" tool in *The Doula Business Guide Workbook, 3rd Edition* for more help.

Start by making a list of what you do every day. How much time is spent on sleep, work, exercise, self-care, household chores, social media, schlepping kids, doctor appointments, family time, time with friends? Just track it for three days without judging it or trying to change. Then sit down with your list and analyze it. Note any patterns. What else is on your to-do list that you didn't get to in those three days? How much does work fulfill your basic needs and how much does it deplete you? What happened to self-care? (Self-care will be needed in direct proportion to how depleting your work is.) How are you *choosing* to spend your time? Can the family do more to help? Could you set better boundaries with your clients, bosses, board members, coworkers, partners, friends and family members? Is there something on the list that is sucking your time—something that you really don't want to be doing and could possibly eliminate? Is there a way to work smarter, not harder? Sometimes we need to make some hard decisions here because we want to do it all.

If you find that you routinely do not have time to complete even the urgent items on your list, then some serious self-evaluation is needed. Just how many balls are you trying to keep in the air and how many are you actually dropping? Wouldn't you rather do four things really well and have people think you are amazing than do eight things lamely and have people constantly annoyed or irritated with you? Who lined up this agenda for you anyway? Who put that one more thing on your plate? Who requires that it all be perfect?

Consider the consequences of cutting out sleep hours or your exercise program in order to get it all done. Maybe here and there you can get away with it, but I'm confident it isn't viable as a lifestyle choice. You can pretty much count on the fact that your body and soul will demand their due so, one way or another, you WILL be required to take care and rest.

My Favorite Time-Management Strategies

- Set aside a chunk of time to focus on one priority task and don't allow anything to distract you (e.g., spend one hour per day completing profiles on social networking sites; commit two hours per day to website development or completing certification requirements). This is known as "time blocking."
- Listen to books or educational/motivational programs as you commute to work or run errands; use the voice recorder function on your phone to capture the low-hanging fruit, two or three notable ideas that you can immediately implement in your business or life.
- Establish control over your phone calls; limit times that you answer and return calls; leave an answering message to this effect.
- Make your website user friendly so that information and answers to frequently asked questions can be easily found online; notice anything that is creating confusion and keep refining this. Create a FAQs page on your site.
- If you sell classes or products, set up online ordering and payment, with auto responders that handle most of the customer interface for you. You can even set up online calendars for making appointments with clients.
- Check and respond to email once or twice per day, rather than indulging your addiction countless times per day. The constant checking means that you are allowing someone else's agenda to take priority over yours. You do not need to interrupt your focused work to respond to their need.
- Contain social media networking to a set amount of time (set a timer!). This will help limit the amount of time you spend going down the rabbit hole.
- Set up systems for essential repetitive tasks. For example, I discovered way too late (but better than never) canned responses in Gmail. Get someone to show you if you don't know how. I am now addicted to canned responses! In case this sounds terrible, I always ensure that they are edited in the moment to match the tone and special needs of the inquirer
- Know when to get help.
- Practice saying "no."

The Difference between a Dream and a Goal is a Deadline

Consider the benefits of setting goals for the month, the week, the day. If we wake up each day and anyone or anything can make a claim on our time, then it's not a big mystery why we can't get our own agendas accomplished. If we are working from home, but we can't shut a door for some undisturbed time and no one respects that we are working, again, it's no big mystery if we become frustrated. If our goals are loosely defined ("make more money"), we never set any priorities, and don't even have an agenda or to-do list compiled, then it certainly is no wonder that we might simply give way to feeling overwhelmed and discouraged by the sheer abundance of possibilities. The work needs to be laid out in bite-size chunks that help us get from point A to point B. In short, we need a plan.

A few years ago, I realized that I needed to keep two running lists rather than one—a To-Do list and an Ideas list. Crossing items off my To-Do list makes me feel happy. My To-Do list is the immediate, day-to-day list of tasks that need to be attended to, calls returned, items purchased, errands run and so on. This list is on top of my schedule for the day—appointments, teaching, Tai Chi class, and social or family engagements. My Idea list is more of a big picture list. It helps me track ideas for marketing or new projects as they occur to me and, more importantly, serves as a tool for prioritizing which items to take action on. The priorities likely will shift over time, so I revisit this list on a regular basis. In setting priorities, I am always looking for the biggest return on my investment of time and money and that is where I choose to concentrate my efforts. But there is one caveat—I have to want to do it. I have learned that some of the ideas that get captured on this list (even good ones) may never rise to the top and make their way over to the To Do list. In fact, they may just stay near the bottom of the list for so long that they drop off altogether (and that's okay!). Not all ideas are equally compelling. The main point is that if every idea gets captured on a To Do list, you will assuredly become overwhelmed. You need to stay focused and purposeful. Work the plan.

The problem of procrastination needs to be addressed. There are three primary causes of procastination:

1. Laziness
2. Fear of failure
3. Perfectionism

If laziness is the cause, then you may not have what it takes to be a successful small business owner. I don't have any help for that challenge. But if that were the case, would you even be reading this book in the first place? Doubtful.

Our "Personal Inventory" tool in *The Doula Business Guide Workbook, 3rd Edition* is designed to help you identify the skills, character strengths, personal habits, assets and motivation required to be successful as a business owner. How can you play to your strengths and minimize your weak areas?

Other readers might identify with fear of failure as a factor in their tendency to procrastinate. Do you have people in your life who make you feel small? Who have made you feel that you are not good enough, smart enough and so on? Who are jealous when you succeed, when you are happy, when you are amazing? These are toxic influences to be banished! Surround yourself instead with positive people who delight in your success. And then accept that some fear is okay. Courage is being afraid and doing it anyway. Honestly, if you don't have a little bit of fear, then you might have blinders on! Feeling daunted is reality-based. Go ahead and get out of your comfort zone. Let me share these words of inspiration from spiritual teacher and author Marianne Williamson:

> *Our deepest fear is not that we are inadequate. Our deepest fear is that we are powerful beyond measure. It is our light, not our darkness that most frightens us. We ask ourselves, "Who am I to be brilliant, gorgeous, talented, fabulous?" Actually, who are you not to be? You are a child of God. Your playing small does not serve the world. There is nothing enlightened about shrinking so other people won't feel insecure around you. We are all meant to shine as children do. We were born to make manifest the glory of God that is within us. It's not just in some of us; it's in everyone. And as we let our own light shine, we unconsciously give other people permission to do the same. As we are liberated from our own fear, our presence automatically liberates others.*

And now we come to perfectionism. This is my home turf. Since perfection will always remain elusive, the biggest challenge is to be able to declare that a task is done—that your website is ready for launch or you are ready for your first client interview. Embrace the idea that there will always be room for improvement and that everything is a work in progress. This requires humility and a willingness to accept imperfection in yourself and others. We perfectionists will always strive. It's just who we are but, at some point, we must simply stop and declare the imperfect "good enough." It's a relief really. Try it.

A Business Plan

If you are not planning to enter the nonprofit world or start a doula program, then you may have understandably chosen to skip reading Chapters 4–6. However, you may want to consider reviewing Chapter 6 because writing a grant proposal is very similar to creating a business plan. Grant proposals are detailed. While articulating goals, objectives and action steps, they also force deadlines and a projected budget for getting it all done. It takes strategic thinking to sketch it all out but once you do, you have a step-by-step business plan to guide your work.

See also our "Goals and Activities Business Planner" in *The Doula Business Guide Workbook, 3rd Edition.*

When we are at the bottom of a mountain looking up, the only way to get from point A to point B is to start the climb, step by step, in manageable chunks. Just like the mama in labor, we may need to be reminded to focus on what we have accomplished, not how much remains to be done.

Next Steps after Doula Training

How can we best harness the enthusiasm, high energy and glow experienced at the close of a doula training weekend? Get yourself an accountability partner (or two or three)! Someone in the same boat, who also has aspirations to set up a business (does not need to be in the same field as yours) and agree to meet on a regular basis. Self-employment can be a lonely undertaking at times, even more so at the beginning because you are not yet busy serving clients. Regular meetings with your support person or group can be used to set goals, brainstorm ideas and strategies, give each other feedback on steps taken, report on progress made or challenges experienced, and so on. It's like having a business coach but, instead of money changing hands, you each invest a little time focused on each other's business. The concept is commonly referred to as a Mastermind group and was introduced by Napoleon Hill in the early 1900s, in his timeless classic *Think and Grow Rich.*

See "How to Form a Mastermind Group" in *The Doula Business Guide Workbook, 3rd Edition.*

A well-designed certification process should lead you through your "next steps" which typically involve reading, gaining hands-on experience as a doula and developing community resources. Begin with the end in mind but set short-term benchmarks for success. *Doing is what will make you feel ready.*

Mentors and Jumping in the Deep End

So many fledgling doulas have inquired about shadowing another doula. There is a strong desire for modeling of the doula role . . . what does it look like in action? I get it. The desire to be an observer with no responsibilities, an opportunity to take it all in and explore your own ideas about the role. What did the mentor doula do well? What would you do differently? It makes sense. Unfortunately, there are few opportunities for shadowing. Unless a family is overwhelmed and in need of an extra pair of hands, a "shadow" doula might be perceived to be an inhibiting influence, an invasion of privacy, yet another factor to integrate. Many experienced doulas are hesitant to take on the mentor's mantle out of a sense of protection for the families they serve.

If mentoring is to be an option, it must come from experienced doulas who feel comfortable presenting this possibility to their clients. If the doula is comfortable with it, there is a good chance her clients will also be, for the most part. Funny how that works. Then it is simply a matter of the mentor evolving a system for mentoring that works for her. I have seen online discussions wherein the prospective doula mentee expects to be paid for her efforts. It would take a very generous mentor to agree to this, in my opinion! In the homebirth arena, it is true that some senior midwives provide a small stipend to their apprentices. Typically, this would only occur *after* the apprentice/mentee:

- has moved beyond the beginner phase and established that she is an asset to the practice,
- has demonstrated good professional boundaries and reliability, and
- shows deference and respect for the primacy of the mentor's relationship with her clients.

In the beginning, the risk is all on the side of the mentor and it is often more work for the mentor as well (coordinating another person's schedule/needs/emotions into the picture, extra effort for good communication, etc.). I have known of cases where an apprentice undermined the primary doula's relationship with her client, questioned her judgment, criticized her to the client behind her back and generally overstepped her bounds. Some mentees have even ripped off copyrighted forms and educational materials developed by the mentor or marketed directly to her clients. Given these considerations, it is not difficult to understand why many professional doulas are not especially eager to serve as mentors. I do not think it is unreasonable for the mentor to charge the mentee for her extra effort or to expect a work exchange—value for value. After all, in essence, the mentor is training her future competitor(s). Whatever the arrangement, it is essential that mutual expectations be *explicit and quantified* to head off any bad feelings on both sides.

It's a bit weird. I think there is natural tension built into the master/apprentice relationship. The student learns from the mentor, initially eager to please. But as the apprentice gains in experience, knowledge and skill, it is only natural that she will begin to critique her teacher. She is beginning to differentiate, to come into her own. She may start to feel resentment that her work is unpaid, feeling "I could do it better." If you are so lucky as to find a mentor, honor the trust she has placed in you. You will learn a great deal, even if one of the things you learn is that you will do things differently when you have your own doula practice (your mentor has earned the right to do it her way). In fact, the purpose of the relationship is to develop the student so that she is ready to go out on her own. As the apprentice, it is your responsibility to speak up once you have outgrown the relationship rather than boil in silent resentment. Do it thankfully and respectfully and you will have an ally going forward as well. Make a rough break and unethical choices, and you have burned your bridges and tarnished your reputation. While it's perfectly right and proper that you want to do things your own way and get paid, don't forget to say "thank you."

If you cannot find a doula mentor, please don't let this stop you! Your "need" for mentoring may be more perception than reality. *It's not courage if there is no fear.* How can we expect our mamas to be courageous if we are not engaging the practice of it ourselves? How can she believe in her strengths if you don't believe in yourself? There is no easy way to gain the wisdom and confidence that comes from experience. It is always humbling to be a beginner, whether learning a new dance step, speaking a new language or becoming a doula. Never misrepresent yourself or exaggerate your experience level to clients; your attempt to live up to the pretense will create a boatload of unnecessary stress. Embrace your beginner status and focus on what you *do* have to offer, not on your insufficiencies in knowledge or experience ("I would be honored to have you be my first client" rather than "I've never been to a birth"). As you dig deep and move outside your comfort zone, so can you encourage the moms you support to move through their doubts and fears. You will quickly see that your presence makes a positive difference for every family served.

Even for your very first client experience, you have something special to offer.

We all find our own way of being with families. If a family chooses you, then they are drawn to you, to your energy. Trust that and do your best for them. Each initial consultation, prenatal visit or end-of-life consultation will get easier as you grow in confidence about your role. There are no shortcuts to experience. You must be humble and simply do your best. Jump in the deep end.

Doula Power!

Perhaps we are drawn to doula work because we need to cultivate in ourselves those very qualities of patience, courage and stamina that the work demands of us. It is not that we are necessarily "patient people" or that it comes easily to us. It's a spiritual practice. We work at it and our work provides us with that opportunity. As we overcome our fears, we grow in courage. As we settle into each moment and practice being fully present in that moment, we grow in patience. As we train our minds not to care that our feet ache after a long, hard ordeal, when our client still needs us and yet another hour of our time is called for, we grow in stamina.

Doulas are moving increasingly into the mainstream culture. As more doulas and visionaries turn service and passion into viable careers, embracing the role of the savvy businesswoman or social entrepreneur, more families will benefit. We can become agents for social change, bringing a humanizing influence to a health-care system in great need. Perhaps you have a less grandiose vision, believing that your role is to provide a humble service with integrity and grace, one family at a time? Think of Mother Teresa and you will realize that there is nothing more powerful. I hope that this book will provide the foundation for more doulas to embrace the businesswoman within, each claiming her own "right livelihood." Dream big and make it so! ◆

Appendix

Doula Programs

The following list is not intended to be comprehensive. There may be many other programs, in all categories. My hope is that the list will give you a jumping off point for further exploration.

Community Based

Ancient Song Doula Services
Brooklyn, NY
www.ancientsongdoulaservices.com

The Birth Doula Program
Markham and Scarborough ON
www.birthdoulaprogram.ca

The Birth Place
Winter Garden, FL
www.thebirthplace.org

By My Side Birth Support, Healthy Start
Brooklyn, NY
www.nyc.gov/site/doh/health/neighborhood-health/healthy-start-brooklyn.page

Healthy Women Healthy Futures
New York, NY
www.bronxhealthlink.org/tbhl/programs/HWHFDoulas

Homegrown Babies
Asheville, NC
www.homegrownbabies.com

The JJ Way®
www.jenniejoseph.com

Mamatoto Village
Washington, DC
www.mamatotovillage.org

Open Arms Perinatal Services
Seattle, WA
www.openarmsps.org

Ounce of Prevention
Chicago, IL
www.theounce.org/what-we-do/programs/doula

San Antonio Birth Doulas
San Antonio, TX
www.sabirthdoulas.org/doulas/sabd.html

South Community Birth Program
Vancouver, BC
www.scbp.ca

Uzazi Village
Kansas City, MO
www.uzazivillage.org

Hospital Based

The Birth Hospital, Ascension Columbia St. Mary's Hospital
Ozaukee Birth Center
Mequon, WI
www.columbia-stmarys.org/oth/Page.asp?PageID=OTH101986

Maimonides Medical Center
Brooklyn NY
www.maimonidesmed.org/obstetrics-and-gynecology/obstetrics/having-a-baby-at-maimonides/free-doula-program

Mount Carmel, St. Ann's
Westerville, OH
www.mountcarmelhealth.com/find-a-service-or-specialty/doula-services

Sharp Mary Birch Hospital for Women & Newborns Doula Program
San Diego, CA
www.sharp.com/hospitals/mary-birch/doula-program.cfm

Swedish Medical Center
Seattle, WA
www.swedish.org/services/doula-services

Village Health System
Ridgewood, NJ
www.valleyhealth.com/ChildBirth.aspx?id=436

WakeMed Health and Hospitals
Raleigh, NC
www.wakemed.org/pregnancy-doula-labor-support

End-of-Life Doula Programs

Hospice of San Luis Obispo County
San Luis Obispo, CA
www.hospiceslo.org/services/end-life-doula-program

Hackensack Meridian Health, Hackensack University Medical Center
Hackensack, NJ
www.hackensackumc.org/health-professionals/education-training/volunteer-programs/end-of-life-doula-program

Holy Name Medical Center
Teaneck, NJ
www.holyname.org/ForSeniors/hospice.aspx

Mount Sinai
New York, NY
www.mountsinai.org/patient-care/service-areas/palliative-care/doula-program

Valley Hospice, Valley Health System
Ridgewood, NJ
www.valleyhealth.com/Valley_HomeCare.aspx?id=3354

Bibliography and Resources

Bibliography

Arnoldy, F. (2018) *Cultivating the Doula Heart: Essentials of Compassionate Care.* Available from ContemplativeDoula.com.

Beckwith, H. and C. Clifford. (2011) *You, Inc.: The Art of Selling Yourself.* New York: Business Plus.

Brennan, P. (2019) *The Doula Business Guide Workbook: Tools to Create a Successful Practice, 3rd ed.* Ann Arbor, MI: DreamStreet Press.

Brewer, E. and C. Achilles. (2008) *Finding Funding: Grantwriting from Start to Finish, Including Project Management and Internet Use,* 5th ed. Thousand Oaks, CA: Corwin.

Browning, B. (2016) *Grant Writing for Dummies,* 6th ed. Hoboken, NJ: Wiley.

Carlson, M and T. O'Neal-McElrath (2013) *Winning Grants Step by Step: The Complete Workbook for Planning, Developing and Writing Successful Proposals,* 4th ed. San Francisco, CA: Jossey-Bass.

Cloud, H. and J. Townsend. (2017) *Boundaries: When to Say Yes, How to Say No to Take Control of Your Life. Nashville, TN: Vondervan.*

Covey, S. (2013) *The 7 Habits of Highly Effective People: Powerful Lessons in Personal Change. New York: Simon & Schuster.*

Crouhy, M., D. Galai, and R. Mark. (2014) *The Essentials of Risk Management,* 2nd ed. New York: McGraw-Hill.

De Becker, G. (1997) *The Gift of Fear: Survival Signals that Protect Us from Violence.* Boston, MA: Little, Brown and Company.

Dodd, P. and D. Sundheim. (2009) *The 25 Best Time Management Tools and Techniques: How to Get More Done without Driving Yourself Crazy.* Chelsea, MI: Peak Performance.

Domar, A. and H. Dreher. (2000) *Self-Nurture: Learning to Care for Yourself as Effectively as You Care for Everyone Else.* New York: Penguin.

Fishman, S. (2018) *Every Nonprofit's Tax Guide: How to Keep Your Tax-Exempt Status & Avoid IRS Problems: A Step-By-Step Resource,* 5th ed. Berkeley, CA: Nolo.

Gerber, M. (2001) *The E-Myth Revisited: Why Most Small Businesses Don't Work and What to Do about It.* New York: HarperCollins.

Gilliland, A. (2018) *Heart of the Doula: Essentials for Practice and Life.* Available from AmyGilliland.com.

Gladwell, M. (2000) *The Tipping Point: How Little Things Can Make a Big Difference.* New York: Back Bay Books.

Godin, S. (2002) *Purple Cow: Transform Your Business by Being Remarkable.* New York: Penguin Group.

Grobman, G. (2015) *The Nonprofit Handbook: Everything You Need to Know to Start and Run Your Nonprofit Organization,* 7th ed. Harrisburg, PA: White Hat.

Hamilton, R.J. (2014) *The Millionaire Master Plan: Your Personalized Path to Financial Success.* New York, NY: Business Plus.

Hayden, C. and Levinson, J. (2013) *Get Clients Now! A 28-Day Marketing Program for Professionals, Consultants and Coaches, 3rd Edition.* New York, NY: AMACOM.

Hill, N. (1937) *Think and Grow Rich.* Book is now in the public domain with many different publishers.

Hutton, S. and F. Phillips. (2017) *Nonprofit Kit for Dummies,* 5th ed. Hoboken, NJ: Wiley.

Kamoroff, B. (2017) *Small Time Operator: How to Start Your Own Business, Keep Your Books, Pay Your Taxes and Stay Out of Trouble,* 14th ed. Guilford, CT: Taylor Trade Publishing.

Karsh, E. and A. Fox (2006) *The Only Grant-Writing Book You'll Ever Need: Top Grant Writers and Grant Givers Share Their Secrets,* 2nd ed. New York: Basic.

Kelleher, J. (Forthcoming, 2019) *Nurturing the Family: The Guide for Postpartum Doulas,* 2nd ed. Publisher information unavailable.

Mancuso, A. (2017) *How to Form a Non-Profit Corporation,* 13th ed. Berkeley, CA: Nolo.

Miner, J. and K. Ball-Stahl. (2016) *Models of Proposal Planning and Writing,* 2nd ed. Santa Barbara, CA: Greenwood.

Morgenstern, J. (2004) *Time Management from the Inside Out: The Foolproof System for Taking Control of Your Schedule,* 2nd ed. New York: Holt.

Pakroo, P. (2017) *Starting & Building a Nonprofit: A Practical Guide,* 7th ed. Berkeley, CA: Nolo.

Pascali-Bonaro, D., and J. Arnold with M. Ringel. (2014) *Nurturing Beginnings: Guide to Postpartum Home Care for Doulas and Outreach Workers,* 2nd ed. Debra Pascali-Bonaro.

Perez, P. with D. Thelen. (2010) *Doula Programs: How to Start and Run a Private or Hospital-Based Program with Success,* 2nd ed. Johnson, VT: Cutting Edge Press.

Petty, S. and E. Verbeck. (2012) *Worth Every Penny: Build a Business that Thrills Your Customers and Still Charge What You're Worth.* Austin, TX: Greenleaf.

Sohnen-Moe, C. (2016) *Business Mastery: A Guide for Creating a Fulfilling, Thriving Business and Keeping it Successful,* 5th ed. Tucson, AZ: Sohnen-Moe Associates.

Slim, P. (2013) *Body of Work: Finding the Thread That Ties Your Story Together.* New York: Penguin.

Thompson, W. (2011) *The Complete Idiot's Guide to Grant Writing,* 3rd ed. Indianapolis, IN: Alpha.

Trudeau, R. and B. Guzman. (2008) *The Mother's Guide to Self-Renewal: How to Reclaim, Rejuvenate and Re-Balance Your Life.* Austin, TX: Balanced Living.

Wolf, T. (2012) *Managing a Nonprofit Organization: Updated Twenty-First-Century Edition.* New York: Free Press.

Resources Online

Free Stuff

My first entry here is not really a resource, just some advice. There is a lot of great, free guidance available to you. Do some web browsing, using different keywords. You will find any number of marketing or business gurus. Pick one or two with whom you resonate and sign up for their newsletters, follow their blogs or join their Facebook groups. That way, regular, informative and inspiring content will show up in your Inbox so you can always be learning, but with very little effort and in small chunks.

Google Alerts

Use Google Alerts to help identify interesting new content on the web. For example, you could create an alert for "doula business" and your specialty (e.g., "end-of-life doulas"). Here's how:

1. Visit www.google.com/alerts
2. In the "create an alert about" box, enter the keywords for which you want to receive notifications.
3. Click "show options" to say how often you get alerts, what types of results you want to get, and more.
4. Click "create alert."

Social Media

There are a few groups on Facebook that are focused on the business side of being a doula (do a search). Go ahead and join a couple of them and explore a little till you find one or two that you like. You may also find reviews or recommendations for different apps and resources. Look for (and join!) relevant doula member groups in your local community. These are great for making connections and identifying local resources.

General Business Resources

BusinessKnowHow.com
Sample articles on the site include: "How to Resolve Business Partnership Issues," "7 Tips for a Successful Business Partnership," "Steps to Finding the Right Business Partner," "Pros & Cons of Business Partnerships," "Business Plan Basics" (includes links to business planning software); plus sample business plans and business planning worksheet. Check out the article "How Do You Separate the Home from the Office?"

BusinessTown.com
This site shows you how to write a business plan, weigh financing options, and review the legal business structures.

Home Business Tools
homebiztools.com
Start-up, expansion, and promotion information for home-based businesses.

Internal Revenue Service
IRS.gov
Tax forms and instructions available in downloadable PDF files. Apply for an Employer Identification Number (EIN) online.

Simple Online Solutions
SimpleURL.com
Check here to see if the domain name you have in mind is available. You can also reserve a domain name.

Small Business Administration
SBA.gov
U.S. government agency that provides support for entrepreneurs and small business owners. Great information for planning, launching, managing and growing your business.

State Government Sites
[StateName].gov
Provides information on developing a business plan, ways to legally structure a business and register a business name, licenses and permits required, and more.

Accounting Software

- QuickBooks.com (If you have employees, you will need the enhanced payroll feature.)
- Wave Financial [WaveApps.com] (free invoicing and accounting software with credit card processing and payroll services for small businesses) (Canadian)

Business Organization/Project Management

- 17hats.com
- AcuityScheduling.com
- BulletJournal.com. Customizable organizational tool; can be your to-do list, sketchbook and notebook.
- Doodle.com. Trying to coordinate schedules with many people? This online tool makes the process more efficient.
- Dubsado.com

- Edoula.biz. All-in-one solution for business management includes client intake, contracts, invoicing, payments and more. (Canadian)
- Evernote.com. Cloud application can be easily used on all devices. Uses the concept of digital "notebooks," like folders on your computer.
- GravityForms.com. Tool for building forms on WordPress sites.
- MobileDoula.com. Business management software designed for doulas.
- PassionPlanner.com. Organize your business goals; free downloads available.
- Tave.com. A couple of doula agency owners mentioned using this software for lead tracking, online booking, workflow and more.
- YourDoulaBiz.com. Doula business management online platform.

Card Readers

- PayPal.com
- Square.com
- Stripe.com

Keyword Identification

- Wordtracker.com. Quickly identify your best-performing keywords.

Liability Insurance for Doulas

Other companies may also provide coverage for doulas. If you do not find what you are looking for on a company's website, call them and ask to speak with an agent. Insurance companies are predisposed to want to sell you insurance, so don't be afraid to do a little advocacy if necessary.

- AON
- CMFGroup
- Doula Care (Canada)
- Liberty Mutual
- ProLiability (Mercer, Canada)
- ProLink (Canada)

Legal Online

- LegalZoom.com. For LLD formation, trademark protection and other legal matters.
- Nolo.com. This legal solutions website has a great deal of accessible information regarding business models and the nitty gritty "how to" details of various models. Look under "Legal Articles" for advice on many topics.
- RocketLawyer.com. For LLD formation, trademark protection and other legal matters.
- USLegalForms.com. For LLD formation, trademark protection and other legal matters.

Logo Design

- 99 Designs
- Fiverr

Phone Apps

- MileIQ (mileage tracker)
- Spending (app for iPhone; for tracking business expenses)

Print and Design Promotional Materials

- CaféPress.com. Online printing services; sells products with business name, logos, slogans (e.g., t-shirts, coffee mugs, posters).
- VistaPrint.com. Business card printing and more; use their templates to create a variety of marketing materials.
- TheWebsiteDoula.com offers free stock photos for doulas and website design.

Video Conferencing/Webinars Platforms

- FreeConferenceCall.com
- Zoom.com
- Vimeo.com

Non-Profit Resources

Alliance for Nonprofit Management
AllianceOnline.org

Center for Nonprofit Management
CNMDallas.org
Brings the most current tools for best practices in nonprofit management to thousands of nonprofit boards, staff and volunteers each year.

GuideStar.org
This website is a free national database of IRS-recognized nonprofit organizations.

Internal Revenue Service
IRS.gov
Contains a link to the 501(c)(3) nonprofit incorporation application kit and instructions.

Nolo.com
Legal website; look under "Legal Articles" for advice on relevant topics; great resources for nonprofit startup.

Non-Profit Risk Management Center
NonProfitRisk.org
Resources on volunteer and financial risk management, employment practices and youth management.

Doula Programs Resources

Beets, V. (2014) *The Emergence of U.S. Hospital-Based Doula Programs* (doctoral dissertation, University of South Carolina). Retrieved from: scholarcommons.sc.edu/cgi/viewcontent.cgi?article=3799&context=etd.

Chapple, W., A. Gilliland, D. Li, E. Shier, and E. Wright. (2013) An economic model of the benefits of professional doula labor support in Wisconsin births. *Wisconsin Medical Journal,* Vol. 112(2).

Gami, S. (2015) *An Enthused Perinatal Team Collaborates to Form a Hospital Based Doula Program,* DONA International Virtual Conference Session. www.vconferenceonline.com/event/sessions.aspx?id=1086&track=2.

HealthConnect One. (2017) *Sustainable Funding for Doula Programs: A Study.* Retrieved from: www.healthconnectone.org/hc_one_resources/sustainable-funding-doula-programs-study.

Hodnett, H., S. Gates, G. Hofmeyr, C. Sakala, and J. Weston. (20120 Continuous support for women during childbirth. Cochrane Database Syst Rev 2011 Feb 16; (2):CD003766.

Levy, L. (2017) Keeping clients' needs first as a hospital-based doula. *International Doula,* Vol. 25(3).

Low, L., A. Moffat, and P. Brennan. (2006) Doulas as community health workers: Lessons learned from a volunteer program. *Journal of Perinatal Education* 15(3):25–33.

Swedish Hospital Doula Services. (2017) *Swedish Hospital Doula Services Annual Report 2016.* Retried from: ohanadoulas.com/wp-content/uploads/2018/04/2016-Swedish-Doula-Program-Annual-Report.pdf.

Visionary Vanguard Group, Inc. (2017) *The JJ Way®: Community-Based Maternity Center, Final Evaluation Report.* Retrieved from: www.commonsensechildbirth.org/wp-content/uploads/2011/05/The-JJ-Way%C2%AE-Community-based-Maternity-Center-Evaluation-Report-2017-1.pdf.

Women's Health Care Physicians. (2017) Approaches to limit interventions during labor and birth. *ACOG Journal.* Retrieved from: www.acog.org/Clinical-Guidance-and-Publications/Committee-Opinions/Committee-on-Obstetric-Practice/Approaches-to-Limit-Intervention-During-Labor-and-Birth?IsMobileSet=false.

Grant Writing Resources

American Fact Finder
FactFinder.census.gov
This website belongs to the U.S. Census Bureau. On the home page, you'll find links for the American Community Survey (an ongoing survey that provides data about your community every year).

Catalog of Federal Domestic Assistance
CFDA.gov
This government resource directory is called the encyclopedia of federal grant assistance. It identifies which federal agencies give grants, where and how much.

Centers for Disease Control, Health Topics A to Z
CDC.gov
This site provides the information you need to talk and write about health-related grant projects.

Federal Grants Portal
Grants.gov

Federal Web Locator
Lib.auburn.edu
The Center for Information Law and Policy maintains this website as the one-stop-shopping point for federal government grant-related information on the internet.

FoundationCenter.org
This site provides information about funding opportunities for nonprofit organizations, a schedule of upcoming proposal writing training programs in various cities around the country, an online budget class, access to an online librarian, a link to the online *Philanthropy News Digest,* and a description of the FC's *Guide to Proposal Writing,* now available in a third edition, by subscription. Extensive information on foundations and corporations is available; however, you will need to subscribe to conduct a funding search for your project area and topic.

FoundationSearch.com
This group is a source of funding information for nonprofits, providing comprehensive, searchable information on 100,000+ foundations, corporations and government funding opportunities. Also provide online grant writing education courses and tracking systems. No-obligation online tours available.

Graduate Women International
GraduateWomen.org
Contains a great brainstorming exercise for developing goals and objectives.

HomeTownLocator.com
Has links for every state and a drop-down window where you can search by city, county, zip code, or area code.

LearnerAssociates.net
Guide for Writing a Funding Proposal includes valuable information on writing an evaluation plan, for both novice and veteran grant writers.

Lone Eagle Consulting
Lone-eagles.com
Grant resources and templates.

MarchofDimes.com
Has a history of funding doula programs and related infant health initiatives.

National Council of Nonprofits
CouncilofNonprofits.org
Find your state association. Grant writing training opportunities and much more.

National Institutes of Health
Grants.NIH.gov
The Office of Extramural Research has developed a website with grant writing tip sheets. This site is helpful in writing health-related or research-directed grant applications.

National Network of Grantmakers (NNG)
chfs.ky.gov
From this website, you can download the NNG Common Grant Application template. The template fits the grant writing requirements of many national foundations. If you don't have a proscribed format, use this one.

Non-Profit Guides
NPGuides.org
Provides detailed information on how to write the project's goals and objectives and the methodology (how you will carry out the activities).

The Chronicle of Philanthropy
Philanthropy.com
The newspaper of the nonprofit world; extensive up-to-date resources.

The Grantsmanship Center
tgci.com
The world's leader in grantsmanship training. Includes federal register announcements; links to local, federal, and international funding sources; top grantmaking foundations by state; community foundations by state; corporate giving programs by state; and state government homepages.

The Philanthropy Roundtable
PhilanthropyRoundtable.org
This site belongs to a national association of individual donors, corporate giving representatives, foundation staff and trustees, and trust and estate offers.

The Robert Wood Johnson Foundation
RWJF.org
Largest single health philanthropy in the world, giving away over $200 million annually. This site includes calls for proposals, guidelines, healthcare–related information, and information about the foundation.

USA.gov
Gateway for all federal and state agencies that make grant awards.

Index

Symbols

A

B

C

D

E

G

H

I

J

K

L

M

N

O

P

Q

R

S

T

U

V

W

Y

Z

About the Author

Patty Brennan has practiced as a doula, childbirth educator, midwife, nonprofit founder/executive director, and birth, postpartum and end-of-life doula trainer in a career spanning 36 years. She enjoys being an entrepreneur, having been self-employed her entire adult life. Patty has been married to her husband Jerry for 40 years. They have two sons and six grandchildren and live in Ann Arbor, Michigan.

Invest in our companion workbook to *The Doula Business Guide*

***The Doula Business Guide Workbook: Tools to Create a Thriving Practice, 3rd Edition* (2019), by Patty Brennan ($19.95)**

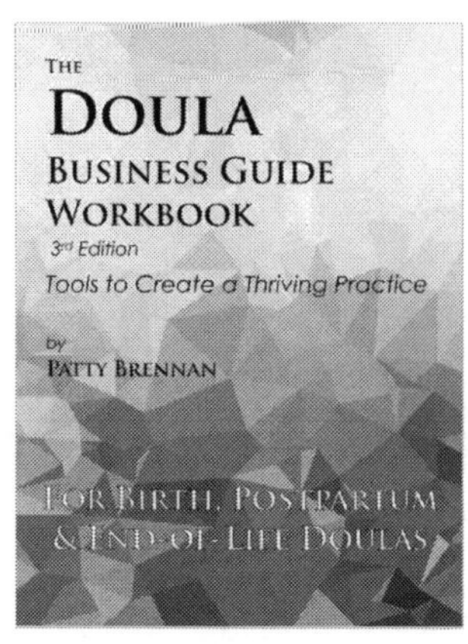

Birth, postpartum and end-of-life doulas will find guidance for visioning, organizing, planning and growing their businesses. Our freshly updated Workbook is filled with practical, interactive tools designed to help you succeed, whether you are just starting out or are already a seasoned doula business owner. Focus your efforts with our checklists, step-by-step instructions, tip sheets, worksheets, exercises, questionnaires, strategies, planners, trackers and more. The notion that heart-centered work and making money are somehow fundamentally incompatible is a false dichotomy. Choose a path of service to others AND thrive financially! The Workbook is a great companion guide to our freshly updated *The Doula Business Guide, 3rd Edition.* While each book stands on its own, the two books are fully integrated and designed to be interactive. Get ready to implement your vision.

Other Books by Patty Brennan

Published by DreamStreet Press, Ann Arbor, Michigan

***Ready for Birth & Baby Workbook* (2016)**

Our *Ready for Birth & Baby Workbook* is a gold mine of essential resources for navigating pregnancy, labor and birth, and the early weeks postpartum. It provides partner exercises, information, proactive strategies and tips to guide you through the childbearing year. Great consumer-oriented and holistic manual for childbirth educators to use with expectant parents.

***Vaccines & Informed Choice: Everything Parents Need to Know,* 6th Edition (2015)**

This book serves as a guide for parents seeking to make an informed choice regarding childhood vaccination. Emphasis is placed on preventing adverse vaccine reactions; how to enhance the immune system naturally; the role of homeopathy in preventing vaccine reactions, disease prevention and treatment, and undoing vaccine damage; and the case against compulsory vaccination and how to exercise parental rights. All vaccines are not equal, each vaccine is a choice, and each family has a unique risk profile. See this condensed resource to sort it all out and make an informed decision.

***Guide to Homeopathic Remedies for the Birth Bag,* 5th Edition (2014)**

This compact book is designed to provide a practical, quick, clinical reference guide that birth attendants can easily slip into their birth bags. Seventy-five key remedies are briefly summarized for their applications in midwifery practice or self-care. Prenatal problems, complications arising during labor and birth, and postpartum complaints of both mom and baby are covered. Short essays are included that answer common questions: How does homeopathy differ from herbalism? How quickly should a person respond to a remedy? How do I know when to repeat a remedy? And more. Written by a midwife for midwives, mothers and anyone who works with pregnant, birthing, or breastfeeding mothers and their babies. Find out why this is the "go-to" reference book for thousands of midwives!

***Whole Family Recipes: For the Childbearing Year & Beyond* (2008)**

From many kitchens to yours . . . *Whole Family Recipes* is more than a cookbook. While being a guide to nutritious meals the whole family will enjoy, it highlights foods that are especially needed by pregnant women, breastfeeding mothers and their growing children. Taking a non-dogmatic and down-to-earth tone, the book focuses on incorporating vitamin- and mineral-rich foods and good quality fats into the diet. Tips for parents and a collection of essays devoted to nutrition during the childbearing year are featured, including a unique piece on "The Birth Marathon–Food & Drink for Labor & Birth." The cookbook is a community effort. Contributors include midwives, doulas, moms and dads, with illustrations by children. Makes a great gift for those parents, doulas and midwives in your life!

About Lifespan Doulas, LLC

Lifespan Doulas was founded in 2016 by Patty Brennan and Merilynne Rush for the purpose of providing professional End-of-Life Doula Training and certification. Additional trainings include workshops on home funeral and green burial, advance care planning facilitation, how to start a Death Café, and doula business development. Monthly mentoring webinars for members are available. LifespanDoulas.com

Special Free Gift from the Author

Select One of the Following:

- Patty Brennan's "Personal Inventory" from *The Doula Business Guide Workbook,* 3rd Edition (PDF), designed to help you capitalize on your business-related skills, personal strengths, habits and motivation to launch your doula business. Identifying areas of weakness, skills to acquire or where help is needed are equally important factors in your success. Sample this tool from our *Workbook.*
- Patty Brennan's "How does the end-of-life doula's role overlap with the hospice team?" (PDF), excerpted from Lifespan Doulas' *End-of-Life Doula Training Manual.* Use the chart to see, at a glance, where/how doulas fit in the picture of end-of-life care.
- Access to five videos (mp4 format) on *Yoga & Your Pelvic Floor* with Iyengar yoga instructor and self-described "pelvic floor enthusiast" Marlene McGrath. Produced by Patty Brennan, these videos are part of a larger collection of videos incorporated into our online childbirth preparation class, *Essential Exercises & Stretches for the Childbearing Year.* Not just for pregnant women!

How to Claim Your Gift:

Visit www.LifespanDoulas.com/FreeGift and simply make your selection.

I hope you enjoyed the book!
If so, I have a favor to ask:
Please go on Amazon and write a short review.
Thank you!

P.S. Did you see what I did there?
I'm modeling self-promotion for you.
Leave no stone unturned.
Go for it!

Made in the USA
Middletown, DE
03 February 2021

33061185R00230